Poverty and Social Welfare in Japan

JAPANESE SOCIETY SERIES
General Editor: Yoshio Sugimoto

Lives of Young Koreans in Japan
Yasunori Fukuoka

Globalization and Social Change in Contemporary Japan
J.S. Eades, Tom Gill and Harumi Befu

Coming Out in Japan: The Story of Satoru and Ryuta
Satoru Ito and Ryuta Yanase

Japan and Its Others:
Globalization, Difference and the Critique of Modernity
John Clammer

Hegemony of Homogeneity:
An Anthropological Analysis of Nihonjinron
Harumi Befu

Foreign Migrants in Contemporary Japan
Hiroshi Komai

A Social History of Science and Technology in
Contempory Japan, Volume 1
Shigeru Nakayama

Farewell to Nippon: Japanese Lifestyle Migrants in Australia
Machiko Sato

The Peripheral Centre:
Essays on Japanese History and Civilization
Johann P. Arnason

A Genealogy of 'Japanese' Self-images
Eiji Oguma

Class Structure in Contemporary Japan
Kenji Hashimoto

An Ecological View of History
Tadao Umesao

Nationalism and Gender
Chizuko Ueno

Native Anthropology: The Japanese Challenge
to Western Academic Hegemony
Takami Kuwayama

Youth Deviance in Japan: Class Reproduction of Non-Conformity
Robert Stuart Yoder

Japanese Companies: Theories and Realities
Masami Nomura and Yoshihiko Kamii

From Salvation to Spirituality:
Popular Religious Movements in Modern Japan
Susumu Shimazono

The 'Big Bang' in Japanese Higher Education:
The 2004 Reforms and the Dynamics of Change
J.S. Eades, Roger Goodman and Yumiko Hada

Japanese Politics: An Introduction
Takashi Inoguchi

A Social History of Science and Technology in
Contempory Japan, Volume 2
Shigeru Nakayama

Gender and Japanese Management
Kimiko Kimoto

Philosophy of Agricultural Science: A Japanese Perspective
Osamu Soda

A Social History of Science and Technology in
Contempory Japan, Volume 3
Shigeru Nakayama and Kunio Goto

Japan's Underclass: Day Laborers and the Homeless
Hideo Aoki

A Social History of Science and Technology
in Contemporary Japan, Volume 4
Shigeru Nakayama and Hitoshi Yoshioka

Scams and Sweeteners: A Sociology of Fraud
Masahiro Ogino

Toyota's Assembly Line: A View from the Factory Floor
Ryoji Ihara

Village Life in Modern Japan: An Environmental Perspective
Akira Furukawa

Social Welfare in Japan: Principles and Applications
Kojun Furukawa

Escape from Work: Freelancing Youth and the Challenge to Corporate Japan
Reiko Kosugi

Gender Gymnastics: Performing and Consuming Japan's Takarazuka Revue
Leonie R. Stickland

Poverty and Social Welfare in Japan
Masami Iwata and Akihiko Nishizawa

Social Stratification and Inequality Series

Inequality amid Affluence: Social Stratification in Japan
Junsuke Hara and Kazuo Seiyama

Intentional Social Change: A Rational Choice Theory
Yoshimichi Sato

Constructing Civil Society in Japan:
Voices of Environmental Movements
Koichi Hasegawa

Deciphering Stratification and Inequality: Japan and beyond
Yoshimichi Sato

Social Justice in Japan: Concepts, Theories and Paradigms
Ken-ichi Ohbuchi

Gender and Career in Japan
Atsuko Suzuki

Status and Stratification: Cultural Forms in East and Southeast Asia
Mutsuhiko Shima

Globalization, Minorities and Civil Society:
Perspectives from Asian and Western Cities
Koichi Hasegawa and Naoki Yoshihara

Advanced Social Research Series

A Sociology of Happiness
Kenji Kosaka

Frontiers of Social Research: Japan and beyond
Akira Furukawa

A Quest for Alternative Sociology
Kenji Kosaka and Masahiro Ogino

MODERNITY AND IDENTITY IN ASIA SERIES

Globalization, Culture and Inequality in Asia
Timothy S. Scrase, Todd Miles Joseph Holden and Scott Baum

Looking for Money:
Capitalism and Modernity in an Orang Asli Village
Alberto Gomes

Governance and Democracy in Asia
Takashi Inoguchi and Matthew Carlson

Poverty and Social Welfare in Japan

Masami Iwata
and
Akihiko Nishizawa

Trans Pacific Press
Melbourne

First published in 2008 by
Trans Pacific Press, PO Box 164, Balwyn North, Victoria 3104, Australia
Telephone: +61 (0)3 9859 1112 Fax: +61 (0)3 9589 4110
Email: tpp.mail@gmail.com
Web: http://www.transpacificpress.com

Copyright © Trans Pacific Press 2008

Designed and set by digital environs, Melbourne, Australia. www.digitalenvirons.com

Printed by BPA Print Group, Burwood, Victoria, Australia

Distributors

Australia and New Zealand
UNIREPS
University of New South Wales
Sydney, NSW 2052
Australia
Telephone: +61(0)2-9664-0999
Fax: +61(0)2-9664-5420
Email: info.press@unsw.edu.au
Web: http://www.unireps.com.au

USA and Canada
International Specialized Book Services (ISBS)
920 NE 58th Avenue, Suite 300
Portland, Oregon 97213-3786
USA
Telephone: (800) 944-6190
Fax: (503) 280-8832
Email: orders@isbs.com
Web: http://www.isbs.com

Asia and the Pacific
Kinokuniya Company Ltd.

Head office:
3-7-10 Shimomeguro
Meguro-ku
Tokyo 153-8504
Japan
Telephone: +81(0)3-6910-0531
Fax: +81(0)3-6420-1362
Email: bkimp@kinokuniya.co.jp
Web: www.kinokuniya.co.jp

Asia-Pacific office:
Kinokuniya Book Stores of Singapore Pte., Ltd.
391B Orchard Road #13-06/07/08
Ngee Ann City Tower B
Singapore 238874
Telephone: +65 6276 5558
Fax: +65 6276 5570
Email: SSO@kinokuniya.co.jp

All rights reserved. No production of any part of this book may take place without the written permission of Trans Pacific Press.

ISSN   1443–9670 (Japanese Society Series)
ISBN   978-1-876843-81-6 (Hardcover)
ISBN   978-1-876843-87-8 (Paperback)

Cover illustration: A homeless person resting in the underground passage at Shinjuku Station, the busiest metro terminal in Tokyo. Plants in the background were installed by Station management to prevent the homeless from sleeping or resting in the area. Photo taken by Yukihiko Kitagawa, the author of chapter 9.

Contents

Figures	viii
Tables	ix
Acknowledgements	xi
Contributors	xii
Introduction: Poverty, Social Exclusion and the Welfare Society *Masami Iwata*	1
1 Policies and poverty: poverty as a welfare policy bracket in post-War Japan and its meaning *Masami Iwata*	12
2 Poverty as a result of exclusion – Tokyo's urban underclass *Akihiko Nishizawa*	39
3 The distribution and dynamics of poverty looked at according to income (the fluctuations of poverty based on a panel survey) *Chizuka Hamamoto*	62
4 Older women and housing poverty: their housing history in home-owning society *Misa Izuhara*	86
5 The interconnection between health and poverty: health and socio-economic well-being *Yūko Hayasaka*	111
6 The spatial spread of poverty in the megalopolis and the state of segregation, 1975–2000 *Keiko Yamaguchi*	136
7 Does the *hi hogo* class represent poor people in general? *Masami Iwata*	157
8 Women, welfare policies and poverty: Poverty and shelter among homeless women *Keiko Kawahara*	185
9 Poverty and the social exclusion of single men: Perspectives on homeless men and their relationship with the welfare administration *Yukihiko Kitagawa*	210
10 Poverty and exclusion as it affects migrant workers from overseas: in terms of employment, housing and consumption *Kahoruko Yamamoto*	226
11 A jail without bars, the social world of the street dwellers *Akihiko Nishizawa*	242
12 Improving poverty stricken areas: A rehabilitation project for *Shima Danchi* public housing *Yosuke Hirayama*	263
Endnotes	288
References	300
Index	319

Figures

5.1:	The annual shift in the male and female suicide rates between 1980 and 2001 (per 100,000)	125
5.2:	The number of households who have failed to pay their National Health Insurance contributions	128
5.3:	The number of households issued with limited term insurance cards or certificates of status	129
6.1:	The ratio of blue collar workers (1975)	141
6.2:	The ratio of blue collar workers (1990)	141
6.3:	The ratio of blue collar workers (2000)	142
6.4:	The ratio of unemployment (1975)	142
6.5:	The ratio of unemployment (1990)	143
6.6:	The ratio of unemployment (2000)	143
6.7:	The ratio of single mother households (1990)	145
6.8:	The ratio of single mother households (2000)	145
6.9:	The ratio of public rental housing (2000)	146
6.10:	The ratio of private rental housing (2000)	146
6.11:	The ratio of owner occupied houses (2000)	147
6.12:	The ratio of elderly single person households (1990)	148
6.13:	The ratio of elderly single person households (2000)	148
6.14:	The ratio of people on the *Seikatsu hogo* benefit (1990)	150
6.15:	The ratio of people on the *Seikatsu hogo* benefit (2000)	150
6.16:	The number of homeless people (2003)	151
6.17:	The spread of kōryoshibōnin, ('vagrants found dead') (1986–1990)	152
7.1:	Transition of the rate of coverage by the *Seikatsu hogo* system	160
7.2:	The transitions of employed and unemployed households among the *Ōhi hogo* class	167
7.3:	Length of time on *Seikatsu hogo* benefits	178
12.1:	Floor plan for the second floor of Green Heights	268
12.2:	Floor plan for Mr. A's residence	277
12.3:	An example of multiple families using multiple homes	281
12.4:	Floor plan for the first floor incorporating a lounge room	282
12.5:	An example of internal yet external space	284

Tables

3.1:	Transition of the poverty rate (%)	66
3.2:	Recurrance of poverty	68
3.3:	Poverty hit and poverty incidence during a given period	70
3.4:	Poverty ratio and poverty gap, according to the poverty hit	72
3.5:	Fluctuations in income over two points of time (poverty ratio) (%)	74
3.6:	Poverty classification based on permanent income approach	76
3.7:	Poverty classification (1994–2002)	76
3.8:	Attributes according to the different poverty types (as at 2002) (%)	77
3.9:	Life events between 1994 and 2002 according to the different poverty types (average±standard deviation)	79
3.10:	Poverty spell (%)	80
3.11:	Increase of chronic poverty	82
4.1:	A brief housing history of the twenty-eight women interviewed	90
4.1:	A brief housing history of the twenty-eight women interviewed—continued	92
5.1:	Classification of occupational classes (Registrar General's Social Class)	113
5.2:	Socio-economic status classification (National Statistics, Socio-Economic Classification)	114
5.3:	Examples of social indicators used in the UK for measuring poverty	115
5.4:	The number of people covered by Medicaid and Medicare in 2001 (out of a total population of 282,082,000)	117
5.5:	The number of AIDS patients according to age and ethnic origin (cases per 100,000 population)	119
5.6:	Poverty in Scandinavia	121
5.7:	Livelihood problems (%)	125
5.8:	The number of participating households in the National Health Insurance scheme (thousands of households)	127

5.9: The ratio of subsidized households on National Health Insurance payments, according to the employment status of the head of the household (as at the end of September 2000) — 127

7.1: The rate of households in poverty and the take-up rate of *Seikatsu hogo* (%) — 162

7.2: The characteristics and transition of the composition of *hi hogo* households (%) — 164

7.3: The types of *hi hogo* households and the transition, and the *hogo* rate for different household types — 165

7.4: Transition of employment among employed poor households — 169

7.5: The reasons for receiving the *Seikatsu hogo* benefit (%) — 170

7.6: Social security recipients among the *hi hogo* class — 174

7.7: Length of time on the *Seikatsu hogo* benefit according to the different types of household (%) — 179

7.8: Households with previous experience of being on benefits and the interval since last benefit received — 181

7.9: The reasons for ceasing to receive the benefit (September 2002) — 183

9.1: The basic attributes of homeless people — 216

11.1: Survey results of street dwellers — 246

Acknowledgements

This book is a translated version of the title 'Poverty and Social Exclusion' [*Hinkon to shakai teki haijo*] (Volume 9 of the Welfare Society Series) which was originally published in Japanese by Minerva Shobo in 2005. First, I would like to take this opportunity to express my gratitude to Keizo Sugita, the president of the Minerva Shobo and the editor, Naho Kōno, for their support and understanding towards the project.

I want to thank especially Rick Tanaka who took the challenge of translating the whole book from Japanese to plain English. This was a particularly onerous task given the fact that the welfare systems in Japan were rather complex and the edited volume written by multiple authors contained many applied studies of poverty using different conceptual and methodological approaches. Darrell Bennetts proof-edited the whole volume, for which I am also grateful.

On behalf of all the contributors, my special appreciation has to go to Professor Yoshio Sugimoto of La Trobe University, Australia. Professor Sugimoto has been working extensively to promote Japanese social science publications to international audiences. Without his support and encouragement, this publication would not have been realized.

Finally, the translation of this volume was supported by the Japan Society for the Promotion of Science (JSPS) under the Grant-in-Aid for Publication of Science Research Result scheme.

Masami Iwata

Contributors

Masami Iwata is Professor of Social Welfare at Japan Women's University, Tokyo and is a member of Japan's national Social Security Council. She is the foremost researcher in the field of poverty, social exclusion and welfare in Japan. She has published extensively on poverty dynamics, the homeless problem and social welfare policies. Her publications include 'Commonality of Social Policy on Homelessness: Beyond the Different Appearances of Japanese and English Policies' (*European Journal of Housing Policy* 2003 Vol3, No2).

Akihiko Nishizawa is Professor of Urban Sociology in the Faculty of Sociology at Toyo University, Tokyo. He specialises in the ethnographic analysis of the social worlds of Japan's urban underclass. He has written numerous articles and books on the urban underclass, focussing particularly on day labourers in *Yoseba* and on street dwellers.

Chizuka Hamamoto, is an Associate Professor in the Faculty of Economics at Daito Bunka University. Her main field of research is social security. Her current focus is a dynamics of poverty. She is a project member on the Japanese Panel Survey of Consumers, at the Institute for Research on Household Economics, Japan.

Misa Izuhara is a Senior Research Fellow in the School for Policy Studies at the University of Bristol, UK. She has worked extensively in the areas of housing and social change, ageing and intergenerational relations, and comparative social policy. She is the author of *Housing, Care and Inheritance* (Routledge 2008). Her recent projects include 'Housing assets and intergenerational dynamics in East Asian societies' funded by the Economic and Social Research Council, UK. Misa is currently the editor of the international journal *Policy & Politics*.

Yuko Hayasaka is Professor of Medical Sociology at Niigata Seiryo University, specializing Social Stratification and Health as well as

Social Aspects of Terminal Care. Holding PhDs in both Medical Science and Social Welfare, she has published articles and books on wide range of health-related research topics.

Keiko Yamaguchi is Associate Professor in the Faculty of Humanities at Hirosaki University. An urban sociology specialist, her current research focuses on the life strategy of homelessness in metropolitan areas and on social mobility for youth.

Keiko Kawahara is Lecturer of Social Welfare in the Faculty of Sociology at Toyo University,Tokyo. She works in the area of poverty and welfare policies, particularly policies for homeless families and women in Tokyo.

Yukihiko Kitagawa is Lecturer of Urban Sociology at Toyo Eiwa University. He is a researcher in the field of urban sociology. He has researched homelessness through interviews with the Tokyo homeless. His particular focus centres on the re-selection process of homeless people by welfare agencies.

Kahoruko Yamamoto is Associate Professor in the Faculty of Urban Environmental Sciences at Toyko Metropolitan University. She specializes in urban sociology and migration. Her publications include 'Newcomer Migrant Workers in the Underclass: A Yokohama, Japan Case Study' in *IJJS: International Journal of Japanese Sociology* no. 9 (The Japan Sociological Society, 2000).

Yosuke Hirayama is Professor of Housing and Urban Studies at the Graduate School of Human Development and Environment, Kobe University. He works extensively in areas of housing and urban change, home-ownership and social inequality, as well as comparative housing policy. He has published widely in numerous international academic journals and he is co-editor of *Housing and Social Transition in Japan* (with Richard Ronald, Routledge, 2007). He is also a founding member of the *Asia-Pacific Network for Housing Research* and chaired its international conference on Housing and Globalization, held in Kobe in 2005.

Introduction: Poverty, Social Exclusion and the Welfare Society

Masami Iwata

Poverty and society

Beauty and poverty

Next to poverty, barely any other social problem has been so widely discussed. Poverty has been constantly problematised since the beginning of modern society. Many critiques have constructed poverty as a form of decay, like a persistent chronic disease in developed countries where 'affluent society' first developed, even in countries where a welfare state had been implemented with the chief aim of its elimination. Of course, that poverty has constantly been discussed does not mean that a single manifestation of it persists. Every time it is looked at afresh, the concept of poverty itself and how it is measured are revised. Discursive difference is more to do with how poverty is perceived. It is measured in numerous ways, not only in terms of developing different yardsticks and improving research methods, but also by introducing qualitative research, listening to the opinions and outlook of the people who are trapped in poverty cycles. As we all know, many scholars and organisations have engaged on whether poverty is absolute or relative, whether it can be defined objectively or subjectively. They argue the relative merits of many various ways of seeing of the problem, including the cost of living approach, the income approach, the deprivation index approach, the capability approach and more.

As to these various views on poverty, Mollie Orshansky of the United States Social Security Administration once compared them to the way beauty is observed. Like beauty, poverty lies in the eyes of the beholder, and is perceived differently according to the viewpoint of the observer. Therefore, we should expect numerous perspectives and opinions on, and interpretations of, poverty. Peter Townsend, a British expert on poverty, after remarking that Orshansky's comment was 'refreshingly candid,' noted that poverty should be defined as much as possible by either independent or external criteria, and that value judgments should play a limited role, though it is impossible to avoid them altogether (Townsend 1974: 19). Elsewhere, Pete Alcock has remarked that poverty, unlike beauty, should not just be observed from across the fence, or end up merely the subject of academic debate (Alcock 1997: 4). From the start, poverty should be judged and discussed as a problem that needs to be dealt with. Different definitions would require different solutions. Alcock stresses that poverty, unlike beauty, should not be left to the eye of the beholder.

Whether we can find objective criteria for evaluation as advocated by Townsend is another matter, but in some definitions poverty is considered as a social problem to be 'dealt with' and to be 'eliminated'. This characteristic is often pointed out in debates over the difference between poverty and inequality. Social inequality is often compared to undulating ground, while poverty is a ravine into which you should not be allowed to fall. The description of undulating ground may be clear enough, but the description of poverty as a ravine certainly needs to be reconsidered. We need to settle on reasons and criteria for why individuals should not stumble and, despite their efforts, fall off.

A good society cannot be affirmed until the deplorable conditions of poverty are eliminated from its milieu. Whatever scientific improvement is made in evaluating poverty, there inevitably remains some ambiguity and room for moral judgment, because poverty is measured on, more: determined by, social criteria. In the elimination of poverty, we demonstrate the basic conditions for an ideal society. In practice, a welfare state which engages in responsible processes for improving the wellbeing of its citizens has to prove that the poverty problem is either already solved or greatly diminished. Critics of welfare models make this matter plain: that despite the extensive efforts by the state, poverty is still increasing. The value judgment, that poverty is something to be eradicated, accelerates the tendency to depict it in a negative way. Debate over the poverty problem, unless based on a deep insight into the lives and thoughts of people actually living in poverty, has the potential danger of jumping to a value-ladened conclusion, that – by whatever means – escape from poverty is good. Poverty, the word itself, embodies a sense of disdain that connotes the kind of value judgment upon which such conclusions are based.

Two Views of Poverty

What is the relationship between poverty and society, from which the former is a problem to be eradicated? Is society obliged to eradicate poverty, because it affects its members, because it is *our* poverty? Or does society see poverty as existing outside of itself, *their* poverty, and does it feel the need for its eradication because poverty poses a form of threat?

In reviewing the history of poverty awareness, the latter perspective first dominated discussion: poor people were portrayed as a mob of vagrants, inhabitants of the sprawling slums in the city and its surroundings, of no fixed address or residents of boarding houses and terrace houses in slum areas, not supporting their families. They were unlike those in ordinary society, and were excluded from regular work, were unemployed, may have been beggars, or undertook odd jobs in the city. The 'leitmotif that ran through them [vagrants five characteristics; poor, able-bodied, unemployed, rootless and lawless] all was disorder.' (Beier 1986: 4) As can be easily understood from terms such as *underworld*, *badlands*, *nether world*, commonly used in the reportage of visits to the slums, poverty stricken societies existed outside of this world. In truth, however, as was pointed out by Kiyoshi Nakagawa, slum dwellers already included some industrial labourers whose living standards were not too different from those of ordinary workers (Nakagawa 1985: 33–35). In the same way, the Polish historian Bronislaw Geremek has stated that up until the middle of the nineteenth century, 'the custom of designating workers under the term "paupers" persisted.' (Geremek 1993: 327) In any case, the poverty of labourers and of others was bundled together and seen as manifestation of the 'other disorderly world.' Past responses to poverty have therefore emerged in the form of control and punishment for disorderly beings, coupled with the provision of charity and philanthropy.

A departure from this way of seeing poverty, as a problem of an other world, took place from the middle of the nineteenth century to the early twentieth century. During this period labourers and the poor were differentiated, and only the poor received pity and punishment because they were considered to be non-citizens. This was later followed by concern about poverty amongst labourers who were now considered to be fully fledged members of society, and hence, their poverty was now the problem of the other citizens.

Poverty among labourers and citizens was not considered to be connected with appearance and disorderliness, but was easily measurable by their savings, income and level of consumption. Poverty now attracted attention as a problem of *our own* society, and was seen as a by-product of industrialisation.

Of course, the central issue in a homogeneous society, one which recognises poverty in its midst, is setting the threshold for poverty delimitation. In any case, a given welfare state was expected to maintain the integrity of *our own* society from the poverty problem *we* had created, by implementing preventive measures mainly through social security.

Our Own and *Their* Poverty

Discovery of *our own* poverty

It is well known that Charles Booth's and Seebohm Rowntree's investigations into English poverty in heralded the discovery of poverty in *our own* society. Praising the importance of this turning point, T.H. Marshall stated that '(t)he importance of these investigations was that they extended the concept of poverty from the pauper sections of the working class, thus giving a new dimension to the problem of poverty.' (1981: 65) Both Booth and Rowntree concluded the problem was derived from an industrial society's living standards. Rowntree went on further to state that poverty was a phenomenon that occurred regularly in the life cycle of workers in general. However, it is doubtful whether these authors perceived *their own* poverty. Rather it was something that was defined just by the income level in *our own* homogeneous society. Booth categorised the population into eight classes from A to H, indexed by living standards. Amongst these, he particularly noted the poverty among the workers of the C class (intermittent wage earners) and the D class (regular small income earners). The point, he argued, was to improve the conditions of the B class of very poor casual wage earners who were dragging down the classes above them. Incidentally, the lowest A class was made up of occasional labourers, street sellers, loafers, semi-criminals and so on, was not considered to be as influential to the higher classes as the B and the C class. Instead, A-category people 'inhabited a world apart.' (Marshall 1981: 37) Karl Marx had made a similar observation in *Das Kapital*, when he described a relative surplus-population and paupers. The latter, according to Marx, consisted of not just those able to work, but also children, the elderly and the disabled, and they were seen as candidates for an industrial reserve army for the active army of labourers, and as such, the lowest layer of the relative surplus-population. But he excluded 'vagabonds, criminals, prostitutes, in a word, the "dangerous" classes.' (Marx, 1965: 643)

Although Rowntree has argued for a poverty line based on the basic minimum cost of living, he often judged people to be in poverty by appearances while he was in the field. He described those living below the poverty line as in primary poverty, and others, in secondary poverty. His poverty line was supposed to be based on a scientific criterion, yet it seemingly was not totally detached from an empirical view of poverty. Secondary poverty could only be understood by means of the people's connection with the particular culture of the poor class.

The discovery of poverty in *our own* society suggested that poverty was a product of stratification, an integral part of a capitalist economy. This demanded a major shift from seeing poverty as a personal problem. Yet, this discovery was not self-reflective. It still ambiguously retained the shadow of *their poverty*, poverty on the margins of our society.

Social Exclusion

The concern over *their poverty*, which existed at the same time as poverty among the working class and the citizens was mainly revealed, resurfaced later, in the following two contexts. The concern for *their poverty* was first raised in the context of the culture of poverty. Second, it came to light in the context of social exclusion and underclass theory, which has become popular in recent times.

The theory of the culture of poverty was derived from Oscar Lewis's book *The Culture of Poverty*, in which he did not treat poverty as something fixed which could therefore be measured. Instead, through ethnographical participant observation techniques, he examined the lives of poor people and analysed why they could not escape poverty. This type of study is often criticised, as it may hide the fact that poverty is the product of industrial societies; it may emphasise certain pathological symptoms of social behaviour. But Lewis's approach convincingly raised awareness that it is absolutely necessary to understand the deprived states the poor are made to endure, the long reproductive process of poverty, and the counter culture people in poverty create. Paul Willis in his seminal work, *Learning to Labour*, pointed out that culture is understood 'not simply as a set of transferred internal structure ... nor as the passive result of the action of dominant ideology downwards ..., but at least in part as the product of collective human praxis' (1977: 4). His discussion rendered meaning and contradiction in *our own* society, the counter culture created by the lower working class and strata below this. He included in his sights a much wider population such as Booth's A class people as well as migrants.

The term *social exclusion* originated in France in the 1980s, describing the emergence of long-term unemployed youth, for whom the existing social security system could not cope (Madanipour et al. 2002). The application of the term has gradually been extended, and now it refers not only to the long-term unemployed, but also to the groups of people, residents of outer fringe suburbs and the ghettos of big cities, who are excluded from the usual opportunities and systems in all aspects of life, economically, politically and culturally. Political movement in Europe has recently sought to install this term at the heart of the EU's new social cohesion policy. As the member nations are working on their common goal of achieving social cohesion and combating social exclusion, the concept is quickly replacing the term poverty. Incidentally, the same socially excluded group of people is in the US known as the 'underclass,' reminiscent of a revival of the nineteenth century style of poverty.

Of course, recognition of social exclusion is not a return to the nineteenth century, but, is rather a fundamental shift in conceptualising *our own* society. This change of perspective has been accelerating in the post industrial and globalised West since currencies were floated and since the oil crisis of 1973 (Harvey 1989). Poverty as understood by Booth and Rowntree was that of workers in an industrial society, while welfare states planned social systems for the permanent industrial workers of the mass production system and their families. The primary concern of welfare states has been the stability of employment opportunities and the maintenance of wages, while risks relating to the whole life cycle, such as the cost of children's education and aged care were looked after by the state. On the other hand, in post industrial societies capital moves freely among the now dominant financial and information sectors and the labour market is reorganised accordingly. This results in the increasing casualisation and contracting out of jobs. Globalisation and intensified competition in the global market has accelerated these shifts even faster. The increasing changes in family relations, such as divorces and unmarried households is another noteworthy feature.

Longitudinal studies now indicate the increase of long-term poverty, and that, due to these changes, our society is shifting from a 'montgolfier' model, with the bulk of income in the middle, to a more extreme 'hour-glass' model where the gap is very wide between the rich and the poor (Lepietz et al 2002). Some call poverty among young people, single parent families and migrants 'new poverty,' because it has been observed that the ratio of these people amongst those who are in poverty has increased, while the number of older people has declined. The social exclusion debate can be understood as a fresh attempt to locate a part of the 'new poor' in relation to the spaces and systems of society as a whole.

This suggests that society at last has come to realise that *their poverty*, existing on their social periphery and excluded from the societal spaces and systems, cannot be addressed by simply measuring it against a threshold which is based on the living standard of homogeneous workers and citizens. It can only be understood as part of the dynamic process of exclusion and inclusion of *our own* society as a whole.

Welfare States, Poverty and Social Exclusion

As shown, to understand poverty purely from the common ground of *our own* society's citizens and workers, the common view of poverty in the twentieth century, of course means not everyone is included. Also, the above studies into the culture of poverty and deprivation point out that poverty is accompanied by exclusion from society. Therefore, it is doubtful if poverty, freshly re-named as social exclusion, can be explained as a wholly new phenomenon peculiar to post industrial society. It is more likely that some of *their poverty* has existed for a long time, but has been hidden from sight in dark corners. The important thing to note here is that *their poverty* has been outside the realm of the welfare state due to a traditionally exclusive policy framework. This framework failed even to see the inside workings of *our own* society, and now has to be revised the point of view of social cohesion, due to changes in *our own* society.

Of course, social exclusion theory has attracted criticism from those who doubt whether exclusion really exists, as, unlike the traditional perspective, it has developed without scientific measures. In a recent investigation in England, Hills and others pointed out that the state of being totally cut off from society is rare. Exclusion and inclusion are a continuum and that the experienced extent of exclusion is heavily influenced by the level of income (Hills et al. 2002). Therefore, integrated research and study of the traditional poverty index and the exclusion theory will soon become more and more important. Also there is a concern that social integration theory might be used short-sightedly to justify the policy of rounding up the poor for the labour market. The significance of social exclusion theory is that it does not just pinpoint poverty as a kind of problem that needs to be solved, but it also deals with the relationship between the poor and the society which creates them. It encourages an understanding of the poor's despair, rebellions, struggles, and the process of exclusion and integration, from the level of the excluded (like the culture of poverty theory, including the very people in poverty).

There is no agreed definition of a welfare state, but Totaro Okada has noted that one characteristic of such a state is that it places emphasis on a nation not just as an association but also on the 'the subject and its responsibility' of society as a whole (Okada 1984: 11). If that is the case, it becomes necessary to examine whether or not the constituency is in a position to fulfil the role of *the subject and its responsibility* in the first place. For example, if Japanese citizens and other residents of Japan were asked about their obligations under *the subject and its responsibility* in welfare service provisions, hardly any attention would be paid to just who exactly are counted as citizens. Nor would attention focus on how many of citizens and residents are in a position to fulfil the role because they are poor and socially excluded. Also unlikely to attract significant focus would be the lack of a work ethic among young part-time workers, and the welfare system dependency of the poor, as to whether or not those people are in a position to fulfil their social role as responsible subjects. Taking these matters into account open us to understanding poverty and social exclusion. This approach may result in highlighting: the social conditions that need eradication in order to minimise or prevent poverty; the lives and consciousness of the people living in such conditions; the competitive relationship between exclusion and integration in society as a whole; and the living conditions of those who are able to fulfil their roles as *the subject and its responsibility* in a welfare state.

By questioning these matters in Japanese society, our understanding of poverty and of social exclusion may elucidate the conditions of life of those who are able to fulfil the role of *the subject and its responsibility*. We need to investigate the contested terrain of meaning between *exclusion* and *integration* in modern society as a whole. This could be achieved though exploring the grounds for exclusion in the life and times of those in poverty that are structurally placed outside society.

In this regard, this book will contribute to the debate on a subject that should be the central theme of the 'welfare society' series of publications.

The aim and structure of this book

The aim of this book

From the above understanding of poverty and social exclusion, this book examines the reality of poverty and exclusion in present day Japanese society through the following perspectives.

First, since the rapid economic growth of the 1960s the understanding of poverty has been limited to reading about the concepts developed in advanced Western societies, or it has been discussed only in the context of developing nations. Only an extremely limited number of empirical studies have been completed. In this book, poverty and social exclusion in Japan today are discussed from various angles, through the opinions and behaviour of the people actually living in these conditions. Second, poverty and social exclusion are formulated by social resources and life opportunities, as well as by the unequal structure of power. Here, we focus especially on locating poverty and exclusion in the huge context of social integration. We will also examine, in particular local areas, how overt or covert measures of separation and exclusion aimed at the poor people are carried out. We also see the process of exclusion and inclusion among the poor. Third, policies and institutions are not merely a reflection of the social recognition of poverty and the struggle surrounding this recognition. They also help to spread specific views on poverty and cause these perceptions to be viewed as fact. Not only do poverty and social exclusion need to be grasped as they are, but they also need to be examined in relation to the policies and institutions set up to manage them, especially in the context of a debate about the welfare nation. In this book, poverty and social exclusion in contemporary Japanese society are looked at through an examination of the level of awareness and typology, apparent in the policy formulation process to do with poverty.

The structure of this book

In the first section, two theses will be discussed examining perspectives on poverty in Japan. The first chapter by Masami Iwata attempts a new approach by relocating poverty through the perceptions displayed in government policies on poverty. This chapter also looks at the characteristics of groups according to the categories used in post-War welfare policies, and discusses the meaning behind this. This is followed by a chapter by Akihiko Nishizawa, who analyzes the way the lower class has been always excluded from the nationalisation process in contemporary Japanese society in terms of treatment, concealment and elimination. This chapter draws examples from Tokyo, from the inception of the urban underclass in the pre-War days to the post-War welfare spost-wartate. In both chapters, the authors discuss not only general definitions of the terms and the reality, but they also argue that a perspective on poverty and social exclusion will come from a reassessment of them in relation to social integration and the welfare system in Japan.

In the second section, covering four chapters, the reality of poverty is portrayed in case studies done from various angles and by various methods. This has rarely been done in Japan before. The first chapter in this section (overall, the third in the book) looks in detail at poverty among young women. Chizuka Hamamoto uses the traditional evaluation of poverty based on the income discrepancy approach, but transforms it into a dynamic analysis of poverty, by applying the longitudinal panel studies technique. The fourth chapter by Misa Izumihara qualitatively analyzes poverty and housing of elderly women, who have lived through the prevailing post-War home ownership ethos, using the 'housing story' technique. In the fifth chapter, Yuko Hayasaka discusses the relationship between health and poverty, comparing experiences in the West and re-examining the existing data in Japan. In the sixth chapter, Keiko Yamaguchi examines the spread of poverty in urban areas, and maps it in the south Kantō region at the beginning of post-industrialisation, using various poverty indices.

The third section contains four different perspectives on how poverty has been objectivised in welfare policies, and how welfare programmes have been formulated in post-War Japan. In the seventh chapter, Iwata deals with the *Seikatsu hogo* (Public Livelihood Protection) programme, the core of the post-War poverty policy. She looks at how the 'public assistance recipient class' produced by the system has gradually come to occupy a prominent permanent position among people without employment, and discusses the meaning of this. The eighth and ninth chapters look at how the poverty of homeless men and women is screened, excluded and graded in the welfare system and in what measure. In the eighth chapter, Keiko Kawahara looks at the poverty of women in Tokyo, examining contradictions in the various welfare policies, while in the ninth chapter, Yukihiko Kitagawa focuses on male homeless people and on the official policy encouraging their self reliance. In the tenth chapter, Kahoruko Yamamoto describes the exclusion from the system of foreign workers, called newcomers, on the grounds of their having no fixed address, and how their predicament is locked into the consumer society.

The final fourth section consists of two chapters. Chapter eleven is by Nishizawa and chapter twelve by Yōsuke Hirayama. They both seek a way out from the current society that produces poverty and social exclusion, into a future welfare society. It is by n o means easy to solve the problem of poverty and social exclusion, but the two chapters stress that the way out from the problem can be found in the mutual relationships among people in dire predicaments. Nishizawa discusses the social environment of homeless people, living in a invisible cage, and sees a potential for them to avoid being reduced to a basic level of existence. Hirayama reports as one of the project organisers on a revitalisation project of a deteriorated residential area in a *Dōwa* area (literally an anti discrimination area, designated for the improvement of the living standards of people of Buraku origin). Making over physical structures was only a part of the project, and the author describes a continual process of community bond building workshops. There, the meaning of improvement and revitalisation was constantly questioned, and the residents had to look squarely at their own still unconvinced state. Through this process we see there is a pathway towards the reinvigoration of their lives.

1 Policies and poverty: poverty as a welfare policy bracket in post-War Japan and its meaning

Masami Iwata

Poverty categories as a product of social policy

The history of poverty is also the history of the policies directed towards the deprived. As we saw in the Introduction above, various views on poverty exist which indicate that it is more than just a 'fact.' Poverty is beyond being a fact; it is something to be fixed and is therefore a socially defined concept. As such, any interpretation itself will be inherently linked to the policies directed at the poor and their actual application. In other words, poverty is on the one hand an 'objective state' measurable by all the specialised scientific studies and a 'subjective state' experienced by individuals. It is on the other hand, an 'intended target category' expressed concretely in various policies.

It is often thought that policy is formulated and applied in reaction to existing problems. However, we should not forget that particular policies and their application actively define a certain state and put people into certain categories. The interpretation of poverty is no doubt greatly affected by definitions of the state of poverty through policy, the state of the poor, and changing official definitions over the years. What we perceive as poverty today is influenced to varying degrees by history as defined and typified by past policies and their application. Of this, Pete Alcock, a social policy analyst in England, has stated:

> Poverty exists within a dynamic and changing social order; and to some extent, as we have suggested, it is created by, or at least *recreated* by the social and economic policies that have developed over time to respond to or control it. Thus the history of poverty is also a history of the policies directed at or developed for the poor. As Vincent (1991) discusses in his history of poverty in Britain in the twentieth-century,

this interrelation between poverty and policy has consistently shaped the position of poor people within all aspects of the broader social structure (Alcock 1997: 9).

In this chapter, I would like to look at poverty as a policy category, which has not been hitherto examined in Japan. My scope here is limited to the official social welfare policies of post-War Japan. A study of the whole history would require a comprehensive historical analysis, stretching right from the beginning of the modern era. In such an analysis we would need to look at poverty not just from the perspective of welfare but also from the perspectives of suppression and crackdown. Polish scholar, Bronislaw Geremek, describes these bluntly as 'compassion' and 'the gallows' (Geremek 1993), but it is not necessarily possible to separate them and they can be combined and included together even in a single piece of policy. As a contribution to such broad and comprehensive studies, I would here like to concentrate on Japan's welfare policies since the end of World War II, and discuss how the poor are defined and categorised.

Here, the welfare aspects of the post War era, are the policies formulated during the era, except for the 'full scale national starvation' time in the immediate aftermath of the War, which have constituted a part of various Welfare State policies during the rapid economic development and right through to the creation of an affluent society. Here we are talking about various welfare programmes during the affluent period, where visible poverty has become less overwhelming, the 'labour issue' is no longer synonymous with the 'poverty problem' (Geremek 1993: 327), and ordinary workers' lives are not, and should not considered to be in a state of poverty. As is generally the case during the process of building a Welfare State, preventative measures against poverty become more extensive, and policies gradually become divided into two distinct types, aimed at prevention or at relief. The preventative measures do not constitute a particular category in the policies directed towards the poor, because the aim of keeping the wage levels of workers and citizens in general 'above the poverty line' and other income policies are embedded in more general social services policies. On the other hand, the relief measures take the more direct shape of government and public intervention, and are aimed directly at the areas or at private individuals, to salvage those people and areas the preventive measures have failed. As we will see later, those types of intervention are classified either as general cases or as a number of specific cases. Some of them may not appear as poverty policies at all, and are embedded in the general social services.

First, in the history of the post-War welfare programmes, the State's definition of poverty must be examined, together with for whom its relief policies were intended, and how the poor were classified. We will start by looking at the development of the *ippan kyūsai* (general relief) policies directed towards them and will explore how to create the category of the *hi hogoso* (service recipient class), a term now used almost synonymously for poor people or deprived people in general.

Selective and entangled general policy categories

According to Hajime Kozawa, the pre-War relief programmes carried out as 'national administrative work' can be divided into the *ippan kyūgo* (general relief) programmes directed at poor people in general, and the *tokushu kyūgo* (specific relief) programmes. As well as these programmes aimed at individuals, the government implemented programmes aimed at 'deteriorating residential areas.' *Ippan kyūgo* programmes were based on the 1929 *Kyūgo hō* (Relief Act). *Tokushu kyūgo* measures, on the national level, had come from several sources. One was the Veterans' Assistance programme, which had begun as the *Kashiheisotsu kazoku fujo rei* (Financial Assistance Programme for the Families of Slain Soldiers), with the *Haiheiin hō* (Establishment of a Care Facility for Returned Soldiers Disabled in Battle) and the *Gunji kyūgo hō* (Veterans' Relief Act). Another source was the 'assistance for sick non-residents', stipulated by the *Kōryobyōnin oyobi kōryoshibōnin toriatsukai hō* (the Act Concerning the Treatment of Travellers found Sick or Dead). The third source was disaster relief, which began with the introduction of the *Bikō chochiku hō* (the National Savings Fund for Future Disasters), followed by the *Risai kyūjokikin hō* (the Relief Fund for Disaster Victims). Relief was also provided to impoverished people from the public health perspective under the *Kekkaku yobō hō* (Prevention of Tuberculosis Act), the *Seishinbyōsha kango hō* (Care of Psychiatric Patients Act), the *Seishinbyōin hō* (Psychiatric Hospitals Act), the *Densenbyō yobō hō* (Prevention of Contagious Diseases Act) and others. Most of these programmes were introduced before the *Ippan kyūgo* programme. The response to poverty in these specific instances preceded that aimed at poor people in general. Masaaki Ogawa explains that these relief programmes for specific cases were 'not aimed directly to aid the poor as such, but their enactment merely had something to do with the poor.' (Ogawa 1960: 120)

We should understand, however, that the programmes to assist poor people could only begin in these specific situations first.

The *Kyūgo hō* was directed at 'those people who are incapable of maintaining life due to poverty.' Therefore, it was applicable in theory to poor people in general but in reality, it was only applied to those: over 65 years old; under 13; pregnant women; and disabled people who could not work. In other words, 'general paupers' were limited to those who had no capacity to work, and were treated individually. These distinctions were used also as a subcategory under general paupers. The *Kyūgo hō* was intended to assist for those at home in principle, but it also included assistance for facilities such as aged care homes, child care facilities, medical clinics and so on. Here, the target groups were lonely and poor elderly people, juveniles and the sick (Kozawa 1934: 183). After *Kyūgo hō* was enacted, relief programmes aimed at the specified groups accelerated because of the country's expanding War effort.

The *Gunji fujo hō* (Veterans' Assistance Act) as well as the *Boshi hogo hō* (Assistance for Single Mother Families Act), both enacted in 1937, the *Iryō hogo hō* (Medical Assistance Act) of 1941 and the *Senji saigai hogo hō* (Protection of War Disaster Victims Act) in 1942, were often described as the 'dispersal of the *Kyūgo hō* Act' (Koyama, 1951; Shigeta 1960). However, it is more appropriate to say that these Acts were enacted to make clear that these were extraordinary measures during wartime, quite distinct from the relief of the poor during peacetime. Hence the word *kyūgo* (relief) was carefully avoided. Instead, *fujo* (assistance) and *hogo* (protection) were used. These acts also declared that 'a single mother and her children,' 'soldiers disabled in battle and bereaved families,' and 'War victims' were given higher priority than 'paupers in general.'

The post-War *Seikatsu hogo hō* (Public Livelihood Protection Act) was a clear declaration that the universally applicable relief of the poor was now in place, instead of the various 'relief programmes aimed at a specific genre of people' of the pre-War time. Various studies have already been carried out concerning how the Act came about in 1946 (Old Act) and revised in 1950 (New Act), and the principles each stood for. The most significant point of the Act was that it was no longer applicable to lonely souls, a clear departure from the *kyugo ho* which were aimed at a specific social genre of people. As a result, we see the emergence of the condition that the poor in general are to be judged only by their living standard, and this does not require any other special qualifications. There were only the *yō hogosha* (people in need of protection) which included those who were eligible but not necessarily on benefits, and the *hi hogosha* (recipients of public assistance) who were actually on benefits.

These two latter groups, however, could not represent all the poor in general, because of the following two reasons. By around 1950, the scholars and commissioned welfare workers (honorary) had identified the existence of impoverished people living slightly above the poverty line. They were called the 'borderline class' or the 'low income class.' The line theses newly identified groups sat on, or above, meant the living standard protection line defined in the *Seikatsu hogo* system. In other words, the poverty among the group slightly above or neighbouring this line, was thus 'discovered' (Onuma 1974: 115). Terms such as the 'borderline class' and the 'low income class' sometimes meant those who were eligible, who should have been on a welfare benefit, but could not actually receive one. Therefore, it became apparent that it is not necessarily the case that the term, beneficiaries represents all poor people, and that poverty could not only be measured by the official poverty line but also by a low income standard. The emergence of the *borderline class* or the *low income class* in itself had much to do with the commissioned welfare workers advocating new social policies aiming at those people. The low income class was examined by commissioned welfare workers known as the *Hōmen iin*, later renamed the *Minsei iin*. They had been appointed under the old Act, but were now excluded from the new *Seikatsu hogo* system. The low income class was identified by these honorary commissioned workers who were on the lookout for a potential area of work (Kida 1960: 332–334). Their hopes were realised in the *Setai kosei shikin kashitsuke seido* {Household Improvement Fund Loan Scheme, which later became the current *Seikatsu fukushi shikin kashitsuke seido* (Life Welfare Fund Loan Scheme)}. Proposals for welfare pensions and other pensions were also made, but they were absorbed into the implementation of the universal insurance and pension scheme. Incidentally, the definition of low income varies widely. According to the aforementioned loan schemes, it includes anybody earning an income between 1.4 and 1.8 times the *Seikatsu hogo* standard. The self-pay portion of various social service provisions, or the exemption of social insurance payments, non-taxable thresholds for residential tax, head tax, income tax and other taxes, may be used to define low income as well. Another standard is also used to determine the income upper limit for eligibility for public housing. Thus, the low income class is defined sometimes as slightly higher than the *Seikatsu hogo* standard, while at other times the definition is based on something completely different. The ceiling for the class is varied and also vague. In recent years, more often than not, the beneficiaries are also included as part of the low income class in policy formulation. In any case, we see various different standards other than the *Seikatsu hogo* standard which was supposed to be aimed at poor people in general.

The next point concerns the complementary nature of the protection offered by the *Seikatsu hogo* system. As mentioned, the *Seikatsu hogo* system expects poor people to utilise all their resources, capabilities and whatever they have for the maintenance of their basic living standard. A capability here means the capability to work, and it is understood that unemployable people can only be assisted after all their efforts to be employed have been exhausted (Koyama 1951: 125). However, in reality, the number of employable people receiving the benefit was decreasing, and they were 'replacing the sort of people who should be on the benefit,' even before Japan's economy entered the rapid high growth phase (Kuroki 1958: 209). This phenomenon was explained either by the fact that those people who could be on the benefit were absorbed into the booming labour market, or the employable poor were in fact actively excluded as a part of the protection adjustment (restraint), exemplified in the existence of the vast low income class we examined earlier. Further, Tadashi Onuma raises the question of society's perception of poverty. He pointed out that the public perception of the poor was locked in on the absolute scale in Japan, and it had not transformed into a more relative perspective (Onuma 1974: 197). In any case, since then the *hi hogosha* (recipients of public assistance) class has become more and more dominated by unemployables and it has been further segmented into smaller sub-genres. Takashi Kagoyama describes this as a 'transition to a system protecting only single mother families, elderly people, orphans, the disabled and anyone else the health care system fails to deal with, rather than a system safeguarding basic living standards for poor people in general' (The Shukan shakai hoken, May 20, 1968). This point is further discussed in Chapter 7.

The complementary nature of the *Seikatsu hogo* system means that any other assistance which can be provided through the other acts takes precedence. Generally speaking, assistance for poor people in a welfare state is considered to play a proactive complementary role in poverty prevention policies. In this regard, the complementary style of assistance is in itself not an issue. Yet, the relationship between the *Seikatsu hogo* system and the other Acts is very tangled in Japan. In general, the complementary role of the official assistance system is explained in the context that the *Seikatsu hogo* system complements the income safety net provided by the pension, for example, and guarantees a minimum standard of living. But in the case of the *Seikatsu hogo* system, the precedence of the other Acts means not just that it complements the other Acts. In some cases, the other Acts are substitutes for the *Seikatsu hogo* system, and vice versa, in a very complicated manner.

One aspect of this is the complexity of the roles shared by the *Seikatsu hogo* system's medical aid and the other Acts. In supplementing the self-pay portion of insurers (or their families) for health insurance or medical costs under the *Seishin hoken fukushi hō* (Mental Health Welfare Act) and the *Kekkaku yobō hō* (Prevention of Tuberculosis Act), medical aid complements these Acts in much the same way as the livelihood aid of the *Seikatsu hogo* system complements the pension payment. But the *hi hogosha* families on benefit are excluded from the National Health Insurance Scheme and the *Iryōhi josei seido* (Medical Cost Subsidy Scheme) provided by the local authorities. They are only covered by medical aid under the *Seikatsu hogo*. Here, the *Seikatsu hogo* system is not complementing the others but substituting for them. Consequently the *hi hogosha* are clearly cut off from the general health insurance systems.

Also, when the *yō hogosha* (People in Need of Protection) utilised any services provided by any other public social service system, they are considered in practice to have received an equivalent economic benefit to *Seikatu hogo* benefit. The other services may be made partially or wholly responsible for providing minimum life security. For example, any *yō hogosha* who use child, aged or disabled facilities are considered to be receiving the equivalent of livelihood aid or housing aid, and cannot apply to the *Seikatsu hogo* system, except for the medical or occupational aid. This substitution is the reverse of the case where medical aid substitutes for the national health insurance scheme, mentioned previously. According to Takeshi Takasawa, those who administered the Child Welfare Act and the Disabled Welfare Act, both enacted at the same time as the *Seikatsu hogo* Act in the immediate aftermath of the War, equated their function of providing the means for the necessities of life in kind to internment in facilities, and ended up confusing the assistance of the poor in those service Acts. This kind of duplication of economic benefits and social services to poverty is being dealt with in other countries. For example, in England, an eligible person would still have to pay for the services they receive, based on the user-pays principle, and the fees are reimbursed through public assistance for income security. In this way, the relationship between the services and benefits designed to maintain a minimum living standard are clearly defined. The need for this kind of clear separation is arising gradually in Japan as well, as welfare services are implemented and put into operation. For example, to go with the nursing care insurance system, a new aid provision for nursing care was established within the *Seikatsu hogo*. The *Seikatsu hogo* recipients can pay for the nursing insurance fee and the user pays portion from their assistance provision, while receiving services through the nursing care insurance. In this case, poverty is clearly subsumed in the concept of the *hi hogo* class, yet, when one is receiving various social services, one is not questioned as to whether one is living in poverty or not.

We should note that, although the measures to replace the economic benefit function of the *Seikatsu hogo* system with services seem to be solving poverty by a universally applicable system, in fact they hold back the *Seikatsu hogo* system in the residual position of the other systems. This is because the *Seikatsu hogo* has to deal with poverty when all other measures fail, not with poverty in general. Under the current *Seikatsu hogo* system, an arrangement with nursing care insurance is exceptional. The eligible people are thus bound to be divided into those who can use other services and who are considered not to be in poverty and the *hi hogo* class who cannot use other services, being cut off from those services because the *Seikatsu hogo* replaces them. The *hi hogo* class was born because the *Seikatsu hogo* system although directed at general poverty, has failed to become an expression of general poverty, which can be defined by the *Seikatsu hogo* standard alone. The *hi hogo* class on the one hand is considered to sit at the very bottom of the low income earning class which is defined by an over-riding standard, or an income standard which differs from the *Seikatsu hogo* standard. On the other hand, it is given a residual status separate from eligible people who are taken in by the social services. Because it is now increasingly made up of the unemployed, the *hi hogo* class has come to signify the more limited extreme poverty of the unemployable rather than poor people in general.

Specific measures: male poverty

Homeless men of working age

With the enactment of the *Seikatsu hogo* Act after the War, as mentioned above, poverty was assessed only by the minimum standard of living and the path of support was expanded to be available universally. Therefore, it was considered that many measures introduced before the War, directed at the poverty of special categories of people, had become redundant. For example, Shinjirō Koyama mentions the following in relation to the *Kōryobyōnin oyobi kōryoshibōnin toriatsukai hō* (the Act Concerning the Treatment of Travellers found Sick or Dead).

> This legislation, as far as its assistance measures are concerned, is almost entirely in competition with the *Seikatsu hogo* Act, because its aims are almost all included in that Act as well. Therefore, as far as the sections concerning assistance are concerned, it can be claimed to have been almost totally incorporated into the *Seikatsu hogo* Act (Koyama 1951: 134).

Koyama states clearly that the only portion of the Act concerning the treatment of travellers found sick or dead which was still valid was the section about the notification and announcement of deceased persons. However it did not happen like that. A proportion of the poor is still assisted by special measures, outside the general assistance offered by the *Seikatsu hogo* system. This relates to its aforementioned complementary role with the other measures, but what we should be concerned with here is not the policies which cover the welfare categories in general (in which poverty is absorbed) such as children, invalids and the aged. Some poor people are put into the *special* category due to their attributes and modes, and separate special policies and measures have been devised outside the general measures of the *Seikatsu hogo* system to cater for these people. One strain of these is the special policy directed mainly at the poverty of homeless men of working age. Although they were developed originally by the large city governments, these policies have been taken up more recently by the national government. What I mean by the *homeless* here is 'either having no residence or residence is unclear' as defined in the *Seikatsu hogo* Act. Residence in the *Seikatsu hogo* system has little to do with one's eligibility, but more to do with the jurisdiction of the local welfare office where one's case should be handled. Even when residence is unclear, the welfare office in the area where one currently is and in need of assistance, is stipulated to be responsible. This clause to assist where one is in need of assistance, has the potential to initiate emergency assistance in a case of emergency, even if one's residence is known. So, as far as the legality of the Act is concerned, the *Seikatsu hogo* system should be able to respond to all types of poverty including the homeless type. However, quite separately from this principle, the poverty of homeless working age people was acknowledged in a different way at the local government level, and special measures directed at vagrants were devised, even at the time the Act was enacted. Poverty was meant to mean the general impoverished condition of any citizen, the poverty of eligible people and the poverty of people on benefits. Yet, at the same time, it was seen as a special circumstance of vagrants as well. According to the operations papers of the Tokyo metropolitan government's public service bureau, the operations classified under 'measures for vagrants' existed not just in the immediate aftermath of the War, but after 1950 when the new *Seikatsu hogo* Act came into force, and right up to 1963, just before the Olympic games opened (Iwata et al 2002). Incidentally, the general welfare categories of the metropolitan government's policies in those days consisted of the *Seikatsu hogo*, vagrants, sick vagrants, invalids (later re-labelled as disabled). Under the emergency assistance classification, War victims, returnees from the former colonies and children were listed. For children, apart from children in general, the distinctive terms of *juvenile vagrant* and *vagrant mother and child* were used. I have already discussed in detail the historical developments concerning the vagrant measures using examples from Tokyo (Iwata 1995), and I will not go over them again here.

The category of vagrants became various other special categories in different local authorities such as 'a person with no fixed address,' 'people sleeping rough,' 'outdoor residents,' 'street dwellers' and so on, to today's more commonly used *hōmuresu* (homeless people). As Kitagawa's contribution in Chapter 9 of this volume gives details of the male *hōmuresu*, I will just refer to three characteristics of the special measures directed at this homeless type of poverty.

Shelter facilities

First of all, the measures directed at vagrants in big cities including Tokyo and Ōsaka have always been handled in a special way, even though the *Seikatsu hogo* system could be applied to them. The local authorities prefer shelter assistance at designated facilities. Instead of going through the usual welfare office channels, they set up dedicated organisations to handle them separately. Alternatively, a dedicated section is established in the welfare office. Special publications like *A Manual for handling people of no-fixed-address* are produced. This kind of attitude has always been there in varying degrees and different measures since the days of the vagrants until quite recently, when the term vagrants has been replaced by other terms such as 'a person with no fixed address,' 'people sleeping rough,' 'outdoor residents,' 'street dwellers.'

To start with, the existence of the shelter facilities is alien to the universal assistance-based *Seikatsu hogo* system. According to Koyama, the *Seikatsu hogo* must naturally be home based, if it is meant to provide income security as a part of social security, on the universal assistance principle (Koyama 1951: 429–439). Unlike universal assistance, shelter assistance offers only genre-based assistance to selected people who are qualified to be interned in particular facilities. Legally speaking, the genres for shelter facilities include elderly nursing (which was later transferred and absorbed into the Aged Welfare Act), aid, rehabilitation, medical aid, vocational aid and accommodation assistance, but in reality, regardless of the type of facilities, they were all used to intern vagrants. To put it bluntly, it is not that the facilities were there first and the internees were selected accordingly. The facilities were built in designated areas to intern vagrants and *hōmuresu* people after they had been rounded up by force or "smoked out," because they were illegally squatting. Having said this, there are variations from region to region when it comes to setting up facilities for different genres. For example, in Tokyo, there are rehabilitation and accommodation aid facilities, while in Ōsaka, there are rehabilitation and aid facilities, and in the rest of the country some aid facilities and rehabilitation facilities have been set up. Whatever the original official functions were, all of them inevitably ended up clustering vagrants, people with no fixed address, people sleeping rough and others into compounds.

It was of course against the spirit of the Act to use the *hogo* facilities for vagrants. The Ministry of Health and Welfare issued a number of notices including a *Guideline for using the* hogo *facilities* in 1957, encouraging the facilities to stick to their original use (Iwata 1995: 96–98). A caution was also issued concerning the use of the shelter facilities to deal with vagrants of working age. It was suggested that aid facilities and rehabilitation facilities should be turned into places to accommodate tuberculosis sufferers and mentally ill people discharged from their institutions, in other words facilities for the unemployable. This kind of attempt to turn *hogo* facilities into places for "unemployables," as well as the fact that the number of facilities is limited, has made it difficult to deal with the poverty of the homeless, and has contributed to the fresh rise in the number of *hōmuresu* people in the 1990s. Incidentally, when the *Hōmuresu no jiritsu shien tō ni kansuru tokubetsu sochihō* (the Act to Assist Homeless People become Financially Independent, hereafter, abbreviated to *Hōmuresu jiritsu shienhō*) was enacted in 2002, the Ministry of Health, Welfare and Labour emphasised, through the Director's directive that the *Seikatsu hogo* applied to the homeless in the same way as to the general public. Yet at the same time, it stressed that they should first be compounded in appropriate facilities, and if employable, in the Centre to Assist with Becoming Self-Reliant. If sick or old, they should be put in the medical and nursing facilities. Only after that could they be assisted at home, as the Director's notice clearly indicated. It also encouraged the local government authorities to develop the *hogo* facilities. In the 2003 Ministry directive, this "compound-ism" had receded somewhat. But it urged that special attention should be paid when deciding whether to apply the *Seikatsu hogo*, to finding out 'if the applicants can continue to live at home or not.' If it was found that it was impossible for them to continue to live at home, it said, they should be compounded in the *Seikatsu hogo* facilities or in accommodation under the Social Welfare Act.

Extra-legal assistance

Secondly, there are extra-legal back-up measures taken by the local authorities at their own discretion. These are directed at the homeless poor by the local authorities when the special measures within the *Seikatsu hogo* system, mostly 'compound assistance,' have been found to be insufficient. In general, the *extra-legal back-up* means supplementary payments, provision in kind, loans and so on, which are outside the service of any of the social welfare related legal framework. In relation to the *Seikatsu hogo* Act, the measures are the assistance given outside the Act at the local level at their discretion. Accordingly, what they are and who receives them varies from region to region, but in general, they are additional assistance to the *hi hogo* households or assistance to the low income earning households. In short, these measures are a "top-up" type of assistance given by the local authorities to the aforementioned general categories of poverty, namely the *hi hogo* households and the low income earning households. In actual terms, they could consist of seasonal relief money in summer and winter, money for children's excursions, book vouchers, bathhouse tickets, grant money for childbirth, congratulatory money for new employment, and various other things. These kinds of top-up measures are very unreliable, easy to review and curtail, especially at a time of fiscal constraint as we have now. Also, there is no right to claim, or a minimum standard. Apart from the assistance measures discussed above, the extra-legal back-up measures have been used to deal with homeless poverty when the application of the *Seikatsu hogo* is uncertain. Some local authorities clearly state this, in dealing with 'people travelling through.' What the Welfare Offices in big cities did to manage the sudden surge in *hōmuresu* people in the 1990s, was to give them emergency assistance using these extra-legal back-up measures. Some of the Welfare Offices had already compiled a manual of how to deal with people of no-fixed-address in the 1980s. Let us look at the example of a manual compiled by a ward in Tokyo. It says, the legal situation 'when assessing people of working age (younger than sixty), is to deal with them strictly unless they are proven to be unemployable by a medical agency, due to illness and so on.'

The extra-legal measures are applied to those people whose 'immediate protection under the *Seikatsu hogo* is difficult.'[1] When these people come up and "claim" they are hungry, give them 'udon noodles or dry biscuits.' When they ask for living expenses or travel expenses, lend them some within certain limits. These are aimed at nobody in particular. These are not part of a positive policy. To put it simply, these measures are directed at poverty which is not immediately recognised as being eligible for assistance under the *Seikatsu hogo* system, but cannot be ignored from the humanitarian point of view. The extra-legal back-up measures can vary from handing out bread vouchers and other food items including the udon noodles and dry biscuits mentioned above, medicine, clothes and groceries, providing access to showers and emergency accommodation, to lending the fares for transport home or going to job interviews. There are some welfare offices which move people on by handing out a universal amount of anything from ¥300 to ¥500, as what they call emergency assistance money. This comes from make-dos and donations of goods and services from various sources, such as making use of the leftovers from disaster relief aid, borrowing from the emergency small amount fund from the council of social welfare, making use of leftover bathhouse vouchers from the extra-legal back-up measures. Some actually come from the special budget too. In any case in order to deal with the homeless problem, extra-legal back-up measures in the big cities, which are quite different from the *Seikatsu hogo*'s top-up assistance, have become emergency assistance from humanitarian concerns, directed at the *hōmuresu* rejected by the *Seikatsu hogo* system. The homeless type of poverty towards which the local authorities direct their emergency assistance is the area the *Seikatsu hogo* system, the last safety net of a welfare state fails. It is literally the "residual" and the extra-legal back-up measures perform the function of residual welfare programme.

The *yoseba*

Thirdly, the homeless type of poverty, mainly affecting males of working age, was rediscovered during the period of rapid economic growth, as something to be dealt with by measures directed at special areas including what is commonly known as the *yoseba*. This kind of poverty was understood first as affecting the *yoseba* area and its lodgers and *yoseba* workers, and then their people sleeping rough, outdoor residents and street dwellers became an issue. The *yoseba* refers also to the labour market for day labourers, and to the areas where cheap rooming houses (flophouses) are concentrated. Among them, Sanya in Tokyo, Kamagasaki (Airin district) in Ōsaka and Kotobuki in Yokohama are large enough to be called the big three *yoseba* of Japan. They are reputed to have propped up the stevedore, construction and other industries during the period of rapid economic growth. These areas seem to have come into being spontaneously, but there has been intervention and guidance from welfare and other administration. After the War, some of the poverty class people with capacity for employment, including vagrants and "shack dwellers" were intentionally compounded into these areas (Iwata 1995).[2] What directly prompted the policy makers to come up with measures directed at the *yoseba* was the riots which erupted in Tokyo and Ōsaka amongst the workers in 1960. The riots were later repeated and became the concern of the central government. After a discussion at cabinet level, the formulation of an integrated policy was suggested for Tokyo and Ōsaka. In this regard, the *yoseba* measures were a public order issue, but the labour problem of the day labourers as well as their family's welfare, health care, education and housing issues, and the comprehensive poverty problems in their backgrounds had also had to be put on the political agenda. To put it in a different way, a proportion of poverty amongst employable people, which had been intentionally compounded into the *yoseba* and excluded from the political agenda, was 'rediscovered' as a result of the riots. Henceforth, the measures involved the provision of consultation and services to individual lodgers in the district, regarding their work and all aspects of life, as well as surveillance and control of the whole district. One of the focuses of the *yoseba* measures in the early days was dealing with the poverty of the families lodging there by encouraging them to move out to public housing. This resulted in turning the *yoseba* into a predominantly single male domain, further accentuating the 'peculiarity' of the *yoseba*. Incidentally, unemployment and sleeping on the streets for people living in these districts are 'permanent' phenomenon, typifying their unstable way of life. Therefore, the measures directed at the *yoseba* inevitably had to include measures for people sleeping rough, outdoor residents and others who might end up in that situation, as well as measures aimed at the lodgers and the district as a whole. The issues became more intensified especially after the oil crisis, along with the ageing population of the districts. In principle, to apply the *Seikatsu hogo* to these people they needed first to be interned to be assisted. Apart than that, special employment enterprises, accommodation assistance which is normally limited to one night, accommodation assistance at the end and beginning of the year, bread (or meal) vouchers and so on are available. These are the *yoseba* variation of the aforementioned extra-legal back-up measures.

Structurally categorising the *hōmuresu*

Various measures directed at the *hōmuresu* people at a local level since the late 1990s and the national legislation of the *Hōmuresu jiritsu shien hō* in 2002 were essentially the result of the national government's attempt to make policies for *hōmuresu* people. The people sleeping rough, outdoor residents, street dwellers and so on, who were no longer contained in particular districts but seen to be spreading all over the country, were bundled together under the term *hōmuresu* for whom the national government attempted to make coherent policies with reference to the previous results of *yoseba* measures, as well as the *Seikatsu hogo*'s compound and assist and extra-legal back-up measures. To put it in another way, the national government only confirmed, although through temporary legislation, the special measures the local authorities had had to employ to deal with poverty, alongside the universal assistance scheme. *Hōmuresu* people were defined here as 'people who live and lead their lives without good reason in the urban parks, on river banks, streets, at railway stations and so on.' Further, when the local authorities were devising the actual programmes, the national government urged them to divide the *hōmuresu* people into three groups, 'unemployed people willing to become self reliant;' 'people in need of welfare or medical assistance;' and 'dropouts from society' and take appropriate measures. The first two classifications are based on the ability to be employed which are reminiscent of the old classifications of the *Kyūgo hō* Act. The important thing here is that those who can be employed are dealt with for their minimum living security, not by the *Seikatsu hogo* system, but by the Centre to Assist Self Reliance and other programmes based on the *Hōmuresu jiritsu shien hō*. Those who failed to become self-reliant as well as the second group would be handled by the *Seikatsu hogo* system. The third group, the drop outs from society have been called by various names including social misfits. But these days they are not so much misfits but escapees from debt or domestic violence at home. In any case, the third category indicates there are employable people who do not fit easily into the programmes for self-reliance. The *hōmuresu* measures are intended to first assist people to become self reliant and not to limit the application of the *Seikatsu hogo* to them. The *hōmuresu* people who cannot be made self-reliant will then be looked after the *Seikatsu hogo*. The compound-ism mentioned above is incorporated into the *hōmuresu* measures as well, as a value judgement about whether or not they can lead their lives at home. When they fail to find adequate housing, an emergency measure, meaning an extra-legal back-up measure, is included in the programme as well, although with a warning that it is to remain strictly for emergencies. How this will develop in practice is far from certain. It will be interesting to see how the general relief and the special measures are going to reconcile and how the *hōmuresu* issue is going to be redefined.

Specific measures: Women's poverty

The *Hōmuresu jiritsu shienhō* does not exclude women from its definition of homeless people. Yet, because its definition is strictly limited to people living in public space, or street dwellers, the measures tend to be formulated for men who are more likely to be *hōmuresu*. The basic guidelines for assistance measures for homeless people, devised by the national government in 2003 stressed, in regards to women's poverty, the necessity for co-ordination with women's counselling services and women's assistance facilities. It suggested that women's poverty should be dealt with within the special framework already in existence. The call to assist single mother families under a special category has been around since the *Boshi hogo hō* (Assistance for Single Mother Families) was debated before the War. The idea was revised in the post-War era under the new term, *mibōjin boshi* (widowed single mother family). The *boshi setai* (single mother households) have been constantly spoken of as being a special poverty category, and special measures have been devised accordingly.

The *boshi*

As the 1949 resolutions by both houses show, the *mibōjin boshi* or the 'issue of assisting bereaved families,' was a huge political concern in the immediate aftermath of the War.[3] According to Shinjirō Koyama, the government was initially 'intent on legislating a stand alone law, which could be called the act to assist the *mibōjin boshi* or something like that, to be the Centre of a programme to help with the assistance of widowed single mother families, but, for one reason or another, it came unstuck.' (Koyama 1951: 40) As he recalls, their poverty was of special concern, but special legislation to deal with it did not materialised. The reason for it failing to happen is not clear, but it is likely that the GHQ occupation authority insisted on a more universally applicable general assistance approach under the *Seikatsu hogo* Act. Yoshisuke Kasai, the head of the Social Welfare Bureau at the time, recalls that the necessity of adding on the disabled veterans and single mother families to the non-discriminatory universal application principle of the *Seikatsu hogo* Act, was much debated on the floor of the national Diet, but it was difficult to gain sympathy from the GHQ. So, the GHQ was lobbied first about the disabled veterans, which bore fruit with the enactment of the Disabled Welfare Act. But by 1950, according to Kasai, hardly any progress had been made on the widows' issue (Kōseishō shakaikyoku 1950: 105–106). Because of this, the *mibōjin boshi* issue was, instead of being given a dedicated legislation, tackled within a framework of welfare programmes for single mother households, a patchwork of various systems. This included thorough implementation and wider application of income security through the *Seikatsu hogo* system and other welfare systems, development of the *boshi* dormitories under the Children's Welfare Act, helping with access to public housing, loans for living expenses, easier access to childcare facilities, special tax concessions and so on. Many of the *boshi* dormitories (now known as Facilities to assist the Lives of Single Mothers and Children) were converted from the facilities that had been used to compound vagrant *boshi*. Many of the single mothers were living in poverty, but, in this specific programme, the accommodation portion was supplied outside the *Seikatsu hogo* system. The loans scheme was set up under the *Boshi* Welfare Fund Act in 1952 with the aim of helping with the problems of single mother households through loans. Unlike the *Setai kosei shikin kashitsuke seido* (Household Improvement Fund Loan Scheme) referred to above, there was no income threshold for this scheme. It was, in reality, financial assistance for households living in poverty, but fashioned as a welfare programme directed at single mother households and added on to the *Seikatsu hogo* system.

With the addition of the 1964 *Boshi* Welfare Act and the 1982 *Boshi* and *kafu* Welfare Act, the entire welfare system for single mother households and former single mothers had been covered by legislation. Here, the special categories to be helped were the *boshi*, 'women without a spouse who have children under the age of twenty in their care' and the 'women who had brought up children in *boshi* households.' If we take into consideration the 1961 legislation of the Childcare Assistance Act, it seems the target for additional assistance has been broadened to single mother families in general from the initial *mibōjin boshi* (widowed single mothers and children) which was prompted by the War. However, in regards to childcare assistance, it was a means to separate *boshi* due to death from *boshi* due to separation and it has been pointed out that the payment is smaller and the income criterion is stricter than for the pension. We must also remember that *kafu* as a welfare category is not the same as *kafu* in common use, as in widows. *Kafu* as a welfare category only refers to women who used to be single mothers. It refers to the welfare of the former single mothers of *boshi* households, after the children have become adult.

Structurally categorising prostitution

In the very early days after the War a special programme was implemented aimed at single women which was not just special assistance for the poverty of women dealt with through the *boshi* category. This was the *Tokushu fujin hogo jigyō* (The Programme to Assist Special Women), directed at the special women known in those days as 'women of darkness' or *panpan gāru* (working girls). The programme originated in the 'Programme to Regulate, Prevent and assist Private Prostitutes' decided on at a vice ministerial meeting in 1946. Following the passing of the Anti-Prostitution Act of 1956, the private prostitution programme was carried over into the more general *Fujin hogo jigyō* (The Programme to Assist Women in Need). The Anti-Prostitution Act had two aspects. One reason for the act was to regulate prostitution from the perspective of public health, to stop the spread of sexually transmitted diseases, and to maintain public morals. The other reason was to protect women and rehabilitate them. The latter perspective is manifested in the *Fujin hogo jigyō*. Here, the poverty of women who had to make a living from prostitution was recognised, although the way out from poverty was not to deal with poverty itself, but to rehabilitate prostitutes. The following three points are worth noting. First, the attitude of Japanese society in general and its government in particular towards prostitution in the wake of the War was vague. It is believed a secret directive was issued to set up brothels specifically aimed at servicing soldiers from the incoming occupation forces, in order to protect ordinary women and girls. The aforementioned Programme to Regulate, Prevent and Assist Private Prostitutes, in which brothels were euphemistically called special eateries, suggested there was a strategy to concentrate brothels and prostitutes in designated districts (red line and blue line districts). This could be interpreted, apart from the public health and moral problems, as acknowledging a solution to women's poverty through prostitution. In the same way that men of employable age were compounded into the *yoseba* to solve their homelessness, women's poverty was left to the prostitution industry. Even after the enactment of the Anti-Prostitution Act, known for its many loopholes, the situation has remained pretty much the same, up to today's overseas migrant women workers' problems.

Second, the special women and women in need of protection, at whom the assistance and rehabilitation programmes were directed, referred not only to those who had already "fallen" and prostitutes who were actually in business but 'those who may fall' and 'those who might become prostitutes' as well. This may be based on an understanding that prostitution might not necessarily be carried out in obvious places and organised by pimps, but could take place anywhere quite easily, in various impoverished circumstances. For example, a runaway girl on the streets is a suspect, even though she is not involved in prostitution. Furthermore, as prostitution took place in a more concealed fashion and in various forms, and as the number of women to be assisted in institutions under the *Fujin hogo jigyō* declined, the definition of likely candidates gradually extended to include those without any organisation to help them as well. More discussion on this point is found below, in Keiko Kawahara's contribution to this book in Chapter 8.

The targets for the *Fujin hogo jigyō* have greatly widened to incorporate the general circumstances of women cut off from their families, including domestic violence sufferers. Third, despite the fact that prostitution is derived from women's poverty and that the *Fujin hogo jigyō* is meant to deal with their poverty in general, the actual programmes, other than medical assistance, exist outside the *Seikatsu hogo* system. Its basic approach in providing assistance is to compound prostitutes into the *Fujin hogo* facilities. It was a fairly commonly held view among the people involved in the *Fujin hogo jigyō* in those days that 'prostitutes were difficult, some intellectually and mentally handicapped, while others were "psychopaths".' Because the Anti-Prostitution Act punishes prostitutes, that is, women over twenty years old who solicit for prostitution are punishable, a correctional attitude may have been brought into the *Fujin hogo jigyō* as well. The women in need of protection and the likely candidates had first to be protected and rehabilitated under the *Fujin hogo jigyō* and not to be dealt with by general assistance under the *Seikatsu hogo* system. Their poverty was, in that sense, considered to be a 'special' case. From the *Fujin hogo* facilities repeated requests have been made to treat the women in need of assistance as ordinary people in poverty, because the level of assistance they get is lower than that available from the *Seikatsu hogo*.

Analysing post-War policy and poverty categories

As seen above, poverty in the post-War society of Japan is on one hand characterised by that of the *hi hogo* class which is increasingly becoming unemployable, and the neighbouring low income earning borderline class. It is, on the other hand, characterised by the special poverty cases to which various special measures are directed. Furthermore, some poverty becomes invisible and included in other social service targets. What is the significance of poverty being scattered all over the place, in different positions, while poverty in general was once clearly defined as affecting people living below the poverty line drawn by the *Seikatsu hogo* standard? Below, I will discuss the meaning of the position of the categories of poverty in the post-War society of Japan, first in relation to welfare policy principles, then in regard to the complex relationship between the policies on poverty and other policies on social security and social services.

Work testing: a double standard

Joel Handler, who has detailed the historical development of welfare policies directed at poverty in the USA, cites three tasks of welfare policy, namely, to help deal with social disorder, to relieve misery and to preserve the labour market. He continues on to say that the last one of these, the thorough implementation of work requirements, which relief should not easily replace, is the most important and the 'most enduring principle' of all welfare policies throughout history.

> The major purpose of welfare policy has been the control of pauperism. Paupers, who were unwilling or unable to work, were considered moral degenerates and were outcasts from society. The goal of welfare policy was to separate the paupers from the deserving poor and to make sure that giving relief would not encourage people to cross that line. The poor were balanced precariously; the surest way to tip that balance and to start the slide into pauperism was the indiscriminate giving of aid (Handler 1992: 37).

Geremek also finds that the 'compulsion to work lies at the root of the contemporary social security system:'

> Work is treated as a medicine to cure poverty and crime. Moral anxiety brought about by poverty goes hand in hand with the fear that indulgence in a lazy life and sacrificing society has dire consequences. Therefore, the compulsion to work always goes back to the modern pursuit of a social policy to eliminate poverty, and provides the basis for the nation to intervene in the establishment of the social security system (Geremek 1993: 333).

Judging from the 'most enduring principle,' the universal non-discriminatory application principle of the post-War *Seikatsu hogo* system has the serious problem of keeping the poor from what Handler calls the dangerous slide into pauperism, as it does not discriminate against those who can work. Criticism has been repeatedly voiced about this danger, from breeding lazy people at the time of the establishment of the system to today's *moraru hazādo* (moral hazard) issue. A careful strategy of double standards has to be employed when putting the *Seikatsu hogo* into practice. On the one hand, the non-discriminatory universal application principle has to be followed, but, on the other hand, the application of it to those who have the ability to work has to be very carefully done, by interpreting the utilisation of assets and abilities in a stricter fashion. Applying the *Seikatsu hogo* to those in the working age group under special conditions and dealing with their poverty using special measures, is all about implementing the work requirement, welfare policy's most enduring principle, within the general assistance principle.

The maintenance of morals

The relief of the poor the cause of whose poverty is suspected to be due to a lack of individual morals, as well as the lack of a work ethic, also causes problems for the defence of poor. The problems are the maintenance of a healthy family life and the morals governing a citizen's social life. These can be more susceptible to changing social values than the work ethic. T.H. Marshall pointed out that single males had been disliked and often punished at the dawn of capitalism in England, because they were thought to lack stability (Marshall 1981: 70). The values applied to marriage and family have become much more diverse today. Therefore, the kind of moral judgments that affect the formulation of poverty policy and how they alter, will have a subtle impact on the special measures directed at poverty. When it was revised in 1950, the *Seikatsu hogo* Act reaffirmed the principle of not imposing a moral judgment by removing what was known as the disqualification clause. It was a very important aspect of the non-discriminatory universal application principle. However this does not mean that the interpretation poverty is due to one's character too disappeared from society as well. For example, the women in need of protection were emphasised on one hand as being victims of poverty, yet on the other hand, at the time of the inception of the *Fujin hogo jigyō*, it was of particular concern that their moral failure might undermine the healthy family life of the general public. Soliciting for prostitution is a criminal act. Single male workers at the yoseba and homeless people are also amongst those who have failed to maintain ordinary family lives. They are often seen as criminals illegally occupying public land. The measures directed at their poverty do not come in the shape of assistance for the general public, even though such measures are initially called for because of what Handler calls the principle of maintaining social public order. Those measures are provided as an inseparable part of the service of correcting their moral problems.

The measures directed at the *boshi* and *kafu*, even though they are all women, are added on to the general assistance, unlike those directed at women in need of protection. This is simply because they are considered to be deserving poor for the following two reasons. Firstly, they were War victims, as in widowed single mothers and children. Secondly, as I said above, because moral judgments alter along with the times and society, the position of 'boshi due to separation in relation to the moral high position of *boshi* due to death has been changing in a subtle way. When divorce is no longer a moral issue, a supplementary assistance given to all single parents equally, based on the welfare of children becomes possible.

Assessment rankings of people in dire circumstances based on social value judgments of their morals are made from time to time, and these in turn are used to influence the particular poverty measures to be taken, and to decide on which people should be helped by particular programmes. For example, the extension of the interpretation of women in need of protection mentioned above means that whether to give priority to prostitutes, women in general in need of protection or the recently added category of domestic violence sufferers is constantly being revised at the actual application level of the *Fujin hogo jigyō*. What kind of poverty is chosen to be the target of special measures, and where the target groups are in society, reflect what kind of morals society demands of people and its priorities.

The issue of belonging

Another important principle in regard to welfare policy aimed at poverty is the legitimacy of belonging to the society as a component of the policy. The *Seikatsu hogo* system is applicable to people of Japanese nationality. It asks in the identification of the poor whether they belong to the Japanese nation or not. In practice, whether or not they belong to the area matters, as each welfare office, the actual operators of the system, and deals only with those belonging to its own territorial jurisdiction. As I have pointed out already, belonging to an area here does not have to mean through residential registration, and physical residence or present location is meant to be sufficient. In reality though, accepting physical residence or present location has not been simple. This is because the local authorities concerned have to bear some of the cost of the *Seikatsu hogo* benefits the resident poor receive and the administration costs. For the welfare office as a part of the local authority, offering its service to people who may not be resident there may be seen as acting beyond their jurisdiction. When more and more basic welfare services are left to the local authorities to administer, it is natural for them to regard the operation of the *Seikatsu hogo* system as no different from other services. Besides, as mentioned already, legality or a lack of social morals are attached to people in the homeless type of poverty, because their type of poverty goes with their illegal squatting in public places such as parks and river banks. The line drawn between the poor and the legitimate residents tends to get more and more marked. Needless to say, the legitimacy of belonging manifests itself most acutely in the measures directed at the poverty of migrants.

The poverty of Japanese welfare policy

There are enduring basic principles which permeate all the poverty policies of any country, at any time. The way the poverty policy targets are set in Japan shows that the basic principles are permeating here as well. Of course, these principles can be manifested more weakly or strongly according to the other factors that affect poverty policies such as the maintenance of social order, sympathy and empathy towards the poor, or the demands and movements of the poor themselves. The actual classification of the poor and their position are bound to change in relation to these factors. In addition, the formulation of poverty classifications and bifurcation in post-War society also reflect the unique position poverty policy occupies in welfare policy at large in Japan. In general, welfare policies are arranged in various ways according to the problems to be solved, the methods employed or the source of the budget. However, income security is considered to be quite separate from the social services which are organised according to different attributes such as youth or old age, and according to various different needs. It is also widely acknowledged that there are preventative measures in income security, as well as after the event type of public relief assistance.

The relationship between income security and social services can vary, as I mentioned already. A person can have a combination of both, like having the pension and other income security, to which nursing services and other social services can be added. A vertically integrated case is also possible, such as the disabled welfare service which will take care of every need for a disabled person including income. Income security can be either a combination of preventative measures and after the event relief assistance, where the relief measures cover what the preventative measures do not, or it could be made up of only relief measures. The historical prototype of this is after the event relief assistance directed at poverty, which takes care of all life's necessities for the poor, no matter how basic that may be. An extreme example is "compounded" care in a facility. The development of the welfare policy is changing this prototype. On the one hand, a combination of prevention and relief in income security has been developed, while on the other hand, social services are organised quite separately from income security. The needs of the people can be met by a combination of these various parts. This has been the direction of welfare policy development. The *Seikatsu hogo* system, which was the starting point for welfare policy development in post-War Japan, had to take on single-handedly the task of meeting all the needs of poor people, as after the event relief assistance for the poor, because social security was underdeveloped and social services were inadequate. In addition to the seven types of aid, the system carried out consultations to encourage self reliance and used the protection facilities as tools to accomplish the task. The reason why the era of the troika system of the *Seikatsu hogo* Act, the Children's Welfare Act and the Welfare Act for Disabled People, is often referred to as the 'relief of the poor' welfare epoch, is because poverty classification in those days represented all the basic needs of everyone.

The relief of the poor welfare system in that sense, however, began crumbling in Japan. One sign was the introduction of universal health care and a universal pension. The other was the development of services according to different welfare needs. Takeshi Takasawa considers it important that in the late 1950s a poverty category for the low income earning class was established and the separate welfare needs of the aged, disabled people, single mother families and other subcategories of poverty were noted. He points out that it was an important turning point for welfare policy which shifted towards satisfying the various different needs of various different attributes of poverty (Takasawa 2000: 188–189). The lower income earning class has many different faces and one size does not fit all now (Takasawa 2000: 189). Later, what is known as the 'six welfare Acts system' was established. According to Takasawa, 'it was at the core a public assistance Act, with the five other fostering acts around it to cater for various welfare needs categories for various attributes,' to carry out social welfare operations. However, looking at the poverty category positions as we have seen in this chapter, the relationship between the *Seikatsu hogo* system and various welfare services has not been as clear cut as Takasawa suggests. In particular because the welfare service has not shifted sufficiently from a facility oriented service to a community oriented one, the service provision and a part of the financial provision to the poor has been confused and constitutes a part of what Takasawa calls a fostering Act. For example, with the enactment of the Welfare Act for Aged People, not only the poor elderly people who had been in the *hogo* facilities but also their financial security were transferred to the old aged care facilities. The measures directed at poverty such as the *Fujin hogo* facilities and the Centre to Assist the Self Reliance of Homeless People, are seen as if they were a general service provision for the various categories of attributes, in the confusion of the financial provisions of the general services system. Seeing them like that, we have to remember that their real negative and correctional natures tend to appear diluted.

As the exclusion of the *hi hogo* class from the national health insurance system and national pension scheme shows, the measures directed at poverty are clearly cut off from general policies. Poverty policy has not been able to completely cast aside the previous historical prototype which neglects the diverse needs of the diverse poor. It has so far failed to establish a supplementary position within the overall system of a welfare nation. In other words, the residual position of today's *hi hogo* class, poverty hidden within the other Acts, or poverty as a special category within a special policy, are partly due to the lack of review of the *Seikatsu hogo* system which had been given the role of administering direct measures to aid poverty relief in the post-War era. The position of the *Seikatsu hogo* system has not sufficiently been reviewed in the expanding landscape of social security and social welfare services since the 1960s, and has been co-ordinated poorly with the various other measures and services. This is indicated by the fact that no fundamental reform has been made to the *Seikatsu hogo* system until today.

The characterisation of poverty, the specialisation of poverty and the latency of poverty by those measures directed at poverty all have to do with the change in the interpretation of poverty, the transformation of people's interest from poverty to the middle class and the optimistic attitude of believing there is no poverty. We can only perceive poverty as a policy category, and, for the time being, have no other means to confirm it other than by the statistics based on that particular category. There is ample possibility for the interpretation of poverty to change, of course, through measuring and studying poverty by new methods and through new approaches, a new interpretation of the work obligation and other policy principles, and raising the possibility for new relations with social services and social security. For instance, the establishment of the Nursing Care Insurance System not only has created a new relationship with the *Seikatsu hogo* system, but also, through its application, poverty among the aged is being freshly discovered. The response to the child abuse problem has the potential to focus attention on the poverty and isolation of the family, which may be behind the problem in the first place. Furthermore, the current long economic slump which has been continuing since the 1990s, due to the transformation of the socio-economic structure, is challenging the prevailing optimistic view of poverty as well. In order to prevent this becoming a passing phenomenon under an economic downturn, we need to create a new language to discuss today's poverty and new policy images as well as a fundamental review of the existing policy categories.

2 Poverty as a result of exclusion – Tokyo's urban underclass

Akihiko Nishizawa

National homogenisation and exclusion

Nationality and *Koseki* (the Family Register)

Gennosuke Yokoyama describes urban underclass couples in his *Nihon no kasō shakai* (The Underclass of Japan) ([1899] 1985: 57) as follows:

> And when we look at self proclaimed married couples, hardly any of them have been through the proper marriage procedure using go-betweens. In one street, properly married couples live in only a few out of several dozen houses. In one row of terraces, there are dozens of children who are only noted in police records and not registered at the ward office. There are many grown-ups with no nationality. Many of them are Japanese but they are not registered as Japanese. They cohabit freely and *shiseiji* (privately born children) are the result. The reason there are so many children without a nationality living in poor areas is that they are born as a result of unwed cohabitation and left by their mothers without adequate care.

Not only Yokoyama but many others also describe the state of citizens without family registration as a state of being 'without nationality.' Much later, Yasoo Kusama in *Donzoko no hitotachi* (People in dire straits) (1936) described 'the person with no nationality, in other words, a person not registered' when discussing 'children in poverty'. According to Kiyoshi Nakagawa, de facto relationships accounted for forty-two per cent of the urban underclass of Tokyo (the lower ten per cent of Tokyo's urban population) between 1891 and 1912, and thirty-seven per cent between 1920 and 1921 (2000: 229). Using 'a divorce rate worked out by measuring the number of divorces compared to marriages, the Tokyo average during the 1880s was a staggering 50.4%, while that for the 1890s was 28.4%. The divorce rate in Tokyo at the turn of the century was extremely high, much higher than the national average during the corresponding period.' (Nakagawa 2000: 246)

Following the Meiji Restoration, the population of Tokyo in 1872 fell to 580,000, barely half of the Edo era population. It began recovering rapidly about 1880, and passed the one million mark again in the 1890s. This was due to an influx to the city of half a million young men. There was no way Tokyo could satisfactorily support this sudden increase in population, and a large class of impoverished people emerged who were too poor to create or sustain families. Not until the twentieth century did Tokyo's natural population start to show an increase. The economy did not improve quickly and the urban underclass continued to 'drift aimlessly.' This underclass has been portrayed from the perspective of 'civilized' writers as 'savages' that displayed ridicule-worthy immorality and vulgarity. Yokoyama and Kusama were the exceptions, who argued that the predicament of the urban underclass was a social problem. Their emphasis on 'nationality' means that even they expected the underclass to be entered in the Family Register in order to become members of the nation state, as an escape route from poverty. Incidentally, when Gennosuke Yokoyama talks about '*shiseiji*' (Privately Born Children), he is not using it in its more usual sense today, meaning illegitimate children, but he was employing the official term of the day, meaning unregistered children. The officially registered children were called '*koseiji*' (Publicly Born Children).

National homogenisation and exclusion

For the Meiji government, the *Kosekihō* (the Family Registration Act) (1871) was a strategy to swiftly nationalise the population within its boundaries. Modern nation states all strive to standardise their populations; they aim for 'good national citizens' who can be the embodiment of industrialism. In order to achieve that, they have to homogenise their entire territories, destroying any status- or locality-oriented differences that had been preserving independent legitimacy. 'In a feudal society such as operated during the Edo period where society is divided into class-based structures and overlaps the physical divisions of the land, a system of ruling by registering all people equally against land space would not be possible.' This is because of a lack of 'homogeneous continuous "space" on which all people can be registered equally.'

Under the Meiji government, the 'standardization of space went ahead alongside the emergence of the new method of government, the "Koseki (family registration)" system'(Wakabayashi 1996: 13). Under the Japanese Family Registration System, everyone is assumed to belong to a family, and perceived as a part of the family, headed by the family leader. Then everyone is standardised as a 'subject' of the emperor, who is assigned to be the one and only ruler of the territory (Fujita 1998: 104).[1] When there is only a primitive control mechanism, the only way of recording everybody is their assembly in one place. With regard to the floating population of the Megalopolis, the 'renters' and 'employees' from other places have to be registered as belonging to the household of the land owners or employers (Temporary Residence Registration). Thus, everybody is recorded according to residence and occupation while their identity is referred back to their place of birth. By registering in this kind of system (i.e. patriarchical family system), they became 'nationals' of the Japanese state. The registration system was used to create such nationals, and this was clearly visible in the way the urban underclass was perceived. This in turn determined how exclusion works through the national homogenisation process. Exclusion means the exclusion of a particular social category from wealth and privilege by the national authorities and by the social class that enjoys wealth and privilege. Exclusion creates a class of people entrenched in poverty and makes them a political minority. A decision is made that a certain class is to be cut off from wealth and privilege and the door is firmly shut on those classified as outsiders. Exclusion, more often than not, is accompanied by a justifying logic, an ideology. The nation state introduced universal public education and universal conscription as pathways towards the compelling and essential goal of 'civilization.'[2] To be allowed to use these pathways, people have to be members of the nation state. Those who cannot comply with the obligatory model of being a member of a family and connected to the land are branded as anational and excluded from 'civilization.' What is unpatriotic about them is that they do not easily fit in with the control mechanism because they tend to move around and not to belong to any organisations, and they are not able to form or be a part of a family, the fundamental requirement of the Family Registration System. The programme to force people to become homogenised members of the nation state is accompanied by aggressive exclusion of those who do not fit in. Of course, as Mikio Wakabayashi remarked (1996: 13–14), 'a programme to connect a place with one's physical body' is simply 'a programme to connect a place with one's name.' The physical body in modern society has a tendency to be detached from its place and to move around. The family system cannot be said to have changed the people's physical body and consciousness overnight. But this programme, as has been discussed, has certainly located those members of the population who had removed themselves from the system, the unorganised and unsettled population, and has persuaded them to join in with the settled families and organisations. It has also provided a standard for the exclusion of those who refuse to comply.

From his examination of textbooks and *Jokunsho* (Moral Textbooks for Women), Masanao Kano concludes that the family life model portrayed there is that of the '"upper class" family model.' He goes on to say that the establishment of the 'family system', 'by portraying in definite terms what constitutes a "desirable" existence has highlighted what is "undesirable."'(1983: 71–73)

Kano cites the following three examples of created and reinforced examples of desirable and undesirable ideas. First, despite the emergence of a large number of displaced people as a result of the modernisation of society, the psychological barrier has been increased against family-less displaced people, and the 'idea of considering a settled life to be normal and a life spent moving around as abnormal has been intensified.' Second, the standardisation of the people, except for the emperor, along with the admiration of the 'upper class,' and the emergence of a consciousness of gentility, has encouraged the formation of a 'tendency to admire pseudo nobility' and on the other hand, a tendency to look down on those who do not or cannot show a connection with the 'nobility.' Third, while the 'gentility' of the 'upper class' has been accepted as desirable, the 'customs of the common people have been despised as vulgar, especially their sexual customs.' Kano then sums up as follows the negative nature of the urban underclass as defined by their lack of conformity to the family register system. Those who do not fit into the family register are on one count abnormal because they do not have a fixed address. Second, they are unconditionally 'without breeding' because they do not have a contact point in the hierarchical family register system. Third, because de facto relationships and 'unregistered children' are often connected with a lack of sexual morals, they are 'vulgar.' Forcing people to become members of the nation state was intended to 'raise up' the population by encouraging a desire amongst them to become civilized. Through responding to the call of the nation, the people could become 'good nationals' according to the values of the nation state. In this national homogenisation movement, it can be said that the recognition and exclusion of unpatriotic elements helped to define what being 'good nationals' meant.

Exclusion and the poverty which results from it accompanied by national homogenisation is not a thing of the past, but it can be found today in the way power has continued to be exercised. The nation state, once having achieved the necessary economic conditions, has become a welfare state. It has remained so since, even though the 'crisis of the welfare state' is often spoken about. As the nature of the nation state needed to thoroughly standardise its people into 'good national citizens,' the construction of a welfare state was a rational choice: it prevented the break-up and preserved the centralised national order (of course, it presupposed the weakness of any opposition forces). The welfare state, of course, provided systematic preventive measures against poverty which helped to stabilize people's lives. No one believes these days that exploitation directly impoverishes people. However, along with the structure of the nation state which has remained the same, poverty resulting from exclusion, which has been hidden in class based poverty and not often talked about, has not changed. In this chapter, we will look at the urban underclass of Tokyo and examine the system of exclusion, which has been operating all along, including its present day transformation.

Nihilation

Therapy, nihilation and physical nihilation

When examining the mechanism of exclusion, I would categorize the intrusions by the authorities of the nation state under three types: therapy, nihilation and physical nihilation (Berger and Luckmann [1966] 1977: 177–196, Nishizawa 2002: 45–73).[3]

Therapy, carried out through discipline and punishment (Foucault) in closed environments such as schools, military institutions, factories and homes,[4] is a process which attempts to condition people into organisation and settlement, and becoming 'good nationals.' In the modernisation process, to produce and reproduce modern labourers, typified by factory workers, this category has a formal significance. Therapy is not in itself the means of exclusion, rather, the means of subsumption and incorporation. But when therapy is employed as a means for the standardisation of people, it becomes a means to select and exclude those anational/denational beings that are considered not worthy of therapy. Working in tandem with therapy, nihilation segregates socially and spatially those anational/denational beings who are not worthy of therapy from the organised and settled zones, and keeps their contact with 'good national citizens' to a minimum in order to render them as invisible as possible. It functions to maintain and reinforce the exclusiveness, as well as the self-evidence, of the national order. Those segregated through nihilation are dehumanised, are turned into ghosts. They 'don't exist' or 'cannot be there,' and are socially isolated and neglected. The connection between the majority and minority is cut off. There is no foundation to make social issues out of the hardships experienced by various minorities. The situation of the minority, if it comes to the attention of the majority, is dismissed as divine justice for fools, and therefore it is not necessary for the majority to concern themselves about it. As Zygmunt Bauman says '(b)eing excluded is presented as an outcome of social *suicide*, not a social *execution*.' (2000a: 86) One thing to note, however, is that nihilation is a conceptual execution, which means those excluded notionally do 'not exist'. In contrast to this, physical nihilation supplements and bypasses the gradual process of nihilation, and directly demonstrates the justice of 'good nationals.' By physical nihilation, the unwanted are physically eradicated either through expulsion or elimination. Whatever the power, therapy or nihilation, it is reinforced by recruiting deputies from society. Therapy is carried out with assistance from families and local communities. For nihilation to work a majority of the population has to take part in isolating anational/denational beings. The segmented labour markets and accompanying segregated communities assist in this process. The process of physical nihilation has as its deputies 'rascals' and 'hooligans' performing a social action. Politicians, media and intellectuals who theoretically support various levels of intervention, have at the ready arguments in support of encouraging such social supplementing actions.

The mechanism of nihilation

What controls the people of the urban underclass directly is the mechanism of nihilation. There are two reasons why nihilation is significant. First, the idea that the national order is unique and that this is self evident inevitably develops nihilation as a mechanism. The eradication of anational/denational beings would only result in acknowledging that areas exist which cannot be nationalised, thereby, negating the uniqueness and self evidence of the national order. For the governing power to be most efficient it would make sense to let anational/denational beings continue to exist but to conceal them, if possible. I say 'if possible', because without the existence of a socio-economic environment to absorb these excluded people, a smooth process of nihilation would not be feasible. Without the concealment of such an environment, the excluded people would be driven out onto the street and exposed. Such circumstances would eventuate in a failed nihilation. I will discuss this in detail later.

Second, there is an inherent problem arising from the nature of the Megalopolis (Nishizawa 2002). The Megalopolis has, against the levelling tide of national homogenisation, a tendency to nurture diverse social worlds apart from the disciplined areas, and to allow for a multiplication of diversity and heterogeneity. The Megalopolis cannot be possibly tamed. There, national homogenisation would always be incomplete. That is why it has always been seen as a problematic place that upsets the national order. Nonetheless, the residents of the Megalopolis are cut off from the community and lack a framework of reference for life. Because they accept social distance as normal, they always respond in a way that fits in with the wish of the majority. They look for a common standard and pay more attention to superficialities than to anything else.[5] The homogenisation tendency based on the sense of vision invites a certain type of interference into society by the authorities. By controlling the landscape (through nihilation) and by convincing people of the uniqueness and self evidence of the national order, authorities intervene to encourage people's subjective assimilation by means of changing their appearance to conform to the landscape. This, unlike therapy, is not a way in which to comprehend a people's whole personality. However, in terms of social intervention by the authorities, appearance can be an important strategic point.

Nihilation is carried out by the different means of separation and segregation. The former breaks up the group to be nihilated and makes them invisible, while the latter collects them together for the purpose of segregation and makes them invisible from the rest of society. Through separation and segregation, either in succession or simultaneously, the people to be excluded are gradually divided into smaller groups, based on minor differences, and removed from the sight of the majority. If separation or segregation proves too difficult, image manipulation may be attempted to neutralise their appearance so they become invisible. Below, I will discuss the exclusion of the urban underclass, using the concepts of therapy and nihilation, with separation, segregation and image manipulation, the subcategories of nihilation.

The reorganisation of the urban underclass

Intervention

Apart from the various forms of exclusion already noted, the urban underclass was also the target of therapy. From the State's perspective, it was unacceptable to have a 'dangerous class' of person in the imperial capital. For the nation state, the homogenisation of its people was of overriding importance. The urban underclass was under pressure to become homogeneous enough to be able to be subjected to therapy. In the end, of course, the integration of the urban underclass called for an economic foundation. It began at last to create families and lead a settled life in the city as the twentieth century dawned (Nakagawa 2000: 236). During the peak of industrialisation, companies began bringing the working class into their organisations, making self employed craftspersons into 'regular company employees.' Furthermore, 'in the late 1920s, the urban underclass began developing and maintaining a regulated life which no longer required communal collective living. Indeed, the dispersal of the underclass from their collective living quarters began.' The state authority started measuring the abstract, statistical living standards of the impoverished and introduced more systematic responses such as the *hōmen iin* (Area Commissioner) system. Due to the 'family register clean up' activities by the *hōmen iin*, the rate of de facto couples among the *yo hogo* households dropped in the 1930s to as low as 8.2%, and a level of more than ninety per cent legal marriages was reached (Nakagawa 1985: 280). The rate of 'unregistered children' also dropped as the schools were recognised as the means of class transference. In the early twentieth century, it seems that hardly any children of the urban underclass in Tokyo attended school, but by the late 1920s, seventy per cent of them were attending day classes, while twenty per cent were attending night classes (Nakagawa 1985: 183–185). It is likely that the desire to become part of 'civilization' through education, and the sense of equality engendered by being the 'emperor's subjects' were widespread even among the underclass. The urban underclass was no longer an 'object of acknowledgement because of its heterogeneity, but rather had become an object of social recognition to be homogenised into society.' By the 1920s, most of the urban underclass formed during the Meiji era had been absorbed into the nation state as a fixable problem. Even though the therapy was to a degree successful, the therapeutic intervention caused differences and friction with the reality of the urban underclass, because national homogenisation is still homogenisation, nevertheless. Therefore, along with therapeutic intervention, the mechanism of nihilation was also becoming established and beginning to work. By far the most outstanding executors of nihilation were the police. Since its inception in 1874, the *Keishichō* (the Metropolitan Police Board) has been an administrative agency whose job is to prevent crime rather than judicial police who are responsible for arresting criminals. The aim of *Keishichō* activities was 'to destroy the people's order and to reorganise them into the national order.' (Obinata 1993: 31–53) The urban underclass was kept under surveillance because it was seen as a hotbed for crime and vice, and sometimes it was segregated and controlled. The 'Prostitute Regulatory Rules' which came into force in 1900 stipulated that working prostitutes be registered at the local police office of *Keishichō*. The police clamped down hard on those operating outside their registered areas and on unregistered prostitutes. Prostitution was only allowed at licensed premises and the number of these was gradually being reduced. The doss houses, flea pits and other forms of cheap rental accommodation that offered a base for this unsettled fluid population in Tokyo, also came under police surveillance. The regulatory rules introduced in 1887 stipulated that any accommodation must be registered at the police office. Because they were considered to be the '"haunt of the poor" and "a gathering place for 'rogue outlaws,'" only one doss house was allowed to operate within each official police area.' None were permitted in the four wards Kanda, Nihonbashi, Kōjimachi and Kyōbashi, which surrounded the imperial palace. With the increase of crime and civil unrest following the war against Russia, the police intensified their regulation of the urban underclass. In that context, a directive was even issued 'that beggars should be expelled from Tokyo, and regulated severely so that they will not return again.' (Obinata 2000: 111–112) Whether it might be prostitutes, flop houses or beggars, it is important to note that the segregation of these unwanted groups was done concentrically from the center (the imperial palace) to the periphery.

A new urban underclass

This style of segregation and dispersal was maintained even after the 1920s. The previously mentioned geographical dispersal of the urban underclass in the late 1920s was not driven by the rise of its living standards alone. There was of course coercive and semi-coercive intervention. Katsumasa Harada describes as follows the urban planning and subsequent large scale redevelopment carried out as national projects following the devastation of the great Kanto earthquake of 1923 (Harada and Shiozaki 1979: 29).

> An increasing number of people in dire circumstances was, because of their economic difficulties, accommodated in low rent collective terrace houses being built on the outskirts. Hence there was the birth of new slums on the periphery. However, the simultaneous trend of dispersal and expansion of the slums after the 1900s due to economic conditions, as well as migration forced by the authorities, was immediately accelerated in the wake of the earthquake. We must note that this dispersal was not motivated by a yearning for the 'genteel country side,' but rather, from the class factor of extending urban areas.

In the early Showa period, most of the 'run-down residential areas' in Tokyo were concentrated along the Nakasendo highway, in Koishikawa ward and in Kitatoshima county which includes today's Ikebukuro. They were created in those places chiefly because of the urban redevelopment and gentrification of the centre following the earthquake. When the space in Tokyo was being filled with the sense of national order as a national project, the urban underclass was excluded and expelled. The concept of extending 'civilized' national space was agreed on almost unanimously by society. Only purely economic reasons could stop it. This means that during the 1920s, national homogenisation in Tokyo was not just carried out by the national authority, but also by the construction of a social conglomerate involving a wide ranging class of people. The same process happened with the exclusion of the urban underclass. Because they were convinced the space filled with the national order was self evident, the majority's consciousness was full of the fear of invisible isolated heterogeneous others when they carried out the massacre of Korean and Chinese residents as well as socialists, in the wake of the earthquake. It is also important to note that *Chōnaikai* (neighbourhood associations) were first being formed voluntarily in the 1920s in the big urban centres. One important characteristic to note about the neighbourhood associations is that there was no territorial overlapping among them and the total sum of their territories was almost the same as that of 'Japan.' It is assumed that such compliance with the nation state indicates that the neighbourhood associations at their inception already presupposed the national homogeneity of the area. In those days, urbanites' initiatives could only be expressed in the form of compliance with and supplementary to the linear system of the national authority, local council and households.

The covering up of unpatriotic behaviour was carried out by image manipulation as well as through dispersal and segregation. The police were heavily involved in this (Obinata 1993: 32–53). Because the government was particularly afraid of the 'old customs, that could be considered uncivilized and vulgar in the eyes of the Europeans and Americans,' they imposed regulations especially in the 'capital city of Tokyo and port cities.' By means of the Road Use Regulation (1900), moral order in public areas was regulated and 'abominations' were eliminated. It is said that geishas enjoying the cool evening breeze in their undergarments and craftspeople that had their clothes 'tucked up' were condemned. 'Civilization' in 'public spaces' was created by this kind of intervention. The Rickshaw Operation Regulatory Rules (1889), regulated the rickshaw drivers' clothes, as well as forcing them to be registered. This was an attempt to conceal and touch up the 'vulgar' behaviour of the rickshaw operators who were of the underclass.

Nihilation by dispersal, segregation and image manipulation thus brought to Tokyo a civilised appearance and extended the space of national order, but this did not mean the whole of Tokyo was completely regulated. As mentioned above, by the late 1920s, most of the urban underclass which was created during the Meiji period had been internalised, and had established families. However, a category of people appeared at the other end of the spectrum that it was deemed was impossible to cure. As has been also pointed out by Nakagawa, 'in the area where the poverty recognition exercise as a part of the homogenisation activity fails, "vagrants," the "interned and protected" aged people' and others who the order could not possibly accommodate surfaced (2000: 440). This new urban underclass included various peoples who were unorganised, unsettled, and not family oriented. The urban underclass did not vanish, but was reorganised. Seen as 'impossible to cure' the new underclass is made up of people from hidden and neglected social areas. The uniformity of 'Tokyo' or 'Japan' can only be guaranteed by the nihilation of these social areas.

The life of the urban underclass

First compiled by the Tokyo metropolitan government's social department, the 1936 report 'The state of the Korean workers in Tokyo' provides insight into the life of the urban underclass after reorganisation. Of course, Koreans were then considered to be nationals of the greater Japanese empire, but their ethnic origin had to be declared to the family registry. Most of the Koreans living in Tokyo at this time had been originally 'imported' after World War I to work in mines as forced labour, or as labourers in the back country. When business suffered a downturn, they were dismissed and drifted into the cities. The devastation of rural Korea brought great numbers looking for work, even though they would be considered to be 'untimely intruders.' (Tokyofu shakaika 1936: 46) In work, forty per cent of them were engaged in labouring and other earth moving and construction jobs, while ten per cent were involved in street selling, hawking and odd jobs. In terms of class, they of course belonged to the lowest stratum. After recognizing that 'more often than not, you cannot say that no hardship exists where there is no chance of getting jobs,' the report concluded that basically the real cause of their predicament was their racial background, even though it admitted that the 'prejudice against Korean workers' was 'one of the factors discouraging them from doing their best.' Although 'their obsession with jobs and money is remarkable, their low standard of living and their inadequacy due to their lack of spiritual life are overwhelming. In short, in the pursuit of material gain, they frequently move from job to job, company to company, and Japanese employers feel dissatisfied with their lack of gratitude, because they believe strongly in reciprocal respect between employer and employees. It appears that employers feel these job changers will never become highly skilled.' (Tokyofu shakaika 1936: 47–48) What is described here as the Korean attitude is simply the attitude adopted by those people who find themselves relegated to the urban underclass. The people of the urban underclass are confined there where their choice of jobs and residence are limited due to social exclusion. They have no option other than moving around and changing jobs, while they try to get by as peripheral workers on low incomes, with bad working conditions and the constant threat of dismissal. Their strategy of pursuing 'material gain, moving frequently from job to job, from company to company' does not help them move out of the underclass, but it is a rational one for survival. The income they received was insufficient to support more than one person and so their opportunities for improving their lives were extremely limited. Their housing supplied the bare necessities for maintaining life at the minimum survival level for labour power. These kinds of limitations prevented future planning from a mid to long term perspective. To plan a life beyond the level of mere survival when faced with these limitations, it is an important strategy to find somewhere where it is possible to fit in into a collective residence. In Tokyo, however, due to the push to nihilate the underclass, collective living was only possible on a small scale on the periphery of the nationalistic homogeneous space. The Korean residential areas were few in number, and as in 1934, they were concentrated in Fukagawa, Honjo, Arakawa, Jōtō, Shinagawa and other wards on the outskirts of the city proper. In other words, they were dispersed and segregated outside the central area. 'Less than ten of them lived in their own place, the rest in rented properties or makeshift shacks,' (Tokyofu shakaika 1936: 131) while many of the 'singles' lived in at the labourers' quarters of the Korean bosses or nearby (Tokyofu shakaika 1936: 2–7).

Here we can see the continuation of the system of dispersal and segregation of the reorganised urban underclass. As well, within the limitations of the urban underclass, the following way of living became established not just among those branded as of 'ignoble origin' in the family registry, like the ethnic Koreans, but also amongst those who broke away from organisations and local communities and slid down the social scale, due to bankruptcy and disaster. First, their way of life was unorganised. In the underclass labour market where they were looking for jobs, the available jobs offered the worst working conditions and always threatened pay cuts and dismissal. The people of the urban underclass had no alternative other than to keep changing jobs and to lead unsettled lives. Second, because their way of life meant they were constantly on the move, the places where they could live were limited just to the areas where the national order was not rigidly enforced, such as the periphery of the city, the inner city, tourist areas and other 'enclaves' of the city, *hamba* (Workers' Shacks) and other temporary accommodation, and *yoseba*, the entertainment district, the red light district and other segregated areas. As their jobs changed, they moved around among these places.

Third, their way of life was not family oriented. Because of their accommodation, they were forced to remain single. It was difficult for them to live with families or partners. Of course there was no possibility of them having children or bringing up young families there. Had they managed to start a family, it would be difficult to maintain it because their lives had no solid basis. Their brief periods of being settled would frequently come to an end. In these circumstances, living collectively and forming 'Oyabun–kobun' relationships (fictive kinship) was one of the limited survival strategies available for them, in order to live outside the world of the 'good nationals.' Although this strategy was based on rationality, their unorganised, fluid and non-family oriented way of life itself would become a mark of their exclusion and keep them forever in the urban underground.

The welfare state and nihilation

Sanya

The style of exclusion based on nihilation, and the segregated social areas of the urban underclass, were continued into the post-World War II era and this has continued to today. Tokyo was burnt out in 1945 by Allied aerial bombing. People with weak contacts with organisations or the local community were thrown out onto the street in their tens of thousands, as 'vagrants,' to the disapproval of the general public. Ueno Park in particular was full of them and this attracted a lot of media attention. The Tokyo government rounded them up and incarcerated them (Nishizawa 1995: 30–42). The vagrants were then graded and sent to one facility or another. First, the aged, the sick and orphans were sent to appropriate facilities. Men who were considered to be able to work, were initially sent to facilities run by nationalists and organised crime groups. After 1946, they were sent to refugee camps set up in the old doss house areas (which had also been burnt to the ground) in Sanya and Takabashi (the Tokyo government lent the large tents and beds supplied by the US army to the operators of the doss houses). The men compounded there worked as day labourers while they were living there. The remaining women were left to their own devices and were absorbed into the entertainment districts and prostitution. Through this process of grading, segregation and dispersal, the group of vagrants disappeared for the time being from Ueno Park. This was far from a solution to poverty. This was the solution of a social problem using the same old nihilation mechanism as before the War.

However, nihilation did not work very well during the time before the economic boom of the 1960s because it had to be supplemented by suitable social and economic conditions. Sanya, for example, had originally been constructed as an accommodation area for single men only. Over the years, the tents were replaced by more permanent constructions like doss houses and after the deflation of 1949, Sanya absorbed the unemployed people including a number of families and became a big *yoseba* of day labourers. Nihilation could not be complete if the population reached a significant figure and included children. Following the rationale of national homogenisation, children were made the target of therapeutic treatment and were offered assistance. Indeed, during the 1960s when there were frequent riots, the Tokyo metropolitan government, local leaders, volunteer citizens groups, economists, entertainers, intellectuals and others combined their efforts and became involved in Sanya for the purpose of 'saving children from the town of riots.' Sanya became a social issue. But the 'Sanya issue' had nothing at all to do with considering the demands of rioting day labourers. Becoming a social issue in any form meant the certain failure of nihilation. Yet, if the problem found a 'solution,' it would only lead to a more sophisticated nihilation of the underclass. This was so much so that the metropolitan government responded swiftly to the issue. It decided on dispersal, offering the families in Sanya public housing at various locations. Poor families living in unsanitary conditions accepted the offer, and by the early 1970s, women and children had disappeared from Sanya. Sanya as a segregated area for single men was established.

We can recognise this form of nihilation if we look back on what had happened a decade earlier (in 1959), when prostitutes moved to Sanya from the neighbouring Yoshiwara district after being ejected from Yoshiwara through the joint efforts of local leaders and the police. In Sanya, only families were selected for therapy and helped to settle down. The unorganised and unsettled single people who did not fit in that framework were graded, dispersed and segregated according to their attributes. The urban underclass that had become visible through Sanya was hidden again and ignored after the women and children were gone, as if 'nothing had been there.' (Imagawa 1987: 295–296) For the Tokyo metropolitan government, the 'Sanya issue' after that period became mostly a security issue.

The social welfare administration and the underclass labour market

The covering up of the urban underclass continued along with the construction of a welfare state in the post-War period. Could the welfare system guarantee that the urban underclass would lead a 'healthy and cultural basic minimum way of life?' The reality is quite the opposite. The welfare system itself grades people and functions to exclude people who belong to the urban underclass. As the welfare state developed further, its monopolisation of the middle class continued (Fujimura 1998). The welfare system had evolved from a 'system to prevent poverty to one which aimed at "social welfare for all",' standardizing the 'legitimate' settled family which belongs to an organised settled society. On the ground level of welfare administration, a Certificate of Belonging was required before assistance would be given, and those without one were excluded from the system (Iwata 1997). This standard corresponds to the settled organised family, the model the family system presupposed. This kind of 'patriotic' model has become even more pronounced under the welfare state, and has further reduced the social space remaining for the unorganised and unsettled population. The people from the unsettled underclass are excluded even from the *Seikatsu hogo* (Public Livelihood Protection) system, which is seen as the last resort for the prevention of poverty. Rather, the Social Welfare Office, following the logic of exclusion and not its legal requirements, has become a grading mechanism to internalise any rescuable people through compassion and therapy, and conversely to actively expel, the unorganised and unsettled urban underclass of people. The Welfare Office is one of the final decision makers which draws a line between 'good national' humans and anational/denational subhumans.

From the style of dispersal and segregation used in dealing with vagrants at the end of World War II through to the handling of Sanya during the period of rapid economic growth, we can see that the mechanism of nihilation was now complete. It constituted the core of the social welfare administration, which was a system of division of labour dealing only with the aged, sick and children, ignoring everyone else who did not fit in with these criteria, and leaving them to the underclass labour market. It was possible to cover up the underclass during the period of rapid economic growth and the subsequent decade or so, because this system of division of labour was somehow functioning with the social welfare administration in tacit agreement with the underclass labour market. In the post-

War period, the underclass labour market, presuming on a constant influx of the underclass, had expanded its space to accommodate the unorganised and unsettled underclass population, offering both 'jobs that do not require CVs' and 'accommodation which does not necessitate guarantors' in a combined deal (Nishizawa 1995: 11–21). The population there was graded purely as labour power according to their age, gender, and family status. There was hardly any connection between *them*. It was the complete opposite of a 'slum' where a diverse population is concentrated. If they were single men, they could be day labourers engaged in construction and earth moving, drifting from the *yoseba* to the workers' temporary sheds. They could be temporary factory workers sent by the labour broker. In the service industry, the underclass people could be brought in to work as door to door newspaper subscription canvasses, to work as pachinko pinball parlour attendants or do other jobs which need someone to live-in. Single women and single mothers would follow the established path of working as attendants at adult entertainment venues or inns and hotels, while living in the 'dorms' provided.[6] Although the grading of the targets of nihilation had been changed to a more complex system, the essential style of the nihilation was the restructured form implemented before the War. Being now divided into smaller groups according to their attributes, as well as being deprived of the chance to reproduce, the unorganised and unsettled population of the urban underclass was moving around, segregated from organised and settled society. This way of living was a continuation of the way they had lived before the War.

Foreign labourers sharply increased in number in the 1980s and were also absorbed in this way of life. Workers from overseas had little choice in this, because of their 'weakness,' that is, overstaying their visas or not having a proper working permit. Even without these 'weaknesses,' it would be difficult for them to find a place to live anyway.[7]

Street dwellers

The transformation of the underclass labour market

Since the 1990s, the '*hōmuresu* problems' can be attributed to the failure of nihilation such as the riots in the *yoseba* in the 1960s. As mentioned above, during the period of rapid economic growth and the ten years or so after that, a kind of coexistence was possible somehow between the social welfare administration and the underclass labour market. Of course, individual people from the urban underclass were facing poverty, but it was invisible and did not become a social issue. Yet, the reduction of the workforce and the intensification of labour control in the construction and earth moving sector, which had began slowly after the oil crisis and accelerated rapidly after the collapse of the bubble economy, led to the scale down or closure of a large portion of the underclass labour market usually filled by single males, namely the construction and earth moving day labourers' market (Nakamura 1998; Yamaguchi 2001). For single males, this spelled the end of the division of labour, which led to the increase in street dwellers, making some parts of the urban underclass visible. The mechanisation of labour on site as well as various labour policies which accompanied it including worker's compensation, the stabilisation of employment, improvement of working conditions, securing young workers and so on brought about a comprehensive identification check and health check-ups such as taking workers' blood pressure on site, resulting in the further filtering and exclusion of workers. The former style of easy going work sites in which the workers from the *yoseba* could mingle no longer exists. Any worker considered too sick or too old, even with no concrete evidence for this, cannot get employment. Following these cut backs and the closure of the day labour market, their chances of getting employment have been drastically reduced.

There have been two major changes in regard to gaining employment in the underclass labour market, as far as single males are concerned. One is the shift of emphasis from the *yoseba* to the *hamba* (temporary workers' sheds) (Nakamura 1998, 1999; Tamaki and Yamaguchi 2000; Yamaguchi 2001). The *hamba* provide a loophole in the intensified labour control regime, because 'by putting them up in the *hamba,* workers can have an "address" of sorts, which functions as a tentative identification' (Yamaguchi 2001: 39). As well, these sheds function as a means to select 'useful' workers leaving it open for the operators to make their own arbitrary assessments. To start with, the *hamba* is a closed compound often ruled by violence, allowing little social intervention by unions and others. However, due to the decline of the *yoseba*, as well as workers moving out of the *yoseba*, 'late comers' who consider the *hamba* to be 'better than sleeping out on the street' arrive there through the employment ads in the tabloid papers or through the labour brokers at railway stations. There is believed to be a hierarchy among the *hamba*, and at the lowest level of them where many street dwellers come, there are not a lot of jobs on offer in the first place. When there is any work, the pay is low due to a general downturn in day labourers' wages, and after deductions for meals and other expenses, not much money is left for the workers. Examples have been noted of dishonest operators failing to pay any wages. On the whole, the wage level at the *hamba* is getting closer to a starvation wage (Nakamura 1999). Because they offer conditions marginally better than the street dwellers status means that the working conditions at the lower levels of the *hamba* are allowed to deteriorate further. They have become long term residences where the workers are simply 'kept in service for life' (Nakamura 1998: 172). As shown by Matsuo Tamaki and Keiko Yamaguchi, *hamba* workers are separated from the street dwellers only by the barest of margins, thus comprising a reserve army of street dwellers. The other change is exemplified in the trend towards seeking jobs from '*tachinbo*' to '*kaozuke*' to '*keitai denwa.*' '*Tachinbo*' means going to the *yoseba* hiring place in the morning and standing there to wait for job offers from the brokers. *Kaozuku* means the applicants getting their 'faces known' to the brokers and recruiters in order to get jobs on an ongoing basis. From the brokers' and recruiters' point of view, this means they can select from a stock of good workers without needing to search for them. Both terms have been in use at the *yoseba* for a long term, but the former is on the way out, while the latter is rarely used any more.[8] The new trend is towards the use of '*keitai denwa*' (cell phones), which relatively young street dwellers use to contact 'temporary staffing companies' to get jobs. The faces of the brokers and recruiters are no longer visible in this system. By registering on the list with the 'temporary staffing companies' and keeping in constant contact by cell phone, they might one day be given a daily hire job like helping a removalist or working at a construction site. They have to keep on proving to the invisible companies their merit and their desire to work. The companies can easily get rid of problematic workers or ones lacking in a proper work ethic. Unlike the *hamba*, no buildings or meals are required. Gilles Deleuze remarks in an interview with Antonio Negri, published in 1990, that our society is in transition from disciplinary societies with their principal means of control as confinement (and therapy) in schools, factories, barracks, hospitals and other facilities, towards control societies that 'no longer operate by confining people but through continuous control' and 'instant communication' (Deleuze 1996: 288). The kind of control mentioned here has already appeared somewhat oddly in the form of underclass workers with cell phones. The transformation I refer to here from the *yoseba* to the *hamba*, from '*tachinbō*' to '*kaozuke*' to cell phones, shows that a system is becoming established where the underclass workers are isolated and belittled made to 'discover' their lack of willingness and ability, and to automatically remove themselves from the labour market.

The sophistication of exclusion

Despite the reductions in the underclass labour market, the social welfare administration continues to stick to its selection criteria standards and to exclude people who have been expelled from the market. According to surveys carried out in various locations where street dwellers live, their generational composition is very similar. They are almost all single males. And, there are a lot of people in their fifties among them (it is important to note they are not in their sixties). This imbalance immediately suggests who the underclass labour markets have rejected. At the same time, the composition of this imbalanced population corresponds exactly to the sort of people the Welfare Office has excluded. Of course, even street dwellers can obtain assistance from the *Seikatsu hogo,* if they are considered to be 'aged. If they are considered to be sick for the time they are sick, they are provided with medical care. But if the street dwellers do not fall into any of these categories, if they are not 'aged,' 'sick' or 'women and children,' they are excluded. The irony of this is obvious. The very process of nihilation that has up till now been based on the pretence that this urban underclass of people does not exist has resulted in exposing the street dwellers and in making them a social issue. To begin with, the social welfare administration and the underclass labour market were not linked together as a willing coalition sharing the same objectives. It is more likely that different entities symbiotically and mutually complemented each other to nihilate the urban underclass during the period of rapid economic growth, on the condition of the exponential expansion of the underclass labour market. Social welfare administration, like so many other organisations, has only developed according to its own principles. Although it has been necessary for the welfare administration to face the volume of street dwellers that could not possibly be hidden, its own momentum does not allow it to put a stop to nihilation. Instead, this pushes it into searching for anational beings that need to be excluded in a more sophisticated manner.

Let us go back to Sanya as a concrete example. With the decline of the *yoseba*, the administration's handling of Sanya also changed. Sanya, redefined as a single male only day labourers' *yoseba*, was indeed the apodosis of dispersal and segregation. It is also somewhere that we can see the incompleteness of the nihilation exercise. An extensive segregation space where a certain number of people are brought together is likely to become visible, as the mass riots showed. Having said that, the decline of the *yoseba* has made it possible to target in a more sophisticated way the people to be excluded. At Sanya, it is reported that the number of *Seikatsu hogo* recipients greatly increased, due to the protection of the doss houses. The administration is also seeking a policy change from a *yoseba* town to a 'welfare town.' (Yamaguchi 2001) Of course, the *yoseba* workers in general will not benefit from the change to a welfare town. Obedient aged people are screened out and compassionately internalised, while the remainder are excluded. As if to deliberately tie in with this, the Tokyo metropolitan government abolished the section specifically dealing with Sanya. With this policy shift and the bureaucratic reorganisation, Sanya is now handled under the general category 'street dwellers problems.' We can see another nihilation here. To start with, by abolishing the symbol of locality the underclass is now reduced to a statistical mass of problematic individuals. Second, by labelling them as street dwellers, it makes it seem that the problem can be solved by taking them out of sight off the street, without dealing with their exclusion and poverty.

Because of the increase in the number of street dwellers, as well as vigorous lobbying by supporting organisations, the *Hōmuresu no jiritsu shien tō ni kansuru tokubetsu sochihō* (The Special Act to Assist Homeless People to Become Self Reliant) was enacted in 2002. The local bodies which had '*hōmuresu* problems,' embarked on their own programmes to 'help with their self reliance' before and after the enactment of the *sochihō*. At last, the '*hōmuresu* problem' was publicly acknowledged. Yet, aiming for a high number of successful examples who had achieved self reliance efficiently would invite action to expel the 'bad *hōmuresu*' people who are not capable of 'self reliance,' causing them to be expelled again. The kind of sympathy gained from some sections of society based on the easy-to-digest fable that these people are the tragic victims of the economic downturn, would not be extended to people who have been once more labelled 'incapable of becoming self reliant.' In this way, the anational nature of the anational people is reconfirmed, and they are pushed out of sight again in a methodical fashion as if they do not exist. The politics of nihilation keep functioning, shifting battle lines, while sharpening the rational for exclusion in a fundamentalist way.

Exclusion and the transformation of 'nationals'

The bringing into view of the street dwellers, as I explained above, no doubt results from a failure of the cover up operation. The '*hōmuresu* problems' is well established. What then is the justification for this continuing exclusion? Along with the increase in the number of street dwellers and their visibility, the polarisation of society caused by globalisation and deindustrialisation is impoverishing a wide range of classes of people. The increase in the single population is remarkable. Following the traditional measurements for exclusion, it has to be said that the reserve army of the urban underground is getting bigger. 'good nationals,' the existence of whom implies the exclusion of others, will no longer constitute the majority of society. However, the process which was meant to have brought about nihilation, still continues through inertia. Impoverished people in contemporary society are only accepted as transitional beings on their way to becoming 'good nationals.' Therefore they are seen as candidates for therapy, but deindustrialisation has increased the demand for low paid casual workers whose work is unskilled, rather than disciplined trained workers, and decreased the justification for therapy. If we are changing 'from disciplinary societies to control societies,' as mentioned by Deleuze (Deleuze 1996: 292–300), see above, the necessity for inefficient disciplinary measures (therapy) will diminish, while the impoverished class, considered earlier to be not worthy of therapy, will increasingly become control targets for security reasons. We can conclude that the conditions which allowed the existence of impoverished people, nationally or socially, have dissipated. The points of conformity for the masses such as civilisation, affluence and the middle class no longer exist, while the goal the impoverished should be aiming for has disappeared. Poverty, from being associated solely with idleness, has become a brand used to dismiss the whole person and is criminalized (Shibuya 2003: 87–96). In this context, the dehumanisation process by nihilation has a different meaning from before and the continuation of the process has support from society as well. The street dwellers whose existence was 'not meant to be' start to become the 'enemies' of the 'good national citizens.' These 'enemies,' by displaying their isolation and ruin to the annoyance of the good nationals, and by relying on the 'justice' of the 'good nationals,' become negative objects which can be interfered with as much as they please. Masao Maruyama said in 1951 that pre-War 'nationalism's most remarkable role was... covering up or suppressing all social conflicts, preventing the masses from voluntary organisation and transferring the frustration of the masses to hatred of certain sacrificial lambs at home and abroad.' He went on to compare that to post-War nationalism and said that the 'mentality of the nationalism of the past vanished from the political surface, not because it was annihilated or transformed qualitatively, but because it was broken down quantitatively to molecules and scattered at the bottom of society.' (Maruyama 1964: 167–169) Today's ideal 'patriot' no longer offers a frame of reference that can be used for therapy treatment. It is as a mockery of love given to the 'good nationals' whose existence takes shape only through attacks on easy to understand 'enemies,' that nationalism, 'broken down to molecules and scattered at the bottom of society' takes shape today. Today's kind of nationalism accepts and utilises through inertia a social exclusion which is based on a different kind of nationalism. Indeed it is true that the expansion of the impoverished class as a result of polarisation and the increase in the single population will challenge the existing notions of 'nationals' and 'human beings,' the 'nation state' and 'society.' If a change to the mode of exclusion does occur at long last, it can only be through the movements of society based on these changes.

3 The distribution and dynamics of poverty looked at according to income (the fluctuations of poverty based on a panel survey)

Chizuka Hamamoto

Introduction

Drawing from a panel survey, this chapter considers impoverishment due to income disparity and the fluctuations of poverty. A discussion based on data about the problem of low income is of course only 'one aspect of the poverty problem, not all' (Iwata et al. 2003: 14), and 'today's poverty should not be blamed solely on low incomes, but should be characterised in relation to the highly sophisticated nature of social life in general.' (Nakagawa 2002: 38) However, by using such measurable means as income, we can gain certain understanding of the experiences of impoverished families. There has been an accumulation of studies done on impoverished households in Japan, based on family income or expenditure. Nakagawa (2002), for example, collated poverty rate statistics from ten studies of the ratio of impoverished households conducted between 1954 and 1995. He notes that there are discrepancies in the results because of different data sets and different methods used in calculating statistics. However, the poverty rate decreased between 1954 and the 1960s, after which, one study concludes it shot up to fifteen per cent, while the other says it decreased further to five per cent. These studies are cross-sectional which means we cannot see whether poverty occurs continuously or temporarily, whether only certain people remain in poverty, or what drives people into poverty.

Poverty is studied dynamically in other countries through panel studies carried out from various perspectives. Consequently, not only the dynamic state of poverty in different countries is revealed in comparison to other countries, but also how many people slip in and out of poverty, and what factors cause this (Bane and Ellwood

1986). Studies have also been conducted elsewhere on the patterns of chronic poverty, to which more policy priority should be given rather than to transitory poverty, and what should be done about it (Hill and Jenkins 2001). In particular, the problem of falling into and climbing out of poverty has been widely discussed since a study conducted by Bane and Ellwood (for example, Stevens 1999; Jenkins 2000). These consider not just the changes in income of the head of the household but also that of the rest of the family members, as well as asset revenue and factors causing transition in the household such as life events. They take censoring problems into consideration, because poverty does not end during the accounting period.

Dynamic studies on poverty have been conducted in Japan, including that by Iwata (1999) and Harada, Sugisawa, Kobayashi et al (2001). Iwata, focusing on women in the family expansion period, finds that the chronically impoverished class experience few life events, while the transient poor experience a combination of employment transitions, as well as life event changes and sickness. On the other hand, Harada et al on elderly people found that a spouse's death is a major factor causing women to slip into poverty. Women more than men, older people and people with a lower functional capacity, found it harder to escape from poverty. These studies, examining poverty dynamically, are still small in number, and the preliminary step understanding the factors contributing to poverty dynamics, the details of poverty transition are still not adequately shown. This chapter's primary concern, therefore, is to look at and discuss the dynamics of poverty in Japan.

Due to the current economic downturn, the number of household slipping into poverty is on the increase. The increase in poverty in the United States between the late 1970s and mid 80s was not just quantitative, as Rodgers and Rodgers (1993) found. It became more chronic, especially among families with women as the head of the household, among African-American families, and among families with a low level of education. Like the US, the recent economic downturn in Japan may be driving more people into chronic poverty. To determine this possibly, this chapter will discuss the state of persistent and transient poverty, using the poverty classifications devised by Rodgers and Rodgers (1993) and Otto and Goebel (2002), where subjects are divided into *chronic* and *transient* poverty sufferers during the accounting period. Looking for the factors driving people into chronic poverty will be the second concern of this chapter.

The analytical framework

The *Japanese Panel Survey of Consumers* data

This analysis uses the Japanese Panel Survey of Consumers (JPSC) results produced by the Institute for Research on Household Economics. This survey has been carried out every year since 1993 at the same places used in the National Census on 1,500 women between the age of twenty-four and thirty-four, selected by the two-stage stratified random sampling method. By the time the most recent survey was conducted in 2002, the women surveyed were between thirty-three and forty-three. The date used here comes, from 1,023 women who have responded continuously since 1994, when the annual income of the whole household was first recorded, to 2002, 333 women have been selected for analysis, because their poverty level incomes and household incomes have all been recorded.

Defining poverty levels

To define poverty, this analysis uses the minimum living expenses as defined in the *Seikatsu hogo* (Public Livelihood Protection) system. Here, I would apply the same criteria for calculation as used by the *Seikatsu hogo* system to calculate the benefit payable. Each household is assessed according to family composition, the age of the family members and their residential location. Minimum living expenses are made 'livelihood assistance', 'housing assistance', 'education assistance' and additions in the case of child birth etc. The minimum living expenses calculated in this way multiplied by 1.2 is defined as each household's income at a poverty level. Then the ratio of each household's income is calculated against the poverty-level income, and this is the poverty ratio. When the poverty ratio is less than 1.0, the household is considered to be in poverty. When I say 'household income,' this means the total from the previous year including 'earnings from employment,' 'business earnings,' 'earnings from assets,' 'social security' and 'other income.' So, for the year-2002 survey, this means the income from 2001. Tax and social insurance contributions are not deducted, because until the 1998 survey, the answer could be either the totals of taxes and social insurance contributions from the previous year or the previous month, that is September, as the survey was conducted in October. Until 1998, the annual income could not be obtained for the entire sample.

A picture of poverty

The sample for the analysis here is limited to those women who, in 1993, were between twenty-four and thirty-four. In order to gain an understanding of the overall picture of poverty in Japan, however, I will briefly examine it cross-sectionally and dynamically using this defined sample.

A cross-section of poverty

Table 3.1 shows the changes to the poverty rate and the poverty gap between 1994 and 2002. The rate of impoverished households (i.e. households with a poverty ratio of less than 1.0) decreased from 9.6% to 7.5% between 1994 and 1995, and then increased continuously to 15.3% in 2001. It decreased the following year to 14.7%, but the rate of impoverished households has doubled since 1995. Households on incomes at more than twice the poverty level occupied nearly half of the total in 1994 and 1995, 45.6% and 46.2% respectively, but managed to hover at forty per cent from 1998. In the rate between 1994 and 2002, we notice a trend towards an increase in the poverty class. The increase is not gradual. There is a clear break between 1997 and 1998. Early 1997 was the time when the post bubble economy recovery slowed down again and this may have contributed the subsequent increase in the poverty class. The same trend can be observed in the poverty gap, which is the poverty intensity rate, worked out by standardizing the difference between the poverty level income and the household income, when the household income is below the poverty level income. It can be concluded that poverty has increased since then.

Frequency of poverty

Counting poverty

One method of dynamically understanding poverty is to look at its frequency according to the poverty hit rate. This is the method of counting the number of times people fall into poverty during the accounting period, has been employed by Coe (1978), Duncan (1988) and others. According to cross-sectional table 3.1, during the period between 1994 and 2002, the poverty class ranged between 7.5% and 15.3%. When we look at this in terms of frequency during the same period between 1994 and 2002, as shown in table 3.2, 31.8% (= 100 − 68.2) of households had fallen into poverty at least

Table 3.1: Transition of the poverty rate (%)

	1994	1995	1996	1997	1998	1999	2000	2001	2002
Poverty ratio/average	2.14±1.10	2.14±1.09	2.08±1.02	2.08±0.97	1.96±0.95	1.98±1.19	1.87±0.95	1.88±0.98	1.92±0.97
less than 1	9.6	7.5	8.1	8.4	11.1	14.1	14.4	15.3	14.7
less than 0.5	1.5	0.9	1.5	0.9	1.2	1.8	2.7	3.6	2.1
more than 0.5 and less than 0.75	2.1	2.4	1.5	2.7	3.9	3.9	3.0	3.9	3.0
more than 0.75 and less than 1.0	6.0	4.2	5.1	4.8	6.0	8.4	8.7	7.8	9.6
more than 1.0 and less than 1.25	9.3	11.1	9.6	10.5	11.7	10.8	14.7	11.1	11.4
more than 1.25 and less than 1.5	13.5	14.1	16.8	10.2	12.3	10.8	11.1	12.6	12.6
more than 1.5 and less than 1.75	9.6	10.2	9.0	13.2	15.0	14.7	13.5	12.0	12.3
more than 1.75 and less than 2.0	12.3	10.8	13.8	12.3	11.4	10.2	8.1	11.4	8.7
more than 2.0	45.6	46.2	42.6	45.3	38.4	39.3	38.1	37.5	40.2
Poverty gap	0.038±0.161	0.027±0.130	0.032±0.147	0.033±0.132	0.040±0.145	0.051±0.167	0.053±0.180	0.067±0.206	0.052±0.173

once. We can see the longitudinal spread of poverty which the cross-sectional study fails to show. However, the households which had continuously been in poverty during the nine year period are relatively small at 1.5 %. In terms of the number of poverty hits, the largest proportion of 10.5% fell into poverty at least once during the nine years. Instead of the same household being in prolonged poverty, we can see that many households experience poverty fluctuations falling into and climbing out of poverty, and more households are in transitory poverty.

Table 3.3 looks at the rate of households at risk of falling into poverty over a given period and at the longitudinal transition over the period. As we saw in table 3.1, the number of households in poverty has been increasing. This trend is confirmed by table 3.3 which shows the rise in the average poverty incidence during the period. As well as the average poverty incidence, the households which had a poverty hit at least once during a given period, as shown in the next column, have also been increasing over the years (although they decreased between 1994–1996 and 1995–1997, while they remained static between 1994–2001 and 1995–2002). The households at risk of poverty compared to the average poverty incidence, as the far right-hand column shows, however, are getting fewer. On the other hand, the rate of households remaining in poverty is increasing. What this means is that, judging the frequency of poverty, not only the number of households in poverty is increasing, but also those in chronic poverty are also on the rise.

Issues

It has been pointed out that there are some problems with fully understanding the dynamics of poverty by examining the poverty hit rate. For example, the method looks at poverty purely as a discrete state. That is, a household is either in poverty or not. The level of poverty is worked out according to the number of poverty hits. For example, we will compare the income of the following four households over three following periods, given a poverty line of three million yen:

Household (a)	3.5	1	3.5	(million yen)
Household (b)	6	2.8	6	
Household (c)	6	2.8	2.8	
Household (d)	2.9	3.1	2.9	

Household (a) went above the poverty line twice but only by a small amount. Household (b) usually earns far more than the poverty line income but can sometimes go below the line slightly. They

Table 3.2: Recurrance of poverty

Poverty hit	1994	1994–1995	1994–1996	1994–1997	1994–1998	1994–1999	1994–2000	1994–2001	1994–2002
0	90.4	86.2	83.2	82.3	79.0	74.8	72.1	70.0	68.2
1	9.6	10.5	10.8	8.7	11.1	12.6	11.7	10.5	10.5
2		3.3	3.6	4.2	2.1	4.2	6.0	6.9	6.0
3			2.4	2.7	3.3	0.9	2.4	3.0	4.5
4				2.1	3.0	3.9	1.2	2.7	1.8
5					1.5	2.1	3.6	1.5	3.0
6						1.5	1.5	2.4	1.5
7							1.5	1.5	1.5
8								1.5	1.5
9									1.5
Total	100.0	100.0	100.0	100.0	100.0	100.0	100.0	100.0	100.0

are obviously in different income classes, but as far as the hit rate is concerned, they are the same because they have only one hit. The depth of poverty of household (a) cannot be measured by this method either. In comparison, household (c) has on occasion earned much more than the poverty line. But by falling slightly under the line twice during this period, it is considered to be in deeper poverty than household (a) which was hit only once. As for household (d), although it experienced a small income fluctuation, because the fluctuation was around the poverty line, the fluctuation is translated into a bigger poverty fluctuation. A case like household (d) should be noted, especially when we examine the factors that contribute to moving into and out of poverty.

Below, we will look at these problems, applying the data used for the analysis here. First, we should make clear the relationship between poverty hits and poverty ratio, that between poverty hits and the poverty gap. Table 3.4 compares the magnification rate and the poverty gap according to the number of poverty hits. The more hits shown, the lower the magnification rate. In other words, we see a tendency that as the rate of household income measured against the poverty level income defined by the *Seikatsu hogo* system becomes smaller, the number of poverty hits goes up. But this is not strictly the case, because those households with three hits have a higher rate, albeit marginally, than those with two hits. Those households with five and six hits have more or less the same rate. So, it is not necessarily the case that more hits means a lower level of household income. As for the poverty gap, it shows that the more hits, the higher the gap. The households with more poverty hits have more intensive poverty, but there is not much difference between those with four or five hits, and those with six or seven hits.

To see if there is a case in the data like household (d) we looked at above, let us examine how many households are hovering around the poverty level line. We divide the poverty ratio into six at the points of time, *t-1* and *t*. Table 3.5 displays income fluctuations and shows us that nearly ninety per cent of higher income earning households, that is, households with a poverty ratio of more than 1.5, remain above 1.5 all the time. On the other hand, the households with a lower poverty ratio tend to fluctuate around the poverty level. For example, more than half of the households with a poverty ratio of between 0.75 and one at the point in time *t-1*, remain between 0.75 and 1.25, in other words, hovering around the poverty level at the point in time *t*. Between 1996 and 1997, it was 76.4%, between 1997 and 1998, it was 68.8%, between 1998 and 1999, it was sixty-five

Table 3.3: Poverty hit and poverty incidence during a given period

	Average poverty incidence of three surveys (1) (%)	Households falling into poverty at least once in three surveys (2) (%)	Households falling into poverty in all three surveys (%)	(2)/(1)
1994–1996	8.4	16.8	2.4	2.00
1995–1997	8.0	13.8	3.0	1.73
1996–1998	9.2	15.3	4.5	1.66
1997–1999	11.2	19.8	5.4	1.77
1998–2000	13.2	21.6	6.0	1.64
1999–2001	14.6	22.5	6.9	1.54
2000–2002	14.8	24.0	7.5	1.62

	Average poverty incidence of four surveys (1) (%)	Households falling into poverty at least once in four surveys (2) (%)	Households falling into poverty in all four surveys (%)	(2)/(1)
1994–1997	8.4	17.7	2.1	2.11
1995–1998	8.8	18.0	2.1	2.05
1996–1999	10.4	21.0	4.2	2.01
1997–2000	12.0	23.1	4.5	1.93
1998–2001	13.7	24.9	4.8	1.81
1999–2002	14.6	25.8	5.4	1.76

	Average poverty incidence of five surveys (1) (%)	Households falling into poverty at least once in five surveys (2) (%)	Households falling into poverty in all five surveys (%)	(2)/(1)
1994–1998	8.9	21.0	1.5	2.35
1995–1999	9.8	23.1	2.1	2.35

Poverty: distribution and dynamics

1996–2000	11.2	24.0	3.9	2.14
1997–2001	12.7	26.1	4.2	2.06
1998–2002	13.9	27.6	4.2	1.98

	Average poverty incidence of six surveys (1) (%)	Households falling into poverty at least once in six surveys (2) (%)	Households falling into poverty in all six surveys (%)	(2)/(1)
1994–1999	9.8	25.2	1.5	2.57
1995–2000	10.6	25.8	2.1	2.43
1996–2001	11.9	26.7	3.9	2.24
1997–2002	13.0	28.2	3.9	2.17

	Average poverty incidence of seven surveys (1) (%)	Households falling into poverty at least once in seven surveys (2) (%)	Households falling into poverty in all seven surveys (%)	(2)/(1)
1994–2000	10.5	27.9	1.5	2.67
1995–2001	11.3	28.2	2.1	2.50
1996–2002	12.3	28.5	3.6	2.32

	Average poverty incidence of eight surveys (1) (%)	Households falling into poverty at least once in eight surveys (2) (%)	Households falling into poverty in all eight surveys (%)	(2)/(1)
1994–2001	11.1	30.0	1.5	2.71
1995–2002	11.7	30.0	2.1	2.56

	Average poverty incidence of nine surveys (1) (%)	Households falling into poverty at least once in nine surveys (2) (%)	Households falling into poverty in all nine surveys (%)	(2)/(1)
1994–2002	11.5	31.8	1.5	2.77

Table 3.4: Poverty ratio and poverty gap, according to the poverty hit

Poverty hit	Poverty ratio (average±standard deviation)	Poverty gap (average±standard deviation)
0	2.32±0.79	0.00±0.00
1	1.70±0.65	0.02±0.03
2	1.37±0.38	0.06±0.06
3	1.41±0.29	0.11±0.07
4	1.16±0.24	0.18±0.11
5	0.96±0.09	0.20±0.13
6	0.94±0.08	0.29±0.08
7	0.89±0.08	0.31±0.08
8	0.75±0.11	0.40±0.15
9	0.62±0.19	0.54±0.28
Total	2.01±0.86	0.04±0.11

per cent, between 1999 and 2000, it was 60.7%, between 2000 and 2001, it was 55.2% and between 2001 and 2002, it was 76.9%. We must bear the income fluctuation in mind when dealing with the poverty fluctuation.

Permanent income

Rodgers and Rodgers (1993), believing that poverty dynamics analysed purely from the poverty hit rate may be problematic, advocate the classification of poverty by the use of the permanent income approach. Hill and Jenkins (2001) work out the average income during the accounting period, and among those who have experienced poverty at least once during that period, they classify people with an income higher than the poverty level as being in transitory poverty. Those who have an income below the poverty line are classified as being in chronic poverty (Hill and Jenkins 2001). Otto and Goebel (2002) as shown in table 3.6, divide what Rodgers and Rodgers term as chronic poverty into two, according to the number of poverty hits during the accounting period. They classify those chronically poor people who are continuously in poverty all through the period as persistently poor, while those with at least one poverty hit are classified as chronically poor. They term those people with at least one poverty hit and an average income above the poverty level transiently poor (Otto and Goebel 2002). {Jalan and Ravallion, using consumption in a similar way to analyse poverty, use the terms chronically poor and persistently poor, to mean the reverse of Otto and Goebel (Jalan and Ravallion 2000).}

Table 3.7 shows the distribution based on this classification. Because we are using the poverty ratio as a yardstick, we apply the average poverty ratio here as well, rather than the average income. When looking at the distribution of the whole surveyed, which includes those who did not experience poverty at all, the combined total of chronically poor and persistently poor, 6.3% and 1.5% respectively, does not amount to even ten per cent, because 68.2% of them are in the never-poor which did not have any poverty hits and twenty-four per cent are transiently poor. The breakdown of those households who had a poverty hit at least once, into transiently poor, chronically poor and persistently poor is shown in brackets in table 3.7. The transiently poor, whose average income during the accounting period exceeds the poverty level, account for three quarters, 75.5%. This is far larger than the persistently poor, 4.7%, whose income has continuously been below the poverty line and the chronically poor, 19.8%, who have periods of escape from poverty although their average income remains below the poverty level. The poverty ratio for the chronically poor is 0.86 while that for the persistently poor is 0.62, which means, during the accounting period these households have had to get by on eighty-six per cent and sixty-two per cent of the level of income the *Seikatsu hogo* system defines as the basic minimum level. What kind of households, then, are in chronic poverty? We will look for the contributing factors next, by looking at attributes and life events according to different types of poverty.

Differing poverty conditions

Attributes

Table 3.8 shows the relationship between the attributes of the panel samples as of 2002 and the four different classifications of poor people we derived from the longitudinal studies carried out between 1994 and 2002. The sample number for the persistently poor is extremely small, only five households. But, as Iwata (1999) reveals the stationary poverty class (what we here call the persistently poor) has different characteristics from the poverty transition class. Partly to see if this is the case, we will stick to the four classifications.

Table 3.5: Fluctuations in income over two points of time (poverty ratio) (%)

	1995					
1994	< 0.5	0.5–0.75	0.75–1.0	1.0–1.25	1.25–1.5	> 1.5
< 0.5		20.0		40.0	20.0	20.0
0.5–0.75	14.3	14.3	28.6	28.6	14.3	
0.75–1.0	5.0	15.0	10.0	25.0	25.0	20.0
1.0–1.25		3.2	9.7	35.5	29.0	22.6
1.25–1.5	2.2		4.4	17.8	37.8	37.8
> 1.5		0.9	2.2	4.0	6.2	86.7

	1996					
1995	< 0.5	0.5–0.75	0.75–1.0	1.0–1.25	1.25–1.5	> 1.5
< 0.5	33.3		33.3			33.3
0.5–0.75	12.5	12.5	50.0		12.5	12.5
0.75–1.0		7.1	21.4	28.6	14.3	28.6
1.0–1.25	2.7		16.2	29.7	40.5	10.8
1.25–1.5	2.1	2.1	4.3	19.1	42.6	29.8
> 1.5	0.4	0.9	0.4	3.6	8.0	86.6

	1997					
1996	< 0.5	0.5–0.75	0.75–1.0	1.0–1.25	1.25–1.5	> 1.5
< 0.5	20.0	60.0	20.0			
0.5–0.75		60.0	20.0			20.0
0.75–1.0		5.9	52.9	23.5	11.8	5.9
1.0–1.25		6.3	12.5	40.6	15.6	25.0
1.25–1.5	1.8			21.4	37.5	39.3
> 1.5	0.5		0.5	2.8	2.8	93.6

	1998					
1997	< 0.5	0.5–0.75	0.75–1.0	1.0–1.25	1.25–1.5	> 1.5
< 0.5		33.3	33.3		33.3	
0.5–0.75	33.3	44.4		22.2		
0.75–1.0		12.5	50.0	18.8	12.5	6.3
1.0–1.25		8.6	11.4	48.6	25.7	5.7
1.25–1.5		2.9	5.9	23.5	50.0	17.6
> 1.5	0.4	0.8	2.1	3.8	5.1	87.7

	1999					
1998	< 0.5	0.5–0.75	0.75–1.0	1.0–1.25	1.25–1.5	> 1.5
< 0.5	25.0	25.0	25.0			25.0
0.5–0.75	7.7	30.8	30.8	15.4		15.4
0.75–1.0	5.0	15.0	40.0	25.0		15.0
1.0–1.25		2.6	25.6	43.6	23.1	5.1
1.25–1.5	4.9	2.4	7.3	19.5	31.7	34.1
> 1.5	0.5	1.4	0.9	1.9	6.5	88.9

Table 3.5 continued

	2000					
1999	< 0.5	0.5–0.75	0.75–1.0	1.0–1.25	1.25–1.5	> 1.5
< 0.5	33.3	33.3	33.3			
0.5–0.75	23.1	15.4	38.5	15.4	7.7	
0.75–1.0	7.1	14.3	39.3	21.4	10.7	7.1
1.0–1.25		5.6	11.1	63.9	11.1	8.3
1.25–1.5	2.8		16.7	25.0	33.3	22.2
> 1.5	0.5		0.5	4.2	7.9	86.9

	2001					
2000	< 0.5	0.5–0.75	0.75–1.0	1.0–1.25	1.25–1.5	> 1.5
< 0.5	55.6		22.2	11.1	11.1	
0.5–0.75	50.0		10.0	30.0		10.0
0.75–1.0	3.4	27.6	34.5	20.7	6.9	6.9
1.0–1.25		8.2	18.4	34.7	26.5	12.2
1.25–1.5			8.1	16.2	37.8	37.8
> 1.5	0.5	0.5	0.5	2.0	6.0	90.5

	2002					
2001	< 0.5	0.5–0.75	0.75–1.0	1.0–1.25	1.25–1.5	> 1.5
< 0.5	41.7	25.0	8.3	16.7		8.3
0.5–0.75		46.2	15.4	23.1	7.7	7.7
0.75–1.0	3.8	3.8	57.7	19.2	7.7	7.7
1.0–1.25	2.7		13.5	54.1	18.9	10.8
1.25–1.5			14.3	16.7	40.5	28.6
> 1.5			1.5	0.5	7.4	90.6

When looking at marital status according to the different poverty classifications, never-married households occupy less than thirty per cent of the transiently poor and the never-poor, 28.8% and 25.1% respectively. However, the rate goes up to forty per cent for the persistently poor, while the never-married household rate is more than half of the chronically poor at 52.4%. As for the ages of the respondents, the chronically poor tend to be older, and forty-two and forty-three year olds make up 47.6%, nearly half. In terms of education level, the never-poor which has not experienced any poverty hits at all, those with post secondary education including vocational school, junior college, specialised high school, university and graduate school, account for 59.1%, nearly sixty per cent. The rate drops to forty per cent for the chronically and transiently poor, and to twenty per cent for the persistently poor. Among the persistently poor, a high proportion of forty per cent finished their education at junior high school.

Table 3.6: Poverty classification based on permanent income approach

Poverty hit	Classification by Otto and Goebel	Permanent income
Once, not in poverty all the time	Transiently poor	Above poverty level (transitory poverty)
	Chronically poor	Below poverty level (chronic poverty)
In poverty all the time	Persistently poor	Below poverty level (chronic poverty)

Table 3.7: Poverty classification (1994–2002)

	Distribution	Poverty ratio	Poverty gap	Poverty gap 2[a]
Persistently poor	1.5% (4.7%)	0.62±0.19	0.54±0.28	0.54±0.28
Chronically poor	6.3% (19.8%)	0.86±0.10	0.30±0.12	0.43±0.15
Transiently poor	24.0% (75.5%)	1.49±0.53	0.07±0.08	0.27±0.26
Never-poor, financially secure	68.2%	2.32±0.79	0.00±0.00	0.00±0.00

a: The average poverty gap is worked out, excluding the time when it is above the poverty level income.

When looking at the number of people in a household, whether married and unmarried households, we can see no significant association to the different poverty classifications. All that is noticeable is that among the persistently poor, all the households, regardless of their marital status, have more than four people. Among the married chronically poor families, the size of the household tends to be bigger, and there is no household smaller than three people, while seventy per cent of them have more than five members. The size of the household may be affected by the fact that the *Seikatsu hogo* system sets a relatively higher level for larger households. Looking at the type of household, there are no households made up of couples among the persistently and chronically poor, while they occupy about ten per cent of the transiently poor and the never-poor. Unmarried households with children or with children and a parent, in other words, sole parent households, occupy 54.6% of the chronically poor and fifty per cent of the persistently poor. Single parent families can be found among the transiently poor, but at a far smaller proportion of 34.8%. Among the never-poor who have never experienced poverty, they account for only 8.9%. It may be due to the small sample number

Table 3.8: Attributes according to the different poverty types (as at 2002) (%)

	Persistently poor	Chronically poor	Transiently poor	Never-poor, financially secure	
Marital status					
married	60.0	47.6	71.3	74.9	d
not married	40.0	52.4	28.8	25.1	
Age of respondents					
33–35	20.0	9.5	36.3	32.6	b
36–38	20.0	28.6	30.0	23.8	
39–41	40.0	14.3	23.8	29.5	
42–43	20.0	47.6	10.0	14.1	
Education level of respondents					
junior high school	40.0	14.3	7.5	2.7	a
senior high school	40.0	47.6	53.8	38.2	
vocational schools	20.0	23.8	31.3	42.2	
university and graduate school	0.0	14.3	7.5	16.9	
Number of family members (married household)					
one	0.0	0.0	0.0	0.6	
two	0.0	0.0	10.5	9.4	
three	0.0	0.0	8.8	15.9	
four	66.7	30.0	33.3	38.2	
more than five	33.3	70.0	47.4	35.9	
Number of family members (unmarried household)					
one	0.0	27.3	17.4	26.3	
two	0.0	18.2	13.0	22.8	
three	0.0	36.4	39.1	24.6	
four	50.0	9.1	13.0	15.8	
more than five	50.0	9.1	17.4	10.5	
Type of household (married household)					
couple only	0.0	0.0	10.5	9.5	b
couple with children	100.0	66.7	70.2	63.1	
couple with parents	0.0	0.0	0.0	0.0	
couple with parents and children	0.0	33.3	19.3	27.4	
Type of household (unmarried household)					
single	0.0	18.2	17.4	26.8	
single with parents	50.0	27.3	47.8	64.3	
single with children	50.0	27.3	17.4	0.0	
single with parents and children	0.0	27.3	17.4	8.9	
Number of children (married household)					
zero	0.0	0.0	10.5	9.4	c
one to two	66.7	60.0	54.4	72.9	
more than three	33.3	40.0	35.1	17.6	
Residential status					
own property	20.0	38.1	58.8	74.0	a
rental property	80.0	61.9	41.3	26.0	

a: $p < 0.001$.   b: $p < 0.01$.   c: $p < 0.05$.   d: $p < 0.1$

of the persistently poor, but among the unmarried households, we do not find any single person households. They either live with parents or with children. Looking at the number of children in a married household, persistently and chronically poor families all have more than one child. At the other end of the spectrum, only 17.6% of the never-poor with no experience of poverty, has more than three children, comparatively less than the thirty to forty per cent among the class who have experience of poverty, whether that is experienced transiently, chronically or persistently. Poverty caused by bringing up children, as highlighted by Benjamin Seebohm Rowntree, still appears valid in Japan. Looking at residential ownership status, far less than half of the persistently and chronically poor own their homes, twenty per cent and 38.1% respectively, while sixty to seventy per cent of the transiently poor and the never-poor own their residences, 58.8% and seventy-four per cent respectively.

Life events

To understand the relationship between life events during the accounting period and poverty types, each year at the time of survey the question was asked whether the following life events had occurred during the previous twelve months:

> [M]arriage, divorce, child birth, relocation, 'serious illness that required an operation or long term hospitalization' (listed in the table as respondent's illness), 'depression or other mental conditions' (listed as respondent's depression), 'accident or disaster' (listed as respondent's accident), 'change of workplace or occupation' (listed as the respondent's job change), 'retirement from work' (listed as the respondent's retirement), 'serious illness that required an operation or long term hospitalization experienced by a family member' (listed as family member's illness),'depression or other mental conditions, or refusal to attend classes by a family member' (listed as family member's depression), 'accident or disaster to a family member' (listed as family member's accident), 'voluntary resignation or unemployment' (listed as family member's job change) and 'bankruptcy or financial ruin' (listed as family member's bankruptcy).

An affirmative answer was counted as one, a negative as zero, and the sum total is tabulated in table 3.9 according to the different poverty types.

Table 3.9: Life events between 1994 and 2002 according to the different poverty types (average±standard deviation)

	Persistently poor	Chronically poor	Transiently poor	Never-poor, financially secure	
Marriage	0.00±0.00	0.05±0.22	0.26±0.52	0.20±0.40	
Divorce	0.00±0.00	0.19±0.40	0.13±0.37	0.02±0.15	a
Child birth	0.00±0.00	0.43±0.68	0.70±0.89	0.60±0.83	
Relocation	0.00±0.00	1.10±1.22	1.14±1.21	0.94±0.97	d
Total life events	0.00±0.00	1.76±1.64	2.23±2.11	1.76±1.72	c
Respondent's illness	0.40±0.89	0.29±0.64	0.19±0.48	0.19±0.51	
Respondent's depression	0.00±0.00	0.52±1.29	0.24±1.08	0.14±0.65	
Respondent's accident	0.00±0.00	0.48±0.87	0.20±0.54	0.24±0.53	
Family member's illness	0.00±0.00	0.48±0.81	0.43±0.63	0.50±0.94	
Family member's depression	0.00±0.00	0.14±0.48	0.08±0.47	0.06±0.37	
Family member's accident	0.40±0.89	0.19±0.68	0.22±0.47	0.29±0.60	
Total of accidental events	0.80±1.79	2.10±2.83	1.24±1.67	1.40±1.92	
Respondent's job change	1.00±1.00	1.19±1.44	0.67±1.31	0.52±0.87	c
Respondent's retirement	0.60±0.89	0.57±0.68	0.59±0.81	0.44±0.68	
Family member's job change	0.60±0.55	0.71±1.19	0.46±0.89	0.24±0.52	b
Family member's bankruptcy	0.20±0.45	0.00±0.00	0.03±0.16	0.05±0.25	
Total of job related transfers	2.40±2.07	2.48±2.34	1.69±2.00	1.23±1.34	b
Total life events	3.20±3.56	6.33±4.16	5.21±4.18	4.40±3.04	c

a: $p < 0.001$.   b: $p < 0.01$.   c: $p < 0.05$.   d: $p < 0.1$

Examining the relationship between life events such as marriage, divorce, child birth and relocation during the past twelve months, and different poverty types, we see that the persistently poor have not experienced any of these during the nine years of the longitudinal following period. Of these life events, we see more divorces occurring among the chronically poor and transiently poor than among the never-poor. As far as total life events are concerned, more events take place among the transiently poor, showing a significant difference between them and the persistently poor. When it comes to the total of accidental events, such as illness, depression and accident, there is not much difference among the different poverty types, but there are again marginally fewer occurrences among the persistently poor. More job related transfers happen to the respondents and their family members among the chronically poor than the never-poor. The job related transfer total confirms that there is a significant difference between the chronically poor and the never-poor. Unlike life events and accidental events, job related transfer events happen among the persistently poor as well.

The chronically poor have experienced more of everything in life, life events, accidental events and job related transfers, than never-poor. The transiently poor sit between the chronically poor and the never-poor, while the persistently poor have fewer events, like the never-poor, although theirs may not be a significant difference.

Judging from the above mentioned attributes and life events, we can say that the never-poor has fewer divorces, fewer job shifts, retirement and unemployment affecting the respondents as well as their family members. The attributes of the transiently poor are much closer to those of the never-poor than to those of the chronically poor. The chronically poor experience more life events than others and unlike the transiently poor, are more likely to be unmarried, older, have more family members, more children and live in rented property. They tend to have more divorces and more job related transfers which make their poverty more chronic. The persistently poor have more family members, finish school more often at junior high school level, and live in rented property. Though they have more job related transfers, their family type made up of singles or single parents living with their parents remains steady, and they have hardly any life events. All these seem to 'lead to a structural hierarchical gap' (Iwata 1999: 190).

In addition to these characteristics, as shown in table 3.10, poverty occurs continuously to the chronically poor. All of the chronically poor experience poverty at least two years in a row. Having once fallen into poverty, these people are stuck there, unable to get out of it again the following year. Then, 90.5% of the chronically poor remain in poverty continuously for three years, 66.7% or nearly seventy per cent of them experience poverty four years in a row. Households which have experienced poverty for

Table 3.10: Poverty spell (%)

	Chronically poor	**Transiently poor**
Twice in a row	100.0	40.0
Thrice in a row	90.5	21.3
Four times in a row	66.7	6.3
Five times in a row	42.9	1.3
Six times in a row	38.1	1.3
Seven times in a row	33.3	0.0
Eight times in a row	9.5	0.0

five years, more than half of the accounting period of nine years, account for 42.9% of the chronically poor. The corresponding percentages for the transiently poor are 21.3%, 6.3% and 1.3%. The chronically poor suffer longer and more continuous poverty than the transiently poor. Furthermore, the persistently poor, as well as the chronically poor, have a bigger poverty gap when they are poor, as the far right hand side column of table 3.7 shows. This is the average poverty gap excluding the time when their income is above the poverty level. The poverty gap is bigger for the chronically poor when they are poor, and their poverty occurs continuously. Because of these factors, it is harder for them to climb out of poverty.

Chronic poverty

As already mentioned, there has been indeed an increase in the number of people in poverty due to the recent economic stagnation, but is this an increase in the numbers of transiently poor or chronically poor? To find this out, we will have a look at the nature of poverty in Japan, referring to Rodgers and Rodgers (1993) who reveal that the increase in poor families in the US during the late 1970s and mid 1980s was not an increase in numbers but also an increase in the chronically poor.

To examine poverty since 1997, when the economy collapsed, and to see if there is any correlation with any particular attributes, we will now compare the following attributes from the period between 1994 and 1997, with those from the period between 1999 and 2002. The attributes for comparison are their age, which represents their basic attribute, the household types (including their life events) which represent their household attributes, and the level of education which represents their socio-economic attributes. We will combine here the persistently poor with the chronically poor, and compare the differences with the transiently poor. As we can see in Table 3.11 (note that the sample for the education level is smaller because of the unavailability of two respondents), both the chronic poverty and the transitory poverty have increased during the period between 1994 and 1997 and the period between 1999 and 2002. The chronic poverty increased from 6.3% to 12.9%, while the transitory poverty increased from 11.4% to 12.9%. Judging from the margin of increase, 6.6% for the chronic poverty and a 1.5% increase for the transitory poverty, we can see that the recent increase in poverty is in fact an increase in chronic poverty.

Table 3.11: Increase of chronic poverty

	Below 34	Above 35	Overall
Chronic poverty			
1994–1997 (A)	4.0	11.3	6.3
1999–2002 (B)	12.1	13.1	12.9
(B) – (A)	8.1	1.8	6.6
Transitory poverty			
1994–1997 (A)	13.2	7.5	11.4
1999–2002 (B)	12.1	13.1	12.9
(B) – (A)	–1.1	5.6	1.5
All poor (chronic poverty + transitory poverty)			
1994–1997 (A)	17.2	18.8	17.7
1999–2002 (B)	24.2	26.2	25.8
(B) – (A)	7.0	7.4	8.1
sample number of (A)	227	106	333
sample number of (B)	66	267	333

		Household				
		Other				
	Sole parent	Total other	Continuously married	Continuously unmarried	Newly married	Experienced separation by divorce or death (no children)	Overall
---	---	---	---	---	---	---	---
Chronic poverty							
1994–1997 (A)	40.0	4.5	4.9	4.7	2.6	11.1	6.3
1999–2002 (B)	57.1	9.5	9.7	9.0	9.1	25.0	12.9
(B) – (A)	17.1	5.0	4.9	4.2	6.5	13.9	6.6
Transitory poverty							
1994–1997 (A)	13.3	10.7	12.4	9.4	5.1	33.3	11.4
1999–2002 (B)	14.3	13.2	12.8	11.9	27.3	0.0	12.9
(B) – (A)	1.0	2.5	0.4	2.5	22.2	–33.3	1.5
All poor (chronic poverty + transitory poverty)							
1994–1997 (A)	53.3	15.2	17.3	14.1	7.7	44.4	17.7
1999–2002 (B)	71.4	22.7	22.6	20.9	36.4	25.0	25.8
(B) – (A)	18.1	7.5	5.3	6.8	28.7	–19.4	8.1
sample number of (A)	15	318	185	85	39	9	333
sample number of (B)	21	312	226	67	11	8	333

To look at the age groups, we will divide the sample into people under thirty-four and above thirty-five in 1997 and in 2002, and compare them with their experience of poverty. The increase in overall poverty is about seven points for both age groups. Yet the chronic poverty among the people under thirty-four jumped from

Table 3.11 continued

	Level finished education				
	Junior high school	Senior high school	Vocational and other colleges	University and graduate schools	Overall
Chronic poverty					
1994–1997 (A)	23.5	8.5	2.4	4.3	6.3
1999–2002 (B)	41.2	14.9	8.7	8.5	13.0
(B) – (A)	17.7	6.4	6.3	4.2	6.7
Transitory poverty					
1994–1997 (A)	23.5	12.1	9.5	10.6	11.5
1999–2002 (B)	17.6	19.1	9.5	2.1	13.0
(B) – (A)	–5.9	7.0	0.0	–8.5	1.5
All poor (chronic poverty + transitory poverty)					
1994–1997 (A)	47.0	20.6	11.9	14.9	17.8
1999–2002 (B)	58.8	34.0	18.2	10.6	26.0
(B) – (A)	11.8	13.4	6.3	–4.3	8.2
sample number of (A)	17	141	126	47	331
sample number of (B)	17	141	126	47	331

four per cent to 12.1%, an increase of 8.1 points, while the chronic poverty among the people over thirty-five increased by only 1.8 points, from 11.3% to 13.1%. Hardly any change is observable for the transitory poverty in the under thirty-four year old age group between 1994 and 1997 and between 1999 and 2002. In other words, the group of relatively young people under the age of thirty-four contained less chronic poverty between 1994 and 1997, but they have been on the increase in recent times.

For the types of households, taking life events into consideration, we divided the sample households into two groups, those which had experienced sole parenthood and those who had not. Those who had not were broken down further into those who had been continuously married, continuously single, newly married, and those households without children who had experienced separation by death or divorce during the accounting period. The households which experienced both marriage and sole parenthood, are categorised as female-headed households. The most noticeable characteristic is the huge increase in the chronic poverty among the female-headed households. They increased by 17.1 points to 57.1% in the period between 1999 and 2002, from forty per cent, higher than other households, in the period between 1994 and 1997. Since there was hardly any increase in number of transitory poverty between these two periods, the proportion of the chronic poverty in poor female-headed households, further increased as well (from seventy-five per cent to eighty per cent). Poverty amongst female-headed households is intensifying. Of the non-female-headed households, both the continuously married and the continuously single households registered an increase in chronic poverty households of between 4.2 and 4.9 points, which is larger than the 0.4 and 2.5 point increase in transitory poverty amongst them, but not as significant as the increase for the female-headed households. Among the newly married households, the chronic poverty households increased by 6.5 points while the transitory poverty increased by 22.2 points. We have to be careful about the fact that this is based on a small sample of households, but this recent deterioration of living standards may be related to some extent to the increase in the number of people remaining single.

In terms of educational achievement, the junior high school graduates who already formed a large proportion of the chronic poverty between 1994 and 1997 at 23.5%, further increased their proportion by 17.7 points to 41.2%, while the proportion of tertiary graduates increased by a mere 4.2 points from 4.3% to 8.5%. Poverty among junior high school graduates is becoming more and more chronic. Of further note is that against the general trend of increasing poverty, the proportion of tertiary graduates experiencing overall poverty has decreased, because the transitory poverty among them have decreased by 8.5 points.

The recent increase in poverty is not merely a quantitative increase, but a qualitative one because poor households are falling into more chronic poverty. Poverty is becoming more chronic in the under thirty-four, relatively young age group, while at the same time, it is intensifying among people who were already poor, such as female-headed households and households of junior high school graduates.

Addressing intensifying chronic poverty

In this chapter, we have looked at the dynamics of poverty and show the state of poverty, using data from the JPSC. The cross-sectional poverty trend reviewed here tells us that between 1994 and 2002, the poverty rate increased from 7.5% to 15.3%. It had already been trending upward in 1994, but accelerated further during and after 1997 and 1998. The proportion of households at risk of poverty amounts to a third of all households, as 31.8% of the households have experienced poverty at least once during the accounting period.

We divided the households which had experienced poverty into three groups. Although they had experienced poverty hits the transiently poor had an average income which remained above the poverty level. The chronically poor are those with an average income below the poverty level, but who have not been suffering poverty all the time, while the persistently poor suffer poverty continuously. Out of all the households, 68.2% of them are from the never-poor which has not experienced poverty at all. The transiently poor occupy twenty-four per cent, the chronically poor, 6.3% and the persistently poor, 1.5%. The persistently poor have been constantly poor, without life events like marriage or child birth, while their household type remained steady, with hardly any accidental events like illness and accident, other than job related transfers. On the other hand, the chronically poor have had life events and job related transfers, and their attributes are much closer to the persistently poor than those of the never-poor. The transiently poor, though their attributes are closer to those of the never-poor, have had life events during the accounting period which contributed to their poverty.

With the current economic recession, the poverty rate is on the increase, and poverty is becoming more chronic. Though the chronically poor and persistently poor constituted less than ten per cent during the accounting period, we found that poverty is becoming more chronic among female-headed households and less educated households. Poverty is also expected to become more chronic among relatively young people. The poverty experienced by these groups of people is very serious. Judging from the pattern that once they fall in poverty they experience it continuously, urgent political action needs to be undertaken at once to deal with chronic poverty on a long term basis, not just by tackling transient poverty. In essence, it is not sufficient to supplement income shortfalls. Further improvement in vocational training is required.

What we need to do includes examining how the transiently poor, who occupy the majority of households with poverty hits, move in and out of poverty, how they move along during the accounting period, and what stops them becoming chronically poor. The sample used here is very small. What is needed are more stable results for examination by, for example, including the sample data which has been added to the JPSC from 1997 onwards.

4 Older women and housing poverty: their housing history in home-owning society

Misa Izuhara

Defining 'older people'

It is often easy to overlook this in statistical analysis, but there are various aspects to the 'ageing society' or the 'older population.' Older people in Japan are not a homogeneous group but comprise approximately thirty million people, which we cannot possibly consider to be one entity. When we define older people as those aged sixty-five years and over, just looking at the age differences alone between those in their sixties and those of over one hundred, there is an age gap of nearly forty years. It is not just their age that is different, but their life experiences are widely varied according to health, financial and other status. It is true that as you grow old, the functions of your body and mind deteriorate, but not every old person requires extensive care. The number of older people who are bedridden, infirm or who have dementia, and require care and support, is estimated to be 2.7 million, about thirteen per cent of people over sixty-five in 2000 (2000 nen kosei hakusho). As a characteristic of an ageing society, the number of the very old, those over eighty-five, is expected to rise and those are people who often require care and support. There are various other factors which make 'older people' diverse, and that prevent us from seeing them as one group. Those factors include gender differences, family composition and living arrangements such as living with family or living alone, the level of social participation, assets and income levels. While it is often overlooked in Japan, the difference in living customs arising from ethnic backgrounds can also be a factor. Moreover, women, because they have a longer life expectancy (77.64 for males and 84.62 for females in 2000), tend to marry older men, making them more likely to be widowed. Considering that long term care is also mostly shouldered by women, the issue of an ageing society can be considered to be a women's issue. With a particular reference to housing, this chapter will focus on the poverty of older women who have lived through the post-War welfare society in Japan. Using a housing history approach, the chapter examines: first, how older women arrived at their current situation; second, the characteristics of their current housing; and third, how the post-War social policies and economic development have influenced the process.

Research method and analytical framework

The qualitative data used in this chapter comes from fieldwork research conducted in a Japanese city during 1996 and 1997. This city is an industrial city from the pre-War era, but the population is in decline due to a recent nation-wide industrial restructuring. A series of semi-structured in-depth interviews with 28 older women were carried out. The criteria were set in advance in order to cover targeted groups of older people. Only women who had been married and had had a child or children, who had become single through either widowhood or divorce, were targeted for interview. However, the research included two never-married women who had alternative means of family support by siblings, nephews, etc. Choosing a 10-year cohort of women who were between 70 and 79 years old as a sample was practical and effective for the research purpose. Older women in this cohort had all experienced a common set of post-War legal, economic and social change.

In order to examine the issues affecting older women in different housing settings, three welfare sectors – the family, the market and the state – were important factors in the selection process for the fieldwork research. It helped to make a clear distinction among older women in terms of their socio-economic status, tenure and dwelling type, living arrangement, or degree of intergenerational solidarity. For example, cases of extended family living were focused on the family sector. For the other two sectors, investigating reasons why those women chose or were forced to live independently from their adult children was one of the major objectives. Older women living in purpose-built housing, both in private and in public housing, were included in those two sectors. Especially for the state sector, women on low income living in public rental housing or a public nursing home were included in the research. Nine or ten women, who met the above criteria, were interviewed from each welfare sector.

This framework allows us to compare women in different situations, but this chapter will mainly focus on older women living in market- and public-sector housing and will discuss their housing poverty and the reasons for it. Table 4.1 shows a brief housing history after their marriages of the twenty-eight female respondents.

Older people and housing

Home ownership

A home functions not only as a shelter to protect people from external hazards but is also a place where people carry out various activities including sleeping, eating, relaxing, communicating, and caring for each other. However, 'home' does not always mean a safe and comforting place for everyone, as exemplified by domestic violence and possible eviction from rental properties. Therefore, living in adequate accommodation is considered to be a very significant 'foundation for welfare' in terms of health and mental well-being, as well as maintaining and improving one's dignity and quality of life (Hayakawa 1997; Hayakawa and Okamoto 1993). For older people to lead an independent life, it is necessary to live in safe, affordable and accessible accommodation. Their need for accommodation is as varied as their ages, backgrounds, hobbies, economic situations and physical condition. Their needs tend to change as they grow older. Therefore policies regarding housing for older people should not just work to reduce or eliminate ageism in all areas, but should also introduce flexible approaches for the social needs of older people. Public policy should cover areas such as building standards, living environments and service necessities rather than concentrating heavily on a medical model dealing with 'disability' arising from ageing (Heywood, et al 2002).

That the rate of home ownership is high in Japan reflects post-War policies encouraging home ownership. According to the 1998 *Jūtaku tochi tōkei chōsa* (A Statistical Survey of Residential Properties and Land), the ratio of home ownership among all residential property was 60.3%. Home ownership was lower in the three megalopolis regions than the national average. In the greater Tokyo area, it was 52.2%, about eight percentage points lower. Home ownership for people over sixty-five years old was even higher. This does not necessarily mean that older people are affluent, because this could refer to properties owned by older people themselves as well as property owned by their children. They might also be living in properties of a lower value. Nonetheless, according to the 1998 statistics, 85.2% of households with older people were owner occupied, and 82.7% owned detached houses. Households which include older people account for roughly a third of households, and typically, the size of the household is shrinking. Over the years, the number of traditional households with three generations has been noticeably declining, while elderly-only households have been on the increase. In 1983, elderly couples accounted for 16.7% of households with older people in general, while single-elderly households accounted for 11.3%. In the fifteen years prior to 1999, those households rose to 25.2% and 17.5% respectively. Nearly half of the households with older people were those living independently from their children. In 2000, while eight per cent of elderly men lived alone, the number of women was 17.9%, indicating that more elderly women are living alone. The rate increases as they grow older. A further increase is expected in the number of older people living alone, because of the increase in the number of unmarried people as well as the rising divorce rate, as older people become more and more financially independent.

Renting alone

The home ownership rate varies according to the household type. Home ownership for single-elderly households was 65%, much lower than the 85% for elderly couples, according to the 1998 survey. The rate for single-elderly households in private rental properties was 22.7%, comparatively higher than the other household types. Older people living in public housing accounted for 11.5%. Of those renting privately, seventeen per cent lived in wooden buildings. It is noted that they may be living with various problems in older buildings, such as inadequate structures and facilities, and lower living standards {2001 *nen 'Kōreisha no jūtaku to seikatsu kankyō ni kansuru ishiki chōsa'* (The 2001 'Attitude Survey of Residents and Living Standards of Elderly People')}. Among elderly women living alone, there were some who were financially well off, those living on their husbands' bereavement pensions and so on, but most were on low incomes. When looking at annual earnings, 22.6% earned less than ¥800,000, and if we included those earning between ¥800,000 and ¥1.6 million, nearly sixty per cent of them fell in this category. Of the elderly women living alone, 21.7% did

Table 4.1: A brief housing history of the twenty-eight women interviewed

Case number	Age (yrs)	Mode of residence	History
Family sector			
1	82	living with the family of her eldest son (already deceased)	rental flat, then moved into a house owned by her son to live with him after the death of her husband.
2	71	living with her unmarried eldest daughter	rental house, rental house (detached), rented room after the death of her husband, bought a house in her name using her husband's life insurance payout.
3	78	living with the family of her eldest son	public quarter, bought a house in her husband's name, moved into her own house (her eldest son with whom she was living got married).
4	73	living with her nephew and his wife	company house, then moved into own house (in her husband's name) with her nephew and his wife immediately after it was built, after her husband's death the house was transferred to a collective title under her name and her nephew and his wife.
5	77	living with her son-in-law (after the death of her daughter)	company house, prefectural public housing (lived together with her daughter and her husband following her marriage, with some time living separately due to her husband's transfer), then to her own house (the title owned by her son-in-law).
6	74	living with the family of her eldest son	lived with her mother-in-law, moved to own house (in her husband's name), inherited the house after her husband's death, and the family of her eldest son moved in.
7	70	living with the family of her eldest son	lived with her mother-in-law in a house owned by her, the house was inherited by her husband following the death of his mother, eviction, purchase of a second hand house (in her husband's name), following her retirement, moved in with the family of her eldest son, renovation (land in her name, the house to the eldest son).
8	72	living with her eldest daughter (whose husband has died)	lived in a rented property, then moved to own house (her husband's), then to another house from which the business was operated as well, after the death of her husband, the present house was purchased and renovated.
9	72	living with the family of her eldest son	lived with the family of her husband in the current house, after his disappearance she moved back to her parents' home, inherited her husband's house and moved back.
Market sector			
10	71[a]	living alone in a commercial old people's home	lived in a training school dormitory, then in a rental property, shared a house with a friend, moved into the old people's home.
11	76	living alone in a commercial old people's home	lived with her husband's mother in a rental property, moved to a house purchased under her husband's name, moved to a flat owned by the family of her second son after the death of her husband, moved into an old people's home.

Table 4.1: continued

Case number	Age (yrs)	Mode of residence	History
12	72	living alone in a commercial old people's home	lived in rental properties (moved around several times), bought a flat under her husband's name, following her husband's retirement, moved back to his old home town and into a detached house, inherited it, seven years after her husband's death, moved into the old people's home.
13	77	living alone in her own detached house	lived in a company house, bought a house under her husband's name after his retirement, before his death, moved into her son's house, inherited it and moved back.
14	77	living alone in her own detached house	lived in a company house, bought a house under her husband's name before his retirement, inherited it.
15	74[b]	living alone in public housing	lived with the family of her husband, divorced and moved into a rental property, bought a house under her name, shared with the family of her sister, transfered the house to her sister, moved to a rental property, moved into public housing.
16	73	living alone in her own semi-detached house	lived with her husband's mother, moved to a rental property, bought a house with a shop under her husband's name, moved to another house, then inherited.
17	70	living alone in her own detached house	lived in a rented flat (moved around several times), moved to a house purchased under her husband's name, moved to another house which burnt down, moved back to the old house, renovated, then inherited it.
18	80	living alone in a commercial old people's home	lived in a company house, purchased a house under her husband's name, inherited it, rented it out and moved to an old people's home.

Public sector

19	72	living alone in a municipally run shirubā haujingu	(serviced public rental property for elderly people) lived in a rental property, moved into municipally run public housing.
20	74	living alone in a municipally run shirubā haujingu	(serviced public rental property for elderly people) lived in a rental property, moved into the municipally run public housing.
21	71[a]	living alone in a nursing home for the elderly	lived in her sister's own house, her brother inherited it, after the death of her sister, moved into the nursing home.
22	75	living alone in an nursing home for the elderly	lived in a rented house, then moved into the nursing home.
23	74[b]	living alone in an elderly nursing home	live-in worked (various places), rented property, then the elderly nursing home.
24	79	living alone in a nursing home for the elderly	lived in a rented property, moved in with the family of her youngest son, moved out to live in a rental flat, then the nursing home.
25	80	living alone in municipally run public housing	lived with the parents of her husband, divorced and moved into a rental property, lived with her daughter for a year, then municipally run public housing.

Continued on next page.

Table 4.1: A brief housing history of the twenty-eight women interviewed—continued

Case number	Age (yrs)	Mode of residence	History
26	77	living alone in municipally run public housing	lived in a rental property, after the death of her husband lived with her daughter for six months, then moved to a rental property, then to the municipally run public housing.
27	75	living alone in municipally run public housing	lived in a rental property, bought a house under her husband's name, evicted and moved into municipally run public housing (long term hospitalization).
28	76	living alone in a rental property (entire rent is subsidised)	lived in her own house, sold the house, moved into her eldest son's flat and they lived together, moved eight times in two years (rental properties).

Notes: a = unmarried; b = divorced.

not have any savings. Thirty-six per cent of *Seikatsu hogo* (Public Livelihood Protection) recipients were people over sixty-five years old. Of them, 16.6% were women living alone (1997). Therefore, even if some of older people wish to move to accommodation that would better cater for their changing needs, it may not be possible for them to do so due to financial and other associated barriers. There is an added difficulty for older people looking for accommodation as there is a tendency in the private rental market to avoid renting to single elderly people. In this regard, among older people living alone or in commercial rental properties, it is more than likely that a reasonable number of them need financial or social support.

Ownership, policy and inequality

The post-War housing policies in Japan have encouraged home ownership. The purchase of a house has been considered to be an individual responsibility. Therefore, provision for housing has been mainly left to the commercial market. Unlike other welfare societies, like the UK where home ownership now surpasses that of Japan but had a period in the past when a massive amount of public housing was provided, the direct provision of public housing in Japan by national or local governments has always been kept to a minimum. Only a small amount of municipally run public housing (accounting for around five per cent of all residential housing), administered by local government with subsidies from central government, offers low cost accommodation for people on lower incomes. Established in 1955, the *Jūtaku toshi seibi kōdan* (Housing and Urban Development Corporation) began supplying accommodation for 'families' living in urban areas but their contribution remains low at about two per cent of over all supply of accommodation. The residential accommodation supplied by the corporation was only for 'families,' and also not intended as housing for life. It was seen as temporary accommodation and as a stepping stone for young families before they purchased their own property. As a result, among older people living in rental housing, the number of those living in public housing is less than half that in private rented housing. Compared to today's standard, such accommodation built within twenty years after the end of the War was of a much lower standard. Even in the latter part of the 1980s there were about thirty thousand unwanted *kodan* units, rejected because of insufficient facilities, poor state of repair, or because they were simply too small. As society became affluent, younger families began demanding much more space and contemporary facilities. Unwanted by young families, the *kodan* units became attractive to older people on low incomes, since the rent was cheaper than private rental, and they were less likely to be asked to leave. The ageing of the public housing tenants is continuing, aided in 1979 by the relaxation of the rules to allow 'single person occupancy.' The central government's intervention into the housing supply was concentrated on stimulating housing demand rather than supplying housing directly. There are no government subsidies to the private sector encouraging higher quality rental property development. There is no (cash based) rental assistance scheme for individual tenants of private rental other than the *Seikatsu hogo* system, like the housing benefits seen in the UK and other European countries.

The government made available long term mortgages with low interest indirectly through the *Jūtaku kinyū kōko* (Government Housing Loan Corporation) only to those buying property, and so, in the most efficient way for the government, it has encouraged private home ownership. Furthermore, after the late 1960s, the housing industry began expanding by the ready-built housing market. To complement the free market economy, private financial organisations began offering housing loans as well. As a result, a housing development system relying on the free market economy was established. During the bubble economy period of the 1980s, however, housing policies encouraging home ownership ran into difficulties due to the soaring land prices. Indeed there are some advantages in housing policies which encourage home ownership. To begin with, they contributed to the improvement of the quality of the housing stock in the post-War housing reconstruction process. In order to ensure accommodation offered larger space and good facilities, it was necessary for people to purchase their own homes, especially in the urban areas which were crowded with low quality rental properties. Also, unlike in rental properties, people could expect more stability in living in their own homes. It is believed to be very difficult to find rental property when people become older, as many landlords and estate agents tend to avoid elderly tenants, partly because they are on a fixed income and may not be able to cope with possible rental price rises, and partly due to the risk of lonely death. Public housing is thought to be more secure, but tenants can be evicted if they fall into arrears or if they cannot meet an increase in rent. Additionally privately owned houses can be inherited by the next generation, which means they can contribute significantly to wealth accumulation over generations and also to the continuation of the family line. Home ownership among households containing more than one generation is high, which can be explained by saying that the relatively larger size makes it easier to share the house, as the houses tend to be detached. However, it is also possible that this is a more efficient way to hand over the family asset to the next generation rather than breaking it up. Finally there is a cultural aspect to home ownership. It brings with it a social status for individuals, especially for married males, as they say 'by owning a home one can be considered to be a full adult,' and help forge their identities. Home ownership development in the post-War period in Japan, however, encouraged by government housing policies was also a means of creating social stratification as in many developed countries. Indeed, inequality and a wealth gap were created between the haves and the have-nots.

The average income for elderly households has increased throughout the post-War period, just like general households, due to the development of the social security system which affects the public pension. Yet there is a significant disparity between the low income households among the elderly population and all the other households. According to the 2000 *Kokumin seikatsu kiso chōsa* (National Livelihood Survey), the most common annual income for an elderly household was between one and two million yen, accounting for thirty per cent of households. Those earning between two and three million yen a year came second, constituting nineteen per cent. Including those on less than one million yen, nearly two thirds of older people are living on less than three million yen a year. This could be a case of 'asset rich, cash poor' considering their higher home ownership, but income no doubt affects their housing situation. It is more likely that people on lower incomes live in the rental properties. The supply of rental property for low income earners is rather limited, as the post-War housing policies focusing on home ownership have dealt a blow to the growth of the rental property market. The recent revision of the Fixed Term Land and Building Lease Act has made life even harder for tenants.

Corporate welfare and company houses

The provision of company houses, a part of employee benefits, has played a unique and important role in the development of the housing system in post-War Japan. Throughout the period of rapid economic growth, corporations provided accommodation for their employees such as dormitories for single people and company houses for families as well as rental assistance. Some leased private properties for this purpose. According to the survey conducted in the 1980s, the average rent for the company houses was a third of that for public housing, and one tenth of that for private rental properties. Among the various employee benefit measures taken by the corporations, accommodation assistance was by far the most important, especially in terms of budget. The amount of accommodation assistance depended on the size of the corporations, but some spent half of their employee benefit budget on it. The average during the 1980s was forty per cent. During the period of rapid economic growth the company housing system made it possible for companies to readily transfer their employees to different locations. Because the companies were offering employees affordable housing the employees in turn had an incentive to stay on with the company. The corporate housing arrangement was indispensable as well in industrial towns where housing was expensive and in short supply. As a result, company housing became established in a unique position, playing a special role supplementing public housing, private rental properties and privately owned houses in the post-War housing system in Japan.

As we shall see later in the empirical data, many employees used company houses as stepping stones on the way to purchasing their own homes. They were able to save enough money to purchase their house because of the subsidised rent at the company houses. Quite a number of older people today have been able to purchase their houses on retirement using their savings and their retirement benefit pay outs, another feature of corporate welfare. Since then, company accommodation assistance has gradually shifted from a direct offer of company housing to home acquisition mortgage assistance and savings schemes for potential home purchases, and more employees buy houses while they are still at work. Take the example of the Hitachi Corporation. In 1967, thirty-eight per cent of households supported by its male employees lived in company housing. Ten years later, the rate had gone down to twenty-seven per cent, while the rate of home ownership among employees had increased from forty-four to sixty-two per cent during the same period (ILO 1982). In recent years, there are still many employees living in company housing and singles dormitories, but not all employees wish to live in company housing. The company's system has also moved away from the direct supply of accommodation to the more indirect assistance given by home acquisition mortgages, savings schemes and interest rate assistance. Like any other welfare provisions, the supply of company housing to employees was not carried out on an equal basis. Company housing was more accessible to privileged regular full-time employees and employees of larger corporations. According to a study conducted in the late 1980s, twenty-three per cent of employees were working for companies with more than one hundred employees while fifty-seven per cent worked for smaller businesses with less than thirty employees, indicating that company housing was a privilege offered to a limited number of employees. Furthermore, single women or households headed by women did not have the same access to occupational welfare including accommodation assistance as their male counterparts. This often led to the exclusion of households headed by women from home ownership and asset building opportunities in their later lives. In consequence, being 'single,' 'female' and 'old' have become the three impedances to finding quality accommodation.

Older women and home ownership

Bearing in mind the housing policies of Japan focusing on home ownership, this discussion will not consider what it means to older people to own houses, based on empirical data. Why older women need to own houses or consider it natural to own houses will first be considered, following which other issues regarding the custom of owning a house will be discussed.

Home ownership, in that a home provides shelter, can be rated highly as it gives a sense of security and assurance. This applies, of course, not only to older people but also to people of any age group.

> She had been living in the house even when her husband was alive. At the time of the interview, she was living in a detached house in her name with her son's family. She said "it would be too hard to live in a rental property. A month passes so quickly, and then it is time to pay rent again". She believed in 'not allowing (my daughter) to marry anyone who does not own a house.' "I wanted my daughter to leave for marriage from our own home as well. If our daughter married someone with a house, her children could also inherit the house." [No.6 aged 74]

For the post-War generation, home ownership was considered to be indispensable and the only sure way to obtain adequate housing. Particularly in her later life, when she had to rely on a fixed income from the pension, home ownership gave a greater sense of security. She felt free from external threats and uncertainty which tenants would experience, such as rental price rises or eviction.

To Japanese people, home ownership is the ultimate goal in the 'Game of Life,' indicating a sense of stability. In this respect, Japanese values are quite different from those of other countries such as the UK where houses are bought and sold frequently according to the changing circumstances of life course, not limited to employment transfers, but also because of marriage, childbirth, children leaving home and retirement.

> Before they built their own home, she moved four times with her husband. They became very tired of moving and when it seemed unlikely that her husband would be transferred again, they decided to build their home. Of course, building a house meant they would live there forever. [No.2 aged 71]

A house can also mean the foundation of a family asset that can be handed down through the generations, and is thus a symbol of family continuity. This is important not just for a family engaged in land based activities, but the process of inheriting a house and creating an asset is also considered important for families in general. Unlike families who have a high regard for family traditions, families without children tend to have less incentive to own a house for this purpose.

> She had been divorced straight after her marriage. She once owned a house, and lived there together with her sister's family, which made her feel constrained, as if she was a 'lodger even though she was the landlady.' After they had lived together for twelve years she moved out, giving the house away, because she could no longer cope with her brother-in-law's violence towards her sister and their children. At the time of interview, she was living alone in a public housing unit. She had no wish to own a house any more. "It would not make much difference, because I have not much time left and no offspring". [No.15 aged 74]

In other word, owning a house prevents one from moving at will according to changes in one's life course. Inheriting a house means continuing to live at the place where the house stands, and the younger generation are expected to live there when they inherit the house. This was not a big issue when living together was common. Selling an inherited house might lead to the severance of the family line. But today (even though there is a trend for people to return to their birth places), people experience higher geographic mobility and being tied to an inherited house may not be practical in terms of schooling, employment, marriage, job transfers and so on. Timing also matters. As people are living longer now, by the time of their inheritance many children have already purchased their own mortgaged homes. Among the women studied, there were some who were not happy with where they were but could not move because of customs. It is quite possible that the children would have no idea what to do with inherited houses, whether to sell them or not due to various reasons. In this respect, home ownership may lack flexibility in providing adequate housing for the changing needs of older people.

> Since her marriage she had lived in rental accommodation. After the death of her husband she moved in with her son's family. She did not consider moving in with them straight after their marriage, since they were living in an apartment. She felt rather relieved to have one less person living with them. She has heard people saying that they are tied to the houses they own (not being able to move as they wish).

Many older people are doing their best on their own in their home simply for that reason. [No.1 aged 82]

A year after her husband's death, she purchased a life-estate in the private purpose-built housing for older people near her son. Although she had no intention of moving back to her own home in Kyoto, she had not yet sold it. A number of residents in her housing sold their own homes before they moved in there because they would not be of use to them. "I had kept the house, rented it out, because I would not like my brothers-in-law who live nearby to make snide remarks about me, like as soon as my husband died, I sold our house and left." [No.18 aged 80]

Pathways towards home ownership

Among the female respondents, home ownership is seen positively as it provides a sense of security and reassurance, as well as contributing to the preservation of family genealogy. However, they have some reservations about being 'bound' by it. With this in mind, let us now look at the pathways this sample group of older women used to achieve home ownership. Among those who managed to own their own houses, the simplest way was through inheritance from their parents. Some of them had sold the houses they had inherited from their parents in rural areas and built new houses in the more convenient urban location. Others had their own houses built on the land they had inherited.

She and her husband moved from place to place living in company housing, while her husband was transferred to different areas. In the late 1960s, they built a house so they could live with her nephew's family, who they had raised like their son. She used the money from the sale of the house she had inherited from her parents and had rented out. It took them five years to pay off the mortgage on the land and three for the house. It was unthinkable to have a longer term mortgage, because her husband was a wage earner. They did not consider 'buying a house and going to all the trouble of borrowing money,' like people these days who have a twenty or thirty year mortgage. She is helping her daughter to buy a house from the sale of some of her other properties. [No.4 aged 73]

She had lived in company housing for six years following the end of World War II. It was public quarters and they did not have to pay rent. She did not like it there, because there was too much attention focused on everyone's lives. The wife of a high ranking official spoke ill of other wives, for example. She had a very hard time dealing with some of the others. There were three male gatekeepers working in shifts. She could not stand them gossiping about 'so-and-so's wife went out shopping in such-and-such clothes, and came back with whatever.' She wished she could come back home without going through the gate, like by climbing over the fence. So much so, she was very happy when her husband had a house built on the land he inherited from his parents. When they were evicted from that house (due to redevelopment), they built another house on land she got from her parents, their former vegetable patch. [No.3 aged 78]

In the industrial city where the interviews were conducted, more than a few of the respondents' husbands had worked for relatively large companies with fairly good occupational welfare. One of the distinctive benefits was company housing. Company housing was indeed convenient for both employers and employees. Some employees, while living in company housing, would be transferred to various locations. For some people, company housing with subsidised rent coupled with an inheritance, have functioned as a stepping stone in the pathway to home ownership. For this generation, it was common practice to buy their own house by the time of their retirement. Their retirement benefits were also poured into this endeavour.

> She lived in company housing until her husband's retirement. They were planning to build a house with his retirement allowance when he retired. When he retired from his job at the age of fifty-five, he had to take up another job for five years because the pension pay out only began at the age of sixty. Unlike today, the company where her husband worked did not have mortgage assistance. It was common to use a retirement allowance to buy a house in those days. They bought a parcel of land with the assistance of the municipal council. They were allowed to stay on in the company housing for an extra twelve months, during the construction of the house. [No.13 aged 77]

"We were all aware that we eventually would have to leave the company housing. It was our common understanding that we would build a house before retirement. My husband built a house before his retirement at the age of fifty-five. It cost a lot to raise the children, so it was common to embark on building a house after the children became independent." [No.14 aged 77]

The have-nots

The elderly women without their own homes obviously did not have any chance of inheriting them, nor any access to the benefits of the occupational welfare system. This had a lot to do with their marital status, whether they had suffered early separation by death or by divorce, or whether they had remained single. Their unstable means of employment also had an affect. The difference in marital status amongst women living in the three residential sectors is clear. A significant number of single women living in public housing had gone through separation soon after their marriage when they were young, either by death or divorce, or they had remained unmarried. As stated in the eligibility criteria 'those who have difficulty residing at home because of health, environmental or financial reasons,' and low income earners are to be given priority for admission to public nursing homes for older people. Many of the residents have no families or are from broken families. There are many unmarried women from the time before the introduction of the universal pension, who have no savings or pension pay out. Because they have not had steady jobs they have been excluded from the occupational pension scheme, and this has contributed significantly to them finding themselves in poor accommodation in their later life. This of course is not limited to women, but taking into account that women's employment conditions are disadvantaged, it is more likely that women will end up in poor accommodation in their old age.

For women without a partner as the main bread winner at home, it would have been difficult to bring stability to their domestic situation from their own irregular and informal employment. It is likely this led to poor accommodation in their old age as well. It is no wonder that more unmarried women end up in the public housing sector. Without a regular and steady job, or without a husband who has a stable job, many of the women now living in public sector housing have not benefited much from the occupational welfare system, such as subsidised company housing during their working life.

She moved into public nursing home in the mid 1990s. She had never married and she used to live with her elder sister. Before moving to the nursing home, she was living with a niece (the daughter of her sister) and her daughter. Initially, she lived in helping at one of her sister's hair salons. She was qualified as a hair dresser, but could not handle chemicals because of her delicate skin. She was living in one of two salons her sister rented, while her sister lived in her own house and operated another one there. Her sister, after her divorce, started running a cafe in the city they now lived in. She later moved in upstairs at the cafe and started helping her sister. When her sister passed away, she had only a small state pension. Her sister had been receiving the bereaved pension from her late second husband, about ¥450,000 a month and when she died she had savings of about ten million yen. Her niece inherited all her sister's assets. The ownership of the house in which she was living was transferred to her brother before her sister passed away, as they were afraid of it going to her niece who was unreliable in money matters and in life in general. She feared that if she kept sharing the house with her niece, who was careless about money, she would end up in the street. She asked the welfare office to find a nursing home for her. [No.21 aged 71]

She was the only child in her family, and was married but divorced after only a year. Her only daughter died from cancer in the early 1990s. After the divorce, she stayed at her aunt's place for a little while before deciding to be independent and finding work as a live-in housekeeper. She saw so much of the negative side of human nature that she could not stay in one place long, moving frequently from one place to another. She could not take her daughter to her live-in work, so she left her daughter at her mother's house. When she began work as a live-in housekeeper at a hospital she was finally able to live with her daughter because her employer said 'a family should not live separately and there is a spare room.' After having worked as a housekeeper for twenty years, she could afford to live in a rental apartment by herself. When her daughter was diagnosed with cancer and her treatment became very expensive, she went on the benefit. After that, she moved into a nursing home. [No.23 aged 74]

These single women who were not able to own their own homes, have had to rely on the small scale rental market or on housing in the public sector which is also in short supply. The quality of the apartments which older women on low incomes could afford to rent was pretty low compared to the average rental property, let alone privately owned houses. It is fairly common for the apartments to be cheaply built, badly maintained and managed dwellings, long past their use-by date. Living in such old rental accommodation means living with the risk of getting evicted at any time, because the rights of the residents were then not very secure. There were some women among the respondents who had moved to current public housing or nursing homes because they had been evicted from such old wooden-built apartments.

> She moved to the city when she was thirty-three after her divorce. Since then, she has been evicted from rental apartments and municipal public housing seven times. She was evicted from the apartments on the grounds that the properties had been sold to other companies and so on. At last she moved into municipal public housing, thanks to the welfare office. She was evicted from that after twenty-three years because the building was scheduled for demolition. She was given priority to move into the newly built housing in situ. The rent was a little higher as it was a new building. She could not go on the public assistance because of her pensions. In other words, she was hovering just above the poverty line. Because she was receiving three pensions including her late husband's military pension, it was enough to meet the required income standard for the new municipal housing. When they were evicted there were many neighbours who could not afford the rental price rise of five thousand yen to move back in the new flats and so they decided to move to other older municipal apartments. [No.25 aged 80]

> After stopping work as a live-in housekeeper she lived alone for a while. A welfare officer persuaded her to move to a public nursing home, saying 'it would be too dangerous for you to live alone.' The officer was afraid that she might start a fire accidentally, despite the fact that the apartment where she was living was not worth much and had a monthly rent of only ¥15,000. As the old building could be demolished at any time, she was living under the constant threat of eviction. For those reasons, she decided to move into the nursing home, even though she was 'well and could manage by herself.' [No.23 aged 74]

There are costs involved when older people decide to move. Due to such moving costs, even when their needs and demands change, it is not easy for low income tenants in their later life to change dwellings when necessary. Whether it is a move made of their own choice or forced on them by others, moving is not a straightforward business for older people without much economic support.

> She had lived in a detached rental property for seven years. The rent had risen every other year, and this was a burden for her. She then moved to a public housing unit in the late 1970s, so that she could get by with what little pension and savings she had. The unit at the time was still available only for 'families' and a single person could not get in. To conform with the eligibility requirements, she borrowed her nephew's name and made it look like she had moved in with him. She was living on the second floor of a four storey building without a lift. In consideration of older tenants, handrails had been gradually installed, starting from the units on the lower floors. Even though it was a small improvement it has been welcomed especially by older tenants living on the higher floors. There was a system 'to move older tenants from the higher floors to the lower floors,' but she was not intending to move from her unit due to the cost of moving. This was not just the cost of the move itself, however, the other costs were also required when one moves out such as fixing up her current unit and the cost of getting rid of all the things she has accumulated over the years. [No.15 aged 74]

When women have to rely on the risk-averse rental market, the problems they face over housing become even more pronounced after they reach a certain age. It is just not easy for older people and almost impossible for single elderly women to find rental properties.

> Her husband passed away when she was sixty. Her sisters invited her to move closer to them and so did her children. She was told that with her pensions, she could get by even if she pays rent. But when she went around to the real estate agents she could not find anyone who was willing to let a house to a single elderly woman over sixty-five. Four of her sisters promised that 'she would not cause any trouble. We will all be her guarantors in case anything happens,' but to no avail. She could not find anything to rent, nor anything to buy. In the end, she bought a life-estate in a private purpose-built housing for older people. [No.12 aged 72]

In more recent years, these problems concerning rental accommodation have been encountered and recognised by younger single women as well. Younger single women in their thirties and forties in urban areas are now buying condominiums, which has been the cause of much discussion. To explain this phenomenon, younger women today who remain single until they are older, have become more financially independent through their advance in the labour market. It may be that among the younger generation, relying on the financial contribution of their husbands is no longer the only and the most desirable way for women to secure accommodation for themselves.

Older women in public housing

For older women to secure their own homes they tend to rely heavily on occupational welfare through their husbands' work and they rely on their family support. Some of the female respondents who did not own their own homes, had not been able to rely on their husbands' economic contribution because of their marital status either being divorced, widowed young or remained single. Others had been forced to support themselves through unstable employment. Home ownership might be inflexible in meeting the changing needs of older people, but it at least provides the security of tenure and it gives peace of mind to older people. On the other hand, people who do not have their own homes suffer from the fear of eviction since older people are perceived as a risk by the rental property market, and they also fear the additional costs incurred in the actual move. The reality is that the housing needs of older people are not met either in terms of quantity or quality, let alone the basic minimum condition of their security. To supplement the argument, using the voices of older women living in the public sector housing, this section will explore how the characteristics of the corporate-centred society and the social security system of Japan have failed not just in eradicating their poverty but have in fact accelerated it. It becomes evident that poor accommodation in their later life was closely connected to disadvantage in the labour market and in the social security system, and associated low incomes.

Women and the labour market

Gender roles and gender inequality are not restricted to the family model but exist in an amplified way in the labour market as well. The post-War employment structure in Japan is male oriented. Therefore, women perform informal duties at home and away from the formal labour market. It has often been the case that women's employment opportunities, promotions and wages are restricted, while their position in the workplace is disadvantaged.

> She was married when she was twenty and divorced six months later. Due to financial reasons, she worked as a shop assistant at a department store for nearly thirty years, until her retirement. She lived in public housing. Since she was not good at 'making up to the bosses' she had not been promoted. Her salary as well as her retirement allowance were lower because she was a woman. The wages and treatment of female workers are very unfavourable compared to those of their male counterparts who have families. Because her wage was so low, her pension was also low. She had to put up with all kinds of discrimination, as there was no Equal Employment Opportunity Act in those days. When she went to the personnel department and complained that she was not getting a pay rise because her boss disliked her, all she was told was 'it must be your own fault.' [No.15 aged 74]

Older women on low incomes now living in public sector housing had had to be employed to maintain their basic living standards unlike women who could rely on male bread winners. Since the employment structure was male oriented quite a few of those women had been employed informally, such as in family run businesses. Some were employed in irregular and insecure part time jobs. One of the reasons that drives women into these difficult economic conditions is the loss of their main bread winner through divorce or death in their younger days. As a result, these women end up entering the labour market without any particular expertise or experience.

> She was divorced twelve months after her marriage. After her divorce, she worked as a live-in housekeeper at several houses. Then she worked at a hospital. At the age of seventy-one, she moved to a public nursing home. "The only jobs I could find were in bars, or housekeeping if I was lucky, because I had only finished my junior high school education. [No.23 aged 74]

> After her marriage, she ran a barber shop with her *yoshi* [adopted] husband. When she divorced at the age of fifty-seven and left the barber business, she worked part time at a kitchen in a restaurant for five years. When she was sixty-two, she spent two months in hospital after she tripped on the stairs at her apartment, fell on the ground and broke her hip. For twelve months after her discharge from hospital she had to wear a corset. After leaving hospital, she went back to live on her own again, but she could not keep going because she

could not work and she had no income. Although her son invited her to move in with him, she declined because she thought it cramped and uncomfortable. In the end, after consulting a welfare officer, she decided to go on the public livelihood assistance for three years until she turned sixty-five and became eligible for the pension. Then she settled in at a public nursing home. [No.22 aged 75]

Women and social security

The development of the post-War social security system encouraged women to get married, and strengthened gender divisions of labour and financial dependence at home. Women were often given access to social security, medical and health care services and social status by gaining the status of 'housewife' through marriage. In other words, their social security access only came through their husbands' status at work and their contributions to the social security system.

The aim of the 'family as a unit' system was to protect married women socially and economically, without them having to go to work full time. From a different perspective, it was a system designed to keep women tied to their homes and away from formal employment opportunities. The position of the housewife was further strengthened by the pension reform introduced to the social security system in 1986. Under the new pension regime, if a housewife registers, as long as her husband works and contributes to the occupational pension scheme, her husband's contribution is counted as her contribution to the National Pension Scheme (without either of them actually making any extra payment). Though the reform was intended to protect against pensionless women in old age (these had been numerous), the privilege given to housewives is obvious, as male employees on the same wage contribute the same amount to the pension scheme, regardless of their marital status. Inevitably women without husbands are often disadvantaged.

> This older woman living in a nursing home was in an uncertain situation. Her national pension was much too low to live on without supplementary support. However, because she was receiving the pension, no matter how small it was, she could not get other financial support from the state. She had some small savings, but no real estate in her name. She had helped with her sister's business for a long time, but she was not entitled to receive the bereaved pension after her sister's death, because she was not registered as a formal

employee, unlike housewives who supported their husbands at home. [No.21 aged 71]

The pension reform in 1986 reinforced the protection of housewives rather than women with a career. Since the system is 'family as a unit,' a married woman with her own record of employment and contributions made by herself to the occupational pension, has to choose at her husband's death whether to receive her husband's bereaved pension (about seventy-five per cent of his pension) or to continue to receive her own pension. Quite a number of women give up their pensions, even though they made the contributions themselves, if the amount of bereaved pension is larger. It is a reflection of the reality that the overall income throughout a lifetime is significantly less for female workers than for male workers in general. Some housewives who have never been employed may receive more from their husbands' bereaved pensions than the women who have toiled all their lives. It is understandable some single women protest against this system, because it reduces the incentive for women to work as full time employees.

> She worked for twenty years as a nursery staff and for another twenty as the head of a day care centre. Her husband was a public servant. Because she had worked for a long time at a nursery set up in the property of a Buddhist temple, which did not have a proper social security system, she had some blank years in her occupational pension contribution. Her pension amount ended up being very small due to the shortfall in the number of eligible years of contribution. She could not make up the missing payment retrospectively, so, when her husband died, she chose to receive her husband's bereaved pension. The amount she received now was almost half of amount they had been receiving when he was alive. [No.17 aged 70]

If one is informally employed, regardless of gender, one cannot benefit from the well-financed occupational welfare system. Many of the single women were so busy making ends meet that they could not possibly plan for their later life. A woman who had worked all her life as a part time employee could not even have access to the occupational pension scheme. In this research, poverty was more prevalent among single women, who had engaged in informal labour since they did not have a male bread winner, the central pillar of the household economy, and were now left with little savings and hardly (if any) pensions.

> When she was in her thirties, her husband became ill and until his death, she worked part-time for ten years while taking care of him. She worked extremely hard to support her family. Since she worked part time, she was offered no occupational welfare or pension. She could not afford to make any contribution to the National Pension Scheme, since her wage was barely enough to make ends meet. It was out of the question for her to put any savings aside for the future. [No.24 aged 79]

> She was living in a wooden terraced house with a full housing benefit from the local council. After they had sold their house, she moved to the city with her husband. They could afford to pick and choose their work as they had enough money from the sale of the house. If her husband did not like a job he quit the job and look for another. He had been a cleaner at a company dormitory, at a condominium, and even an attendant at public bath house. While they had plenty of money, they could do whatever they wanted. That is probably why he did not get a regular job. They moved eight times in two years. By the time he fell sick, they had hardly any money left. They had no security from the occupational welfare system. She had to go out and earn some money herself, but she fell ill as well, because of the stress. When both of them were too ill, they had no alternative but to go to the welfare office. [No.28 aged 76]

On the other hand, more formally employed women were guaranteed a better life including their own pension. Women in professional jobs, the public service, teaching or with their own businesses tend to attain financial independence in their old age, without depending on their husbands.

> She worked as a civil servant for thirty years until her retirement at the age of sixty. At the time of the interview, she was living with her son's family in a newly built detached house. She chose to live on her own pension at the time of her husband's death, because it was much better than his bereaved pension. He was employed in a small business, while she worked at a public office. Ten years ago, she purchased the neighbouring plot of land with her retirement allowance. [No.7 aged 70]

Conclusion

Not all older people now live in ideal housing. In particular the housing available to them does not necessarily meet the needs of old age. Some older people without alternatives put up with the uncomfortable situation of living with others, while others continue to bravely live alone. As a result of the post-War housing policies favouring home ownership, there is an unequivocal gap between the haves and have-nots in terms of the security of housing, its availability and quality. The gap is likely to widen over time between the haves and have-nots, since family wealth can be built on home ownership. As a result, older people on low income are often tenants of rental properties, the insecurity of which increases their poverty.

It was evident that for those women outside a conventional family structure, the system placed them at a considerable disadvantage. There were many difficulties facing single women or female-headed households which prevented them from benefiting fully from the system establishing a means for independent living in their later life. The disadvantages become clearly manifested in the later life of women who from their very early days were not dependants. The research found that being female and single as well as a tenant represented probably the worst combination of factors in housing for later life.

5 The interconnection between health and poverty: health and socio-economic well-being

Yūko Hayasaka

Introduction

In 2003, the average life expectancy for a Japanese woman was 85.33 and 78.36 years for a man. These were the world's highest life expectancy rates (Asahi shimbun, July 17, 2004). If measured using the healthy life expectancy (HALE) index advocated in recent years, a Japanese woman, at birth, can expect to live up to 77.7 years before being bed ridden or becoming senile, while for a man, the corresponding expectation is 72.3 years (The World Health Report 2004). But this index, after all, is concerned with the average of the overall population. When you classify the degree of health with socio-economic status, various groups emerge with distinctive attributes. The disparities among them become apparent as does their relationship with poverty, which is the theme of this chapter.

The socio-economic status I refer to here includes employment status, job classifications, status at work, income level, marital status, educational level, home ownership, car ownership and so on. Unfortunately, data based on socio-economic status is extremely difficult to find in Japan in comparison to Western nations. This might be because the Japanese do not want to be surveyed on matters like these, or due to their middle class consciousness, the Japanese people do not want to be measured by certain standards. If we consider the way the national morbidity rate and the mortality rate are worked out just on the basis of sex, age and locality, and the way the health issue in general is perceived, in comparison to the West, especially the UK, it is hard not to think the Japanese are missing the point.

In this chapter, I would like to analyze how much a person's health is affected by poverty, low income, unemployment and other socio-economic factors. The chapter's first half will review the situation in the West, while the second half will compare this with Japan.

Health and poverty in the West

Western health care systems and national health services vary from country to country. The common characteristics of poverty studies in the West are the size of the studies, most of them utilizing the census and other national scale data, and most of them drawing on long term data. I would here like to focus largely on the UK, which has undertaken outstanding investigation in the study and accumulation of policies on the relationship between health, poverty and social classes, but also provide some reference to similar programmes in the US and in Scandinavian countries.

United Kingdom

In 1977, the United Kingdom investigated the connections between socio-economic conditions and health as a national project. The result revealed a wider inequality in health than had been anticipated, according to different socio-economic conditions. This inequality persisted even with the basically universally accessible NHS (National Health Service). The Black Report[1] had a huge impact not only in the UK but also in other developed nations. The question of inequality in health is still keenly studied today in the UK. A wide range of people have been surveyed, and the criteria investigated was also wide-ranging (the yardsticks to measure the degree of health, such as the mortality rate and the morbidity rate).

When dealing with issues arising from poverty – whether we are looking at 'absolute poverty' or 'relative poverty' – it is necessary to judge the social status of those affected. Among UK citizens, class consciousness is very strong, it is almost a central part of their cultural identity. Television and newspapers frequently use terms like 'working class' or 'middle class.' Even in daily conversation, a person's own class origin is often openly mentioned. Furthermore, they do not seem to mind being classified as to what class they belong to by others. For example, a university in the UK has published on the internet the social class, as well as the selected subjects of their applicants and successful students. This is something which the Japanese might consider discriminatory and would possibly cause sensational media coverage. In short, in the UK, social class is an important indicator or yardstick when judging social phenomena, social issues and human relations.

Social class

Table 5.1 is the Registrar General's 'Classification of Social Classes based on occupation' commonly known as RGSC, used until 2000. First introduced in 1911 and drastically revised in 1921, the classification focused on 'occupational skills and the level of qualifications.' Since then, at the time of the national census every ten years, the occupations each social class contain have been revised. Although it has been criticised for having no logical basis, the RGSC has had a long history. Most existing research papers have used the RGSC.

Table 5.2 is the socio-economic status classification, officially introduced in 2001, commonly known as the NS-SEC (the National Statistics Socio-Economic Classification). Replacing the RGSC as the socio-economic index, the NS-SEC is based on such criteria for classification as 'whether someone is an employer or employee,' 'the size of the organization,' 'required managerial capability,' 'level of profession' and 'employment status.'

Measuring poverty

Many earlier studies in the UK employ the 'Townsend index,' 'Carstairs index' and 'Jarman index' when measuring the level of poverty. These indices are to measure not individuals but neighbourhoods based on electorates or post code areas.

Table 5.1: Classification of occupational classes (Registrar General's Social Class)

Occupational class	Example
Social class I Professional	Accountants, doctors and lawyers
Social class II Intermediate non-manual	Teachers, nurses, most managers and senior administrators
Social class III N Skilled non manual	Clerks and shop assistants
Social class III M Skilled manual	Bricklayers, coal miners and bus drivers
Social class IV Semi-skilled manual	Bus conductors and postmen
Social class V Unskilled manual	Porters, cleaners and labourers

Compiled by the author using data from Taylor, S and Field, D (1993) *Sociology of health and health care.*

Table 5.2: Socio-economic status classification (National Statistics, Socio-Economic Classification)

Social class	Typical employment
1.1 Higher managerial occupations	Company directors, police inspectors, bank managers, senior civil servants, military officers
1.2 Higher professional	Doctors, barristers, solicitors, clergy, librarians, teachers
2 Lower managerial	Nurses and midwives, journalists, actors, prison officers, police and soldiers (below NCO)
3 Intermediate	Clerks, secretaries, driving instructors, computer operators
4 Small employers	Publicans, farmers, play group leaders, window cleaners, painters and decorators
5 Lower supervisory and craftspeople	Printers, plumbers, butchers, bus inspectors, TV engineers, train drivers
6 Semi-routine occupations	Shop assistants, traffic wardens, cooks, bus drivers, hairdressers, postal workers
7 Routine occupations	Waiters, road sweepers, cleaners, couriers, building labourers, refuse collectors
8 Never worked	Long term unemployed and non-workers

Compiled by the author using data from Sociology at Bryn Hafren school and the Barry Sixth Form *School of Sociology.*

Our Healthier Nation

It is clearly stated in *Our Healthier Nation*, the White Paper on Health Strategies, that the health inequality based on social factors is widening, and that the lowest class of people are suffering most in most causes of death (United Kingdom Department of Health 1999). The government, aiming at both 'improving the national health standard of all' and 'correcting health inequalities,' sets a reduction target to be achieved by 2010, covering five particular areas, cancer, coronary heart disease, stroke, accident and mental illness. It does not just list the reduction targets, but also various concrete measures to achieve them. *Our Healthier Nation* states that when making individual lifestyle decisions concerning diet, exercise and sexual behaviour, various factors beyond an individual's control directly affect their health. These factors include poverty, social exclusion, employment status, housing, education, environment and more. Even taking these factors into account, *Our Healthier Nation* goes on to note, it is vital also to be responsible for one's own health, and that improving one's lifestyle vastly improves one's health.

Table 5.3: Examples of social indicators used in the UK for measuring poverty

---

Townsend Index (Townsend et al., 1988)
Economically active residents aged 16–59 (female), 16–64 (male) who are unemployed;
Non private car ownership;
Non owner-occupied households;
Private households with more than one person per room.

Carstairs Index (Carstairs and Morris, 1989)
Overcrowding;
Unemployment among men;
Low social class;
Non private car ownership.

Jarman (1983, 1984)
Children aged under 5;
Ethnic minorities;
Single-parent households;
Elderly living alone;
Low social class;
Highly mobile people;
Non-married-couple families;
Overcrowding factor;
Poor housing factor;
Unemployment.

Compiled by the author using data from Whitehead, M (1992) 'The Health Divide' in *Inequalities in Health*, p 349, table 20.

It should be noted here that *Our Healthier Nation* acknowledges that the health issue is not totally an individual responsibility, but is affected largely by socio-economic factors which include factors that are the government's responsibility. When thinking about where the responsibility lies for national health this is very meaningful, especially in comparison to the attitude of the Japanese government. It is especially telling when compared to the rampant 'diagnosis' of 'lifestyle related diseases' in Japan.

Earlier studies in the UK

Poverty, infants and children
In 2000, the UK's infant mortality rate was 5.6 per 1000, higher than that for the EU, 5.2 per 1000 (1997). Sixty-four per cent of infant deaths occurred in the families of manual workers. The infant mortality rate for social class V is 1.9 times higher than that

for social class I (United Kingdom Office for National Statistics 2000). Accidents are the main cause of child deaths in the UK. Nearly one in five children who die between the ages of one and four are killed in accidents. Accidents claim eighty-three children per ten thousand in social class V, but only sixteen in social class I (Roberts and Power 1996).

Adult health

The relationship between tuberculosis and poverty was examined by studying 1,516 tuberculosis sufferers from thirty-nine constituencies in Birmingham between 1989 and 1993, in terms of morbidity rate and the degree of poverty. The degree of poverty was measured by the 'number of residents per room,' 'no home ownership,' 'homes without central heating,' 'no private car ownership' and 'the ratio of unemployed.' The result showed a correlation with overcrowding. When it came to the morbidity rate from tuberculosis and poverty, there was some correlation among white people, but none among the residents of south Asian descent (Hawker et al 1999). Similar findings concerning morbidity rates and poverty were made in a study on 344 tuberculosis sufferers in thirty-three constituencies in Liverpool between 1985 and 1990 (Spance et al 1993). Elsewhere, a study on data from the Fourth National Survey of Morbidity in General Practice (covering sixty medical clinics in England and Wales, out of a total of 283,842 adult patients and their consultations between September 1991 and August 1992), determined that the attributes of patients who made more than twelve consultations a year included divorcees and widowers, people belonging to social classes III M and IV/V, people of south Asian origin, and the unemployed. Isolation and poverty were linked to the frequent consultations (Scaife et al 2000). Also, prolonged poverty increases the risk of morbidity from chronic illness more than temporary poverty. Income changes, as well as income levels, have a significant correlation with health (Benzeval and Judge 2001).

Mortality and poverty

The mortality in the UK's deprived areas worsened compared to other areas and affluent areas. A study of the relationship between mortality and poverty (using the Carstairs index) based on the census taken in Scotland in 1981 and 1991 reveals that the postcode areas considered in 1981 as deprived were even more deprived in 1991. The mortality in the most deprived area between

1991 and 1992 was 162% higher than that of the most affluent area. Furthermore, the increase in the death rate in the poor areas for men (twenty-nine per cent) and women (eleven per cent) between the age of twenty and twenty-nine was mainly due to an increase in suicides (Mcloone and Boddy 1994). In the relationship between mortality and poverty based on the 1981 and 1991 census data, mortality differentials in all age groups under seventy-five between the most affluent and most deprived widened in 1991 (Phillmore et al 1994). Last, people of social class V are three times more likely to die from coronary heart disease before the age of sixty-five than their counterparts in social class I (United Kingdom Office for National Statistics 1997).

United States

The only public health insurance in the US is Medicare for elderly and disabled people, and Medicaid for low income earners. The lack of universal public health insurance coverage is the fundamental cause of health inequality and the health gap in this society. While Medicare is run completely by the US Federal government, Medicaid is run by each state and responds to needs more flexibly. Funded by both the state and federal governments, Medicaid is generous towards children and pregnant women. However, other people, especially those who are on a low income but not considered sufficiently poor, are often excluded from Medicaid. Apart from those who are not covered by any health insurance it is believed that there are a vast number of under-insured people as well.

The most popular health insurance coverage in the US is private health insurance (as at 2001, out of 70.9% of people with private health insurance coverage, 62.6% were employment based). In the same year, 14.6% of the country's population, or about 41.21 million

Table 5.4: The number of people covered by Medicaid and Medicare in 2001 (out of a total population of 282,082,000)

	The number of people with health insurance	
	Actual number	%
Medicare	38,043,000	13.5
Medicaid	31,601,000	11.2

Compiled by the author using data from the US Census Bureau, Current Population Survey, 1988–2002 Annual Demographic Supplements in *Health Insurance Coverage*: 2001, p. 13 table A-1.

people were uninsured (Current Population Survey 2001). We can see huge discrepancies among the uninsured people. The ethnic group that has the largest uninsured proportion is the Hispanic group at 33.2%. They are followed by black people at 19%, Asian and Pacific islanders at 18.2%, white people at 13.6% and (non-Hispanic) white people at 10%.

Medical insurance

In 2001, the number of people in poverty in the US had increased to about 32.9 million or 11.7% of the population, an increase of 1.3 million from the previous year of 31.6 million or 11.3%. Of these people, 40.5% or 13.3 million are covered by Medicaid. 30.7% of the people in poverty, or 10.1 million people have no health insurance cover at all. This ratio is twice that for the total population. Uninsured poor people constitute 24.5% of all uninsured people (US Census Bureau 2002). Having little access to medical care, on top of deplorable housing conditions and poor quality food, obviously worsens the existing problems for deprived and low income people.

Healthy People 2010

The *Healthy People 2010* initiative launched in 2000 by the US Federal government is a statement pinpointing the causes of serious threats to the nation's health, and setting goals for the nation to eliminate those threats. To 'increase quality and years of healthy life' and 'eliminate health disparities' are its two goals. The 'eliminate health disparities' goal focuses on health inequalities caused by gender, race and ethnicity, education and income, disability, physical location, sexual orientation and so on (US Department of Health and Human Services 2000). The US government admitted that poverty and socio-economic factors have an effect on health. Yet, *Healthy People 2010* is only setting 'goals' for existing systems and activities to achieve them, rather than initiating fresh programmes. In this sense, it is more of a 'public relations exercise.'

Earlier studies in the US

There are a lot of earlier studies done in the US on the issue of ethnic minorities and health, many of them comparing white people and black people. They tend to agree that the obvious discrepancies found in the social class index such as occupation, educational background, housing and residential area, affect health directly and indirectly. In relation to poverty, generally speaking,

Table 5.5: The number of AIDS patients according to age and ethnic origin (cases per 100,000 population)

Race and ethnic origin	Male	Female
White, non-Hispanic	13.8	2.2
Black, non-Hispanic	106.7	46.1
Hispanic	42.8	11.2
American Indian or Alaskan Native	18.3	6.1
Asian or Pacific Islander	7.4	1.5

Notes: These are patients diagnosed between June 30, 2000 and June 30, 2001. Hispanic people may be of any race. American Indian or Alaskan Native, Asian or Pacific Islander do not include Hispanics.
Compiled by the author using data from the Center for Disease Control and Prevention, the National Center for HIV, STD and TB Prevention, the Division of HIV/AIDS Prevention-Surveillance and Epidemiology, AIDS Surveillance, 2001 Special Data, *Health, United States, 2002*, p. 182 table 54.

the least healthy group is the most deprived group with the lowest level of education. We can see a strong correlation between health conditions such as heart disease, diabetes, obesity and high blood pressure, the birth rate of low-weight babies and the mortality rate, with the income level, education level and ethnic origin. Table 5.5 shows the number of AIDS patients in the US diagnosed between June 30, 2000 and June 30, 2001.

Many of the earlier studies concern the relationship between AIDS, race and poverty. Below are some examples.

A survey of 1,445 Medicaid covered HIV/AIDS sufferers concerning housing conditions and availability of medical care revealed that six per cent of them were homeless, while 24.5% were sharing housing with others and 69.5% were in stable accommodation. Compared to those in stable accommodation, the homeless and those in share houses were less likely to see doctors as regularly (Smith et al 2000).

Interviews were conducted with 2,898 reported AIDS sufferers in eleven states between June 1991 and January 1993. The result indicated there was a correlation with failure to complete twelve years of schooling, unemployment, and racial/ethnic differences (Diaz et al 1994).

A survey of the 15,805 AIDS cases reported to Los Angeles County from 1987 through to 1992 revealed that the rate of patients was highest in the low income areas (252.8 per 100,000). In the middle class areas, the rate was 161.2 per 100,000, while in the high income areas, it was eighty-two per 100,000 (Simon et al 1995).

Scandinavia

Compared to the other developed countries, poverty rates in Scandinavia are lower, but poverty exists there as well. Table 5.6 shows the proportion of people living on less than half of the national median income in each country according to data from the United Nations Development Programme.

Although they are reputed to have the most advanced social welfare systems in the world, and they are seen as models for welfare nations, earlier studies have revealed that even in Sweden, Denmark, Norway and Finland there are deprived people and health inequalities caused by socio-economic factors. We often talk about Scandinavia as if it were all one country, but Scandinavian health insurance systems vary from one country to the other. For example, in Sweden, the *Landsting*, or county council, is responsible for provision of health and medical services. The portion of user payment for medical care is decided by each *Landsting*, though the upper limit is set by the national government. For a general consultation the patient pays no more than 900 SEK for the first twelve months of consultation, while the maximum an outpatient pays for prescription is 1800 SEK (The trend of insurance and pension, 2003).

In Denmark, the total cost of the health service is borne by the government. In recent times, a few private hospitals have appeared, but they only constitute one per cent of existing hospital beds, because some of them have been closed due to financial difficulties. Accordingly, most of the citizens depend on the public health services. No payment is required at the time of consultation (Eijing sōgō kenkyū sentā 1998).

Norway and Finland

Among the Scandinavian nations, Norway and Finland have launched clear guidelines on health. The government's guidelines on health in Norway and Finland – the Norwegian *National Environment and Health Action Plan* and the Finnish *Government Resolution on Health 2015* public health programme – are both based on the WHO's 1977 *Health for all by the year 2000* (HFA). The Norwegian government's guidelines place more emphasis on environmental factors such as noise, water quality and food quality, but pay little attention to health inequalities arising from socio-economic factors. The Finnish guidelines indicate a framework for the health programmes between the years 2001 and 2015. They focus on the promotion of health itself by improving the health service system. They make a reference to health

Table 5.6: Poverty in Scandinavia

Nation	Poverty rate	Year of survey
Sweden	6.6	1992
Denmark	9.2	1992
Norway	6.9	1995
Finland	5.1	1991

Compiled by the author using data from The United Nations Development Programme *Human Development Reports 2002.*

inequality, stating their aim to reduce the discrepancy in mortality rates to one fifth, based on gender, educational background and occupational differences. They warn of the danger especially to young people with a low level of education who lead unstable social lives, of descending into drug and alcohol abuse and unhealthy lifestyles. They also point out that, for the elderly section of the population, social exclusion and a lower status in society contribute to a higher mortality rate and a decline in physical health. They aim to reduce the health inequalities among the different socio-economic groups. In this programme, the local governments are expected to perform a central role and close working links with NGOs, business organisations and the media are encouraged. The programme, however lacks concrete data which would give conviction to the necessity for reform and is not persuasive enough.

Earlier work in Scandinavia

Overall, most studies and investigations look at the effect of educational background and employment on health. According to a follow up study of 37,789 people aged between twenty and sixty-four in Sweden between 1983 and 1993, unemployment was the most important risk factor for suicide and suicide attempts. Living alone, living in rental accommodation and self perception of poor health were attributes (Johansson and Sundquist 1997). According to a longitudinal study of 25,728 residents, both men and women, in 149 parishes in metropolitan Copenhagen, the mortality rate showed a correlation with the average level of household income in the area. When divided into four, the most affluent quarter showed a mortality rate of 17.5 per 1000, while the lowest income quarter showed a mortality rate of 28.4 per 1000 (Osler et al 2002).

According to a 1993 study of 1,557 Finns which looked at the association between socio-economic factors and mental health, the most influential factors causing mental disorders were unemployment and an adverse financial situation. Mental disorders were more common among women than men and they were further exacerbated by long term unemployment, financial difficulties and insufficient social support. The sufferers tended to take sleeping pills and sedatives because they were feeling uncertain about their future (Viinamäki et al 1995).

Health and poverty in Japan

As mentioned above, Japanese data on which to base a discussion of this issue is very limited. Therefore, this chapter will concentrate on four specific groups, recipients of the *Seikatsu hogo* (Public Livelihood Protection) benefit, the low-income elderly, the unemployed and those who have failed to pay the national health insurance dues and taxes.

Seikatsu hogo and health standards

Personal health status has a notable correlation to this increase in *Seikatsu hogo* beneficiaries. However, the relationship between individuals meeting the necessary entry qualifications for accessing this benefit, and their personal health statuses is not clear.

It is not straight-forward to suggest that a significant correlation exists between illness and injury, and *Seikatsu hogo* benefits. The number of *Seikatsu hogo* beneficiaries reached 1,281 million people in February 2003. This is one per cent of the Japanese population. At that time, the increase was considered due to an economic downturn and an ageing society. The number of households on benefits was 896,000, the largest since the system was first introduced in 1950 (*Asahi Shimbun*, 14 June, 2003). Among the households to receive benefits for the first time in 2001, 42.5% did so because of illness or injury. In the same year, among those households to exit this benefit system, 11.7% exited because of recovery from illness and injury. Unlike the UK, where a study on the correlation between illness, injury and welfare has been conducted as a national project, there has been no comprehensive study done on the relationship of these phenomena in Japan. We have to rely on earlier work done by individual researchers, though their number is limited. Only a handful of studies are available, carried out in the 1990s, on the relationship between the tuberculosis morbidity rate, medical services utilisation, poverty and low income, and on alcohol dependency and poverty.

Depression, suicide, low income elderly and health

A year-2000 comparison of household incomes, the *Heisei 13 nen Kokumin seikatsu kiso chōsa* (2001 National Livelihood Survey), found that the largest representation among the 'elderly households'[2] category was those with an annual income of between 1 and 1.5 million yen. In comparison, the 'single mother household' category topped the income bracket of between 1.5 and 2 million yen. Both these household categories (14.6% of 'elderly households'; 14.8% of 'single mother households') lay similarly within the bracketed combined totals of 'less than half a million yen' and 'between half and one million yen'. It is difficult to generalise about their actual standard of living for single mother households, because they may have access to various social welfare provisions. However, it is obvious that many of them are living on a limited income. Yet when one tries to learn what the level of health is like for single mothers, no information can be found. We can at least find some earlier work on the health of elderly people, as mentioned above, concerning the relationship between 'depression' and 'melancholia' and level of income.

The elderly over 75 years old have the highest statistical suicide rates. The suicide rate among the elderly is staggering and their respective levels of relative income must have something to do with this. The *Heisei 13 nen jinkō dōtai tōkei* (2001 Dynamic Statistics of Population report) showed that, among people aged between eighty-five and eighty-nine, 68.1 men and 35.8 women in every 100,000 committed suicide. The figures for people over ninety years of age, is 72.8 for men and 32.4 for women in every 100,000. Next highest, are the group aged between fifty-five and fifty-nine, with 67.1 for men and 18.2 for women per 100,000. According to the police agency, the most common reason for suicide for people over the age of sixty (note that the agency puts anyone over sixty in the same bracket), is 'financial and livelihood problems' accounting for 20.5% of men and 29.4% of women who kill themselves. The rate is less than half for men in the age group between fifty-five to fifty-nine, as in that age group the same reason accounts for 42.2% of men and 36.9% of women, yet, for elderly people, 'financial and livelihood problems' are still serious enough for them to take their own lives. This issue requires significant, intensive investigation, concerning, for example the medical costs that elderly people have to pay.

Suicide and unemployment

As of April 2003, the Japanese unemployed numbered 3.85 million. The national unemployment rate for men was 5.6%; 5.1% for women (Statistics bureau, the Ministry of Internal Affairs and Communications *Rōdōryoku chōsa* (Labour Force Survey)). Care is necessary when discussing the unemployed, because among the total unemployed number voluntarily and involuntarily unemployed, the latter being those who have been made redundant. 'Unemployed people' sometimes includes retirees as well. How does unemployment affect one's health? Studies on mortality rates and life expectancy of the Japanese population, along with suicide, mortality, mental illness, sleep disorders, alcohol abuse and stress have been published in medical journals since the 1990s. Yet, again, the studies with a rich base of data are those undertaken in North America and Europe, especially in the UK.

The most notable studies on unemployment and health in Japan are those on the relationship between suicide and unemployment. When categorised by occupation, 4.1% of those who committed suicide in 2001 were unemployed. However, this does not take into account those on the brink of becoming unemployed due to bankruptcy or restructuring at work. The mental and physical health of this 'reserve army' of unemployed is a real concern.

The overall number of people taking their own lives in 2001 was 29,375 (21,085 men and 8,290 women). Figure 5.1 shows the annual suicide rates between 1980 and 2001. The Economic Planning Agency considers the period between November 1986 and February 1991 as the 'economic bubble period,' during which we can see the suicide rates for men slightly declining. After that period, they started climbing slowly, then in 1998 surged to 36.5 per 100,000 population. This was the highest number since statistics on suicide were first compiled in 1899 (Aihara and Iki 2003).

The Japanese Trade Union Confederation (JTUC) conducted face to face interviews on the economic status and health of unemployed people in early 2002. This determined that half of those surveyed did not have enough money to cover their living expenses. The survey, carried out over a month between mid February and mid March, was called the 'Second National Employment Survey (on the unemployed and job seekers).' Those surveyed were the 'currently unemployed;' workers 'contemplating a job change;' and 'fresh school leavers and fresh job seekers.' Out of 8,321 surveyed, 78.6% fell into the 'currently

Figure 5.1: The annual shift in the male and female suicide rates between 1980 and 2001 (per 100,000)

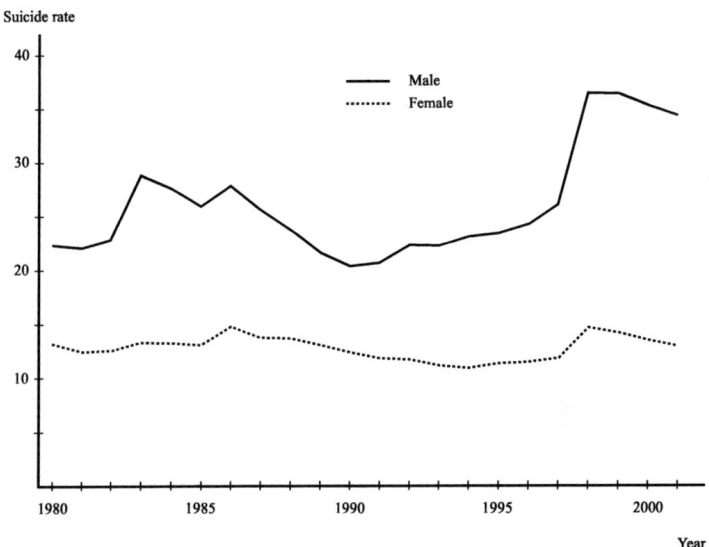

Table 5.7: Livelihood problems (%)

	Total	Age (years)				
		≤29	30–39	40–49	50–59	≥60
Lacking adequate income for living expenses	48.8	50.1	51.7	51.4	48.8	42.6
Unable to survive without unemployment benefits	30.3	20.2	29.4	36.0	39.0	27.7
Medical costs too heavy	17.4	13.9	14.8	14.1	18.8	30.6
National pension, health care contribution too high	43.7	42.8	45.5	44.0	47.2	39.6
Health and mental stress	26.4	26.8	27.9	26.7	26.6	25.0

Compiled by the author based on Nihon rōdō kumiai sōrengōkai (2002) *Dainiji zenkoku koyō (shitsugyōsha/kyūshokusha) ankêto.*

unemployed' category. Some of the results from the survey, about their livelihood and health problems, are shown in table 5.7.

National health insurance

Post-War Japan has maintained public healthcare under the 1959 National Insurance Act. The Act was intended to be a universally available national insurance system for all in need. However, in recent years an increasing number of citizens have failed to pay their national insurance dues and taxes, the consequence of which has been restricted access to medical care. This has been met by the issuing of limited term insurance cards or certificates of status to them, until their arrears are resolved. Welfare lobby organisations, including the Central Association to Promote Social Security (a network organisation of various organisations including labour unions, medical and welfare organisations and feminist organisations, aiming for the improvement of the social security system), have criticised this development.

As Table 5.8 shows, the rate as a whole is on the increase. The rate insurers above sixty years old is increasing, while that for the under sixties has been in slight decline up until 1997, but has steadily picked up since. As of 2000, 23.9% of people under fourteen years of age took part in the scheme, constituting 9.4% of all participants overall. 27.5% of those between fifteen and fifty-nine years old in the general population took part, making up 45.8% of all scheme participants, and seventy-one per cent of people over sixty years old were in the scheme, filling the remaining 44.8%.

Since 1998, the increasing participation by the young and middle aged has been especially noticeable, and is due to the increasing number of jobless people and working poor, a result of bankruptcy and/or the restructuring of smaller businesses caused by the economic downturn. Some smaller businesses, supposed to take part in the employment –based health insurance scheme administered by the national government, have withdrawn from it, forcing their employees to join the National Health Insurance Scheme (Ainoya 2002).

When looking at the contributors to the National Health Insurance Scheme by householder occupation, 49.5% are unemployed, while 24.1% are employees, 18.3% are self-employed, 5.5% are engaged in primary industries and 2.6% in other occupations (excluding households where the head of the household is covered by employment-based insurance). Among the unemployed, eighty-eight per cent are older than sixty and 56.7% are older than seventy. Table 5.9 shows the households whose dues and taxes are subsidised.

The huge proportion of elderly and unemployed contributors is the main characteristic of the National Health Insurance Scheme. A third of contributors is those with a low income, who have their dues and taxes subsidised. It is no surprise to see many contributing families failing to pay their dues and taxes, regardless of any

Table 5.8: The number of participating households in the National Health Insurance scheme (thousands of households)

	1997	1998	1999	2000	2001	2002
Number of households	18,887	19,519	20,338	21,153	21,948	22,834

Note: The numbers are all as of June 1 of each year. The data for 2000 excludes that of Miyake Mura village in Tokyo.
Compiled by the author based on Kōsei rōdō shō hoken kyoku kokumin kenkō hoken ka *Kokumin kenkō hoken tainō setai s ū tō no suii* (The Change in the Number of Households which have not paid their National Health Insurance Scheme dues).

Table 5.9: The ratio of subsidized households on National Health Insurance payments, according to the employment status of the head of the household (as at the end of September 2000)

	Overall	Primary industries	Other self-employed	Employees	Other occupation	Unemployed
Subsidized household	36.9	2.0	2.7	5.2	0.5	26.6
General household	39.2	2.1	3.0	5.6	0.5	27.9
Retired household	20.4	1.4	0.5	1.7	0.2	16.7

Notes: The overall number of contributors is 47,235,000. This is calculated excluding households where the head of the household is covered by employee insurance. The first columns showing general households and retired households indicate the ratio of subsidized households compared to the overall number of general households and retired households respectively.
Compiled by the author based on Kōsei rōdō shō hoken kyoku (2002), *Heisei 12nendo kokumin hoken jittai chōsa hōkoku* (The 2002 Report on the Reality of the National Health Insurance Scheme), p 13, table 6.2.

subsidy. Under the current sluggish economic circumstances, the increasing number of households failing to pay their dues poses a serious problem. Limited term insurance cards are issued by insurers and local governments to those who fail to pay their dues to the scheme, under terms set depending on the individual's case and the amount owing. Here, a certificate of status is issued to certify that the bearer is a contributor to the National Health Insurance Scheme and is issued to those who have failed to pay their dues and taxes for more than twelve months. When receiving a medical service, the certificate bearer has to pay up all medical costs incurred. The insured portion will only be refunded when the amount owed is fully paid up. Figures 5.2 and 5.3 show the number of households who have failed to pay their contribution, and the

Figure 5.2: The number of households who have failed to pay their National Health Insurance contributions

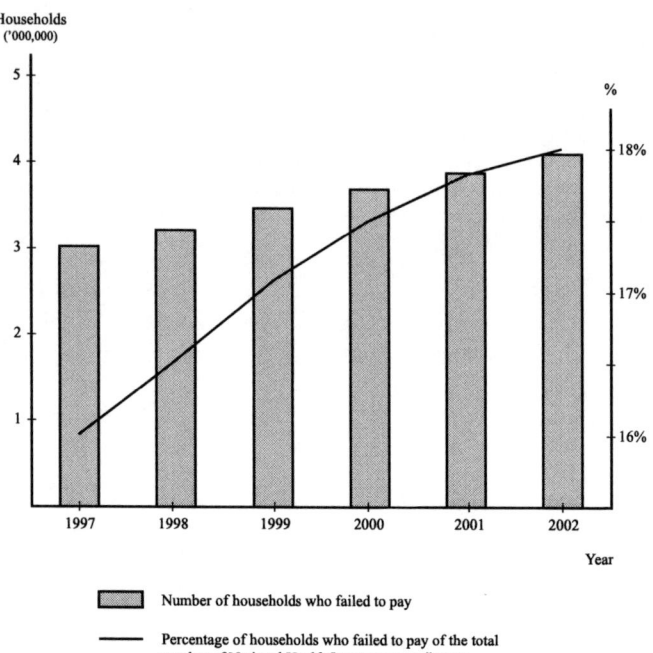

number of subsequent issuing of limited term insurance cards or certificates of status.

These cards and certificates were introduced at the end of 1986 under an amendment to the National Health Insurance Act. Then, the issuing of cards and certificates was voluntary, and it was left to each local government whether or not to issue them. In a further amendment to the Act in 1997, the issuing of these items became mandatory in April 2000.

Depending on the amount of funds respective local authorities have available for local operationalisation of the National Health Insurance Scheme, differences in response persist toward those who have failed to pay their dues. Public debate needs to address how these differences affect the residents' health in different localities. More, consideration of the repercussions of mandatory issuing of limited term insurance cards and certificates of status should not just focus on the improvement in management, resulting from the improved rate of contributions. It should also review how the status associated with these new processes has affected the health of those who had

Figure 5.3: The number of households issued with limited term insurance cards or certificates of status

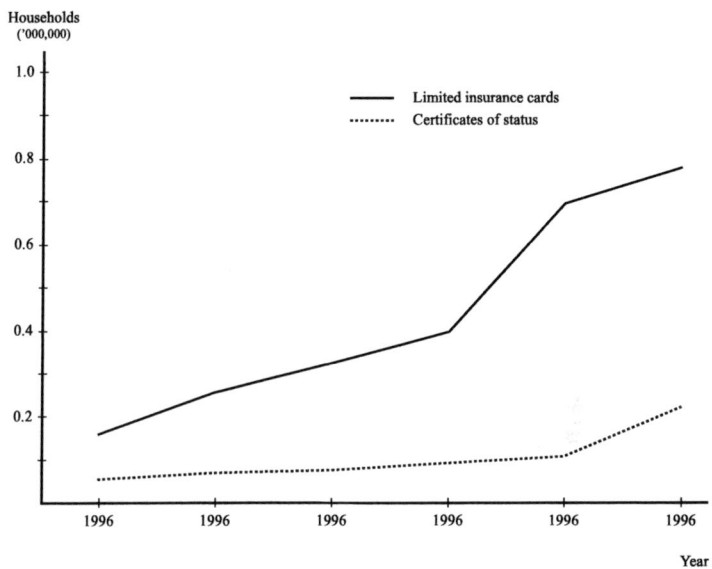

failed to meet their dues. Little research has been done on whether or not these people are now more reluctant to ask for medical services, and the repercussions for their health are presently unknown. A wide ranging study is necessary. One study, conducted in Fukuoka in 2000, revealed that those who had ordinary health insurance cards utilised medical services on an average of 10.2 times in a year. Comparatively, those with a certificate of status only used medical services 0.09 times a year. The latter, in other words, utilised medical services at the rate of one hundredth of the former (Hiejima 2002).

Healthy Japan 21 guidelines

Japan's national health policy has been developed from 1978's '*First Programme for National Health*' through to 1988's '*Second Programme for National Health.*' From this foundation, an eleven year programme, '*Healthy Japan 21 (The movement to create a healthy nation in the twenty-first century)*' was devised and launched in 2000. One of the major differences between the *Healthy Japan 21* programme and its predecessors is that the former involves clear numerical targets. In concrete terms, *Healthy Japan 21* sets targets for nourishment and diet, physical exercise and sport, rest, smoking, alcohol consumption, dental care, and prevention of diabetes, cardiovascular disease and cancer. Another notable difference is that the programme is more inclusive. Its predecessors focussed on people in particular conditions and of a particular age group, although these also advocated 'creating a healthy life through living.' A third significant difference is that *Healthy Japan 21* enlists the co-operation of government bodies, medical insurers, medical organisations, education organisations, media, business bodies, volunteer groups and more to create a supportive environment. This seeks to encourage individuals to maintain their own health.

However, the framework employed for *Healthy Japan 21* lacks perspectives on the 'effect on health of socio-economic factors' and the subsequent 'health inequality caused by social factors.' Apart from the direct effects socio-economic and social factors have on health, such as health inequality and premature death, the programme fails to grasp the enormous indirect effects on health consciousness, health behaviour and lifestyle routines. More, the *Healthy Japan 21* movement has introduced the concept and the term 'lifestyle related diseases' into popular discourse. This is not the name of a disease, but is rather an administrative term. Many of the symptoms traditionally associated with 'adult diseases' (this is also an administrative term) are now listed under 'lifestyle related diseases,' putting stress on the individual's lifestyle as the reason for the occurrence and development of the symptoms. The term 'adult diseases' used before the introduction of the term 'lifestyle related diseases,' was purely a Japanese invention, and was first recorded officially in 1956 by the then Ministry of Health and Welfare. The term referred to such diseases as cerebral strokes, malignant tumours such as cancer, and heart disease. The reason for the introduction of the term was for the early diagnosis and early treatment of these diseases which often affected and sometimes caused the death of forty to sixty year olds.

When we look at the way the term and concept of 'lifestyle related diseases' was introduced, we find that the Ministry of Health and Welfare, rather than the advisory body of the council section for public health, dealing with adult diseases and difficult diseases, was behind it. Yet, the determination of what these terms mean remains unresolved. For example, the Council for Public Health, which deals with 'adult' and difficult diseases, has issued a recommendation that 'adult diseases' were illnesses caused by old age, and different from 'lifestyle related diseases' which were caused by a particular lifestyle. The Council's understanding was that many diseases were common to both categories and they existed side by side. Yet, the media and experts have understood that the term 'lifestyle related diseases' replaced 'adult diseases,' and the Ministry of Health and Welfare has not really tried to explain the difference. In the US and the UK, we cannot find any term corresponding to 'adult diseases' or 'lifestyle related diseases.' It is common in those countries to instead use the term 'chronic diseases.' An internet search on the term 'lifestyle related diseases,' almost exclusively produces texts written by Japanese authors in English. According to a participant in the meetings of the Council for Public Health, dealing with adult diseases and difficult diseases, an equivalent term for 'lifestyle related diseases' is used by the French, but not in day to day usage. The term is not in use in German, but if you have to, I am informed, there are some similar terms used on occasion like 'civilization diseases,' 'diseases of adulthood,' or 'senile diseases.'

Now, the term 'lifestyle related diseases' is known far exceeding *Healthy Japan 21*. While it is important to stress the significance of diet, exercise, sleep and other lifestyle customs for the maintenance of health, the following problems need to be pointed out in regard to 'life-style related diseases.' First, some lifestyle related behaviours are created under particular socio-economic situations. Japan lacks the perspective that lifestyle customs are often influenced by external elements and health inequalities are caused by social factors. While in the West, eliminating health inequalities caused by socio-economic factors is considered to be the core of public health policy, this is not the case in Japan. Many measures related to health should be pursued as national projects, such as dealing with unemployment, and improving working and housing conditions. Yet, the Japanese government has shifted the responsibility for individual health care on to individual consciousness and behaviour. Second, the emphasis on lifestyle customs weakens the relative importance of various elements which affect health such as environmental degradation, and the quality of drinking water and food. Third, the hegemonic prescription of personal responsibility creates stigma for those who are suffering from diseases classified as 'lifestyle related diseases.' They are seen as 'people lacking the ability to manage themselves.'

Summaries of past studies

Mortality rates indexed by social class

The remainder of this chapter will briefly summarise existing literature on health inequality and poverty. Data on mortality rates across Tokyo, and across Japan, reveals local variation. Mortality rates compared between the twenty-three wards and twenty-six cities of Tokyo and the rest of the country, the demographically adjusted mortality rate for middle aged people throughout the whole of Tokyo was only slightly higher for both men and women than the national rate. Yet, in the twenty-three wards mortality was significantly higher, while in the twenty-six cities it was significantly lower. Tokyo's counties and islands registered slightly a higher rate than the rest of the nation.

The standardised mortality rate in each individual ward and city of the twenty-three wards and twenty-six cities comprises local variations, especially for men. The downtown area generally has a higher mortality than other locations. The seven downtown wards of Taitō, Arakawa, Sumida, Kōtō, Edogawa, Katsushika and Adachi recorded well above the national rate. A similar result was recorded for Shinjuku as well. On the other hand, in what is usually called the uptown areas, the rate was low. The mortality for Setagaya, Suginami and Nerima was significantly lower than that for the nation. The difference between the higher eight wards and the lower three wards was 1.58–1.24:1. As for the cities, there was no city registering a significantly higher mortality rate for men. Six cities, Chōfu, Machida, Hachiōji, Hino, Higashikurume and Tama recorded well below the national figure (Mizota et al unpublished).

For the ward by ward mortality rate for middle aged women, while we can see a strong similarity with the rate for men ($r = 0.71$, $p < 0.01$), the variation among the twenty-three wards was lot smaller than that for men. Only Adachi's figure was well above the national rate. A similar trend was observed with women's mortality rates for the twenty-six cities, that is, they were similar to those for men ($r = 0.71$, $p < 0.01$). The difference among the cities was far smaller than that for men, and there was no city which had a significantly higher rate than the rest of the country. The same tendency could be observed for the standardised death rate for the sixty to sixty-nine year old age group of Tokyo residents (Mizota et al unpublished). This research showed similar results to the preceding research of the same type, conducted between the late 1970s and the middle of the 1980s (Yamazaki 1989).

Tuberculosis and poverty
Tuberculosis morbidity is clearly linked to poverty. Using the 1995 research into tuberculosis occurrence in all tuberculosis and smear-

positive patients, and the census results of the same year, among the various social indices of each prefecture only the 'rate of households on the *Seikatsu hogo* benefit' and the 'total unemployment rate' showed a significant correlation to tuberculosis morbidity. The only social indices of each prefecture showing a positive correlation with the age adjusted smear-positive tuberculosis morbidity were also the 'rate of households on the *Seikatsu hogo* benefit' and 'total unemployment rate' (Horie 2001). Also analysed, have been the social backgrounds and the reasons for late diagnosis for the ninety-five cases of advanced cavitary type (b13) from among all the tuberculosis patients hospitalised and treated in a hospital between 1987 and 1998. This study revealed that thirty-one patients were unemployed (either before or after their hospitalisation), twenty-four were day labourers and twenty-five were on the *Seikatsu hogo* benefit (Sasaki et al 2002). Similar studies, with regard to the delay in diagnosis and the subsequent aggravation of the illness, also made similar findings (Sasaki et al 1996; Oki et al 2001).

Alcohol dependency and poverty
The backgrounds of forty-two male patients who had been hospitalised in the specialised alcohol treatment ward (with 131 beds) for more than three years were analysed. Nearly seventy per cent of them had only completed secondary school or lower. They had had various occupations and most of them had frequently changed from one job to another. At the time of hospitalisation, nearly half of them were on the *Seikatsu hogo* benefit. Also, nearly half of them had no fixed address. We can see as a background to their long-term hospitalisation, their long-term financial dependency. Nearly half of them had also suffered from mental illness, and nearly a third from an alcohol-related physical disorder. In a different study, the prognosis of 703 alcohol dependent patients who came for consultations at a public health care centre was analysed. 154 men had since died, while nine women had died. The average age of death was 56.5 for men, 50.0 for women. The age for unmarried men and women was 48.9, 51.6 for living alone and 51.3 for those on the *Seikatsu hogo* benefit (Tokunaga 1996).

The elderly poor, depression and melancholia
An analysis of 928 elderly residents over sixty-five years old by income, in the public health centres of Ishikari, Sorachi and Atoshi in Hokkaidō revealed those with less than one million yen occupied the largest group of melancholia sufferers (28.8%). Another

significant finding was that the lower the respondents' income, the worse her or his depression (Sato and Nakajima 1997). Elsewhere, a 2001 study of melancholia in 2,719 elderly residents over sixty-five years old in three cities, towns and villages in Hyōgo prefecture showed a strong correlation between melancholia and 'short on cash for living expenses', in both under and over seventy-five year old age groups (Kuroda and Sumida 2002).

Suicide rates and unemployment

The relationship between the high suicide rate of recent years and economic as well as demographic factors has been examined, using data recorded between 1995 and 2000 on suicide rates from forty-seven prefectures. The standardised mortality rate for male suicides (above the age of fifteen, per 1,000), the number of bankruptcies (per month), and the aging rates of men (the rate of over sixty-five year olds compared with the overall population) showed a positive correlation, but a negative correlation with household savings. The standardised mortality rate of female suicides was associated with the job application rate for the period from 1997 to 2000, and the aging rate for 1996 and 1997 (Aihara and Iki 2003). A separate study of the suicide rate in Ōsaka showed a strong correlation between the job application rate and the suicide rate of middle aged men between 1980 and 1999. In the Higashi Ōsaka area, the female suicide rate held a clear correlation to *Seikatsu hogo* benefit (Aihara and Iki 2002). Third, according to an analysis of the total of 17,234 suicide cases (11,507 men and 5,727 women) in Hokkaidō between 1979 and 1994, the annual rate of suicides for men in Hokkaidō was 26.3 per 100,000. This was well above the national average. The suicide rate for both men and women was closely associated with the unemployment rate (the correlation factor for men was 0.59 while for women it was 0.42). Especially of note was the surge in the suicide rate for men in and around 1983, at the time of the economic slump caused by a strong yen. The rate was high for both men and women in the old coal mining area, while it was low in the capital city of Sapporo and its suburbs (Okamoto 2000).

Health inequality and poverty

Assessing only the data available, health inequalities caused by socio-economic factors are becoming more serious world wide. Due to the limitation of available space, this chapter has not discussed the increasing number of studies on this subject that have been carried out in Asia, revealing the extent of inequality and the structure of

The interconnection between health and poverty

inequality. The deprived people in this region are again the least healthy. Material, environmental and educational factors either directly damage their health, or contribute to a harmful lifestyle. To conclude, with regard to the Japanese data, two recommendations are made:

- The method of calculation across various Japanese public offices must be standardised, so as to avoid variations in the same data.
- Japan's social stratification and social mobility survey should include health related items in order to increase its usefulness.

6 The spatial spread of poverty in the megalopolis and the state of segregation, 1975–2000

Keiko Yamaguchi

The spatial structure of the megalopolis

Social classes and spatial structure

A polarisation of social classes in Japan's largest cities has been noted since the middle of the 1970s. This polarisation has arisen through deindustrialisation and globalisation. Concern for this trend has prompted the study of Japanese social classes' relationship to urban space. A number of discussions on the inner city relating to urban spatial structures and poverty have arisen since the late 1970s. In certain areas of the Japanese megalopolis, studies undertaken from various angles have revealed that many social issues now have overlap with each other in this urban context. These issues include the decline in the economy, unemployment, rundown housing, concentrations of minority groups and other social problems (Narita 1987; Takahashi 1992). However, those discussions about the inner city were concerned more practically with the discovery of the concentration of problems and their possible solutions. By the late 1980s, they soon diminished due to the recovery of the economy in general and of the city governments' finances in particular.

Analyses of the relationship between social classes and urban space have persisted. During the 1990s, in a study based on the situation in Tokyo, Masahisa Sonobe advocated an urban polarisation hypothesis. Sonobe's argument arose from recognition that the polarisation of occupational and income classes affected the emergence of a new class of poor in the city. Sonobe stated that, compared to the case of New York or London, 'what you can see in Tokyo is only the "threat" of polarisation.' (Sonobe 2001). His hypothesis drew upon case studies of the Shinjuku area of Tokyo where it is possible to see 'homeless' people; the inner city of Tokyo; its suburbia; and areas where the gentrification process was under way (Sonobe 2001). Though his work illustrates the characteristics of the social classes of each area very well, its analysis of the relationship between them is insufficient. Elsewhere, Takashi Machimura has advocated a world city hypothesis, based on an analysis of Tokyo, which incorporated the polarisation of social classes. Across the twenty-three wards of Tokyo and its neighbouring cities, he has analyzed how income disparities changed during the decade which included the era of the bubble economy. His study revealed that there are distinctive characteristics in each local area with regard to the average income standard and its pattern of change (Machimura 1998). In a similar fashion, Tetsuya Toyoda has noted local disparities in occupations and income when he studied class polarisation in the twenty-three wards of Tokyo, around the time of the bubble economy. According to Toyoda, a reduction of the population took place in the centre of the metropolis, thus increasing the proportion of the specialised managerial white collar population, and causing a striking contrast with other areas. The spatial spread in the twenty-three wards of Tokyo, where the west is dominated by white collar workers and the east is dominated by blue collar workers, is less marked. But in particular wards such as Shinjuku and Toshima where, he observes, a new dimension of spatial polarisation is appearing (Toyoda 1999). After taking into account the collapse of the financial bubble, both Machimura and Toyoda carried out an analysis of class polarisation in relation to spatial structures. However, their scope was limited as far as the breadth of the metropolis was concerned, as it dealt only with the twenty-three wards of Tokyo. Other studies have extended their scope to also include suburbia.

In their social geographical analysis, *Tokyo no shakai chizu* (A social atlas of Tokyo, 2004), Kurasawa et al. have constructed mesh maps of the twenty-three wards of Tokyo using the 247 indices essentially between 1975 and 1978, and set out the spatial structure patterns. More recently, in an updated *Shinpen Tokyo ken no shakai chizu* 1975–90 (New edition: A social atlas of metropolitan Tokyo), these authors extended the study area as far as the south Kanto region and analyzed the spatial structures of the area (Kurasawa and Asakawa 2004). The spatial alteration of the occupational classes in the south Kanto area between 1975 and 1990 has revealed that the increasing concentration of blue collar workers at the megalopolis's periphery. This 'blue collar areas in the periphery' formed a concentric zone structure with the white collar area in the outskirts of suburbia. It also highlighted the emergence of a wedge shaped blue collar belt stretching from the eastern part of the twenty-three wards of Tokyo to the eastern part of Saitama prefecture (Nishizawa 2004). Last in this review of existing literature, in my 2004 study I had analyzed poverty indices, taking into account the overall trend of the changes in social strata, and pointed out that there were three main geographical types in greater Tokyo. The first of these was the centre of the south Kanto region, represented by the area around the Shinjuku ward in Tokyo and the coastal area of Yokohama city in Kanagawa prefecture. These are the areas where a low proportion of blue collar workers and 'mixed urban area' characteristics were observable through cluster analysis. The second was a part of the 'population reproduction and industrial area,' also situated in the centre of the megalopolis, around the eastern part of the twenty-three wards and around Kawasaki city in Kanagawa prefecture. The third was suburbia and its peripheral areas, where the ratio of blue collar workers was larger, and this was mainly included in the 'population reproduction and industrial areas,' and 'population reproduction and blue collar areas' by cluster analysis (Yamaguchi 2004).

As seen above, through an understanding of the extended spatial structures of greater Tokyo, the characteristics of the spread of poverty in this megalopolis have become apparent. However the period of the study ended in 1990. Since the collapse of the bubble economy, the subsequent prolonged economic downturn and higher unemployment rate must have had a huge impact on poverty. Current analysis in terms of housing is not sufficient and leaves a lot to be desired.

Chapter aim and methods

Based on the aforementioned premise, and supplementing the data from 1975, 1990 and 2000, this chapter will look at the changes that did and did not take place in those three geographical types, in the south Kanto region (a part of Ibaraki prefecture, Saitama, Chiba, Tokyo and Kanagawa prefectures) in the period of post industrialisation. In the process, I will also look at the relationship between deprivation and spatial structure. Compared to the West, poverty in Japan is often said to be spread out and not really 'visible,' but the hidden urban structure can be made visible by mapping like this and we can picture it. Until now, studies of the urban lower classes of Japan have tended to focus on individual social minority classes. Of course there are distinctive situations which need to be analyzed separately up to a point, but minorities from different backgrounds would tend to be concentrated in particular areas because of deprivation. In this

Poverty in the megalopolis: spatiality and segregation

chapter, I will examine the spatial structures in the megalopolis and poverty, placing importance on poverty as a category and analyzing it horizontally across the region, while paying attention to changes in social classes as a whole.

This chapter will describe poverty using various maps, with easy to analyze indices, even though I am well aware that poverty has various analytical aspects including qualitative and quantitative measures. Here, I will use various indices such as the unemployment rate, the single mother family rate and the elderly single person household rate, which are likely contributors to poverty, as well as the accepted indicator of poverty, the number of people who are on the *Seikatsu hogo* (Public Livelihood Protection) benefit, and a prime consequence of poverty: homelessness. Unless otherwise stated, the raw data are derived from the national census. These indices are proportionalised and standardised, and then the average is given showing the standard deviation and divided into six groups. The darker colours in the maps signify the larger figures. The accompanying legends show, at the bottom, the figures making up those six groups and at the top, the number of local councils that fall into those groups. Accordingly, the gradation indicates only the relative position in the subject area of this chapter, the south Kanto region. Because the smallest spatial unit in this analysis is the council, these maps do not directly show whether poverty is concentrated in a particular area of the council or spread out across the council area.[1]

Below, I will show firstly how the occupational classes are spread across the south Kanto region, and then look at how this correlates to the poverty indices. Based on this, I will arrange the types of poverty into categories. Finally, I will examine the spread of poverty and segregation.

The spatial spread of poverty

Occupational classes

As already noted, the biggest alteration that took place between 1975 and 1990 in the south Kanto region in terms of the spatial shift in occupational classes was the concentric formation of blue collar areas on the periphery and white collar areas in the outskirts of suburbia, and the emergence of a wedge shaped 'blue collar belt.' Beyond this period, Figures 6.1 to 6.3 show the distribution of the ratio of blue collar workers from 1990 to 2000. From these maps it can be seen that not a lot has changed in the basic spatial structures in the south Kanto region. However, if we look into the detail, we can see that the blue collar ratio has become slightly lower in the eastern part of the twenty-three wards of Tokyo and the neighbouring south-eastern part of Saitama prefecture, while going up in the coastal north-eastern region of Chiba prefecture. In other words, what we can see is a further slight continuation of the trend of an increase in white collar workers in the centre and the suburbs, and an increase in blue collar workers on the periphery.[2] The period between 1975 and 1990, which covers the time of economic depression following the oil crisis through to the heights of the bubble economy, saw aggressive urban development, the exodus of the manufacturing industry from the city centre, and the resulting major shift in spatial structures. After the burst of the bubble economy, we can see the same trend still persisting although perhaps on a much smaller scale.

Thus we can see that the basic spatial structures of occupational classes in 2000 remain pretty much the same. Here, following the earlier work done in this field, we shall call the areas in the outer edge of the south Kanto region where the blue collar proportion is high, the 'peripheral blue collar area' and the 'periphery,' and the blue collar area stretching from the eastern part of the twenty-three wards of Tokyo to northern Saitama, we shall term the 'blue collar belt.' Bearing these spatial structures in mind, let us examine the spread of poverty and its characteristic shifts.

The unemployment rate

First, let us examine the index considered to be directly linked with poverty. In Figures 6.4, 6.5 and 6.6 we can see the changes in the unemployment rate in chronological order. In 1975, the highest unemployment index was concentrated in Tokyo, excluding the centre, the neighbouring south-eastern part of Saitama prefecture, the north of Kanagawa prefecture and the coastal area of Tokyo Bay. In 1990, we can see the higher index figures in the peripheral areas as well. In 2000, the trend became clearer in particular suburbs and peripheral areas. The high employment rate is visible in the 'blue collar belt' which stretches from the northern and eastern parts of the twenty-three wards of Tokyo to the north of Saitama prefecture, the area stretching north to south from the south of Saitama, through the Tama area of Tokyo to the centre of Kanagawa prefecture, the border area between Ibaraki and Chiba prefectures, the north-eastern coastal parts of Chiba prefecture such as Mobara city and Togane city, and Kawasaki city and the coastal part of Yokohama city in Kanagawa prefecture. It is worth noting that the average unemployment rate had

Figure 6.1: The ratio of blue collar workers (1975)

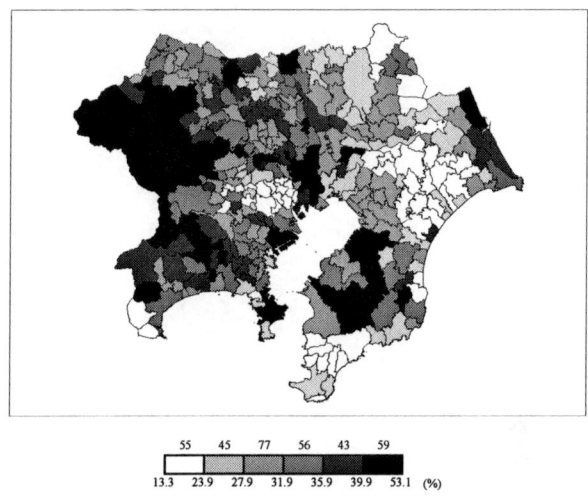

Figure 6.2: The ratio of blue collar workers (1990)

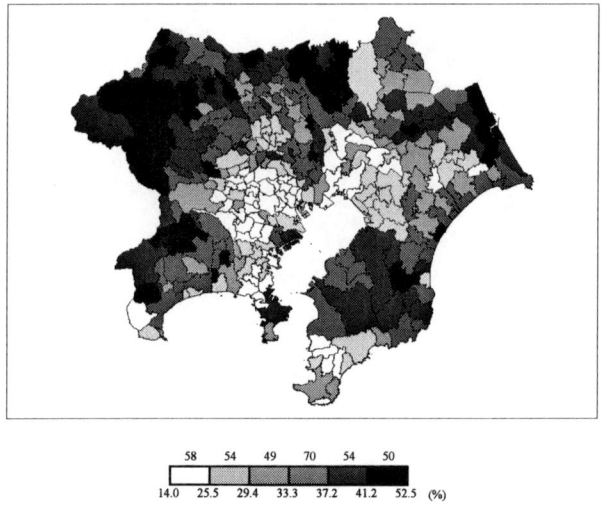

risen dramatically from 1.9 per cent in 1975, to 2.6 per cent in 1990 and to 4.5 per cent in 2000.

The spread of the higher unemployment rate seems to correspond to the blue collar rate mentioned above. The areas which showed a high concentration of blue collar workers in 1975 such as the 'blue collar belt' and the area stretching from north-eastern Tama in Tokyo

Figure 6.3: The ratio of blue collar workers (2000)

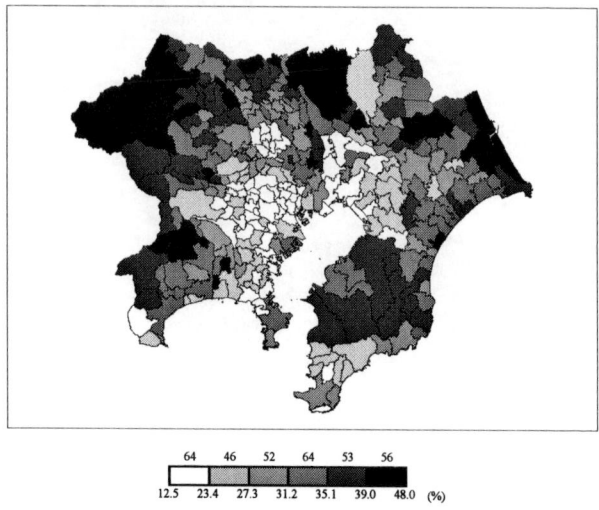

Figure 6.4: The ratio of unemployment (1975)

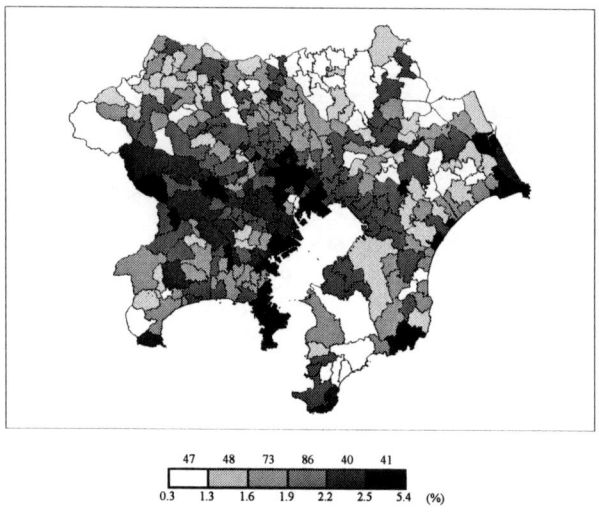

to the centre of Kanagawa, recorded a lower concentration in 2000. The former region was traditionally the area where light manufacturing industries were concentrated in the centre of the megalopolis. The latter is the newer industrial area on the outskirts of the megalopolis, consisting of mostly metal and machinery businesses, developed since 1965, and also absorbing factories that have been relocated from

Figure 6.5: The ratio of unemployment (1990)

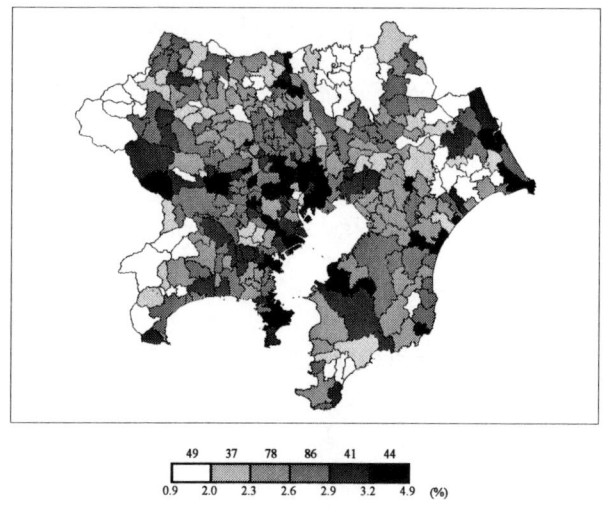

Figure 6.6: The ratio of unemployment (2000)

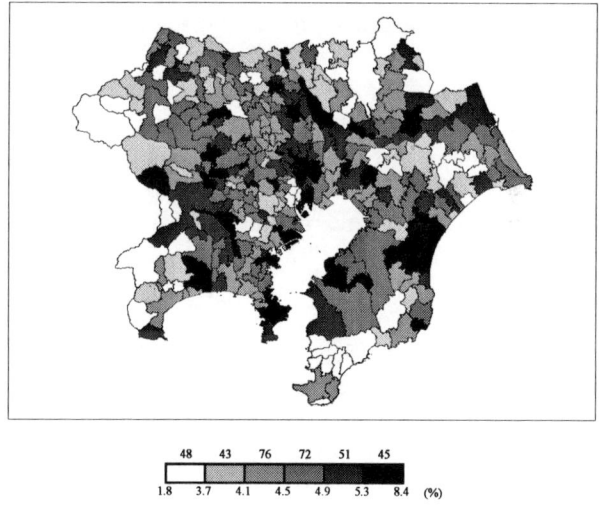

the centre. Both areas are thought to be affected by deindustrialisation, the spread of urbanisation and the serious economic downturn.

The concentration of a higher unemployment rate emerged in 2000, in places like the north-eastern coastal part of Chiba prefecture including Mobara and Togane, and the border region between Ibaraki and Chiba prefectures, including Kashima city. These places have a history of creating a concentration of manufacturing industries, through aggressive subdivision for industrial estates and other measures to attract business enterprises. For example, Mobara in north-eastern Chiba had had its share of success as a manufacturing base, and began attracting factories in 1952 by passing a local ordinance to provide them with a cheap supply of natural gas. Industrial areas like this, however, have suffered from the economic downturn as well as the fact that the exodus of the manufacturing industry did not just stop at the outskirts of the megalopolis, but continued its movement right offshore. Concerning the area surrounding Kashima, we also should take into account the stagnation and the demise of the huge industrial complex developments, along with the decline of smaller associated businesses in the area (Yamaguchi 2004).

Single mother households

Let us now look at single mother households. According to the *Heisei 10 nendo zenkoku boshi setai tō chōsa kekka no gaiyō* (The summary of results from the 1998 national survey of single mother households), the average annual income for a single mother household for 1997 was 2.29 million yen. Compared to the average income for general households in the same year of 6.58 million yen, this was about a third, an extremely low level. Out of all single mother families, 84.9 per cent were employed, of which 38.3 per cent were in part-time or casual employment. The low level of income must be related to the instability of their employment. As far as home ownership is concerned, 26.6 per cent live in their own home, 16.6 per cent are in public housing, 3.1 per cent are in public corporation housing, 25.9 per cent live in private rental housing, 13.6 per cent live in shared accommodation, and 12.6 per cent are in other types of accommodation. Compared to households in general, the rate of home ownership is low, while the number in public housing is very high (Kōsei rōdō shō 2002).[3]

Figures 6.7 and 6.8 show the concentrations of single mother households. The areas with the higher index figures in 2000 are in the 'blue collar belt,' the north-eastern part of Tama area around Musashimurayama city in Tokyo, the northern parts of Saitama and Ibaraki prefectures, the eastern coastal regions of Chiba and Ibaraki prefectures, the eastern part of Chiba prefecture near Mobara and Togane cities and the southern part of Chiba prefecture around Kisarazu city. Compared to the 1990 data, a greater concentration of higher index figures is visible as a whole in 2000, especially in the peripheral parts of northern Saitama and Ibaraki prefectures where new areas are visible. The average remained almost steady from one

Figure 6.7: The ratio of single mother households (1990)

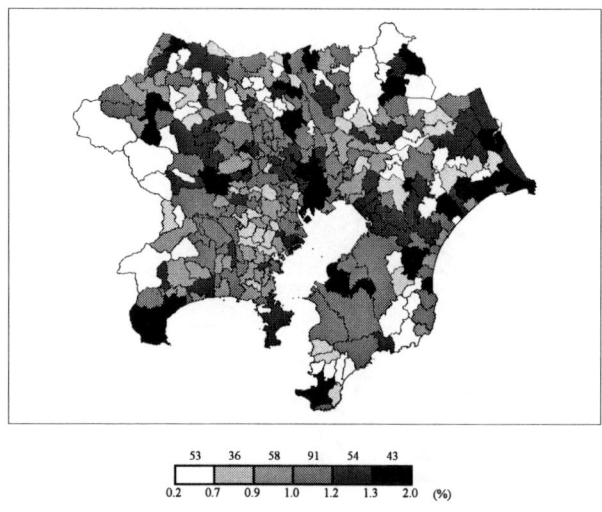

Figure 6.8: The ratio of single mother households (2000)

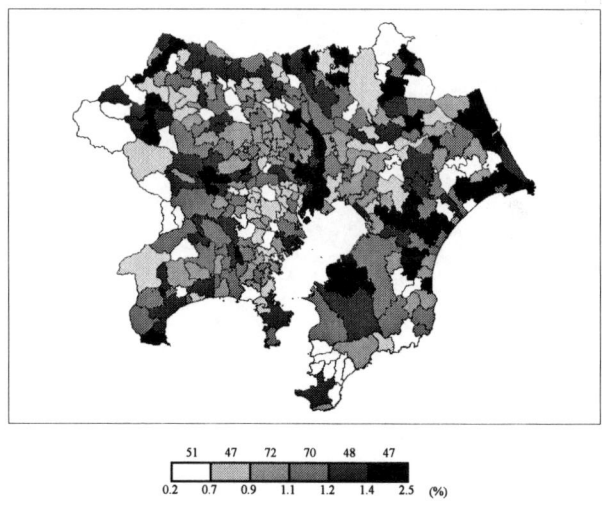

per cent in 1990 to 1.1 per cent in 2000. However, the background for the spread is believed to be complex. As the survey result referred to above suggests, the availability of accommodation must be playing a vital role. Figures 6.9 to 6.11 show the kinds of accommodation there is available. The areas with a higher concentration of single mother households in Tokyo and Kanagawa prefectures correspond to the areas with more public housing (as seen in Figure 6.9) and private

Figure 6.9: The ratio of public rental housing (2000)

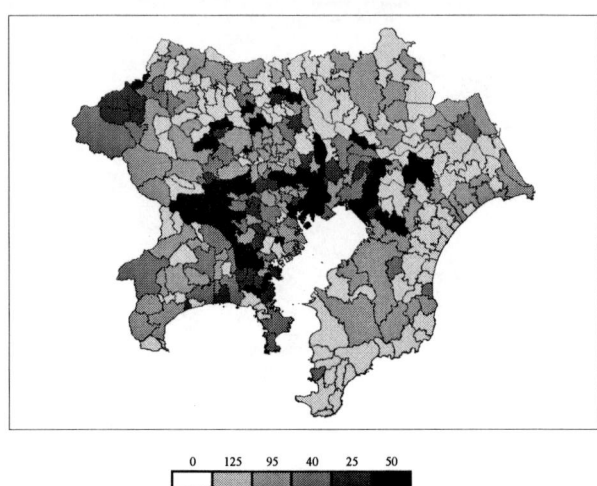

Figure 6.10: The ratio of private rental housing (2000)

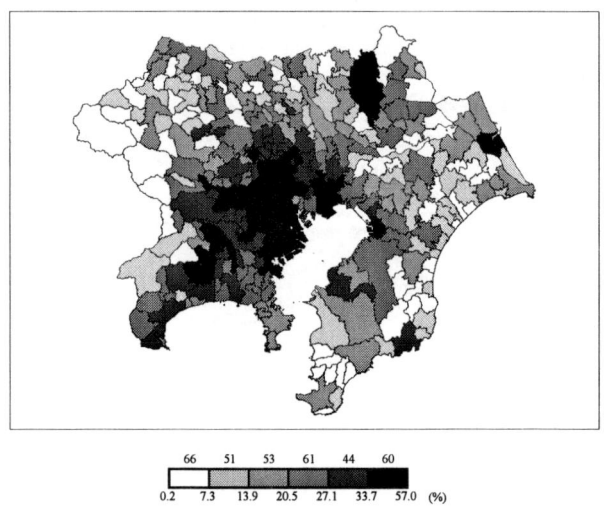

rental properties (Figure 6.10). The peripheral area has a relatively higher rate of home ownership (Figure 6.11), but a higher concentration of single mother households can be found among them in areas where there is a lower rate of home ownership. If they were able to get accommodation in public housing, they would have done so. If they have not been able to, they need to look for private rental properties. Further to this, Yoshimichi Yui and Keiji Yano have pointed out that,

Figure 6.11: The ratio of owner occupied houses (2000)

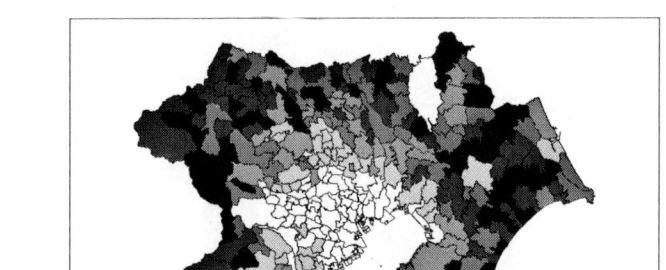

compared to households of single men with children who tend to stay on in the same house when they are parted from their partners by death or separation, women with children tend to be forced to look elsewhere for their accommodation. They face a much more challenging situation because of their difficult financial status. They also have a very limited choice of accommodation because of their children. They are more disadvantaged because they have a limited network of relatives to turn to as guarantors for renting private properties. They may also find it hard to scrape enough money together to pay for the bond and commission needed upfront to rent a private property (Yui and Yano 2002). Apart from this, the concentration of single mother families in south of Kanagawa prefecture and the eastern coastal areas of Ibaraki and Chiba may be because of the existence there of tourism and food and beverage service industries which tend to employ women more readily.

Elderly single person households

Figures 6.12 and 6.13 show the ratio of elderly single person households. Of course not all the elderly single person households are impoverished. Some of them, because of their assets, houses and savings are not really poor at all. However, as Yasuhiro Tsukahara found out from his study of elderly people in the twenty-three wards in Tokyo comparing their annual pension income and the general *Seikatsu hogo* benefit, fifty-five per cent of single elderly people would

Figure 6.12: The ratio of elderly single person households (1990)

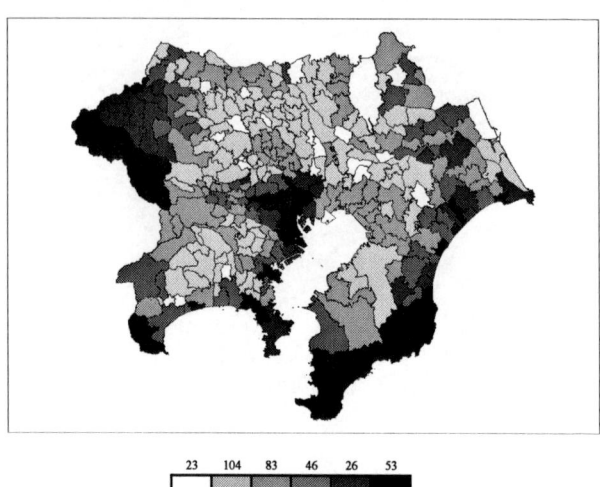

Figure 6.13: The ratio of elderly single person households (2000)

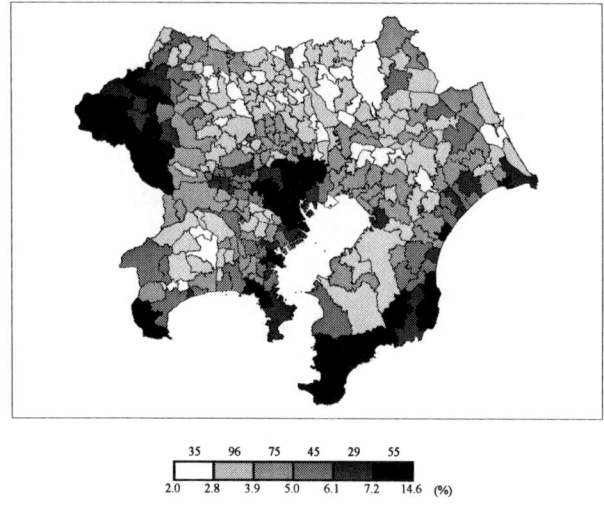

fall below the poverty line if they only had their pension to support them (Tsukahara 2001). No doubt the single elderly households are socially disadvantaged if they have only the pension, and no other family members who might bring in an extra source of income.

Single elderly people are found throughout the entire twenty-three wards of Tokyo and the adjacent north-eastern Tama area, and the coastal area of Kanagawa prefecture. On the periphery, a higher concentration can be seen in western Saitama and the eastern coastal area of Chiba. Because western Saitama, the eastern coastal area of Chiba, and the south-eastern part of Kanagawa around the Miura Peninsula have a higher level of home ownership, they may not necessarily be living in poverty. On the other hand, the bay areas of Kawasaki and Yokohama cities in Kanagawa prefecture and the wards and city areas of Tokyo are traditionally noted for a higher concentration of single person households and also for a higher rate of private rental properties. When looking at the shift between 1990 and 2000, the spread pattern remains almost the same. Only a slight increase in the index figure is observed in the northern and eastern parts of the twenty-three wards, and the area adjacent to north-eastern Tama, as well as the bay area of Yokohama. Despite the general population exodus from the centre of the megalopolis since the 1960s, elderly people have stayed on. This trend has now spread further out to the entire twenty-three wards and the surrounding city regions. It is hard to imagine elderly people moving house frequently, especially as single elderly people would be most likely to have difficulty finding accommodation in the private rental property market.

The *Seikatsu hogo* benefit

Next we will look at the rate of people on the *Seikatsu hogo* benefit, the direct indicator of poverty. Proclaiming to 'guarantee a basic minimum healthy and civilized standard of living,' the *Seikatsu hogo* system, however, has severe restrictions when it comes to approving people who can receive the benefit. To receive rent assistance, for example, the beneficiaries have to choose from low rent housing within set limits. Looking at the *Seikatsu hogo* recipients in 2000 according to family type, 45.5 per cent of them are elderly single people, 8.4 per cent are single mother households, 10.2 per cent are disabled households, 28.5 per cent are sick or injured households, and 7.4 per cent fall into the category of others. The most represented types of family are elderly single people and sick and injured households. On a monthly average, 88.0 per cent have 'no employed household member.' (Kōsei rōdō shō 2002)

Figures 6.14 and 6.15 show the ratio of people on the *Seikatsu hogo* benefit (the actual number of people on the benefit).[4] The original data is derived from the demographic statistics of each prefecture. We have to note that the number of benefit recipients can be affected by the policies of the administering local councils. In 2000, the areas

Figure 6.14: The ratio of people on the Seikatsu hogo *benefit (1990)*

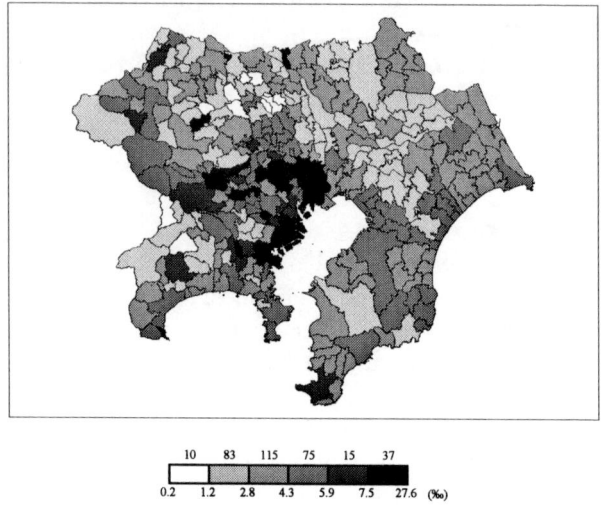

Figure 6.15: The ratio of people on the Seikatsu hogo *benefit (2000)*

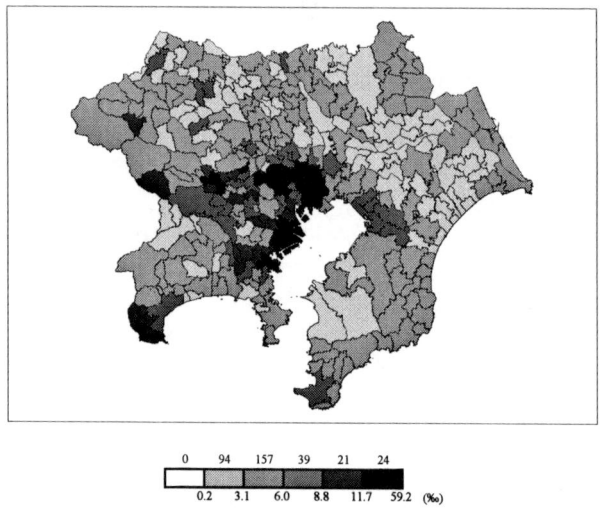

showing a higher concentration of *Seikatsu hogo* recipients are the twenty-three wards except for a section in the west, and the areas to the north east of Tama in Tokyo, the adjacent coastal part of Kawasaki and Yokohama and along the railways heading inland of Kanagawa, and also the south-western part of Kanagawa around Hakone. In comparison to 1990, we can see that the welfare recipients have

Figure 6.16: The number of homeless people (2003)

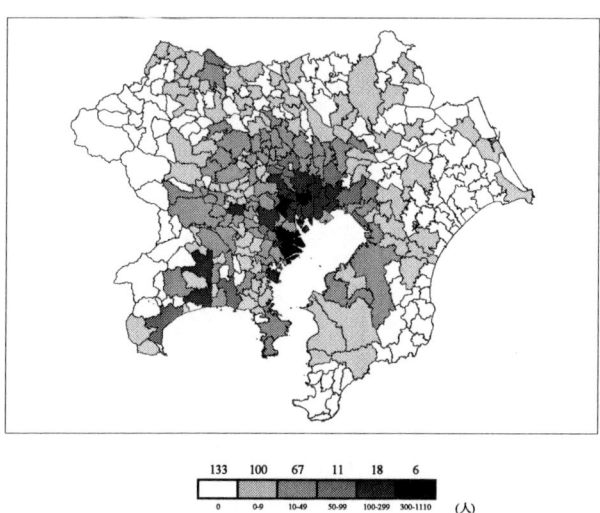

become more concentrated in the limited number of areas of Tokyo's twenty-three wards, which is the centre of the south Kanto region as a whole, the coastal region of Kanagawa, and the north-eastern Tama area. A slight increase has also occurred in the south-western part of Kanagawa around Hakone. In relation to the housing situation, the areas with the highest numbers of welfare recipients coincide with areas with high numbers of private rental properties. Some of them are also areas with a high concentration of public housing as well.

Street-homelessness

Next we will look at the spread of people living on the street, the people who are 'homeless' as a result of poverty. The raw data is drawn from the result of a rough estimate done by counting all the homeless people who could be seen on the streets, parks or somewhere outdoors which was carried out throughout the nation under instruction from the Ministry of Health, Welfare and Labour in January 2003. This number is, needless to say, the minimum number that could be counted by eye witnesses. According to this, there were 25296 homeless in the whole nation. In the south Kanto region, they counted 6361 in Tokyo, 1928 in Kanagawa, 829 in Saitama, 668 in Chiba, and 130 in Ibaraki. Figure 6.16 shows the spread of these people according to local council areas. The areas with the greatest concentration were Shinjuku, Shibuya, Taitō, Sumida and Ota

Figure 6.17: The spread of kōryoshibōnin, ('vagrants found dead') (1986–1990)

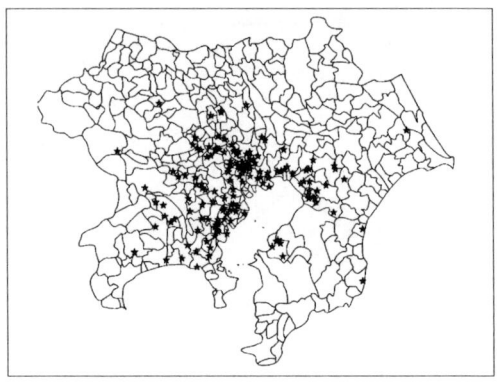

wards of Tokyo and Kawasaki ward of Kawasaki city. Then came the twenty-three wards in general and their neighbouring areas. It is noted that there were large numbers of homeless people in the middle of Kanagawa prefecture, around Atsugi and Hiratsuka cities. Figure 6.17 shows the spread of kōryoshibōnin, or 'vagrants found dead' between 1986 and 1990. Kōryoshibōnin means those who are found dead without an address or without anyone, such as a relative, to claim their bodies.[5] It can be assumed that these 'vagrants found dead' include some who had been living on the street. So, assuming this is a compatible sample, let us examine this for a chronological comparison. One dot on the map represents one case, and there are 275 dots in total on this map. The dots are concentrated in Tokyo and Kanagawa, especially in the east and the centre of Tokyo, in Shinjuku, Toshima and Taitō wards, and Yokohama and Kawasaki in Kanagawa. It is difficult to make an accurate comparison, as the counting units are different, but we can at least see that the trend is increasing.

One characteristic of the areas with a high concentration of homeless people is the existence of *Yoseba*, or day labourer markets. Some of the relatively large *Yoseba* in the south Kanto region are 'Sanya' in eastern Tokyo stretching across the Arakawa and Taitō wards, 'Takadanobaba' in Shinjuku ward, Kotobukichō in Yokohama city in Kanagawa and 'Harrapa' in Kawasaki city. *Yoseba* traditionally have played a role as areas in the city with a concentration of lower class workers, and as such, have numerous flophouses, cheap and temporary apartment blocks and other types of low rental accommodation. Labourers who had been living in these sorts of accommodation might have had to move out onto the street.

The other characteristic of these areas is the existence of places where homeless people can find shelter from the authorities and neighbouring residents without too much difficulty. On the river banks, for example, they find they can remain for longer and are less likely to be hassled than in a densely populated residential area. It is not too difficult to see the connection between the river and the high concentration of homeless people, as the Sumidagawa river and the Arakawa river flow through the eastern part of the twenty-three wards, while on the prefectural border between Tokyo and Kanagawa flows the Tamagawa river, and the Sagamigawa river flows through the middle of Kanagawa.

Incidentally, the index relating to this is the ratio of households in institutions. The national census lists various household types under this classification which do not fit into the general one, including those interned in social institutions, those who are hospitalised, those locked up in prison or the watch house and single people with no fixed address. These are the unsettled class who do not have a permanent residence, who are homeless people in the broad sense. I have not reprinted the map here, but although some of these 'people in institutions' are in the peripheral areas, the highest concentration of them also falls in the central Arakawa, Taitō, Sumida, Chiyoda and Chuō wards of Tokyo, the Kawasaki ward of Kawasaki city in Kanagawa and Naka ward of Yokohama city.

Three types of impoverished areas

Looking at these indices, we can see that the areas of concentrated poverty and the three types of deprivation we saw in the analysis of the 1975–1990 data were more or less still the same in 2000. There were, of course, some new characteristics emerging in some areas, because of the shifts which had occurred since then and after taking the housing situation into consideration. Below we will examine these new area-determined characteristics.

First, we will look at the geographical centre of the south Kanto region, where the rate of blue collar workers was originally not particularly high. Typical areas were the northwest of the twenty-three wards, like Nakano and Shinjuku wards in Tokyo and the coastal area of Yokohama city in Kanagawa prefecture. These areas, as we saw in the indices from 2000, show extremely high rates of unemployment, of elderly single person households, of people on the *Seikatsu hogo* benefit, of homeless people, and a reasonably high rate of people in institutions. More people now live in private rental properties. These areas can be called 'inner-city type' impoverished areas. As a background to these areas was the existence of the dense low rent housing areas, which had been saved from large scale development or redevelopment. In short, not much money had been invested in these areas either privately or publicly during the high economic growth period, or the bubble period.

The second kind of typical area was the eastern part of the twenty-three wards and the coastal area of Kawasaki in Kanagawa prefecture. These show higher figures in almost all categories including unemployment, single mother households, single elderly people, people on the *Seikatsu hogo* benefit, and homeless people. These areas had a high number of people in institutions as well. Here also, the main kind of accommodation was private rental properties. There was a high concentration of public housing in the north-eastern part of the twenty-three wards of Tokyo, too. To be offered a place in public housing, the income has to be below a certain limit and it will be evicted if it goes over this limit. Public housing therefore tends always to be full of low income earners. Few of the residents think of moving out because if they did, their level of poverty would deepen, as they would lose the protection of the system, and they would have to put up with higher rents and worse housing conditions. This phenomenon of a particular social class of people ending up concentrated in particular areas or particular housing blocks is called the 'housing trap.' (Takenaka 1990; Yui 1999; Hirayama 2004) This phenomenon must be taking place in part in these areas. With that understanding, we will now look at class based occupations. These areas had a high blue collar ratio in 1975, but there is a definite trend towards white collar workers since 1990. Traditionally, these areas had a concentration of manufacturing industries which must have been directly affected by deindustrialisation and economic stagnation. The impoverishment here can be seen in terms of being left behind. These areas are affected by the traditional blue collar type of poverty.

The third type was suburbia and its peripheral areas, where the ratio of blue collar workers was high. The areas either registered a high rate of unemployment and single mother families, or these have been rising continuously since 1975. These areas include a part of the blue collar belt which stretches from the north-eastern part of the Tama area of Tokyo to the middle of Kanagawa prefecture, the north-eastern coastal part of Chiba prefecture around Mobara and Togane, and the border region between Ibaraki and Chiba prefectures, including Kashima. This third type can be classified as a peripheral blue collar type of poverty. Basically the biggest influence in these areas is deindustrialisation. The area in the middle of Kanagawa prefecture, in particular, has seen a decline in the rate of blue collar workers between 1975 and 2000, while the unemployment rate has gone up, as well as the number of homeless people. Most of these homeless people were formerly workers in the local area, many of whom came from the country. During the prime of their working lives they had relocated to work in Kanagawa prefecture which was why they ended up sleeping on the streets in that area, according to a survey of 251 people living on the street conducted in Kanagawa prefecture (at Atsugi, Ebina, Odawara, Sagamihara, Chigasaki, Hiratsuka, Fujisawa and Yokosuka) in 2000 (Kanagawa toshi seikatsu kenkyūkai 2001). Here we can see the clear link between the stagnation of industry caused by deindustrialisation, and the fact of the workers losing their jobs and housing. The north-eastern Tama areas had already had a high unemployment rate in 1975 and a high rate of public housing. The rate of single mother households, single elderly people, people on the *Seikatsu hogo* benefit was also recorded as high in the area in 1990 and 2000. Because this area has a relatively high concentration of public housing and facilities, it is conceivable that a suburban 'housing trap' phenomenon is occurring.

Impoverishment and segregation

The spatial structures of the south Kanto region in 2000, as seen mainly from the occupational classes, appeared concentric with the areas with a higher number of blue collar workers and those engaged in primary industries on the outer edge, then suburbia mostly inhabited by the families of white collar workers, then the ward areas of Tokyo in the middle. In part, we can see the 'blue collar belt' stretching north from the eastern part of the twenty-three wards of Tokyo. Compared to what it was like in 1975, a clearer concentric zone structure formation has emerged with the blue collar areas on the periphery and the white collar areas in suburbia, as a result of the continuing concentration of blue collar workers on the periphery. In the gaps between these basic structures, there are areas where poverty is concentrated, though they are sometimes more difficult to see. We have identified three types of these areas. The first is the 'inner-city type' which exists in part of the urban complex landscape, typically in the north-western part of the twenty-three wards of Tokyo and the coastal area of Yokohama city. The second is the 'traditional blue collar type', typical to the eastern part of the twenty-three wards of Tokyo and the coastal area of Kawasaki city, and the third is the 'peripheral blue collar type' which is observable in some suburbs and peripheral areas with a higher concentration of blue collar workers. The other characteristics we noticed are deepening poverty and the concentration of poverty in particular areas. The areas with higher rates of unemployment and single mother families, indicative of the existence of poverty, were spread widely and included the peripheral areas. On the other hand, in the areas with a higher concentration of elderly single people, who are unlikely to move residence frequently, there is some overlapping with areas that have a higher number of private rental properties, such as the ward and city areas of Tokyo and the coastal area of Kanagawa prefecture, near the city centre, where the conditions for elderly people are thought to be tougher. In much the same way, the higher rate of people on the *Seikatsu hogo* benefit, which is a direct reflection of poverty, is concentrated in the ward and city areas of Tokyo and the ward area of Kanagawa prefecture. Some of these areas also have a higher concentration of people in institutions which include homeless people in the broader sense. In addition, the twenty-three ward areas and their adjacent areas in Tokyo had more homeless people.

Though these results are derived from limited indices, we can see the concentration of the disadvantaged towards the city centre as their poverty deepens. As mentioned above, the existence of traditional cheap accommodation and lower class labour markets in the city centres have played a key role. What accelerates the concentration is economic reorganisation through deindustrialisation and stagnation, as well as welfare, housing and other public policies. For example, 'Sanya,' the biggest *Yoseba* market in the south Kanto region, had become a town of single men, as a result of the policy adopted by the metropolitan government throughout the 1960s and 1970s of promoting the dispersal of the family members (Nishizawa 1995). Now, it has been transformed into a place of residences for impoverished elderly people because of the policy initiative to utilise the flophouses and other low rent accommodation in the area for those on the *Seikatsu hogo* benefit (Yamaguchi 2001). The previously mentioned 'housing trap phenomenon' has had an effect as well. It is important to note that public policies aimed at particular classes have had a big impact on the spatial concentration of poverty.

7 Does the hi hogo class represent poor people in general?

Masami Iwata

Poverty under the *Seikatsu hogo* system

A definition of poverty

The principle of equitable access

In Article 2, the *Seikatsu hogo* Act declares that 'everyone is entitled to the protection set forth in this Act, equally and without discrimination, as long as he or she meets its conditions.' This therefore stipulates that the protection of living standards is a right applicable to everyone, equally and without discrimination. Shinjiro Koyama, who was involved with the drafting of the Act, explains its equal and universal application principle as follows:

> This Act does not treat anyone preferentially or in a discriminatory fashion based on how they have come to be in need of protection, whether through illness, injury, disaster, the death of the head of the family, being physically handicapped or through unemployment. Differences in race, faith, sex, social status, family origin and so on, do not make any difference (Koyama 1950: 106).

The Act was intended to apply universally and equally. It could not define specific institutional 'eligibility' other than by mentioning 'nationals.'...

The *Seikatsu hogo* Act initially prescribed categories for individuals who would be ineligible for its benefits (old Act in 1946). These included persons with no intention of working; a lazy person or a person of delinquent character. Later revisions to the Act (new Act in 1950) clearly stated its character as one of general and broad assistance to alleviate modern poverty, which can be measured only by living standards. In this way, the universal and equal application principle of the Act has been seen for a long time as proof of its modernity, and hailed as an asset for the public assistance systems of Japan.

The *hi hogo* class

Translated, in the context of the *Seikatsu hogo* Act, *hi hogo* in Japanese means people on welfare benefits. The *hi hogo* class represents all kinds of poverty because it is measured solely by living standards, which incorporates every kind of poverty in Japan. Compared to the *Kyūgo hō* Act of the pre-War era, which excluded workers and people with families, and was limited in its application only to those who could not work, the post-War *Seikatsu hogo* system has had a broader scope. It was directed not only at poverty outside the modern labour market, but also at the poverty of the working poor, the poverty of working families as depicted by Charles Booth and Seebohm Rowntree. It also embodied a judgement that those 'lazy people' and 'people of delinquent character' which the pre-War Act had excluded, should be given a chance and their self reliance should be encouraged. As a result, the *hi hogo* have become synonymous with the poor in Japan. The *hogo* rate, the rate of the number of *hi hogo* measured against the entire population, has become broadly known as the poverty rate. Yet, does the *hi hogo* class actually represent the poor of Japan? Does the *hogo* rate really indicate the magnitude of poverty? Discussion elsewhere in this book has noted several aspects of the Japanese experience of poverty. Apart from assistance measures directed at the poor in general, various 'special measures' also operate, intended to alleviate the poverty of homeless people, *yoseba* workers and 'women and children in need of protection.' The poverty of aged people and disabled people is handled within the institutional welfare policy framework. This is because poverty cannot be understood solely by looking at income or living standards and therefore, the principle of general assistance offered by the *Seikatsu hogo* system can exist only alongside these special measures (see further discussion in Chapter 1).

There is another reality, where various different poverty alleviation measures are in use that differs from the *Seikatsu hogo* system, such as the policies directed at low income earners. Many past studies on public assistance have commonly assumed that the *hi hogo* class is exclusively unemployed households. Whether or not the *hi hogo* actually represent the poor in general is now constantly under scrutiny. In light of this, this chapter set out to determine the proportion of the various poor amongst modern working families that could be considered as a genuine *hi hogo* class. This can also determine the proportion of the poor not represented by the *hi hogo*. If the *hi hogo* class is only a response to a specific area of poverty, the position it occupies in society is of importance. Below, we will examine these issues by focusing on the *hi hogo* class in and of itself.

Measuring poverty by the *hogo* standard

The *hogo* rate

The proportion of poverty in general which the *hi hogo* class represents can be measured by its position in overall poverty in terms of quantity and quality. Of course, it is very difficult to define poverty overall, but here, let us say the sum total of the *yō hogosha* households (People and households eligible for protection) defined by the *Seikatsu hogo* standard is the sum total of people in poverty. It should be noted that poverty can be measured by other means than the *Seikatsu hogo* standard and that measuring it by various means is important.

In recent years, attention has been given to the poverty rate and the take-up rate of the *Seikatsu hogo* system. From these studies, we can determine the quantity and quality of the *hi hogo* class. Once we can work out the overall number of poor people (= the *yō hogo sha* households), we can determine the percentage of *hi hogo* amongst them. In this way, we can count the proportion of poor people which the *Seikatsu hogo* system looks after. Second, if we compare the overall number of people in poverty and the *hi hogo* class in terms of quality, we may be able to ascertain if the *hi hogo* represent poor people broadly or only partially. For this we need to rely on the accumulated empirical studies of poverty.

To begin with, we need to trace the transition of the *Seikatsu hogo* rate for people over time, which is the ratio of the *hi hogo* class in the population (the *hogo* rate), as well as the rate for households (the household *hogo* rate). As Figure 7.1 shows, the rate of the *hi hogo* class both in terms of population and households, has been in decline in general since the rapid economic boom, with a few fluctuations. In terms of the total Japanese population, the rate has declined from 23.8 per thousand in 1952, all through the period of rapid economic growth, through the time of the bubble economy and afterwards, to an all time low of 7.0 per thousand in 1995. It has increased slightly after 1996. The trend for households is pretty similar. It decreased from 39.6 per thousand in 1953 to 14.0 per thousand in 1993. Since then, it has increased slightly.

Figure 7.1: Transition of the rate of coverage by the Seikatsu hogo *system*

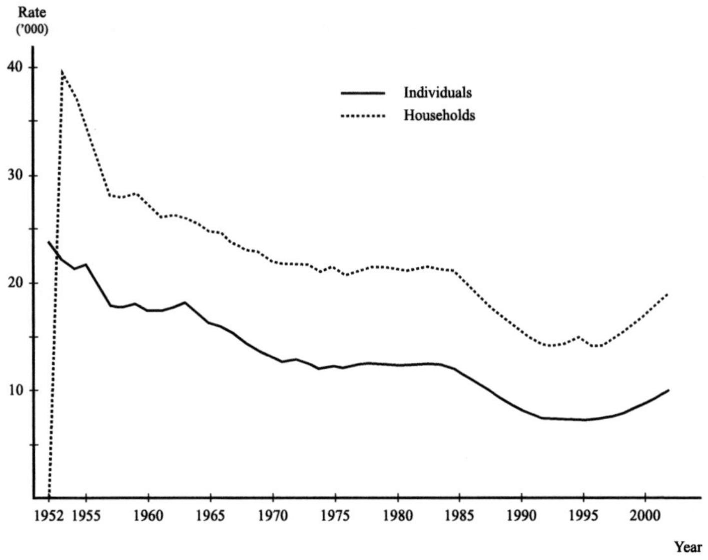

Source: *Shakai fukushi gyōsei gyōmu hōkoku* (Operating report, social welfare administration).
Origin: *Seikatsu hogo no dōkō Heisei 16 nendo ban* (The 2004 trends for *Seikatsu hogo*).

If the *hi hogo* class represents poverty in general, we could conclude that poverty in post-War Japan has been constantly in decline and only in the aftermath of the collapse of the bubble economy has it begun to increase. But, of course, the *hogo* rate is not the same as the poverty rate.

Poverty rate and the take-up rate by *Seikatu hogo*

Next, rather than use the number of *hi hogo* who are on welfare, we should use the number of *yō hogo* people, those eligible for benefits under the *Seikatsu hogo* Act, who are below the *hogo* standard set by the Minister for Welfare. Against the overall population, the rate of these people and households is the real poverty rate. However, because the *Seikatsu hogo* rate has long been considered to be synonymous with the poverty rate in Japan, and because there have not been many studies to challenge this commonly held notion, the real poverty rate has not really been measured. This is further not assisted by the ban on the use at a micro level of national income and consumption data such as family expenditure surveys under the statistics legislation.

Listing three of the very few surveys conducted under these restrictive circumstances, Table 7.1 shows the measurement of poverty based on the *Seikatsu hogo* standard. All three surveys define households as being in poverty if they are below 1.0 times of the *Seikatsu hogo* standard. In other words, they consider what the *Seikatsu hogo* Act defines as the state to be eligible for protection, or *yō hogo*, as poverty. While agreeing with each other on the definition of poverty, the three surveys differ slightly from each other on how to measure minimum life expenditure and the size of income which is drawn from the minimum life expenditure. Eiichi Eguchi's measurement is a pioneering example of this kind in Japan, though the area of measurement was limited just to Nakano ward in Tokyo. The other two measurements by Shinya Hoshino and Kōhei Komamura deal with the national statistics, using recounts of the micro data from the National Survey of Family Income and Expenditure. The Komamura measurement is a ground breaking one, covering all four surveys done between 1984 and 1999. Table 7.1 shows quite different poverty rates, reflecting the different standards and different definitions of income used in their calculations. When looking at Komamura's calculations, four of them worked out using the same methods, we can see the poverty rate hovering around ten per cent, except in 1989, which was during the peak of the bubble economy boom. The *hogo* rates for households at the corresponding times were 21.1 per thousand to 15.7 per thousand.

Applying this to the poverty rates shown above, we can estimate the ratio of the *hi hogo* class among the poor, using the take-up rates of the *Seikatsu hogo* system shown in Table 7.1. This again reveals a huge discrepancy. According to Komamura, about twenty per cent of people in poverty are covered by the *Seikatsu hogo* system, while Hoshino estimates a higher forty per cent. Either way, only twenty, or forty per cent at best of people in poverty are covered by the *Seikatsu hogo* system, defined as the *hi hogo* class.

Qualitative characteristics of the poor
While limited by the coverage of the surveys, these three measurements also determine the qualitative characteristics of the households in poverty. Despite the differences in measuring times and calculation methodologies, all three come to a fairly similar conclusion. For household numbers and types, they point out that

Table 7.1: The rate of households in poverty and the take-up rate of Seikatsu hogo *(%)*

	Ratio of households in poverty	Ratio of take-up/ household	Ratio of coverage/ person	Characteristics
Eiichi Eguchi				
1972	26.2[a]			Single person households.
	19.1[b]			Women's households.
				High geographical fluidity full time employed in small businesses.
				Part-time/day labour.
Shinya Hoshino				
1984	4.15	40.0	24.0	Women.
				Single mother households.
				Aged and young unsteady employment.
				Single person households.
1984	10.43	16.51		The poverty rate is higher in employed households, women's households, single person households, amongst the young and people over forty years old.
Kōhei Komamura				
1989	4.02	25.22		
1994	9.44	12.02		
1999	9.32	18.47		

Notes: Eiichi Eguchi's measurement is based on the tax register of Nakano ward residents. It uses annual income.

a: This is the poverty rate in Nakano ward.
b: This is an estimate worked out by multiplying the *Seikatsu hogo* standard for the overall Tokyo metropolitan area by 1.5 (low income standard) (Eguchi 1979).

Shinya Hoshino's measurement uses the recounts from the national survey of family income and expenditure from 1984. He works out the poverty rate and the coverage rate both from annual income and from expenditure, but here we list only the one calculated from annual income. He works out the coverage rate for people as well as households (Hoshino 2000).

Kōhei Komamura's measurements use the recounts from the national survey of family income and expenditure from 1984 to 1999. For income, the approved income, which is the annual income adjusted for income tax, social security payments and other deductions, is used (Komamura 2003).

a higher poverty rate is observed among single person households and female households. In terms of life cycle, poverty is more frequent amongst both young and old, creating a U-shaped curve. In relation to employment, the poverty rate is higher among small business employees and people in unstable employment, such as part-time workers and day labourers. They also measure poverty among employed people (i.e. the working poor). In his measurement of poverty among the residents of Nakano, Eguchi refers to the relationship between poverty and the duration of residence. He suggests that the more geographically fluid they are, the poorer they will be.

If these are the characteristics of the households in poverty in general, what are the characteristics of the *hi hogo* class? It may not represent the poor in general sufficiently in quantity, but the *hi hogo* may be representative when it comes to quality. If that is the case, the *Seikatsu hogo* system may be considered to be addressing its general service obligations reasonably well. Various studies carried out on public assistance, based on data from the *Seikatsu hogo* statistics, have already made similar suggestions with regard to the characteristics of the *hi hogo* class. Here, we will examine this matter again, but from the following perspective. Taking into consideration the above mentioned characteristics of households in poverty, we will first look at the characteristics in terms of the types and sizes of the households. Then we will examine how well the poverty of the working poor is represented. And third, we will look at the reasons why they came to be on a benefit and how they became the *hi hogo* class in the first place.

The *hi hogo* class

Household type and size

Table 7.2 shows the composition of households and the transition of the *hi hogo* class over the years based on the general simultaneous survey (baseline survey) carried out on 1 July every year of all Japanese on the *Seikatsu hogo* benefit. In the measurements of households in poverty discussed above, the poverty rates were worked out for the households without looking at the composition of the households. Here, we compare this data with data from the Population Census. From the outset, the *hi hogo* class has had a higher proportion of single person households. The ratio went above fifty per cent in 1970 and seventy per cent in 1995. The growing rate of single person households among the *hi hogo* is far greater than that for the general population. What the poverty measurements discussed above suggest, that the poverty rate is highest among single person households is clearly accurate, and

Table 7.2: The characteristics and transition of the composition of hi hogo households (%)

	1960	1965	1970	1975	1980	1985	1990	1995	2000	2003
Hi hogo *households*										
Overall	100.0	100.0	100.0	100.0	100.0	100.0	100.0	100.0	100.0	100.0
Single	31.5	39.0	50.0	55.8	55.7	57.3	64.7	72.0	73.5	73.3
Two persons	14.6	19.0	20.8	20.7	20.3	20.2	19.3	17.3	16.8	17.0
Three persons	13.0	14.0	11.9	10.2	11.2	11.5	8.9	6.3	5.6	5.7
Four persons	12.9	12.0	8.7	7.0	7.2	6.7	4.4	2.9	2.6	2.6
Five persons	10.7	8.2	4.9	3.6	3.3	2.7	1.7	1.1	0.9	0.9
More than six persons	13.6	7.8	3.8	2.7	2.4	1.7	1.0	0.6	0.5	0.5
General households from the national census										
Overall	100.0	-	100.0	100.0	100.0	100.0	100.0	100.0	100.0	-
Single	16.5	-	20.3	19.5	19.8	20.8	23.1	25.6	27.6	-
Two persons	11.2	-	13.8	15.6	16.8	18.4	20.6	23.0	25.1	-
Three persons	14.0	-	17.6	18.6	18.1	17.9	18.1	18.5	18.8	-
Four persons	16.4	-	22.7	24.7	25.3	23.7	21.6	18.9	16.9	-
Five persons	15.0	-	12.9	11.6	11.1	11.1	9.4	8.0	6.8	-
More than six persons	26.9	-	12.6	9.8	9.1	8.1	7.3	6.1	4.5	-

Sources: *Hi hogosha zenkoku issei chōsa (kiso chōsa)* {The national simultaneous survey of *hi hogo* people (baseline survey)} and Kokusei chōsa (The national census).
A different household composition criteria was used for the census in 1965, which cannot be converted for comparison and has been omitted.
Origin: *Seikatsu hogo no dōkō Heisei 16 nendo ban* (The 2004 trends for the *Seikatsu hogo*) and the national census data.

this group is well and truly representing the poverty of single person households.

Table 7.3 shows the types of *hi hogo* households and their transition. It also shows the *hogo* rate according to the different household types. The *Seikatsu hogo* statistics use their own unique household type categories which have more to do with the original reasons for people being covered by the system in the first place, among them that households of aged people have increased significantly from 22.9% in 1965 to 46.3% in 2002. Looking at the *hogo* rate of aged households was 46.2%. The higher poverty rate among aged households is reflected here as well. It looks quite different, however, for single mother households which also show a

Table 7.3: The types of hi hogo *households and the transition, and the* hogo *rate for different household types*

	Household type (per cent)					
Year	Total	Aged household	Single mother household	Household suffering illness	Injured household	Other
1965	100.0	22.9	13.7	29.4		34.0
1970	100.0	31.4	10.3	35.9		22.4
1975	100.0	31.4	10.0	45.8		12.9
1980	100.0	30.3	12.8	46.0		10.9
1985	100.0	31.2	14.6	44.8		9.3
1990	100.0	37.2	11.7	42.9		8.1
1995	100.0	42.3	8.7	42.0		6.9
2000	100.0	45.5	8.4	28.5	10.2	7.4
2001	100.0	46.0	8.5	27.6	10.1	7.7
2002	100.0	46.3	8.6	26.7	10.0	8.3

	Coverage rate ('000)			
	Total	Aged household	Single mother household	Other
1965	23.2	173.5	248.2	15.5
1970	21.0	165.2	175.9	13.0
1975	21.4	136.7	189.2	13.4
1980	21.1	93.0	211.5	13.1
1985	20.9	78.2	225.3	12.5
1990	15.5	55.2	135.0	8.9
1995	14.7	45.3	108.7	8.5
2000	16.5	43.9	106.1	9.3
2001	17.6	45.2	117.4	9.9
2002	18.9	46.2	112.3	10.7

Sources and origin as Table 7.2.

higher poverty rate in the poverty measurements mentioned above. The proportion of single mother households among the *hi hogo* has decreased from 13.7% in 1965 to 8.6% in 2002. After having hovered around ten to fourteen per cent for a couple of decades, the proportion decreased slightly to eight per cent in about 1995 and has stayed there since then. The *hogo* rate was 112.3%, much higher than that for aged households, but it fluctuates significantly from year to year. In other words, single mother households, although having a higher poverty rate, are not consistently covered by the *Seikatsu hogo* system.

We cannot get a clear picture of the poverty rates for young households because the *Seikatsu hogo* statistics do not have such a household category. Looking at the number of people on benefits who are between six and nineteen years old and the twenty to thirty-nine year olds the rate was 29.73% and 15.24% respectively in 1955. It went down to 6.01% and 1.94% in 1996. It went up slightly after 1997 to 9.77% and 3.39% in 2003, which was still the lowest among all the age groups. Komamura and others pointed out the existence of a U-shaped poverty distribution curve when talking about the poverty rate, indicating that youth poverty is not necessarily covered adequately by the *Seikatsu hogo* system.

The working poor

Households without working members

What are the characteristics of the *hi hogo* class in relation to employment? How well does the *Seikatsu hogo* system cater for the working poor, which characteristically form one of the household types in poverty? The first thing to note here is that, as has been pointed out by many already, the *hi hogo* have increasingly become unemployed or incapable for work. Figure 7.2 clearly shows that initially among the *hi hogo* there were slightly more households with working members (working households) than there were without working members (non-working households). This trend was reversed in 1964, and since then the proportion of non-working households has kept on growing. From 2000 it has accounted for more than 88%. Nonworking households include households that have the capacity to work but are unemployed. So this trend does not directly suggest the *Seikatsu hogo* system is excluding the employed, rather the poor (working poor) households. However, taking into the account the transition of the household types (Figure 7.2), such as the growing proportion of aged households as well as disabled households (which jumped from 29.4% in 1965 to 45.8% in 1975, in only a decade, although there has been a slight decline recently), it is fair to conclude that the significant increase in nonworking households suggests that the *hi hogo* class does not adequately represent the working poor.

The majority of households with working members amongst the *hi hogo* are single mother households and others. In 2003, approximately fifty per cent of single mother households and about thirty-five per cent of the others on the benefit were employed households. Looking at the transition since 1992, working households in both groups are in slight decline. As Table 7.4 shows, commonly among the working households it is the head of the household who works. To have more than one member of the family

Does the hi hogo *class represent poor people in general?* 167

Figure 7.2: The transitions of employed and unemployed households among the hi hogo *class*

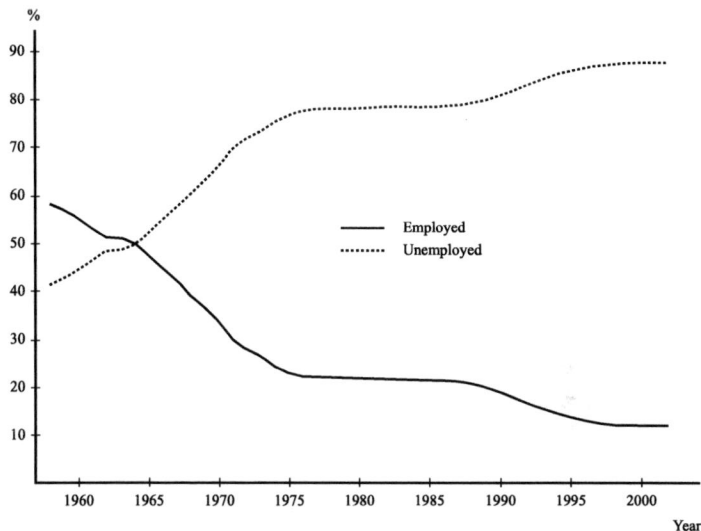

Source and origin as Figure 7.1.

working was not common among poor families even before the 1960s. The dominant type of work was, until 1965, the traditional kind of unstable occupations such as day labouring and piecework at home, as well as self-employment. Since then, especially after 1985, regular employees have become the majority. We must note, however, that the term regular employment used in the *Seikatsu hogo* criteria is not defined in the same way this term commonly is. It does not refer to full time employment and regular employment in the usual sense at all. Under the *Seikatsu hogo* definition, it means one is 'employed by others in a contract for longer than one month, and receives a wage or fee, whatever the type of employment is.' It includes many part time employees, casual employees and other 'regular employees with limited employment terms.' Regular employment in this sense is gradually increasing and becoming the dominant style of employment, replacing day labouring and other unsteady types of employment which were predominant during the 1960s and 1970s among employed poor households. Obviously because the payment from this regular employment is not enough for minimum living expenses, there are some measures, modest as they may be, directed at these working poor households. Incidentally, single mother households have a very high percentage of 'regular employees with limited employment terms,' while other household types have unsteady types of employment such as day labouring as well as 'regular employees with limited employment terms.'

Reasons for receiving benefits

In order to ascertain further the trend of the *hi hogo* class being dominated by nonworking households, the reasons why they started receiving benefits is relevant. This is reflected in Table 7.5, which is based on the annual dynamic survey of *Seikatsu hogo* recipients conducted every September. The most common reasons for receiving the benefit were 'sickness and injury' and 'other.' The reduction in income has floated around the ten per cent level, with the lowest level at 3.5% in 1990. It is gradually increasing as the economic woes continue to deepen. 'Sickness and injury' has kept on rising, with the exception of 1970, to a peak of 80.8% in 1990 since when it has been decreasing. The accelerated decline since 2000 is because of the change in criteria. Under the new classification, hospitalisation (often affecting homeless people) and other emergency admissions into the system which used to be filed under 'sickness and injury,' are now filed under 'others.' Apart from this, the 'loss or diminishing of savings' and 'separation from the dominant income earners' are relatively important in the 'others' category.

Looking at these reasons according to the household types, among the aged households receiving benefits, 'loss or diminishing of savings,' 'sickness and injury to the head of the household,' and 'loss of income due to old age' are the common ones, according to the 2002 dynamic survey. Among the disabled households, 'sickness and injury,' and 'other' are the dominant reasons. For the single mother households, 'separation from the dominant income earner' is the major reason, while for the others, the 'loss or diminishing of savings' is the most dominant.

Of course, these classifications are for bureaucratic convenience only. If the *Seikatsu hogo* system was truly *directed at* poverty among the general public, the reasons for receiving benefits would naturally be diverse and complex. Still, the dominance of the 'sickness and injury' category and the relatively small proportion relating to 'reduction in income' suggest it is no doubt easier for the aged and disabled households to be admitted into the *hi hogo* class than for the working poor households. The administrative authorities still consider 'separation' to be the dominant reason for

Table: 7.4: Transition of employment among employed poor households

Actual numbers

Year	Overall total	Head of household at work					Other members at work
		Total	Regular employment	Day labour	Piecework at home	Other	
1958	341,684	250,948	34,057	81,644	45,416	89,831	90,736
1958	346,112	249,372	33,195	83,494	41,834	90,850	96,740
1960	333,744	236,713	32,171	81,477	37,063	86,002	97,031
1965	302,707	213,004	36,547	71,546	25,804	79,108	89,703
1970	220,130	151,021	33,709	42,506	19,131	55,675	69,109
1975	160,767	109,542	29,936	27,637	15,230	36,740	51,226
1980	161,217	113,254	43,476	25,768	14,459	29,552	47,962
1985	166,190	122,909	62,486	21,761	14,168	24,494	43,281
1990	116,970	90,200	51,065	13,144	10,226	15,765	26,769
1995	81,604	63,705	37,546	8,788	7,076	10,294	17,899
2000	89,660	71,151	45,552	9,318	6,360	9,921	18,509
2001	95,295	75,726	49,397	9,910	6,339	10,079	19,569
2003	113,967	91,082	60,651	12,443	6,456	11,532	22,885

Composition ratio (per cent)

Year	Overall total	Head of household at work					Other members at work
		Total	Regular employment	Day labour	Piecework at home	Other	
1958	100.0	73.4	10.0	23.9	13.3	26.3	26.6
1959	100.0	72.0	9.6	24.1	12.1	26.2	28.0
1960	100.0	70.9	9.6	24.4	11.1	25.8	29.1
1965	100.0	70.4	12.1	23.6	8.5	26.1	29.6
1970	100.0	68.6	15.3	19.3	8.7	25.3	31.4
1975	100.0	68.1	18.6	17.2	9.5	22.9	31.9
1980	100.0	70.2	27.0	16.0	9.0	18.3	29.7
1985	100.0	74.0	37.6	13.1	8.5	14.7	26.0
1990	100.0	77.1	43.7	11.2	8.7	13.5	22.9
1995	100.0	78.1	46.0	10.8	8.7	12.6	21.9
2000	100.0	79.4	50.8	10.4	7.1	11.1	20.6
2001	100.0	79.5	51.8	10.4	6.7	10.6	20.5
2003	100.0	79.9	53.2	10.9	5.7	10.1	20.1

Note: These are the monthly averages from each year. The total number is the 'actual number of households who have been on benefits' excluding those suspended. Sources and origin as Graph 7.1.

receiving benefits even for single mother households, rather than the inadequacy of their income, though there are many 'employed' households.

Table 7.5: The reasons for receiving the Seikatsu hogo *benefit (%)*

	Total number	Sickness and injuries	Reduction in income	Other
1960	100	56.8	11.1	32.1
1965	100	68.9	8.5	22.6
1970	100	80.9	4.5	14.6
1975	100	75.1	6.6	18.3
1980	100	70.4	8.0	21.6
1985	100	72.2	6.9	20.9
1990	100	80.8	3.5	15.7
1995	100	78.1	6.8	15.1
2000	100	43.2	13.9	42.8
2003	100	38.6	15.5	45.9

Note: based on the annual survey in September.

Source: *Seikatsu hogo dōtai chōsa* (Dynamic survey of the *Seikatsu hogo*). Since 1999 it has been in *Shakai fukushi gyōsei gyōmu hōkoku* (Operating report, social welfare administration).

Origin: *Seikatsu hogo no dōkō Heisei 16 nendo ban* (The 2004 trends for the *Seikatsu hogo*) and the population census data.

Poverty and the *hi hogo* class

Summary

The *hi hogo* class reflects to some degree the high poverty rate among single households as well as among elderly people. Yet, as we have seen in the proportion of people receiving benefits out of all people who are eligible, it is not fully reflecting poverty among those people in terms of actual numbers. It also does not necessarily reflect the higher poverty rate among single mother households and young people. Relating to this point, the measures directed at the working poor are not really adequate. Only some part-time workers and households of day labourers are looked after by the system, accounting for only about forty per cent of the single mother households and other types of households. As has been already pointed out, nonworking households dominate the *hi hogo* class. The door may be open for 'sickness and injury,' 'loss or diminishing of savings' and 'separation from the dominant income earner,' but not necessarily for the simple 'reduction in income.'

Prescribed restrictions at the gate

Judging from the available poverty measurements and the *Seikatsu hogo* statistics, though limited, we can conclude that the *hi hogo* class does not represent people in poverty in general. The *Seikatsu hogo* system has served only about twenty per cent of eligible people. Its service is limited mostly to nonworking households, especially to those with disabled and aged households. The *Seikatsu hogo* system, because of its universal general service nature which is directed at poverty in general, has eliminated the necessity to set up separate services such as assistance for the unemployed. Yet the reality is that its service scope is extremely limited. As the system has concentrated its assistance on the disabled as well as aged people, one cannot help feeling that it is becoming similar in practice to the old *Kyūgo hō* Act of the pre-War era, which only applied to those isolated people. What then has happened to the *Seikatsu hogo* Act which was meant to serve the poor in general? Many previous studies have blamed the administrative bureaucracy for tightening restrictions through administrative directives and notices limiting the availability of the benefit (or tightening the rules for eligibility). But the real issue is that although the system was meant to be universally and equally open to all poor people, with no restrictive eligibility criterion, there has been a fear of applying the system to assist the poor in general, and there have existed elements, both within the Act itself as well as within the welfare administrations, wanting to steer away from a universally and equally applicable system. On this point, Shinjirō Koyama mentions in a discussion with Yūichi Nakamura in the strong fear held by the welfare administration at the time that a universally applicable system might breed lazy dole cheats, *Seikatsu hogo 30 nen shi* (the 30 year history of the *Seikatsu hogo*).

In the beginning, 'even though the system was open to everyone equally in principal, we thought there should be certain criteria to be met in order to become a recipient. No matter how universal and equal the system was meant to be, we believed those not meeting the criteria should not be eligible.' (Kōseishō shakaikyoku hogoka 1981: 118) He admits that this was interpreted by the welfare administration to mean that it was essential to have a filtering device to select the 'deserving poor' from the undeserving, when applying the universal and equal service principle. This is why, according to Koyama himself, he included the suggestion 'to clarify ineligibility criteria' in his 'advice to improve and strengthen the *Seikatsu hogo* system' given to the Advisory Council on Social Security in 1949. His suggestion was not included in the new *Seikatsu hogo* Act in 1950 because it was vetoed by the General Headquarters (GHQ) occupation authorities. This reluctance to apply the principle can also be found in the Act itself. The fourth clause, in declaring the complementary nature of the Act states one's assets, one's capability to work and the other Acts and benefits should be considered before this Act applies. These are described as the prerequisites. At the same time, the Act warns in a contradictory manner against the strict application of its emergency admission criteria.

Despite the Act's universal application principle, it has been possible to restrict its range of application because of its complementary nature. Although they are described in such a vague manner, the prerequisites in practice function as a test of eligibility. The central government and the local welfare offices are able to use their discretionary powers to place more importance on depending on family assistance, on the utilisation of the capability to work and imposing limits on cash in hand and assets. By reducing the size of the gate, it is not too difficult to reduce the rate of eligible people on a benefit. Not just in terms of quantity, but also quality, it is also possible to limit services to the working poor to only a part of the single mother households. In relation to this, Shinya Hoshino remarks that even though generally applicable assistance sounds good, non-general assistance measures by separating employed and unemployed would serve poor single mother households much better (Hoshino 2000: 196). His remark concerning the contradictions of the general assistance system in Japan is accurate.

Exclusion of the *hi hogo*

The *hi hogo* and social security

Complement to social security in general

The *Seikatsu hogo* system was meant to deal with poverty on an equal basis, without discrimination. But its recipients do not necessarily reflect poverty at large. The system now mostly deals with the poverty of single aged people and the disabled. In consideration of this, what sort of position does the *hi hogo* class occupy in society when it only represents a limited proportion of poverty? Let us examine first the position of the *hi hogo* in the overall social security structure.

In general, the decreasing number of people on benefits is attributed to the increase in national wealth as a result of economic growth, and to the development of the social security system. Yet, the fact that single aged people and the disabled, and single mother households have a higher poverty rate means the development of the social security and welfare services apart from the *Seikatsu hogo* system, has not achieved the eradication of preventable poverty for elderly people and single mother households. For the *hi hogo* class, the *Seikatsu hogo* system is inadequate as far as its measures for the working poor are concerned, but for aged people and the disabled it complements the inadequacy of the general social security structure. When I say the *Seikatsu hogo* complements the others, I mean this in two senses. In one sense, it makes up the shortfalls in the minimum living costs of pensions, child care allowances and other payments received. In another sense, it is a complement for those who have no access to any other social security or welfare service. In the first sense, we can gauge its extent by examining the social security payments the *hi hogo* receive. Table 7.6 shows that, as at 1 July 2003, 14.5% of all the *Seikatsu hogo* recipient households received employee's pensions, while 23.4% received a national pension. This means at least more than thirty per cent receive the pension and complement the shortfall with the *Seikatsu hogo* payment. In terms of the rate of composition, the child care allowance (8.6%) which most of the single mother households receive and the child allowance form the main part, apart from pensions. Although this is often referred to as an example of the low standard of social security in Japan, this kind of supplementation was the original role of the *Seikatsu hogo* system, because various pensions are considered simply as replacement for a part of one's previous income, and not intended to provide a minimum cost of living.

The example above shows social security and the *Seikatsu hogo* mutually supplementing each other. In this, the *hi hogo* class is not separated from the social security system. In much the same way, the *hi hogo* class is clearly linked to carer insurance because since the inception of carer assistance, the '*hi hogo* class' can receive a nursing care service, as if they were covered by Nursing Care Insurance. There are about 100,000 people who benefit from the carer assistance service at the moment. They are considered to be covered by nursing care insurance, rather than it being the '*hi hogo* class' using the service.

Separation from universal coverage

The *hi hogo* class is not allowed to join in the national pension scheme, and on the health care front, is not allowed to join in the national health insurance scheme. When universal health care was introduced, it was argued that the health care of the *hi hogo* should also be covered by the national health insurance scheme,

Table 7.6: Social security recipients among the hi hogo class

	1995			2000			2003		
	Number of recipient households	Number of cases	Recipients (%)	Number of recipient households	Number of cases	Recipients (%)	Number of recipient households	Number of cases	Recipients (%)
(hi hogo households)	600,980		100.0	724,561		100.0	906,184		100.0
employees' pension/ mutual aid pension	58,213	60,013	9.7	92,059	95,127	12.7	131,016	136,051	14.5
old age (retirement) pension	33,588	34,886	5.6	47,520	49,325	6.6	64,927	67,623	7.2
disability pension	6,303	6,359	1.0	8,502	8,556	1.2	10,265	10,337	1.1
bereaved family pension	9,130	9,231	1.5	13,113	13,248	1.8	17,778	17,933	2.0
other	9,192	9,557	1.5	22,924	23,998	3.2	38,046	40,158	4.2
national pension	174,689	183,248	29.1	183,526	191,224	25.3	211,753	220,567	23.4
basic aged pension	16,516	17,168	2.7	38,696	40,430	5.3	59,828	62,851	6.6
basic disability pension	36,910	37,989	6.1	44,146	45,475	6.1	50,838	52,315	5.6
basic bereaved family pension	1,340	1,417	0.2	1,227	1,314	0.2	1,525	1,610	0.2
aged pension	97,865	104,276	16.3	85,298	89,646	11.8	85,486	89,500	9.4
disability pension	5,624	5,732	0.9	7,126	7,241	1.0	9,198	9,354	1.0
single mother pension	160	160	0.0	45	47	0.0	36	36	0.0
orphans' pension	121	124	0.0	37	41	0.0	92	94	0.0
aged welfare pension	14,890	15,083	2.5	5,362	5,387	0.7	3,139	3,151	0.3
other	1,236	1,304	0.2	1,589	1,643	0.2	1,611	1,656	0.2

pension and relief	4,767	4,777	0.8	4,632	4,650	0.6	4,795	4,803	0.5
unemployment insurance	495	500	0.1	744	752	0.1	844	852	0.1
special child care allowance	2,420	2,455	0.4	2,728	2,754	0.4	3,498	3,532	0.4
special disabled allowance	1,941	1,964	0.3	2,573	2,609	0.4	2,999	3,035	0.3
disability child welfare allowance	921	935	0.2	956	980	0.1	1,239	1,262	0.1
child allowance	7,705	7,760	1.3	10,513	10,638	1.5	35,672	36,055	3.9
child care allowance	50,360	50,883	8.4	59,276	59,659	8.2	77,558	78,357	8.6
other	9,316	10,325	1.6	12,007	13,428	1.7	13,808	15,230	1.5

Source and origin as Table 7.2

as the *Seikatsu hogo* system operates on the principle of giving priority to other Acts. This suggestion was 'somehow, turned down' (Kōseishō shakaikyoku hogoka 1981: 226). Presumably, this was for financial reasons. The principle of 'universal health insurance' had to be sacrificed because national health care could not cover the health care of the *hi hogo*, nearly half of whom were at that time unemployed.

As a result, the trend towards cutting them off from the general social security system was strengthened. In other words, the direction was towards the latter meaning of supplementing, that the *Seikatsu hogo* system looks after those whom the other systems and securities fail. The medical aid given through the *Seikatsu hogo* system does not supplement medical insurance. It is aimed at those people who are not able to receive medical insurance, by issuing its own medical coupons in order to meet their medical needs. This service is only available to those who do not conform to the social standard of universal insurance. Hoshino criticises the fact that at a time when an increasing amount of tax money is being poured into national health insurance and the national pension, there is no reason why only the *hi hogo* are excluded from receiving them (Hoshino 2000: 194). It could be argued that the introduction of such unrealistic social standards as 'universal insurance and a universal pension' was only possible by excluding the extra burden of the *hi hogo* class.

Climbing out of poverty

In regard to other legal framework, the relationship between the living security offered under the *Seikatsu hogo* system and the social welfare service is complicated. If they are residing at home, the *hi hogo* class can have access to social welfare services, just like anyone else. The only difference is that they are exempt from fees. Incidentally, there is a view that these fee exemptions should be abolished and fees should be charged and reimbursed from the livelihood aid of the *Seikatsu hogo* system. If the person is interned in the *hogo* facilities, the minimum living standard is provided in kind within the *Seikatsu hogo* system as well as counselling and assistance in becoming self reliant.

But there are cases where *hi hogo* climb out of *Seikatsu hogo* protection, when they are receiving integrated services at facilities operated under different welfare Acts. Their minimum living standard as well as various other welfare services is provided under the auspices of different frameworks. For example, since the enactment of the Welfare Act for Aged People in 1973, the aged care facilities of the *Seikatsu hogo* system were converted to welfare facilities for the aged. As a result, the lives and care of the *hi hogo* was transferred from the *Seikatsu hogo* system to the jurisdiction of the new law. This was revised under the Nursing Care Insurance Act, and the separating of integrated services (such as food, accommodation, nursing care and so on) was begun, but the same situation still occurs in facilities for disabled people and women. In short, the poor are divided into those who remain in the *hi hogo* class and those who climb out of it by means of the other laws, even though they are poor nonetheless. Because the *Seikatsu hogo* places priority on other Acts and systems, the *hi hogo* may be seen as left over people who the other Acts and systems could not deal with. Within social security overall, as we have seen, the they are clearly linked with the other systems and are not placed in any special category in that sense. However, in another sense, the *hi hogo* class is cut off from the other systems and placed outside the welfare nation. How these two contradictory aspects are balanced will determine whether the *hi hogo* become increasingly segregated and sidelined or whether they have a place in the wider society.

Entrenched poverty

Transient and chronic poverty

Another factor that has separated the *hi hogo* class from the social standard is the protracted period of their protection under the *Seikatsu hogo* system. The fact that the *hi hogo* are increasingly unemployed inevitably means that unless the conditions for other social security change, their period under protection will be prolonged. Generally speaking there are two types of poverty. One is transient poverty which is relatively short term and moves back over the poverty line. The other is chronic poverty, where people get locked in for a long time. More recently, with the use of the panel study technique by which poverty experiences can be measured and followed up for a certain period, it has become common to recognise poverty accordingly. The study by Iwata and Hamamoto (2004), and the dynamic analysis of poverty in Chapter 3 of this book show an aspect of the poverty experience in Japan. What is of most concern is the tendency for transient poverty to become chronic. Public assistance schemes such as the *Seikatsu hogo* system are expected to play the role of halting poverty in its transient period, and pushing it back above the poverty level. In particular, the general assistance

Figure 7.3: Length of time on Seikatsu hogo benefits

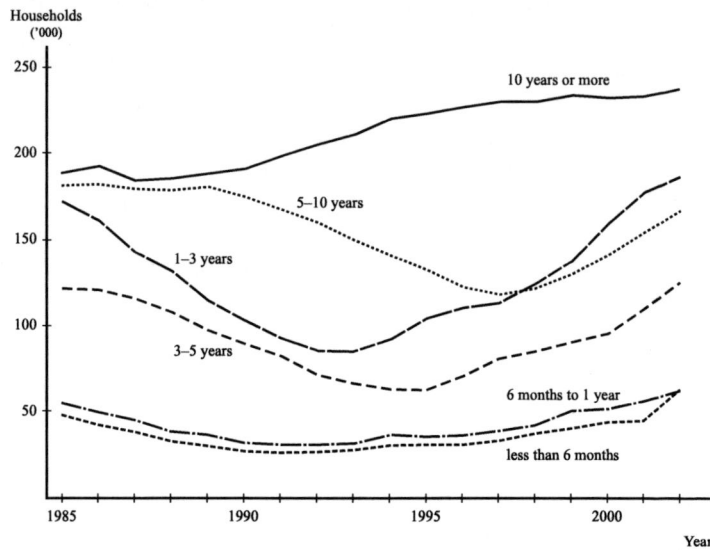

Source: Hi hogosha zenkoku issei chōsa [kobetsu chōsa] (The national simultaneous survey of the *hi hogo* people [individual survey]).
Origin: Kōsei Rōdōshō Shakai Engo-kyoku Hogo-ka shiryō (Data at the Public Assistance Division, Social Welfare and War Victims Relief Bureau, Ministry of Welfare and Labor).

service of the *Seikatsu hogo* has a strong potential to deal with transient poverty among the working poor. However, the trend of the *hi hogo* to become increasingly nonworking suggests that the *Seikatsu hogo* system kicks in only when poverty becomes chronic, instead of dealing with it when it is still transient. As mentioned above, due to the stricter application of the benefit, poor people are not able to be assisted until their poverty progresses from transient to chronic, until they turn sixty-five, until their illness becomes chronic, until their disability becomes permanent and until they lose all their assets. This inevitably prolongs the period they are on benefits. This can be seen in Figure 7.3 and Table 7.7.

Time spent on benefits

Figure 7.3 shows the number of households on the *Seikatsu hogo* benefit according to the length of time they have been on the benefit, based on the *hi hogosha zenkoku issei chōsa (kobetsu chōsa)* {National simultaneous survey of the *hi hogo* people (individual survey)}. As far as the long term trend is concerned, all households

Does the hi hogo class represent poor people in general? 179

Table 7.7: Length of time on the Seikatsu hogo benefit according to the different types of household (%)

	Total	> 6 mth	6–12 mth	1–3 yr	3–5 yr	5–10 yr	≥ 10 yr
Aged							
1960	100	7.7	6.3	22.6	14.6	48.8	
1970	100	9.5	7.5	22.8	17.4	27.4	15.5
1976	100	3.0	5.0	23.1	17.4	26.8	24.8
1981	100	4.5	4.8	16.6	14.4	28.7	31.0
1985	100	3.1	4.1	16.1	14.4	26.9	35.4
1990	100	2.2	3.2	12.1	12.6	28.9	41.0
1995	100	2.8	4.0	12.9	9.2	22.9	48.2
2000	100	4.0	5.0	17.4	12.1	19.7	41.8
2003	100	4.7	5.1	18.2	14.8	21.6	35.5
Single mother							
1960	100	10.9	9.8	29.9	17.8	31.7	
1967	100	10.1	9.0	27.9	19.7	23.4	9.9
1970	100	11.5	9.9	27.9	18.4	24.6	7.7
1976	100	8.4	13.3	31.8	17.3	20.3	8.9
1981	100	13.8	12.5	32.1	18.0	17.7	5.9
1985	100	8.5	11.4	34.8	19.5	19.6	6.3
1990	100	5.2	6.9	24.2	19.8	33.9	10.1
1995	100	6.7	8.3	28.3	14.7	26.6	15.5
2000	100	9.8	10.6	31.6	18.0	20.0	9.9
2003	100	9.6	11.5	33.0	19.4	19.7	6.9
Invalid							
1960	-	-	-	-	-	-	-
1970	100	13.6	9.9	24.3	16.4	22.2	13.6
1976	100	7.3	10.7	26.4	15.3	20.9	19.4
1981	100	10.9	8.4	22.2	15.2	21.8	21.4
1985	100	7.6	8.2	22.8	15.2	22.6	23.6
1990	100	6.0	6.4	18.7	15.0	26.1	27.8
1995	100	6.7	7.1	20.4	11.6	21.2	33.0
2000	100	7.3	8.2	24.5	14.1	19.2	26.7
2003	100	8.8	8.5	24.3	16.2	20.1	22.2
Other							
1960	100	16.1	12.5	31.5	15.4	24.4	
1967	100	14.2	10.0	28.7	18.5	21.477	7.2
1970	100	12.4	9.7	24.3	17.1	25.0	11.5
1976	100	7.4	10.6	27.4	15.8	21.1	17.7
1981	100	9.8	8.0	24.7	17.0	22.3	18.2
1985	100	7.0	8.0	24.6	17.6	23.2	19.7
1990	100	3.1	4.8	17.9	14.9	30.5	28.8
1995	100	5.5	6.3	19.1	10.8	23.6	34.7
2000	100	10.9	10.6	28.3	11.5	16.3	22.4
2003	100	15.4	12.6	28.4	14.6	14.2	14.8

Note: 'Other' in 1960 includes 'invalid households.'
Source: *Hi hogosha zenkoku issei chōsa (kobetsu chōsa)* [The national simultaneous survey of *hi hogo* people (individual survey)].
Origin: *Seikatsu hogo no dōkō Heisei 16 nendo ban* (The 2004 trends for the *Seikatsu hogo*).

except for those households which have been on benefits for longer than ten years, had been in decline until the recent economic downturn. It is noticeable that households on benefits for more than ten years had been on the increase even before the current economic slump. Table 7.7 looks at this trend according to the household types. The households on benefits for longer than ten years, naturally, are more numerous among aged households. Since 1990, more than forty per cent of aged households have been on benefits for more than ten years. There are two peaks among the disabled households, those which have been on benefits for between one and three years and for more than five years. This may be due to the differences between sickness and injury. Single mother households are fairly evenly spread, with those on benefits for between one and three years the most predominant. When looking at the transition over the years, the proportion of longer term beneficiaries has been on the increase among aged and disabled households.

This, however, only indicates the duration of receipt of benefits for those on a benefit now. This does not show the record of the *hi hogo* class, that is, how many times they have been on benefits before. To find this, we will look at the record of those who just started on benefits from the statistics showing the dynamics of the *Seikatsu hogo*. Table 7.8 shows from among the households which started receiving the *Seikatsu hogo* benefit during September 2002, the households which had received the benefit before. They are divided according to their reasons for receiving the benefit and according to the time which has lapsed since the last time they received the benefit. During September 2002, a total of 16,994 households started receiving the benefit, and 23.3% of these had been on the benefit before.

Forty percent of the households which had been on the benefit before were receiving it again after less than three months' interval. More than 62.2% were receiving it again within twelve months. When analysing this in relation to the reasons why they needed the benefit, the emergency admittances record an extremely high percentage. For those suffering from sickness and injury, more than sixty per cent returned to the benefit within twelve months. A similar trend can be observed for those with a loss or reduction in income, and those going through separation, but there are slightly more of those cases returning after a five year interval. It is not just the lengthening duration of the time they are on benefits that matters. There seems to be about ten per cent of households which keep coming on and off benefits, even though the time of duration

Table 7.8: Households with previous experience of being on benefits and the interval since last benefit received

Interval since benefit	Total no.	Total %	Injury and sickness no.	Injury and sickness %	Separation by death or divorce no.	Separation by death or divorce %	Loss or reduction in income no.	Loss or reduction in income %	Other no.	Other %	Emergency protection no.	Emergency protection %
Total	3,041	100.0	1,798	100.0	141	100.0	488	100.0	1,514	100.0	789	100.0
<3 mth	1,613	40.9	670	37.3	23	14.9	142	29.1	780	51.5	561	71.1
3–6 mth	466	11.8	206	11.5	11	7.8	54	11.1	195	12.9	113	14.3
6–12 mth	392	9.9	198	11.0	17	12.1	49	10.0	128	8.5	50	6.3
1–2 yr	368	9.3	188	10.5	20	14.2	59	12.1	101	6.7	28	3.5
2–3 yr	194	4.9	105	5.8	11	7.8	22	4.5	56	3.7	8	1.0
3–4 yr	124	3.1	59	3.3	11	7.8	18	3.7	36	2.4	8	
4–5 yr	89	2.3	46	2.6	5	3.5	16	3.3	22	1.5	5	
>5 yr	695	17.6	326	18.1	45	31.9	128	26.2	196	12.9	16	

Source: Heisei 14 nendo *Shakai fukushi gyōsei gyōmu hōkoku* (The 2002 business report, social welfare administration).

is short. This is the case with chronic poverty, but the system (and the *hi hogo* households themselves) makes them look like transient cases because they come on and off the benefit frequently. In other words, there is a *hi hogo* class locked in deep inside the *Seikatsu hogo* system, as well as one hovering in and out of the same system. For both these cases, the *Seikatsu hogo* plays the role of keeping those in chronic poverty down around the minimum living standard level and does not let them go.

The continuous return to benefits, as well as the lengthening period on benefits can be seen in the reasons for their leaving the system. As shown in table 7.9, there are a smaller number of positive reasons, such as recovery and an increase in income. There are more cases of death, going missing, or discontinuation of medical assistance due to emergency admittance into other types of assistance in the *Seikatsu hogo* system. Their repeated admittance to the system is manifested in the form of coming back to the system through emergency admittances and the cycle of onset and treatment. During this process, a proportion of the *hi hogo* class, instead of representing the contemporary poor in general, gains a special position as long term *hi hogo* or people with a multiple record of being *hi hogo*.

Re-integration of the working poor

As I have pointed out repeatedly above, the fact of the *hi hogo* class becoming increasingly non-working and the lengthening of their time on benefits, indicates that the original function of the *Seikatsu hogo* system to assist social security services by dealing with the poverty of the modern working household, especially with transient poverty, is weakening. As several poverty rate measurements suggest, poverty is not restricted to chronic poverty among unemployed households. The measurements unanimously point to a high poverty rate among people with unsteady employment and poverty among the young and single mother households. As we look at the poverty dynamics of young women in Chapter 3 of this book, we cannot help being surprised by the magnitude of transient poverty among young people. The issue of the working poor, who are not part of the *hi hogo*, is often discussed using terms like the low income earning class.

Historically speaking, conscious mention has been made of the low income earning class at the beginning of the era of high economic growth, at the time of the oil crisis and in the

Table 7.9: The reasons for ceasing to receive the benefit (September 2002)

	Households ceasing to receive the benefit	
	Number	%
Total	10,817	100.0
Invalid	2,124	19.6
Death	2,252	20.8
Missing	1,265	11.7
Increase in income	1,255	11.6
Increase in social security	508	4.7
Increase in allowance	82	0.8
Taken over	295	2.7
Moved into facilities	200	1.8
Other	3,891	36.0
Emergency admittance	2,294	21.2

Source: Heisei 14 nendo *Shakai fukushi gyōsei gyōmu hōkoku* (The 2002 business report, social welfare administration).

current economic stagnation. All of these are economic slumps accompanying structural change. I have already discussed the vagueness of the yardstick used to measure what constitutes low income in the first chapter. Recently, low income is often referred to as either the bottom ten or bottom twenty per cent of the income scale. Either way, it means a lower position in the relative spread of income. Since the *Seikatsu hogo* standard became the relative standard, its poverty line has been determined in comparison to the income and consumption levels of low income earners. In other words, poverty is thought to be associated with low income earners. Maybe because of this, the *hi hogo* class, which has increasingly become nonworking, is often brought out into the open and compared with the low income earning class as a whole. This may sound contradictory, but on the one hand the existence of a class that is cut off from the social standard and left at the bottom of society, is becoming clearly visible. On the other hand, it is more likely to be examined critically as the *hi hogo* for its relatively higher standard of living and security in comparison to the low income earning class, especially the working poor.

The lack of adequate policies directed towards the working poor, and their exclusion from the *hi hogo* class through the strict application of the qualification for the *Seikatsu hogo* system, have made them look critically at the fixed existence of the *hi hogo*, resulting in friction between them. Workers who pay for the pension contribution, may find it unfair that the *Seikatsu hogo* payment is set above the basic pension pay out. Working single mother households may consider unemployed single mother households on benefits to be having an easy life. Once considered to be synonymous with poverty, the *hi hogo* have become the target of criticism from the larger poverty class surrounding them. Only when many low income earners are admitted to the *Seikatsu hogo* system and become a temporary 'class with *hogo* records,' when the *hi hogo* class is constantly renewed from poverty groups with a wider range of risks and needs, as a result of widening the narrow door of the system or through more public assistance and when benefits such as youth housing assistance and child benefits become available, I believe only then will the *hi hogo* become reconnected to social standards and in a position to represent poverty in general.

8 Women, welfare policies and poverty: Poverty and shelter among homeless women

Keiko Kawahara

Poverty, social and welfare policies

It has been argued that welfare policies meddle in people's daily lives (Takegawa 2001: 33). The grounds for this claim are clearly observable but are, of themselves, variable. Social policies concerning women in particular have a lot to do with the household as the basic unit of private life. How women are perceived in relation to a family, to their partners and children, determines justification for policy intervention in women's lives. Social policy is in the first place designed and formulated to remove and eliminate unacceptable conditions in social life. Yet, how a given policy intervention occurs depends on the predominant values of society at the time.

The basis for social policies is 'poverty'. Poverty is not just a state of affairs, it is an unacceptable state of affairs (Alcock 1997: 3–4). Central understanding of the need for social policy intervention (here, the 'object' of an intervention) rests on identification of social conditions. In all policy interventions, two processes must be followed to define an object as a social welfare concern. The first is *problem recognition*, in which a social condition is initially identified as 'unacceptable to be ignored,' and therefore requires a 'solution'. Then, second, the acknowledged problem is re-defined as an *object* in the context of social welfare policy. Definition of the object of a policy intervention follows examination of its conditions and circumstances from particular social welfare angles. Judgment is here made on whether or not a situation should be brought into the social welfare field. This process determines the aspects of the problem that policy could address and how solutions could be achieved. Therefore, the aims of a social welfare policy can be understood through how it is framed and what it means (i.e. a value judgment) (Iwata 2001: 28–29).

This chapter discusses how women's poverty has been defined and handled in Japanese social welfare policy. As Alcock (1997) has shown, poverty is something society cannot accept and must address. Social welfare policy analysts have called for measures, and have implemented interventions to address women's poverty. The definition of 'conditions unacceptable to be ignored' however, varies widely and so does opinion and perception on where to focus the issue (i.e. how to frame the object). They can contradict and overlap each other and need to be prioritized. First, the chapter discusses the relationship between women and poverty, and then how poverty has been recognized by welfare policy using the shelter-protection policy in Tokyo as a case study. Then, an examination will follow of the characteristics and meaning embodied in the welfare policy designed as a social response to the poverty of women.

Women and poverty

First, a few things must be noted about women and poverty. This is important because poverty among women tends to manifest itself differently from poverty among men, and women's risk factors for poverty are different. These differences, which arise from the difference in genders, are based on respective social and economic position.[1]

The feminisation of poverty

Since the late 1970s, the feminisation of poverty has been discussed earnestly, mainly in the US. Behind this were demographic factors, as an increasing number of households were then headed by women. The growth was due to an increase in longevity, the rising rate of divorce, higher extramarital child birth, among lesser factors. A subsequent relative increase in poor households headed by women, featured in the trend, and the proportion of women on welfare assistance had grown.

The study of the feminisation of poverty examined the following perspectives on the relationship between women and poverty, which had often been neglected in the study of poverty. First, the nuclear family, which constituted the basic unit in modern society, presupposed a sexual division of labour, where a male breadwinner and his dependent wife who does in the home including housework, child rearing and caring for the sick. Although engaged in labour in much the same way as men, women worked mostly at home and were unpaid. Therefore, they are economically dependent on their husbands. To women, the breakdown of a family means the loss of the main wage earner, thus increasing the risk of living in poverty. Second, women are tended to be considered as second-rate in the labour market, because of gender biased discrimination based on the fact that their primary work is domestic duties. This is one of the reasons for their lower pay. It is difficult for them to participate in work outside the home on an equal footing with men because women with a husband and children have to perform unpaid domestic work in the home. When women engage in work outside the home, they tend to break off their careers or to be engaged in part-time jobs and have shorter working hours than their male counterparts because of their domestic role. Their employment is also seen as only supplementary to their husband's main income, justifying the payment of low wages to women. Furthermore, because of the still prevailing traditions such as gender occupational segregation and discrimination in the workplace, women's job opportunities are concentrated in lowly paid work. It has been pointed out that this relatively lower position of women in the labour market has contributed to their poverty (Goldberg and Kremen 1990: 3–5).

Third, not only the labour market but also the welfare and taxation systems presuppose and hence reinforce the traditional notion of sexual division of labour. This is where men are seen as the main wage earners, and women are assumed to be unpaid domestic labourers. Criticism has been levelled at the fact that women's rights to receive benefits, especially the rights of married women, are judged in conjunction with their marital status, because they are primarily seen as the spouses of the main income earning husbands, as dependents and homemakers, while men are guaranteed various income replacement benefits, as full-time workers and breadwinners.

These and other issues raised in the discussion of the feminisation of poverty point out that the preventive measures previously put in place such as income insurance for the reduction or loss of income arising from unemployment or sickness of the main wage earners are not sufficient. They also point out that the loss of the main wage earner, due to divorce, separation or death, especially for women who rely financially on their husbands or partners, increases the risk of the women casting into poverty. On the other hand, the traditional full-time, life-long and permanent labour market, which the typical social security system has presupposed, has been undermined by the more flexible new labour market, characterized by part-time, temporary, short-term (in other words, lowly paid) employment contracts, because the corporations are seeking to maintain their international competitiveness in the globalised market. Women are increasingly called for in that flexible labour market, which has been discussed in relation to their marginalization and to their growing poverty (Doherty 2001: 11).

Recent studies have concentrated on women's poverty and the magnitude of poverty in households headed by women. This has emerged through a number of concurrent factors, including demographic change in Western society, (i.e. a departure from the traditional household made up of two adults and children to a greater number of non-traditional households -single-parents, single-person households and female-headed households), increasing participation by women in the work force and expansion of the new labour market with its low-status and low-paid employment (Glendinning and Millar 1987). At the same time, feminist analysis of the welfare state that focuses on the experience of poverty and the risk factors involved, has noted that these experiences and factors vary between men and women within households. These studies revealed the structural differences between men and women in the socio-economic system which studies on poverty until recently had failed to see.

Labour and household differences

Though discussion of the feminisation of poverty was introduced into the country in the late 1980s (Sugimoto 1986; Ozawa 1990), those studies did not delve as deeply into labour studies as corresponding research the West. Meanwhile, Japan's industrial structure changed in response to global competition, with a resultant growth in irregular employment such as part-time and temporary work (Furugori 1997). Consequently, women, especially married women, were pushed into the margins of the labour market (Nomura 1998).

As Kimiko Kimoto has noted, contemporary female workers do not necessarily fall into two primary groups, an 'elite class' which strives for upward career development in much the same way as their male counterparts, and part-timers who also do housework and child rearing. There are many who do not fit into either of these groups. Having said that, in the countryside where the 'modern family model' based on gender division of labour is still dominant, women are still seen principally as homemakers and child-rearers. Hence 'traditional' employment practices which rely on the modern family model continue (Kimoto 2000: 10–11). In traditional employment practice, male workers are expected to be fully committed company men, who devote themselves to working long and irregular hours without being responsible for housework or child rearing, and are paid compensating family wages.[2] Female workers, on the other hand, especially those who are married, are burdened with the primary responsibility at home, and their work outside the home is considered to be secondary. This family model is, in reality, the accepted one in Japanese society. The participation rate in the labour force according to women's age and class still continues to form an M shaped curve, where most women choose a reemployment pattern, retiring temporarily from paid work to rear children and do housework and then returning to the work force when their children are older.[3] When they return to work, women tend to opt for part-time work which takes less time away from their domestic responsibilities.[4]

As in the West, and noted in Japanese studies of the feminisation of poverty, the collapse of families can also present a higher poverty risk to women here. Along with the fact that the traditional perception of the household permeates through the labour market, the relatively lowly position of female workers increases their risk of poverty. This is especially so where women are the sole or main household income earners, such as in homes made up of women with children, single women, and women with unemployed or sick husbands. Though they are the main wage earners in these scenarios, their wages are unavoidably influenced by the lowly position of part-time female workers in general, in a society where most of the married female workers are employed part time (Nomura 1998; Kumazawa 2000). Furthermore, part time employment does not usually come with the various rights and fringe benefits afforded to full time employment. The level of unionization, one of the means of creating stability and improving working conditions among part time female workers, is extremely low (Pāto taimu rōdō kenkyūkai 2002).

There have not been many studies done on women and poverty. One of the rare examples is by Masami Iwata, utilizing panel data. In the third chapter of this book, Hamamoto gives her analysis of the relationship between women and poverty. According to these studies, the significant factor in women's poverty is the existence of a fluid 'temporary poor' class, who move in and out of poverty, as well as those locked into long term poverty. It is pointed out that women are forced into poverty due to changes in family circumstances such as separation and divorce, and because of child birth and changes to employment. Those locked into long term poverty, are characterized by a lack of partners, employment and disability (Iwata 1999).

Visible and submerged poverty

As we have seen, women are more vulnerable to changes arising from their life cycle and their family relations, and their relatively lowly position in the labour market. Of course, the depth and condition of women's poverty varies. When a woman escapes from a violent husband, for example, losing her shelter and livelihood temporarily, the social assistance required to help her to rebuild her life differs. In such cases, if she does not have much in the way of material assets, no help from other family members and little experience of work, or if she has tertiary qualifications and has had regular long term employment, she will face different challenges and future possibilities. Because of this, the depth of poverty is not necessarily the same.

These characteristics have lot to do with how women's poverty is manifested. Women's poverty may manifest itself because of unstable employment, low income, unemployment and other factors relating to the lower position women in general occupy in the labour market. Alternately, poverty can be triggered directly by the collapse of relationships such as in divorce, separation, death, running away from home or desertion. Poverty that results from the collapse of relationships can be easier to understand, as its development tends to be sudden and it presents with more urgency. A typical example of this would be women leaving home, escaping from their abusive husbands and domestic violence. For women, domestic violence, and their escape from it means the total loss of the lives they have created up till then. Their hardship can be extreme, as they might have to quit the jobs they have had for a long time, or they might have to limit their contact with their relatives and friends, simply to prevent their husbands finding them.

Even in the case of poverty directly resulting from unemployment and unstable employment, women may have experienced the collapse of relationships beforehand.⁵ Yet this does not necessarily involve a break up, as in the case of unmarried women suffering from sickness, the loss of their job, or unemployment due to old age. Also, the difficulty of obtaining employment due to factors relating to being a single parent such as unmarried pregnancy, birth and child care is rather to do with the relationship between a life event which relates particularly to women and the labour market, than to do with the collapse of relationships. When women are brought into poverty through the collapse of relationships or because of reasons to do with the labour market, more often than not as well as these factors various other complex factors overlap and can cause a chain reaction. For example, the collapse of relationships could be preceded by various types of friction between the couples or within the families. These could include multiple debts from consumer finance, relentless exaction attempts by debt collectors, bankruptcy of the business, incidence and revelation of extra-marital relationships, physical violence, pregnancy, child abuse, juvenile delinquencies, or substance abuse. It is noted that domestic violence and child abuse do not manifest as themselves so much but as various factors that destabilize the household finances, such as loss of jobs, business bankruptcy, illness, pregnancy and child birth, child rearing, physical disorders, accidents, irregular employment, prostitution, gambling, lack of informal networks, overstaying and vagrancy (Shōya 1996; Eguchi 1979; Aoki 2003; Otomo 1985).

There are also cases where women's poverty is concealed. Because their poverty often manifests itself through the collapse of relationships, it can be concealed when the relationship is maintained. For example, in families seemingly not in dire straits women may be in de facto poverty, because of a disproportionate distribution of resources at home (Alcock 1997: 135–136). Though the household income level may be above the poverty line, the husband may have to pay off consumer loans, he may spend it all on gambling or drinking, or he may not contribute at all to living expenses. These hidden poverty cases of women are, more often than not, revealed only after the collapse of relationships.⁶ Osamu Aoki notes that from his research into single mother on welfare assistance, more than a few of them revealed that their livelihood had improved and more stable after their separation because of receiving means-tested welfare benefits as single mother even if their living standard is minimum. Aoki concludes this is because 'they feel more stable in comparison with the poverty, uncertainty and the state of mind they had had to endure before divorce, and they feel more secure because they can control over their lives by themselves.' (Aoki 2003: 226)

Even though the family might be in extreme difficulties, if the relationships were loose and constantly changing, the poverty of the household including that of the woman, could often be concealed. According to my own research among poor families, family relationships can be very loose, with marriages and de facto relationships constantly following divorces and separations.[7] In these cases, the instability of family life is not clearly visible, as the women lodge with friends or relatives after separation, or start new live-in work with new partners. In other words, poverty becomes apparent only when, after marriage breakdown, women cannot find anywhere to live, or they cannot find any live-in work and are in dire straits. In such cases, they are accommodated in welfare facilities, these can be a married household, or single mother household, depending on when they come under protection.

Tokyo homeless women

Welfare policy and women's poverty

While women's poverty has the above mentioned characteristics, it can manifest itself in many different ways. In general, it is likely that hidden poverty tends to remain unnoticed and so no real welfare policy response can be expected. On the other hand, when poverty surfaces it attracts a response. Because women's poverty tends to occur due to the collapse of relationships and to their relatively lowly position in the labour market, the response will also tend to focus on some of these characteristics. The exact characteristics of women's poverty on which the actual welfare measures focus have naturally changed according to the dominant value judgment of the time and the society. Some of those measures, aimed at the problem of the collapse of relationships, may not have been recognized as a response to women's poverty. The welfare programmes considered to have been aimed specifically at women's poverty, range widely from the *Izoku nenkin* (pension for the bereaved), *Jidō fuyō teate* (childcare allowance for single mother with low income), *Shikin kashitsuke seido* (fund loan scheme), *Hoiku seisaku* (childcare policies), *Ikuji shien* (child rearing support) and others.

What these programmes consider unacceptable varies as to the level of poverty of women and the factors and the channels through which they got there. These different programmes have at least one thing in common, in that they directly deal with women in extreme predicaments such as having lost the basis for their daily existence and having nowhere to go. That is, being in a state of homelessness, living at one or another welfare facility. Therefore, I will focus on the most explicit condition of women's poverty, the state of homelessness, for which every welfare programme agrees that provision of some kind of assistance at a welfare facility is required. Using the example of Tokyo, I will examine the welfare policies concerning *whose* and *what* is the problem and what response is called for.[8] In the following section I will particularly examine the types of policies implemented, and how the recipients of the policies are defined.

Homeless women in Tokyo

There are various welfare programmes for homeless people based on the 2002 *Hōmuresu no jiritsu shien tō ni kansuru tokubetsu sochihō* (hereafter, abbreviated to *Hōmuresu jiritsu shienhō* or the Act on Special Measures to assist Homeless People become Financially Independent). In greater Tokyo, most of these are aimed at homeless single men. Accordingly, for women who have no home or anywhere to go it is very difficult to access those programmes, though individual women may be legally entitled to be considered homeless, as they are living on the street. The welfare programmes available for homeless women in Tokyo are very complicated, including temporary protective care based on the *Baishun bōshi hō* (The Prostitution Prevention Act), temporary protection based on the *Haigūsha karano bōryoku bōshi oyobi higaisha no hogo ni kansuru hōritsu* (The Act for Prevention of Spousal Violence and the Protection of Victims, hereafter, abbreviated to the Domestic Violence Prevention Act), emergency temporary accommodation at facilities for fatherless family under the *Jidō fukushi hō* (The Child Welfare Act), emergency temporary accommodation at facilities operating under the *Seikatsu hogo hō* (Daily Life Security Law, *Seikatsu hogo* means public assistance in Japan) and the *Shakai fukushi hō* (The Social Welfare Service Act). This confused state of affairs is, in a way, a reflection of the history of how welfare programmes aimed at homeless women have developed.

In short, the interpretation of the Acts for which these welfare facilities were originally set up, has been extended to accommodate these women. The facilities are accommodating women they were not originally intended for. This extended interpretation of the Acts and their application to those for whom they were not originally meant is not done in a consistent manner throughout the nation. Instead, it is done on the spot, where an individual case is assessed, understood and dealt with. Therefore, what is going on in Tokyo is just an example, not necessarily a general rule. One important thing we must note is, however, that homelessness is generally a more urban phenomenon, due to more unstable employment and the various modes of living which accompany this. Women's homelessness is no exception. In a way, those implementing Tokyo's welfare programme have had no choice other than to face this problem, and, as we will see later, in dealing with it they have helped other local authorities with the issue. In that respect as well, it is worthwhile following Tokyo's example.

Responses under the *Fujin hogo jigyō*

In dealing with homeless women, a pivotal role has been played by the *Fujin hogo jigyō* (The Programme to Assist Women in Need of Protection), stipulated under the *Baishun bōshi hō* (The Prostitution Prevention Act). Most of these homeless women have been sheltered as women in need of protection, at the temporary shelters attached to the Women's Counselling Centre, which operates under the programme. Japan has a long history of prostitution along with the *Haisyo undo* (Prostitution Abolition Movement). Public prostitution under state regulations existed even after the end of the last War. Quite a large number of women had to resort to prostitution for survival in the economic collapse that followed the end of the War. In those days, a flesh trade racket for prostitution was rife, and many poor children were traded all over the country to disreputable bars in order to make money for their family. The policy dealing with women involved in prostitution in the immediate aftermath of the War was called *Tokushu fujin hogo jigyō* (The Programme to Assist Special Women), and even before the enactment of the Prostitution Prevention Act, in order to prevent the spread of sexually transmitted disease and protect public health, 'harmful' people were institutionalized, medically examined, and put into rehabilitation {*Tokyo to minsei kyoku* (Bureau of social services, Tokyo metropolitan government) 1948}. As was the case with the subsequent Prostitution Prevention Act, *Tokushu fujin hogo jigyō* which was also aimed at preventing the fall of women and children into prostitution, it included in its scope not just those already in the business, but also those who 'might fall.' Those who might fall included 'street loiterers,' 'fresh home leavers,' and other single young women estranged from their family or who had lost their family, which covered in some degree what we call homeless women today.[9]

The 1965 Prostitution Prevention Act defined prostitution as 'harmful to human dignity, violating sexual morals, and downgrading the public morals of society.' It was enacted in order to prevent prostitution by institutionalizing and reforming the 'women who might commit sexual intercourse and prostitution (hereafter, abbreviated to women in need of protection)' (The Prostitution Prevention Act, article one).[10]

The 'women in need of protection' that the Act was intended for were made up of 'women already in the prostitution business' and 'women, who through running away from home, vagrancy and so on, have the potential to fall.'[11] The criteria for this potential continued to gradually widen. For example, at the time of enactment, the women considered to have this potential were defined as runaways and vagrants, just as they were under the *Tokushu fujin hogo jigyō*, and they constituted only about eight per cent of the women handled by the Women's Counselling Centre. But, in the 1969 edition of the annual report of the programmes summary, it is stated that 'it is extremely difficult to ascertain what condition they can be in,' and it goes on to list some real life examples of 'women who might fall,' drawn from the cases the centre handled in 1967, such as 'runaway girls, delinquent girls, and women who have been deserted by men and have nowhere to go – more often than not, these women are pregnant'. The number of these women had increased until they had become a third of the women the centre handled (*Tokyo to fujin sōdansho* [the Tokyo Women's Counselling Centre] 1969: 14). The annual report of the programmes summary notes that, because prostitution was becoming more implicit and difficult to police, preventing women from taking up prostitution should be considered as the top priority for the Women's Counselling Centre, that the interpretation of who should be protected should not be too rigid, and that the application should be flexible (ibid: 23). The potential candidates for prostitution continued to increase, and a report from 1971, only four years later, shows these women were now three quarters of the cases handled, the majority of the women being given temporary protective care.

The tendency to widen the interpretation of potential candidates is to do with the fact that right from the start a smaller than expected number of women turned up looking for shelter and protection under the *Fujin hogo jigyō* (the Programme to Assist Women in Need of protection), and that within just a few years following the Act coming into force, the prosecution rate dropped drastically (Nakano 1973: 293). In other words, there was a significant decline in the number of legitimate cases for which the programme was originally intended.[12] Therefore, the *Fujin hogo jigyō* facilities including the Women's Counselling Centre could afford to use their spaces and resources to respond the rise of potential candidates. While, from around 1965, it was noted on the ground, that a number of women were fleeing from violent drunken partners. 'We sheltered those women who were escaping from domestic violence and had nowhere to go, no money and nobody from whom to seek help, under the category of "potential candidate",' I heard.[13] Also some domestic problems were brought to the social welfare office, but were passed on to 'the women's counsellors, because the welfare office was not staffed with anyone who could handle them.' (Kamano 1997: 8) In this way the general domestic problems of the women were dealt with within the framework of the *Fujin hogo jigyō* established under the Prostitution Prevention Act.

The recognition of the problems on the ground led to the first notification of the Ministry of Health and Welfare (now the Ministry of Health, Labour and Welfare) in 'Government contributions and subsidies to the *Fujin hogo jigyō* in 1970 (bulletin #33),' which accepted that the programme should cover a wider target group.[14] The Ministry's statement, though reluctant and merely confirming the fact of the widened interpretation and the necessary responses being provided on the ground, instructed the *Fujin hogo jigyō* to extend the net to help women who did not actually have the potential to fall but had a number of life problems, because there was no other appropriate institution (Nishimura 1984: 36–37). Following these instructions, as referred to above, the number of women who were homeless for various reasons, given temporary assistance, surged suddenly. To give some idea of the sorts of women were given help at that time, I will quote the following detailed account.

> Recently, numerous and varied cases have been depending on the counselling facilities, particularly because of their temporary protection capacity and the accommodation facilities for women in need. Those seeking help from us are referred to us from other public authorities including the police, as there are no other appropriate facilities or organizations under other laws and programmes they could turn to. Some require extremely urgent attention, including

temporary accommodation at once. Those seeking help include, for example, mothers with children seeking temporary respite from the violence of their husbands, (remitted) psychiatric patients who have no guardians (guarantor), unidentifiable mentally disabled runaway vagrants, psychopaths (including women with personality disorders) who cannot fit into society, pregnant women who have been deserted (left behind) by their men and have nowhere to go, syphilis carriers who cannot find a job, and so on. Society's need for emergency protection is getting greater and greater, year after year. In 1971, the Women's Counselling Centre assisted 580 people (actual number), and among them, 25% were prostitutes (with a history of prosecution) while the remaining 75%, the overwhelming majority, were from the various groups mentioned above who required urgent assistance.

We expanded our interpretation of the Act to help prevent them from becoming prostitutes, taking on a supplementary role to the other Acts and systems, because there are no other appropriate organizations (*Tokyo to minsei kyoku* (Bureau of Social Services, Tokyo metropolitan government) 1973: 326–365, emphasis added by the author).

Later, with the rise of the feminist movement which was partly spurred by the International Year of Women in 1975, as well as through having a more progressive government in power, the Tokyo government passed the 'Metropolitan Women's Counselling Centre Ordinance' in 1977. Under this ordinance, not only those defined under the Prostitution Prevention Act, but also '*All* women and the children under their care, who are in need of urgent protection or help to support themselves (emphasis by the author)' would be given equal (as those defined under the Prostitution Prevention Act) opportunity to receive counselling, guidance and assistance (*Tokyo to fujin sōdan sentā* [Tokyo metropolitan women's counselling centre] 1978: 1).[15] This, by confirming what had been done at the coalface, clearly stated for the first time that there would be provision for emergency assistance to 'women and children, fellow human beings in need for whatever reason,' in other words, to women in general. In 1985, the '*Fujin hogo jigyō* operation procedure' was revised, and the widening of the net began to extend to the rest of the country. In 1992, the Japanese name for the Tokyo metropolitan Women's Counselling Centre was changed from *Tokyo to fujin sōdansho* to *Tokyo to josei sōdan sentā*, using the word *josei* instead of *fujin*. The Ministry of Health and Welfare's notification in the same year, 'On the operating procedure for *Fujin hogo jigyō* (Ministry notification/

shasei #95)'[16] and its partial revision in 1999 (Ministry *shaenho* #17), reaffirmed the widening of the definition of the women to be assisted. The Tokyo government now considers that the rest of the nation has caught up with their extension of the safety net for women.[17]

As we have seen, homeless women including victims of domestic violence, have been able to be given temporary protection at the women's counselling centre through the expedient of widening the interpretation of the target group defined by the Prostitution Prevention Act. This measure was taken because 'there was no alternative,' there were no other organizations that could help. Even though temporary protection of the women under the *Fujin hogo jigyō* was an inevitable temporary measure in relation to the other laws and programmes, it is gradually gaining legitimacy. Let us now see the response of other welfare programmes apart from the *Fujin hogo jigyō* to homeless women.

Other welfare measures

Under the welfare programme put in place after the end of the War, homeless people in Tokyo were impounded for their protection into public facilities.[18] The overwhelming number of people of no fixed address including vagrants and shanty residents in the central districts of Tokyo were routinely rounded up from the winter of 1945 to the 1950s. As a result they had almost disappeared by the opening of the 1964 Olympic games in Tokyo {*Tokubetsuku jinji kōsei jimu kumiai shakai fukushi jigyōdan* (the Association of the Tokyo 23 special wards for personnel and welfare affairs) 2000: 23–28}. Those who were rounded up at this time ranged from children, single persons (male/female), and single women with children and families. They were impounded mostly in facilities built under the *Seikatsu hogo hō* (Public Livelihood Protection Act). In order to cater for different needs separate shelters for single people, families, and the disabled were built.

The compound (*Seikatsu hogo* facility) to accommodate *vagrant women with children* who were picked up *loitering* around the underpass at the railway station at Ueno and elsewhere, was called *Furō boshi ryō* (the shelter for vagrant women with children) and clearly differentiated from the ordinary *boshi ryō* built under the *Jidō fukushi hō* (The Child Welfare Act) (ibid: 30). The Tokyo metropolitan government, which had carried out measures for the 'protection (welfare) of women with children' since before the War, placed special emphasis on the accommodation of the father-less families who were in dire straits in the immediate aftermath of the War. The core of the programme was through the *boshi ryō* built under the *Jidō fukushi hō* to 'give support to families of women with children who lost their husbands and houses due to the War, by providing a roof over their heads and jobs' (Matsubara 1999: 11). In this way, even though they were suffering similar consequences, the measures for suffering women with children in general such as the families of War widows and families of single mothers returning from the former colonies, were clearly differentiated from measures directed towards the 'special' ones including vagrants, and put in place separately.[19]

At the *Furō boshi ryō* (the Shelter for Vagrant Women with Children), the prostitutes and the potential prostitutes rounded up under the previously mentioned special *Fujin hogo jigyō* were also impounded, indicating how 'special' the 'vagrant' was considered in those days. Since the late 1950s, due to recommendations from the Ministry of Health and Welfare and others, upgrading of the facilities for protection in general, including accommodation facilities for vagrants, has been carried out in the metropolitan area. Finally, as a result of the revision of the Local Autonomy Law in 1965, and the subsequent transfer of the welfare programmes from the metropolitan government to the ward governments, most of the remaining *'boshi ryō* accommodation facilities for families of women with children were transferred from the jurisdiction of the *Seikatsu hogo* to that of the *Jidō fukushi* {*Tokubetsuku jinji kōsei jimu kumiai shakai fukushi jigyōdan* (the Association of the Tokyo 23 special wards for personnel and welfare affairs) 2000: 33–48}.[20] This meant that the homeless 'vagrant women with children,' who had been differentiated under the category 'special', were now handled in the same manner as the rest of the families of single mothers, under the *Jidō fukushi hō*.

Furthermore, the annex of the *Seikatsu kosei sodanjo* (the Counselling Centre for Life Rehabilitation, a rehabilitation facility under the Public Assistance Act) which had been set up in 1961 to provide temporary protection for single women, was abolished in 1965 when the transfer of power took place between the metropolitan government and the wards. Since then responsibility for dealing with single women in need of help has come under the metropolitan government's jurisdiction, and has been handled mainly through the *Fujin hogo* facilities under The Prostitution Prevention Act (ibid: 48). In this way, from the period immediately following the War, there have been three separate programmes existing alongside each other,

Tokushu fujin hogo jigyō (the Programme to Assist Special Women), then after the enactment of the Prostitution Prevention Act, *Fujin hogo jigyō*, there was the *Furōsha hogo jigyō* (the Programme to Assist Vagrants), and the *Boshi hogo jigyō* (the Programme to assist women with children in need), dealing with homeless women.

In about 1965, when the transfer of power between the metropolitan government and the wards took place, the foundation of the current means of welfare assistance for women in need was established. This was based on the makeup of the household. Families made up of women with children were compounded in the *Boshi ryo* (later renamed as the *Boshi seikatsu shien shisetsu*, or the Facilities to Assist the Lives of Women with Children) under the Child Welfare Act, while the single women were dealt with by the women's counselling centres or other *fujin hogo* facilities under the Prostitution Prevention Act. I should add that single homeless men continued to be dealt by the *Seikatsu hogo* facilities (shelters and rehabilitation accommodation under the Public Assistance Law).

Thus, the *fujin hogo jigyō* was extending its responsibilities to cover not only prostitutes and potential prostitutes, but also other women and women with children in general that were in dire circumstances. It should be noted that the timing of the transfer of welfare programmes between the metropolitan government and the wards, and the handing over of the single women in need of help from the *Seikatsu hogo* to the *fujin hogo* jurisdiction, coincided with welfare providers finding a 'significant increase in cases requiring urgent protection around 1965'. It is possible that the operational changes to the welfare programme as a whole might have brought about changes which affected the welfare service recipients.

The Tokyo metropolitan government launched a programme specifically targeting women with children, called the 'Emergency Protection Programme for Women with Children' in February 1973. This programme, utilizing the designated accommodation facilities for fatherless families, is still in operation today. At the launch of the programme, its target was defined as 'households of women with children in need of urgent protection,' in particular it recognized, 'women with no partner, or in an equivalent condition, seen to be lacking in the resources to provide welfare for children in their care, and in dire circumstances who require urgent protection.' This, apart from the section about 'in dire circumstances who require urgent protection,' was exactly the same as article 23 of the *Jidō fukushi hō* (The Child Welfare Act) of the time, which set out the qualifications for admittance to the *boshi ryō* shelter accommodation. In other words, the target of this programme was just the same with that of *bosi ryo*, except for following the necessary procedures before entering the accommodation. The director of the facility at the time of the launch explained this in an interview conducted by the author as follows.

> Before (the Emergency Protection Programme) was put in place there were social conditions which called for it, and a social need for it. There were a great many women with children fleeing their homes, needing emergency help in Tokyo, and there was a strong demand from the metropolitan government to set up (the programme). Because of the (husbands') violence, welfare facilities like ours (which would have to take on the responsibility) turned down (the demand from the government). We replied saying that the Tokyo metropolitan government should build a special shelter separately (from the existing *boshi ryō*), safe from violent husbands. However, the government thought that would be carrying things too far. The metropolitan government insisted (the programme) should be set up by designating some of the existing *boshi ryō*.
>
> Q: Why did it start in the middle of a budget year?
> There were plenty (of women with children who needed emergency protection). There were too many of them and a day could not be wasted. The urgency was there, that the programme had to be started immediately, even in the middle of the budget year. (Supplements in brackets are added by the author.)

From the start, the Emergency Protection Programme was clearly aimed at those women with children fleeing from their husbands' violence. That is why the existing shelters, because of the fear of physical reprisal from the husbands, initially turned down the government's demand, insisting instead on separate dedicated 'government owned and properly guarded' facilities. But, due to strong pressure from the metropolitan government the programme eventually got off the ground in the middle of the financial year, which was extremely unusual. We do not know exactly why the metropolitan government launched the programme with such a degree of haste. The previously mentioned report on the *fujin hogo* in Tokyo by the *Tokyo to minsei kyoku* (Bureau of Social Services, Tokyo metropolitan government) came out in March 1973, and the metropolitan government might have recognized the urgent need for the protection of women with children from their husbands' violence. Also the same report warned that *fujin hogo jigyō* is based on the Prostitution Prevention Act, which, unlike other welfare related acts, has a strong taint of criminal law. An extended interpretation of 'women who might become prostitutes' to cover all women in need means the welfare service providers tend to treat them as "potential candidates," and this may be against their will and may violate human rights.' The metropolitan government may have felt it necessary to offer an alternative for dealing with 'women in general' and their children escaping from violent husbands.

Incidentally, most of the *boshi ryō* shelters tended to prefer as their 'legitimate customers' the already divorced, the 'fully fledged' single mother families, or those with their divorce process already in set in place, to those 'yet to be divorced,' fleeing temporarily from violence in the home. It is possible that there was reluctance on the part of the social welfare system because 'a public authority should not meddle in domestic affairs,' and it only recognized the kinds of 'family/household' officially sanctioned by the domicile and resident register. The emergency protection programme for women with children ended up accepting de facto divorcee families into the *boshi ryō* which was not necessarily an accepted idea in those days.[21] The programme widened its scope to include those in 'dire circumstances who required urgent protection,' making homelessness the sole criteria.

Later, in 1982, in the notification 'on admittance to the *boshi ryō* (jihatsu #514),' the Ministry of Health and Welfare made it clear that the 'equivalent conditions' in article 23 of the *Jidō fukushi hō* (The Child Welfare Act) should include 'women whose marital union is as good as over, such as those who have run away from home due to their husband's violence, but *have not yet submitted a divorce notification due to circumstances beyond their control*' (emphasis added by the author). This is another example where Tokyo led the way for the rest of the country.

Today, in the Tokyo metropolitan area, the Emergency Protection Programme for Women with Children is carried out on the city and ward level as well, mostly at *boshi seikatsu shien shisetsu* (facilities to support the lives of father-less families), the *fujin hogo* facilities and contracted private sector shelters. Most of them began their operation after the previously mentioned notification #514 was issued by the Ministry. The emergency protection programme at the city and ward level is applied when it is believed that the women or women with children, if they are residents or running away from their home to a resident, are in 'dire circumstances which require urgent protection.' Nearly half the number (48.6%) of the *boshi seikatsu shien shisetsu* (facilities to assist the lives of father-less families) in the metropolitan Tokyo area, implement the emergency protection programme {*Tokyoto shakai fukushi kyōgikai boshi fukushi bukai* (The Subcommittee for the Welfare of Women with Children, Tokyo Council of Social Welfare) 2000: 35}.

Lastly, we should examine the Emergency Temporary Protection Programme implemented at the *Seikatsu hogo* facilities. As mentioned above, before the transfer of the jurisdiction of welfare programmes from the metropolitan government to the ward governments in 1965, the *Seikatsu hogo* facilities were actively involved in housing homeless women and women with children, whom they classified as 'vagrants.' But after the transfer a clear separation procedure was put in place, whereby the single women were to be looked after at the *fujin hogo* facilities, while the women with children were cared for at the *boshi ryō*. The *Seikatsu hogo* facilities from then on, handled the other people in need, such as single father households, general households (excluding the households of women with children), single males and returnee families from China. As mentioned above, however, the majority of the *boshi ryō* were not necessarily meant to cater for 'fleeing women with children,' victims of domestic violence, nor those separated de facto families who had not had time to go through the proper procedure. Under these circumstances, from the middle of the 1970s, the 'fleeing women with children' were also sheltered at the *seikatsu hogo* facilities under the 'de facto single mother household' classification {*Tokubetsuku jinji kōsei jimu kumiai shakai kōsei gyōmu iinkai* (Welfare Service Committee, the Association of the Tokyo 23 special wards for personnel and welfare affairs) 1979}. The 'de facto single mother household' meant that they were not the officially recognized single mother household as defined in the *jidō fukushi hō*. Because the *Seikatsu hogo hō* includes a clause to give priority to other acts and programmes, to function as an alternative to the *boshi ryō* which is under the *jidō fukushi hō*, and to give protection to de facto single mother families fleeing from the 'alcohol dependency, violence and abuse of the husbands (ibid: 14),' the 'de facto' classification was justified as a necessity. In those days the majority of family households including 'de facto single mother families' were admitted for temporary protection without having gone through official channels because they were fleeing from violence, exaction of consumer credit debts and so on (ibid). Furthermore, at the shelter for people in dire need built under the *Shakai fukushi jigyō hō* (The Social Welfare Services Act, currently the *shakai fukushi hō*) to provide free accommodation, or accommodation for a very small fee, there has been a significant increase in the single parent households lodging there since the late 1970s {*Tokubetsuku jinji kōsei jimu kumiai shakai fukushi jigyōdan* (the Association of the Tokyo 23 special wards for personnel and welfare affairs) 2000: 82}.

The existence of households in need of emergency protection was perceived by the workers on the ground as 'qualitative changes among service recipients' and 'needs lost in the gap between welfare systems' and seen as an issue for the welfare programmes and facilities to tackle in a proactive manner.[22] This later led to the beginning of the Emergency Temporary Protection Programme at the *Seikatsu hogo* facilities. The Programme at the *Seikatsu hogo* facilities and shelters which was started on an experimental basis in 1993, was intended to give one to three months temporary accommodation to those 'referred by the *fukushi jimusho* (Municipal Welfare Office), including households which receive *Seikatsu hogo* benefits (public assistance) and in need of protection , households other than recipients of *Seikatsu hogo* benefits and in need of protection, and households which would in future be taken care of by other acts or other programmes, but which were in need of temporary accommodation, until they could be admitted to the welfare facilities' (ibid: 113). To be more exact, three groups, families, single women and single men who had lost their homes as a result of disaster, were accommodated at the rehabilitation facilities or shelters in the *Seikatsu hogo* facilities, or the *shakai fukushi* shelters, depending on whether they were on a *Seikatsu hogo* benefit or not and on the extent of the care and help required.

We can see here that the temporary emergency protection programmes led the way for a more flexible application of the acts, by understanding and interpreting the actual situation, instead of adhering to a rigid interpretation of what constitutes a family, and therefore making the service available to more people, de facto families and individuals.

The Domestic Violence Prevention Act

The Domestic Violence Prevention Act was enacted in 2001 and came into force the following April. As we have seen already, women fleeing from violence and consequently without homes, with nowhere to go, had long been considered a 'common' problem by social welfare organizations (Sudo 2003). With the increase of concern about the incidence of domestic violence in society, the enactment of the Act clearly stated that violence even in a private environment constituted a bona fide crime and a violation of human rights, and gave the police and the public authorities power to pro actively intervene in the domestic problems of families and couples. The Act stipulates the prevention of violence to victims and the protection of victims, and this is the responsibility of the national and local authorities (the second clause). Under the Act, the prefectures are mandated to set up Spousal Violence Counselling and Support Centres where victims can seek temporary protection and counselling (the third clause). Victims are now able to apply for apprehended violence orders against the perpetrator (the tenth clause). Temporary protection is to be provided either at the women's counselling centres or by their contractors, and the Act makes it possible for the *fujin hogo jigyō* resources, counsellors and facilities, originally set up as a service under the Prostitution Prevention Act, to be utilized for the protection and the support of domestic violence victims. As such, the Domestic Violence Prevention Act can be said to have legitimized the practice of taking care of domestic violence victims. These women made up a number of the homeless women who had been looked after through the extended application of the 'potential to become prostitutes' interpretation by the *fujin hogo jigyō* which had made it possible to make this a nationwide approach. As a result, after the implementation of the Act, the Women's Counselling Centres naturally became full of women with no home and nowhere to go, who were looking for help. For example, before the Act came into effect, those seeking temporary protection were equally divided into 'homeless people or de facto homeless people, women and women with children escaping from their partners' violence, and people with psychiatric problems {the *Tokyo to fukushikyoku* (The Welfare Department, the Metropolitan Tokyo government) 2000}, but in 2002, 60% of these women were escaping from their husbands' or other relatives' violence {the *Tokyo uimenzu puraza* (the Tokyo Women's Plaza) 2003: 6}. It should be also noted that the occupancy rate of the temporary shelters these days is almost 100%, and they are nearly always full. Because of this, the homeless women who are not victims of domestic violence have now to resort to other facilities than the ones attached to the Women's Counselling Centres.[23]

The poverty of homeless women

Classifying homeless women

As we have seen so far, the welfare system has responded flexibly to homeless women, women in the worst visible predicament, by stretching the existing welfare system or changing the interpretation of the existing Acts, and by treating these women as 'potential prostitutes' who are 'in need of emergency protection.' Homelessness has, in other words, been tackled by accommodating homeless women in a welfare facility so that the condition of homelessness is eliminated. Most of the homeless women, in this way, are seen as 'potential prostitutes' who, if not given assistance, may commit a crime or become prostitutes. However, their situation is not understood from the point of view of poverty. Based on this perception and in order to prevent them from 'falling' into prostitution, emergency protection of homeless women has been justified. The conclusion from the particular understanding of the poverty of women is that the separation from family leads to a deviation from the social order and hence 'protection' is required. Homeless women, it can be seen, are separated from their families by 'running away,' for example or by being deserted by men. Therefore, they find themselves in an 'extraordinary' state which might lead to their becoming prostitutes. In Japan, family ethics based on the gender division of labour is still dominant, and accordingly the status of women in the labour market, generally speaking, is low. It is hard for women to become independent as 'workers' and they tend to be portrayed as 'economic underdogs'.

Based on that kind of general view of women in relation to the labour market, it is easy to conclude that single women when cut off from their supporting families or husbands could easily take up prostitution, by commodifying their bodies. Hence, out of concern for the maintenance of the social order, public intervention has been called for and is considered justified. This kind of thinking emphasizes on simply the result of the breakdown of family or couple relations among the various aspects of the poverty of women and views the poverty of women in the context of a social order issue and gives hardly any consideration to the possibility of independent women workers. Furthermore, the welfare policy aimed at homeless women with children also has placed more emphasis on vagrancy, meaning deviation from the social order, as well as deviation from the usual makeup of the family. Initially, they were called *furō boshi* (vagrant women with children), clearly differentiating them from the ordinary *boshi* such as those of the War widows.

The term *boshi* itself embodies the women's position, which can only be understood in relation to the family. With the gender based presupposition, women are seen first and foremost as mothers. Only when women perform the social role of the mother, when they are carers of children, do they come under the consideration of the children's welfare programme.[24]

Extending the welfare target group

The interpretation of just who should be protected, based on a rigid understanding of family relations, has had to be continuously widened and reinterpreted. This is because the existence of various different kinds of women who share the commonality of homelessness challenges the legitimacy of the official definition all the time. Generally speaking, a welfare programme has a specific target group, and is operated within those boundaries. The specific target group to whom the programme is applicable is separated from the rest, and the others, in principal, are discarded and excluded from the programme. But in actual practice, women in dire circumstances cannot be turned away just because they are not part of the specific target group. It was believed that they should be protected and they have been. In order to make the decisions about who should receive help as painless as possible, the decisions had to be given authorization. Hence the extended interpretation of the acts, the 'Metropolitan Women's Counselling Centre ordinance' and the setting up of the 'Emergency Protection Programme for Women with Children'. The target group had to be extended beyond potential prostitutes to include women in general, and all the women with children fleeing from violent husbands, because not only the properly divorced single-mother families needed to be accommodated. It could be said that the framework of the existing welfare jurisdictions was extended because there exist various different kind of women sharing one of the worst predicaments imaginable, homelessness. This is one of the reasons why the existing welfare programmes for homeless women have become so complicated, and homeless women have been prevented from having to live out on the streets only by the extended interpretation of the Acts.

Once the problem of homelessness is resolved by protection, however, instead of looking at the problems arising from poverty, attention tends to be focused on the factors and pathways that caused the homelessness which initially exposed the poverty. It is easy to conclude that the reason for homelessness which leads to conditions which require 'urgent protection' is always the result of poverty, but the contributing factors are varied and various. On the one hand common homelessness has drawn more flexible responses from the welfare service providers, but when it comes to their actual responses, it has led to a classification of the factors leading to homelessness and a prioritization of the targets. Of course, the factors and pathways which lead to homelessness are complex and complicated {Williams 1998; *Tokyoto shakai fukushi kyōgikai boshi fukushi bukai* (The Subcommittee for the Welfare of Women with Children, Tokyo Council of Social Welfare) 1998}. Whichever one of the contributing factors happens to be focused on from amongst the whole chain reaction depends on the dominant values and standards of the particular time and society. It is also highly likely to be influenced by the point of view of the individual welfare workers responsible for each case. For example: when a woman has to seek shelter after fleeing from a violent husband, and because she does not feel very comfortable staying with relatives and she has run out of money, what then is the reason for seeking shelter? Is it the violence of her husband, the lack of accommodation or economic hardship? Which should we choose? What if she had been under extreme pressure for the exaction of payment for consumer credit debts, as well as her husband's violence? Which do we choose the factor which directly triggered the homelessness, or the background factors which contributed indirectly? These sorts of difficulties arise all the time. It may be important to understand and analyze each and every individual factor but there always is going to be difficulty in pinpointing one, or stressing one, amongst the complex layers and chains of factors.

This difficulty is evident, as a new preferential system is coming into being following the enactment of the Domestic Violence Prevention Act, concerning who should be given emergency temporary protection. Until this it has been possible for the welfare facilities from their limited resources, to make flexible responses and to help homeless people. This was partly because the number of their 'rightful clients' was dwindling and they had found themselves with some spare capacity. But since the Domestic Violence Prevention Act came in force, helping domestic violence victims has become the responsibility of the national and local authorities, and it has become possible to mobilize facilities and related organizations of the *fujin hogo* programmes to provide this service. There is an emerging tendency to allocate the limited social resources to the newly redefined 'rightful clients,' domestic violence victims, who receive preferential treatment over others who have become homeless from factors other than domestic violence. On the other hand, in relation to this, we can see that the interpretation of domestic violence can be extended (or other factors can be reinterpreted as domestic violence) as well. For example, the poverty of women at home as a result of strict control over family finances by their husbands and so on, is considered to be psychological violence. Or domestic violence can be emphasized as the leading cause among many layers of contributing factors that lead women to become homeless. That is another example. It can be understood that the welfare programmes by stretching the boundaries of the existing systems in order to respond to homelessness which they saw as unacceptable and something that could not be ignored, may have begun the same process again with it. In any case, the welfare programmes for homeless women having the core principle of a need for protection for those separated from their family support mechanisms, have constantly been forced by the existence of women in related plights, to blur the boundaries of who is entitled be rightful clients and to change their preferential order.

9 Poverty and the social exclusion of single men: Perspectives on homeless men and their relationship with the welfare administration

Yukihiko Kitagawa

Administering welfare to the homeless

Since the middle of the 1990s, the so-called 'homeless people' have drawn public attention in Japan. These are people who can not find any other accommodation than sleeping rough out on the roadsides, parks and river banks in urban areas. The 'homeless problem' has become controversial; how to best deal with the homeless has become problematic. Relief efforts to help these people have been mounted by both official and non-official organizations. Prior to the 1990s, people have – of course – lived on the streets of major Japanese cities, though they were not as numerous as they are now.[1] Over time, various policies have been implemented to assist the homeless (and to those without a permanent address who might be likely to join them) and help them from their poverty. However, these programmes were not intended to include all people who were (or who might become) homeless. The programmes had their rightful targets, and their selection processes always aimed at including some and excluding others. In other words, Japan's welfare systems have separated the homeless into those who deserve protection and support and those who do not. These systems have given help to the former while excluding the latter. The widespread increase in people living on the streets since the 1990s could be in part due to the various welfare programmes that exclude the some of the homeless from protection and support.

New programmes launched since the late 1990s have sought to help homeless people become self reliant. These programmes have sought, at least on the surface, to include those who had so far been excluded at helping them rehabilitate themselves into society. Even though the selection criteria and background of these new approaches have changed quite markedly from those prior to 1990, a fundamental process still exists of separating people into those who are worth helping and those who are not. The purpose of this chapter is to look at the change in the criteria for social inclusion/exclusion applied by Japan's welfare programmes to the poor people who are roughing it (and to those without permanent home, mostly single males). In concrete terms, the period during the 1990s – when homeless people had become numerous and visible enough to constitute a 'homeless issue' and subsequent programmes to address the issue were planned and implemented – is used as the turning point in this chapter's analysis. I will concentrate on changes in the selection criteria used during this period and how these criteria were applied to the people in the worst circumstances, the people living on the streets. My focus here is limited mostly to Tokyo. In addition, because there has been a detailed study already done by Masami Iwata on the development of welfare systems aimed at people with no fixed address, I will refrain from looking at the overall picture and instead, will concentrate on analysing what seem to be the important changes which took place before and after 1990.

The day labourer market

Exclusion from *Livelihood Protection*

By definition, the *Seikatsu hogo* (Public Livelihood Protection) system guarantees a basic standard of living for all Japanese nationals.[2] Through its application, those who have lost their flat, their house, or other residence in a traditional sense (including those living on the street), are separated into those who can work and those who can not. In reality, the former have been excluded from the system. Those who have lost their place of residence, unless registered with the local welfare office, are seen as having no fixed address.[3] Those considered as having no fixed address, no matter how bad the plight they are in, if they are found capable of being able to work, will not be given much assistance (other than medical assistance) on the grounds that it is difficult to assess their material possessions due to their lack of a fixed address, or that they could not be classified as unemployed as they could find a day labourer's job tomorrow (which does not require a fixed address).[4] Here, the ability to work is strictly regarding physical ability, certified by a doctor. Because of this, such social factors as whether one has the opportunity to utilise this ability and whether this ability is called for in the job market of the day, are rarely taken into account.[5] As for medical certification, though a person might be suffering from sickness or injury, unless he or she needs to be hospitalized, he or she is more often than not classed as being able to do light duties, not as being unable to work. In that case, it is likely that the majority of assistance other than medical assistance (for example, livelihood assistance and housing assistance) would not be applicable to someone who is homeless. As for the criteria applicable to people with no fixed address to determine whether they are qualified for *Seikatsu hogo* assistance or not, the applicant's age is as significant as a medical certificate or the ability to work defined in the narrow sense mentioned above. If a person is considered elderly, he or she is past the working age and would be likely to get the *Seikatsu hogo* protection.[6] In short, those who are living on the streets have been excluded from the *Seikatsu hogo* protection scheme, unless they are considered to be too sick or too disabled to carry out light work, or are elderly. This policy framework more or less remains the same today.

In a 1995 survey of the workers at welfare offices throughout the Tokyo metropolitan area, Masami Iwata found that at most of the welfare offices, the support for homeless people came from extralegal measures outside the *Seikatsu hogo* programme (Iwata 2000: 290). Then in March 2001, the Ministry of Health, Labour and Welfare issued a notice on the basic application of the *Seikatsu hogo* programme to homeless people at the National Conference of Directors in charge of the *Seikatsu hogo* Programme for Local Government. In this notice the Ministry stated that

> [the] *Seikatsu hogo* programme is a programme designed to provide necessary assistance to people who cannot maintain a basic standard of living, no matter how hard they try to make use of their abilities, assets and so on. In other words, it is for those who are genuinely in dire straits. Accordingly, just because a person is homeless does not by that fact alone qualify them for assistance under the *Seikatsu hogo* Act. The same criteria apply as they do to the general household. Homelessness, or the ability to work alone, does not make one excluded from protection.

The very fact that the Ministry had to issue a renewed notice like this to local governments, though paradoxically, indicated that there was a tendency for them to apply different criteria to homeless people from 'ordinary' households.

As we will see later, demographically speaking, those living on the streets are overwhelmingly male. However, this does not necessarily mean that a smaller number of women find themselves in a similar predicament, unable to maintain a roof over their heads. Instead, this demographic imbalance only means the welfare systems have more options available for women in dire poverty, such as protection through the Anti-Prostitution Act and the Child Protection Scheme. Should they fall through the safety net of the *Seikatsu hogo* system, it is likely that they would be to be protected at the anti-prostitution related facilities or the emergency shelter for women with children, and they would not be visibly roughing it out on the street (Iwata and Kawahara 2001: 9).

Absorption into the day labourer market

People with no fixed address who were practically excluded from the *Seikatsu hogo* welfare system were absorbed into the *Yoseba*, where they got temporary food and accommodation. The *Yoseba* is, in short, the day labourer market. Employment contracts are agreed in direct negotiation at the *Yoseba*, (mostly only verbally) between the day labourers (i.e. job seekers) and employers such as construction contractors and illegal labour recruiters. At the *Yoseba*, employers or recruiters hardly ever ask for personal information and addresses. The *Yoseba* grew by absorbing seasonal workers from the country areas, drop-out farmers and the urban unemployed, at a time of rapid economic growth, to satisfy the growing demand for labourers from construction, stevedore and other transport and manufacturing industries (Komai 1969; Eguchi et al 1979; Matsuzawa 1988; Tamaki 1999). During the process, flop house (cheap hotel) townships had sprung up around the *Yoseba*, in the Sanya district in Tokyo, Kamagasaki in Osaka and Kotobuki in Yokohama, where job seekers flocking to look for work could find temporary beds as well. Men came to the *Yoseba* and moved between the doss houses and temporary workers' lodgings,[7] and from one temporary workers' lodging to another while they worked. These flop houses and temporary workers' lodgings, unlike ordinary flats, are not at all a stable form of accommodation, as one can get evicted as soon as one can no longer afford the hotel charge or one loses a work contract. The employment to be found at the *Yoseba* is mostly day to day, casual employment, not regular stable employment. Therefore, the life of day labourers is extremely unstable. They can avoid sleeping out on the street so long as they are able to get a job and stay at a flop house or a temporary workers' lodging, but once they get sick, injured or become too old to work, they will be forced out on to the street.[8] The fragility of existence for those who flock to the *Yoseba* had been understood as early as the immediate aftermath of the War, and some programmes were implemented to give workers more security, especially at the time of the *Yoseba* extension, which also coincided with the outbreak of riots. We must note that those programmes were not intended to incorporate the slum and flop house dwellers into the general welfare structure, but they were specific programmes aimed at specific people in specific areas. The programmes were also aimed at dispersing these people from the *Yoseba* areas, encouraging them to find a permanent address elsewhere (by such means as offering financial loan assistance to those seeking accommodation outside the *Yoseba* areas, and by giving them preferential treatment for entry to public housing). Finally, the programmes were almost entirely aimed only at the couples (and the households with children) in the shanty areas. To sum up, single males without family living in a flop house or a temporary workers' lodging, were more or less excluded from the programmes, except for the emergency relief supplied from outside the *Seikatsu hogo* system (Imagawa 1987; Nishizawa 1995). As a result, the *Yoseba* areas became almost entirely places for single males without stable employment.[9]

To paraphrase, the *Yoseba* and the day labourer markets absorbed as labour power those people who had lost their permanent address for various reasons. They had functioned as a shock absorber, by keeping these people off the street and away from extreme conditions by giving them a means of support, jobs and dwellings, no matter how much they engendered uncertainty in and of themselves (Nishizawa 1997). From this, it can be concluded that the practical exclusion of those people with no fixed address from the social welfare system linked up with the shock absorber function of the *Yoseba*.[10]

Changes in the day labourer market

Since the oil crisis of the 1970s and subsequent changes to the day labourer market, the *Yoseba* gradually have become unable to act as a shock absorber. This was due to the following reasons. Manufacturers have moved out of the market due to mechanization, and with the introduction of freight containers, so has the stevedore industry. Vacancy advertisements in tabloid papers and magazines for employment opportunities have become more generally used, replacing the *Yoseba*. Finally, workforce reorganization (such as mechanization and rationalization of the work, and the employment of younger more permanent workers) has finally taken place in the construction industry which had been clinging onto the *Yoseba* in order to obtain casual labourers. Because of this, the selection process for day labourers is getting fiercer. At the *Yoseba*, it has become more common for workers with some skills and experience, who are familiar to the recruiters to be given preference. Also it has become common to hire those workers with skills and experience for a longer term, either housing them in the temporary workers' lodgings or sending them to the work sites directly from their flop houses No matter how skilled and qualified the worker is, the age limit is being more strictly imposed, and recruiters are shunning the older workers.[11] The labour management at the construction sites (especially those involving big corporations) has become stricter, and any worker who is found at the medical check to have health conditions such as high blood pressure, is likely to be excluded.[12] As a result, it has become very difficult for older workers with little experience or few skills, and with health problems, to find work at the *Yoseba*. The same trend can be observed in the classified employment ads and employment magazines that have replaced the *Yoseba* as the dominant method of recruiting for the day labourer market. The older people are screened out purely on an age basis when they make a phone enquiry about a job. Single males, of middle age and older, who have no skills and no qualifications, are no longer seen as useful labour power even in the day labourer market.

Table 9.1 shows the basic attributes from surveys of homeless people in the big cities, conducted since the late 1990s. From this table, we can see some trends. Homeless people are predominantly male with the middle aged and older groups being dominant. People in their 50s make up the principal age group, while the number of over 70s drops off drastically. This discrepancy in the attributes shows that the increase in people living out on the streets since the 1990s is due to people being forced out on the streets, either through being squeezed out of the day labourer market due to the age limit or a lack of skills and qualifications, or through being excluded from the welfare system, because they are not old nor sick enough.

Poverty and 'self-reliance'

From amongst those people excluded from the *Seikatsu hogo* programme as well as from the day labourer market, and forced to live out on the streets, there have emerged some people who

Table 9.1: The basic attributes of homeless people

	Tokyo Metropolitan	Osaka	Nagoya	National Census (2000)
Gender				
Male	694 (97.6)	652 (97.0)	258 (98.9)	
Female	15 (2.1)	20 (3.0)	3 (1.1)	
Total	709 (100.0)	672 (100.0)	261 (100.0)	
Age				
Under 40	47 (6.7)	21 (3.2)	7 (2.8)	(52.4)
40s	138 (19.6)	114 (17.1)	28 (11.1)	(13.1)
50s	337 (47.9)	300 (45.0)	109 (43.3)	(15.3)
60s	161 (22.9)	205 (30.8)	93 (36.9)	(11.1)
70 and more	20 (2.8)	26 (3.9)	15 (6.0)	(8.1)
Total	703 (100.0)	666 (100.0)	252 (100.0)	(100.0)
Average	54.0	55.8	57.5	39.3

Note: National census data indicate the ratio of age groups in proportion to the males in the populated areas.
Compiled from the *Toshi seikatsu kenkyūkai* (2000), the *Osaka shiritsu daigaku toshi kankyō mondai kenkyūkai* (2001) and the *Kiso seikatsu hoshō mondai kenkyūkai* (2002).

put together shanties or shacks on the streets or in the parks as a temporary base for their existence, from discarded materials such as cardboard, pallets and tarpaulin sheets. They go around regularly collecting recyclables such as drink cans and old magazines (though scarcely making an income above the *Seikatsu hogo* criteria,) but still leading, to a degree, self sufficient lives (Kitagawa 2001).

The sight of people living on the streets, however, has drawn very negative responses such as hostile stares, harsh words and even violence from passers-by and neighbouring residents.[13] These negative reactions have also taken the shape of complaints to the local government over 'illegal occupation.' As well there is a growing number of demands to public authorities from the organizations assisting homeless people and from the homeless people themselves, for assistance so that they can get off the street.

In response, the local governments including the Tokyo metropolitan government, have devised and implemented a policy to ensure *appropriate use of public space*, meaning wholesale or gradual eviction of homeless people from the streets and parks, and various programmes aimed specifically at helping those people living on the streets to become self-reliant.[14] These programmes, in essence, are intended to create a new and alternative support system for street homeless people, rather than to incorporate them into the general welfare system including the existing *Seikatsu hogo* system.

The Assistance for Self-Reliance programmes are devised and implemented by the local government outside the framework of the relevant act, and paid for from the coffers of local governments. As they get more implemented, they naturally become more costly. In response, since the late 1990s, Osaka, Tokyo and other big cities with large street dwelling populations have passed special ordinances asking the national government to clarify their responsibility (including the amount of expenditure expected of them).[15] Demands were also made by the groups assisting the homeless people and from the homeless people themselves, asking that the national government to take responsibility for the welfare programmes and for them to expand public assistance measures as soon as possible. Subsequently, in July 2002, a special Act aimed at homeless people (*Hōmuresu no jiritsu shien tō ni kansuru tokubetsu sochihō* (The special Act to assist homeless people to become self reliant)) was enacted.

During its draft stage, the organisations assisting homeless people as well as from the homeless people themselves lobbied to include in this act some acknowledgement that the administration of the *Seikatsu hogo* welfare system had failed to include the work capable street homeless people.[16] Yet the Act went through without reflecting any of these demands. In the following month, the director of the assistance division, the social welfare and War victims' relief bureau of the Ministry of Health, Labour and Welfare, issued a notice to local governments asking them to deploy their 'self-reliance' programmes rather than applying (or not) the *Seikatsu hogo* programme to homeless people capable of working.[17]

When it came into force, the Act gave legal support (as well as a budget from the national government) to the local governments' self-reliance programmes that were devised and implemented to make up for the exclusion of street homeless people from the *Seikatsu hogo* and other general welfare programmes. In the forthcoming section, the Tokyo government's actions in this arena will clearly illustrate the effects of such programmes to assist self-reliance, implemented under the Act in more than one local government area.

Filtering and exclusion of self-reliance

In 1997 the Tokyo metropolitan government launched its *programme aimed to assist those living on the streets to become self reliant.*

It was a programme aimed at people who were not too old or too sick, in other words, those people who had been excluded from the *Seikatsu hogo* system, helping them to become independent by assisting them to find dwellings and jobs. The Tokyo metropolitan government went on to release a report on the homeless people in Tokyo, in March 2001. In the report it announced the revision and expansion of its *programme aimed to assist those living on the streets to become self reliant* into the *system to assist self-reliance*. The Tokyo metropolitan government is in the process of implementing the report's recommendations, and at the time of writing in February 2004, there were two Emergency Temporary Protection Centres (with a maximum accommodation capacity of 400 people) and four Centres to Assist Self-Reliance (with a maximum capacity of 346 people). In the following, we shall see how the filtering process works at each procedural step, referring to the 2001 business summary.[18]

Emergency Temporary Protection Centres

First, anyone who needs the assistance of the programme has to present themselves at a welfare office in their ward. After a brief interview, they will be admitted to an Emergency Temporary Protection Centre. The existing programme to assist self-reliance can only be applied after the applicant has been admitted to an Emergency Temporary Protection Centre. Therefore, if someone living on the street in a makeshift shanty, like those mentioned above, who was earning some money from regular miscellaneous jobs and leading a self sufficient life up to a point, were to apply for protection from this system, they would first be told to leave their shanty or wherever they were living, and sever any ties they might have with fellow street homeless people.

Based on interviews with the residents accommodated at the Emergency Temporary Protection Centre in Ōta, 20.9% had 'permanent' shanties or shacks (40.9%, according to a survey conducted on the street), while the ratio of residents who previously used to have cash income work was 37.1% (49.4%, according to a survey conducted on the street) (Tokubetsuku jinji kōsei jimu kumiai 2003). In other words, the *programme aimed to assist those living on the streets to become self reliant* in actual fact excluded from their target those street homeless who had some kind of self reliant life already.

At the Emergency Temporary Protection Centre, the residents share a room with a number of other people. Sometimes there can be dozens of others. (This is also the case at the Centre to Assist Self-Reliance). Various strict rules are imposed, such as a ban on alcohol and a curfew. At the Emergency Temporary Protection Centre, during the regulation month of residence, the residents are provided with 'accommodation, meals, consultations, health checks and so on,' while going through a 'rehabilitation of the health of body and mind'. Contracted social welfare counsellors and others also assess them during their stay for their 'motivation, ability, wishes and so on'. During their stay, the residents are not allowed to apply for jobs and can only wait for their turn for assessment and their results. At this stage, those who cannot cope with sharing a space with others, those who cannot stand rules such as the drinking ban, and those who cannot stand a life of doing nothing except waiting, leave the Centre either because of 'voluntary withdrawal,' 'withdrawal without notice,' or 'violation of rules (and subsequent eviction),' and find themselves back on the street. These reasons constitute 9.3% of overall reasons for leaving the Centre. When the assessment result is due, the welfare office makes a decision based on the assessment as to whether it is appropriate to send the resident to the Centre to Assist Self-Reliance, which is outside the *Seikatsu hogo* jurisdiction, or to correction facilities or other accommodation including flop houses, under the *Seikatsu hogo* system. If admitted at the Centre to Assist Self-Reliance, the internees are provided with 'accommodation, meals, and counselling on line, employment, and accommodation.' From the Emergency Temporary Protection Centre, 48.9% go to the Centre to Assist Self-Reliance, while 15.5% to other accommodation under the *Seikatsu hogo* system. We can thus conclude the central pillar of the programme is the Centre to Assist Self-Reliance.

The Centre to Assist Self-Reliance

On leaving the Emergency Temporary Protection Centre, the residents move to the Centre to Assist Self-Reliance. Here, they register the Centre as their place of residence, and go looking for jobs. Once they find employment, they commute from the Centre until they have saved enough to move into a flat or other accommodation. While they are at the Centre, employment counselling is offered as well as transport costs (to assist with job searching as well as commuting to work) and other sundries necessary for starting to work are provided, but there is no guarantee that the residents will find a job. They have to look for one themselves through the official employment service agency or through job magazines. Whether or not they can find employment depends largely on the state of labour market. In 2001, the average age of the Centre internees was about 50. At the same time, the number of job offers to job seekers (excluding temporary and seasonal jobs, but including part-time jobs) in Tokyo for the age group between 45 and 54 was around 50%. (For the 55 to 59 age group, it was between 20 and 30%).[19] In these circumstances, it would not be easy to find a job, while having to deal with the stigma of being a former homeless person. In principle, the internees can stay at the Centre only for two months during which they are expected to find permanent work. The stay at the Centre can be extended at the end of two months (to a maximum of four months) if the internees have got jobs, and have started commuting, so that they can save enough money to move to other commercial accommodation. But if they are not employed at the end of the two months, they are asked to leave the Centre, and deemed to be 'difficult to help to become self reliant.' This accounts for 9.8% (but does not include those seen as having 'no possibility of finding a job and becoming self reliant, due to sickness' and those who actually left the Centre for medical reasons).

Those deemed difficult to help to become self reliant are, according to a notice sent from the metropolitan government to individual welfare offices, to be 'dealt with appropriately, including the application of the *Seikatsu hogo* measures' by the welfare office who processed them in the first place. They are not necessarily thrown out on to the street all of a sudden.[20] Yet, the decision whether or not to apply the *Seikatsu hogo* is left to each ward's welfare office to decide, as the Tokyo metropolitan government does not specify the criteria for those deemed 'difficult to help to become self reliant'. The metropolitan government does not officially have any idea, or statistics, about what happens to those deemed 'difficult to help to become self reliant' after they are handed over to the ward's welfare office. There is no record of whether they are protected under the *Seikatsu hogo* system, or whether they are back on the street. According to a volunteer helper working in Tokyo, however, hardly any of them are given protection by the *Seikatsu hogo* system and most of them go back on the street (personal interview with a volunteer helper, Mr. A on November 1, 2003). To get protection under *the Seikatsu hogo* system, one has to apply first. Even if a resident fails to find a job during the two months stay at the Centre, if he is not aware of the *Seikatsu hogo* system, it is unlikely he would know how to apply.

According to Tsuyoshi Inaba who is involved in volunteer work to help the residents of the Centre (such as finding guarantors for them when renting a flat), it seems the workers at the Centre for Self Reliance believe the residents are naturally lazy, and that if they are told about the *Seikatsu hogo* system, then they won't seriously look for jobs. It is common for the Centre workers to put intense pressure on the residents to find jobs within four months. Some of the internees are worried about 'getting kicked out at the end of two months,' and come to seek help from Inaba's group (Inaba 2002: 59–60). Even if a resident knew of the possibility of being covered by the *Seikatsu hogo* system, in the employment and self reliance first atmosphere he has to have ample knowledge of the system and the appropriate communication skills to explain and convince the welfare workers in charge that this is what he really wants.

The use of the Centre for Self Reliance is limited to one opportunity only, so as to maximize the use of the limited resources for as many street homeless people as possible and to put pressure on the residents themselves to become employed and self reliant.[21]

This pressure is one the reasons some of the residents can not cope with staying at the Centre, as well as sharing a room with others, which also applies to those who leave the Emergency Temporary Protection Centre. These residents are categorized as leaving the Centre 'without a notice or voluntarily of their own reason.' This accounts for 23.7% , while the other 12.8% are evicted from the Centre as a result of a violation of rules like those evicted from the Emergency Temporary Protection Centre.

Being 'employed and self reliant'

The ratio of residents who leave the Centre, after putting up with the intense pressure, and managing to become employed and self reliant at last, is 49.9%. This is just about half, but this does not mean that all of them lead a stable life with a stable job, which was what the Tokyo metropolitan government set out to achieve as the programme's goal. As mentioned above, the kind of jobs the Centre to assist for self reliance recommend is limited to 'regular employment' (Tamaki 2002). Therefore, the 49.9% of residents who leave the Centre having become employed and self reliant, means they have regular employment. However, the biggest proportion of these, 24.2%, found jobs in administration and security, 16.6% in the construction and 15.2% in the cleaning industry.[22] These jobs generally do not offer a fixed monthly salary. Their payment system is usually on a daily basis, paid monthly according to the number of days worked. These jobs, especially those in the construction industry, are practically no different from those of the day labourers, as far as employment status is concerned. It is presumed that many of the residents who have left the Centre with supposedly regular employment are in fact in unstable employment with unstable wages.

As far as accommodation goes, an overwhelming majority of 65.4% left the Centre for flats and other accommodation, yet 34.6% have ended up in 'live in work' accommodation such as temporary workers' lodgings and dormitories attached to work. As mentioned in the previous section, 'live in work' is not necessarily stable, as a loss of work leads to the loss of accommodation. Matsuo Tamaki quotes a worker at a Centre to assist self reliance, saying that some of the residents who had worked for many years as day labourers, steadfastly 'refused to go to job interviews where they were required to wear ties,' though 'the Centre has dozens of suits and ties for such interviews' (Tamaki 2002: 28). What this episode tells us is that the kind of jobs that the Centre demands the residents apply for are ones requiring them to wear suits and ties for the job interview, and that some of the residents, like those employed for a long time as day labourers, have no experience with that sort of work, nor (probably) the necessary ability (which they had not needed to acquire previously.) If these people have to obtain 'regular employment' within the short given time of two months, they would have no choice other than to take (in practice, unstable) jobs. Following is an example of someone who, after going through the intense pressure of finding a job within the two month period, was forced to take a live in construction job, and then lost the job and the accommodation and was back on the street again.

> 'S.,' 40 years old, went from living on the street to the Centre to Assist Self Reliance, via the Emergency Temporary Protection Centre. Because he was suffering from a chronic disc hernia, it was not easy for him to find a job. As the end of the initial two months got closer and as he had found no employment, it was unlikely they would extend his stay. His relationship with the welfare office worker in charge was turbulent. He found the worker arrogant and had had a quarrel with the worker already. Hence, because it was impossible to apply for the *Seikatsu hogo*, S. had no alternative other than taking a live in job at a construction firm, and though he was unsure of his health he moved into a temporary workers' lodging. Because he had a bad

back, he was deemed 'incapable of working,' and was fired within a month. He was forced to leave the temporary workers' lodging, and he went back on the street (40 year old Mr S. interviewed on the street in Shinjuku, on November 30, 2002).

The Centre to Assist Self Reliance separates street homeless people into those who have the desire, necessary experience and the ability to find stable jobs and stable accommodation and those who have not, and they send the latter into unstable employment and unstable accommodation, which often comes with shocking working conditions. While there are people 'who want to have live in work from the start,' Inaba reports that 'some residents are persuaded by the Centre to go for those sort of jobs and even if they get the jobs, they are unlikely to get the accommodation within the designated four month period' (Inaba 2002: 59). Some of these live in jobs are not very different from the ones obtained at a *Yoseba*, and sometimes they are worse. Nasubi, who is involved in voluntary activities to assist day labourers and street homeless at Sanya, Tokyo's *Yoseba* district, reports on a typical case.

> A typical example is the Mitsue Construction case, which came into the open last year, and a strike was organized against the company. As a paper it submitted to the official employment service agency stated, the jobs were 'for people from the Centre to Assist Self Reliance.' The company clearly targeted the street homeless from the beginning, and the official agency and the counsellors knew that and acted accordingly. As far as we know, at least ten resident job seekers were introduced to the company by the Centre and were given work. They moved from the Centres in Taito and Sumida districts to the company's dormitory in Kawasaki. They soon realized there was hardly any work there. All they did was fix up the dormitory building. The rest of the time they waited around. Hardly any construction work. Of course, they were not paid at all. With 'employment' like that it seems that after twelve months nearly everybody had left (Nasubi 2003: 176–177).

The System to Assist Self Reliance, in essence, is just a screening process for human beings, based on the premise of the traditional *Seikatsu hogo* policy of excluding 'people with no fixed address (although they might be capable of working)'. Through the System to Assist Self Reliance, those excluded people are either sent to the labour market (to demanding and unstable work, not very different from that obtainable from the *Yoseba*), or discarded as 'difficult to help to become self reliant.'

Summary: subsumed and discarded people

To summarise this chapter's discussion, street homeless, people with no fixed address and others in dire circumstances, unless they are categorically elderly or sick, have in reality been excluded from the *Seikatsu hogo* system which guarantees all people a basic minimum standard of living. The *Yoseba* and other day labourer markets have functioned as a shock absorber, providing impromptu beds and jobs to people with no fixed address, thus concealing their existence as unemployed and poor. Also concealed here is the failure of the general welfare system which has excluded those people. When the decision is made as to who is more worthy of assistance and the necessary help to become part of the local community, it is the families with children rather then the single men who receive this help. The single men are screened out and as a result, the instability of life for single male day labourers has not really been allowed to become an issue. The increase since the 1990s of people living out on the street, and the fact that most of them are middle aged or older males, indicates the collapse of the interlocked system, and the fact that the day labourer market can no longer absorb 'people with no fixed address' who the *Seikatsu hogo* welfare system policy has excluded.

The programmes to assist self reliance, which had been devised and implemented first by local governments in the late 1990s and legalized later by the Special Measures Act, are essentially an attempt to replace the failed day labourer market and to send homeless people to the labour market, as the programmes stand on the same old premise to keep those people with no fixed address excluded from the general welfare structure, instead of correcting the system failure. As we have examined above, the System to Assist Self Reliance introduced in Tokyo, in the form of the Centre to Assist Self Reliance is in essence a screening system for street homeless people. Those who fail to achieve what the metropolitan government expects them to achieve, that is to become employed and self reliant, are simply discarded as lacking in the 'desire to become self reliant' or in 'self help effort.' The Tokyo system first rounds up street homeless people, some of whom have shacks and shanties and work at miscellaneous jobs and in a way, have a relatively stable life. Then it separates from the rest those people who cannot obey the rules, who cannot put up with living with others, and discards them as 'lacking in the desire to become self reliant' or 'failing to live with others'. The residents are then told it is totally up to them and their efforts whether or not they become employed and self reliant, the goal the system sets for them. In the process of becoming employed and self reliant, another screening process takes place, separating those who have the necessary experience and skills to find stable employment and accommodation from those who do not. The system screens those people who can motivate themselves and complete the whole process of finding jobs, attending job interviews, working, commuting, saving money and finding accommodation, using the 'assisting' system, which is in no way adequate. Those people who cannot, are either sent back to the unsatisfactory unstable work and living conditions, or turned out onto the street, and branded as 'difficult to help to become self reliant.'

What we are witnessing now is the screening process of those people, who (at least officially) have not or could not belong to a corporation, a local community or a family, and consequently are not even considered to be citizens of our society. They are structurally placed outside the general welfare system. They are forced to make an effort to fit into a certain self reliant model (with inadequate assistance). Depending on the result, they are again screened into those who are worth bringing back into society and those who are not.

10 Poverty and exclusion as it affects migrant workers from overseas: in terms of employment, housing and consumption

Kahoruko Yamamoto

> Everybody forgets everything rapidly
> Only the desire remains there unchanged
> What passes through it
> has had different names
> (Okazaki 2003: 309)

> Just as the most diabolical characteristic of the devil is not that he actually exists but that he convinces us that he exists, for affluence to become a useful myth it only needs to convince us that it exists, when it does not really exist (Baudrillard 1995: 305)

Are migrant workers from overseas all living 'in poverty?'

Recalling 1996

> I would like to help foreigners who are in trouble

I remember hearing many volunteer candidates making this statement over the several years that I had volunteered at an organization based in the Greater Tokyo Area dedicated to helping foreign migrants. When I began in 1996, my motivation was not very different from theirs. Yet I soon realized how arrogant my thinking had been when I started getting to know the migrants that visited the office. To be honest, I was amazed how affluent they looked, certainly much more than I had expected. The kind of images I had had about migrant workers were stereotypical, imagining that they sent money home by living on a shoestring budget; just making ends meet while living in poverty. My first task as a volunteer, in

October 1996, was to go and see a migrant worker who had suffered a workplace injury. This is how I recall the day.

> I had taken a few minutes to walk up to the front of the convenience store, and there was a guy already there who looked like the person I had come to meet. He asked me if I was Yamamoto. He was tall with a chiselled well-defined face, rather noble looking. He was wearing a collared shirt with a cardigan over it and dark green woollen pants. I know it is only a stereotype, but I had thought that a 'male foreign worker' would be wearing a pair of jeans (not a brand name make like Levis, a non brand make of course), a T-shirt and a wind cheater. So I thought at the time, 'wow, he's dressed rather smartly.' (Yamamoto 1998: 3)

Most of the migrants from overseas I came in contact with were single and in their twenties and thirties. Their patterns of consumption did not seem to be too different from those of their Japanese contemporaries. Apart from the fact that cell phones are a must for work and keeping in touch with friends, it was not too uncommon to see them owning PCs and other electronic gadgets such as CD and MD players. Above all, I had not expected to encounter migrant workers who were familiar with the latest trends in pop music, TV programs, especially popular soap and variety programs, the latest TV ads, the new releases at convenience stores and more.

The poverty of foreigners

Migrants and poverty. These two have long been considered to be inseparable. In pre-War Japan, several research projects were conducted, looking at migrant labourers from the Korean peninsular and China. We can imagine the hardship they endured from reports compiled by the Tokyo municipal government's social bureau, such as *Shinajin rōdōsha ni kansuru chōsa* (Research on Chinese workers) (1923) and *Tokyo zaijū senjin ni kansuru chōsa* (Research on Korean residents in Tokyo) (1925). Koreans from the former Japanese colonies had to endure harsh living and working conditions in post-War Japanese society. Many studies have shown that they have been discriminated against as 'Korean residents in Japan'.

What about the so-called 'new comers,' the short term migrant workers from overseas who have come to Japan to make quick money since the boom time of the 1980s? For the newcomers, especially for the over-stayers among them, their background, and the state they are in is precarious. Previous studies and NGOs' reports have revealed such issues as workplace accidents and unpaid wages. These issues arise from the fact that undocumented migrants are not covered by medical insurance and social security. These studies, repeatedly points out that their volatile legal status, stemming from their lack of proper residential status, is the major cause problems concerning migrant workers.

Yet, the circumstances of some of them seem to be at variance from 'poverty,' and the stereotypes we hold of their status and fortunes. According to the survey on Korean workers (from Chejudo and so on) conducted by Koh Sun Hui at Kotobukichō in Yokohama, a well-known *yoseba* district (day-labourers' town), more than half of them were earning over ¥300,000 a month, and a quarter of them were earning more than ¥400,000 (Yamamoto 1998: 148–150). In other words, when looking solely at their income levels, we cannot immediately conclude that 'migrant workers are poor.' Not all the migrant workers live in slums and in other urban underclass areas. They are not necessarily the poorest in the country.

So, are they completely free from poverty? We cannot say that. In this chapter, I will attempt to bring some order to the discussion on the relationship between foreigners and poverty in contemporary Japanese society, to help gain an understanding of the real picture. I will analyse how the issues are constructed and discuss the background that makes the poverty of migrant workers less visible. First, I will begin with their housing, and then medical, welfare and other social security issues. I will then examine the connection between economic migrant labourers and poverty, from the perspective of migrant workers in contemporary consumer society.

The state of migrants' housing

Not squatting, not out on the street

Various studies have revealed that both migrant workers from the Korean peninsular in pre-War Japan, and ethnic Korean residents in post-War Japan, endured shocking living conditions. After the War, Korean workers and their families who had been forced to work in Japan for the construction and munitions industries during the War were just left at places like Utoro district in Kyoto, practically abandoned without any compensation. In several places in the country, their housing began as 'illegal occupation,' and still persists as such today. Most of these districts have problems affecting their residential areas. For example, they are more susceptible to natural disasters. From overseas examples, many migrants participated in the 'movement for residential rights' which developed in France in the 1990s. One of the movement's strategies was squatting in unoccupied houses. In contrast, hardly any newcomers have since the 1980s employed squatting to secure their housing in Japan . In France, for example, forty per cent of all homeless males (street dwellers) and forty-nine per cent of homeless females were born overseas, while in Berlin in Germany, nearly a quarter of those who used the various facilities set up for homeless people in the first half of 2002 were migrants (Kodama et al. 2003: 150–151, 219). In Japan, street dwellers that number among the so-called 'old comers,' or long-standing post-War Korean residents, are barely mentioned in discussion of the newcomers. Of course, they do exist. I have conducted a face to face interview with a male migrant street dweller whose ancestors were of Japanese origin, near a railway terminal station in Kanagawa prefecture (Yamamoto 2000). Through my fieldwork, I have met a pair of Korean men who had no work or place to sleep, a Filipino who built a shanty and lived next to a creek among Japanese street dwellers. In addition to these, the numbers collected by the NGOs show there are a number of new migrants living on the street. But their proportion compared to all the new migrants, and compared to the entire population of street dwellers, is absolutely minuscule.[1]

Public housing and convergence

How should we deal with the housing problems that face the newcomers? Discrimination against them over access to housing is the first issue to consider. Several previous studies have noted this problem for both long-time migrants and for the newcomers (see, for example, Ishii and Inaba 1996). At the local government level, a similar point has been raised and suggestions made for improvement, such as in Kawasaki city's *Gaikokujin shimin daihyōshakaigi* (The Kawasaki City Representative Assembly for Foreign Residents) and Kanagawa prefecture's *Gaikokuseki kenmin Kanagawa kaigi* (the Kanagawa Foreign Residents' Council).[2] Conducted in 2000, the *Kanagawa ken gaikokuseki jūmin seikatsu jittai chōsa* (Research into the State of Living of Residents of Foreign Nationality living in Kanagawa Prefecture) asked migrant workers about the difficulties faced in finding housing. Responses to the multiple answer survey included the most common answer as 'nothing in particular,' with 47.6% (762 new migrant respondents). However, 26.6%, more than a quarter, said they were 'turned away because of their nationality (Kanagawa jichitai no kokusai seisaku kenkyūkai 2001: 87).

One way to avoid this discrimination over access to rental properties is for migrant workers to purchase their own homes. Yet hardly any new migrants had done this. Most of them have been in Japan for a decade. The Kanagawa survey found that out of 720 new migrant respondents, 19.3% lived in their own homes while the rest lived either in rental properties (such as detached houses, condos and apartments), company housing or company dormitories (Kanagawa jichitai no kokusai seisaku kenkyūkai 2001: 87). Elsewhere, Ikuo Kawakami has surveyed families of Vietnamese origin over 1989–1990. He found a very low level of home ownership among them. Among the sixty households surveyed, half lived in relatively cheap commercial rental properties (apartments) and forty per cent lived in public housing (housing provided by the Employment and Human Resources Development Organization, Prefectural Public Housing and others) (Kawakami 2001: 160).

Looking at the Kanagawa survey, of 139 migrants from South America, most of whom are supposedly in possession of 'legitimate' status, an overwhelming 52.5% live in private rental apartments. Comparing this to the survey conducted by Kawasaki city in 1993 which found more than sixty per cent of the respondents were living in 'either company housing or properties rented by the company,' we may be able to conclude that migrants are now less reliant on job brokers and employers for their housing (Kanagawa jichitai no kokusai seisaku kenkyūkai 2001: 78–79). This trend is confirmed in Takamichi Kajita's survey on Brazilians of Japanese origin living in Aichi, Shizuoka and other prefectures in 1998 (2054 appropriate responses). He described it as the 'trend of becoming independent from the brokers' (Kajita 1999: 7).

Then again, can these examples be taken at face value? In the past, securing employment directly led to the security of housing. But with the recent restructuring trend now being extended to new migrants, and with more and more of them being employed irregularly, their insecure employment may affect their housing conditions. In fact, according to the survey done by the Kanagawa prefecture government, thirty-five out of sixty-seven migrants who live in public rental housing, more than half are employed irregularly as 'part-time' and 'temporary staff.' Of course, the overall sample has a higher proportion of the irregularly employed as well as the unemployed to start with, but more than sixty per cent, or 161 of the total 251 migrants who live in commercial rental apartments are in irregular employment. This is much higher than those living in their 'own home,' 'company housing or company dormitories,' and other 'rental properties (including condos).' (Kanagawa jichitai no kokusai seisaku kenkyūkai 2001: 87)

Because the rules for public rental housing do not discriminate against migrants, public housing certainly has advantages, as well as offering lower rent than private sector rental accommodation. However, some of the easier properties to rent (that is, the less popular), are often found in very inconvenient locations. As has already been pointed out in previous studies, some convergence of migrants has been reported at some of the public housing estates in Kanagawa, Aichi and other prefectures. Concerning the background of the convergence of new migrants in public housing, especially those of Japanese descent, Kiyoto Tanno offers this explanation, based on examples from Toyota City in Aichi prefecture. Because they had plenty of empty units in their local *Danchi* complex, the Jūtaku toshi seibi kōdan (Housing and Urban Development Corporation) began letting them out to businesses. This was just what the local contractors and subcontractors needed to provide accommodation for their employees. As a result, according to Tanno, a local labour market supply system of migrant workers of Japanese ancestry came into being (2003: 211–2). In other words, this convergence in public housing was not born out of individual choice. Just like moving into accommodation supplied by their employers in the past, the migrant workers now move into public housing in group, once they are incorporated in the particular employment structure.

At some public housing estates, the concentration of new migrants and the accompanying problems such as friction with local and neighbouring residents comes under close scrutiny.[3] Often, cultural differences are cited as the cause of most of these cases. However, it may be more accurate to take into account that most of these troubles occur in geographically isolated places, miles outside of urban centres, where the aged, people on low incomes and migrants are socially segregated. In France, the concentration of migrants in housing built for low income earners (*Habitation à Loyer Modéré* or HLM, housing at moderated rents), especially HLMs in suburbs, is so dense that the problems there are often discussed synonymously with immigration problems. Some HLMs are built by private businesses, most of whom have connections with the companies employing migrant workers. Migrant workers end up congregating in these HLMs which are built on the urban outskirts because the land is cheaper. Just like the example from Aichi prefecture, we can clearly see this is just publicly funded company housing and the concentration of migrants is artificial, the direct result of their employment. In France, the delinquency of the young second generation of migrants is often seen as a deterioration of law and order caused by the concentration of migrants, and it has been reported that the local residents often resort to xenophobic action (Ishii and Inaba 1996: 54–60). As a matter of fact, most neighbours of migrants are low income earners or unemployed people, who cannot escape from where they are because of their economic predicament. They may be just venting their frustration about their own predicament through xenophobic action directed towards migrants.

The concentration of legitimate migrants from South America of Japanese descent, who are often regarded as having a steady status, can be understood as a kind of segregation. They are made invisible to the residential areas, yet they are secured as labour power. If we reduce any troubles and social issues to their 'differences,' be they ethnic or cultural, rather than to unemployment and poverty, even though the migrants constitute part of the low income earners, this kind of essentialist way of thinking is dangerous because it leads to residents abandoning their efforts towards mutual understanding and ceasing to try to solve the problems.

Overstayers' insecurity of housing

Despite the collapse of the bubble economy and the prolonged economic stagnation, there are more than 170,000 overstayers living in Japan (2007). Being an overstayer means that you cannot sign a rental agreement under your name, including public housing. In many cases, because you do not have much social contact outside your work, you have to rely on your employer for many essentials of your life as well, including accommodation and the guarantee of your status. A Pakistani man in his thirties (an overstayer) made the following remark in an interview (conducted in 2000) regarding housing.

> (As for my apartment,) someone from my company rented it for me. Been in Japan for twelve years. I have left several companies, and I

have been fired by many companies as well. I've been living in this place for five years, but it takes an awful long time to set it up. You know, even if you get some stuff for the house, decorate the house, you have to chuck it all out if you are fired. I have moved so many times in these twelve years. I have had to throw away TVs and everything. Until I find my next job, I have to stay at someone's place. When you find a job, you buy the stuff again. That is the hardest part (Kanagawa jichitai no kokusai seisaku kenkyūkai 2001: 322).

The apartment he was living in then was rented by the company. As he says, a dismissal means the loss of the housing. Apparently, he has repeatedly had to move house because he changed jobs several times. He had to sometimes stay at friends' places temporarily as well. Even though he has been in Japan for more than a decade, he has not got a lot of household goods to speak of because he throws away furniture and electrical goods, and then buys them again every time he has to move. This is very similar to the lifestyle of the day labourers. The actual proportion of day labourers among the new migrants including overstayers is not necessarily large. At the aforementioned Kotobukichō in Yokohama, there was a situation at one time in the 1990s, when the number of Korean newcomers surged. In a district with less than six thousand labourers, one in five was a migrant labourer. The number, however, has since dwindled drastically. The reason the number of overstayers surged in Kotobukichō, albeit briefly, is the existence of doss houses where they can stay (dwell) without producing identification and guarantors. The means of survival for the overstayers, who were 'not meant to be there in the first place,' renders them literally homeless. However, hardly any cases are found in Japan where they are forced to live on the street.

This is often explained by the existence of strong networks of people from the same country or region (helping each other when needed). It is also an important factor that the migrants can go back to where they come from if they are stuck. But the Japanese do not have that choice. For them, the loss of home means living out on the street. Also, the relative youth of the newcomers who are mostly in their twenties and thirties, can assist them on the employment front, compared to Japanese street dwellers who are mostly middle aged or elderly men. But we must remember, once the migrant workers lose their jobs and housing and have to live on the street, they become people to be 'smoked out,' not to be officially helped and protected.

Healthcare and social security

Exclusion because of 'no fixed address'

We have so far seen the housing problems that new migrants face at a basic level. Let us now deal with the housing problem of overstayers from the aspect of the official policies. No matter how long they have lived in Japan, migrant workers without proper visas are considered to be of no fixed address, though in reality, they have an address. They can be called institutional home-less people. This constitutes the reason for them being excluded from the healthcare system. Migrant residents without a proper visa are not entitled to join the National Health Insurance Scheme, which means they have to pay for all medical treatment. The problems arising from this exclusion have been raised repeatedly already (see Ōkawa 2001). Their exclusion from healthcare has been raised since the early 1980s when the surge in the number of new migrants became newsworthy. To begin with, the main healthcare issue for overstayers is thought due to the fact that they are not insured, and therefore have to pay for all medical costs. Medical bodies have had to be compensated by the local authorities and the national government for unpaid bills left by migrant residents. Because the individual migrant is not entitled to benefit from the healthcare scheme from the start, the issue of unpaid bills has been seen more as a 'financial management issue of the medical institutions,' rather than a 'healthcare issue for migrants.'

In 1981 and operational policy interpretation was made on the inclusion of foreigners and refugees in the National Health Insurance Scheme. The interpretation determined that migrant residents 'who have been living here or are likely to live here for twelve months' can join the Scheme (*Hoken hatsu dai 84 gō kokumin hoken kachō tūchi*). At that time, there were some cases where migrants were accepted after showing a record of residence for more than twelve months, despite lacking a proper visa. However, since then a further interpretation was announced in 1992. *Hoken hatsu dai 41 gō kokumin hoken kachō tūchi* (The no. 41 Directive on Healthcare, from the National Health Insurance Section Manager) determined that, as the 'duration of the visa at the time of entry is (or is likely to be) longer than twelve months,' many foreigners (especially those arriving in Japan on a tourist visa and overstaying) are excluded. Despite this, several cases have been heard by the courts appealing against exclusion from National Health Insurance on the grounds of the lack of a proper visa, and some overstayers have been allowed access to healthcare. The contentious point in every court case has been whether the overstayers could have a residential address or not. In 1998, a Chinese woman took Musashino City to the district court over the city's refusal to grant a National Health Insurance Certificate to her because she did not have residential status. The Tokyo District Court handed down the verdict, saying it was unlawful of the city not to issue an insurance certificate. Yokohama city was sued by a Taiwanese man without residential status for not issuing him with a Healthcare Insurance Certificate. In a ruling handed down in 2001, the Tokyo district court judged the national government's announcement not to give insurance because of a lack of residential status was unsound and the city's action was pronounced unlawful, although the man's claim for compensation was not recognized.[4]

Until recently, there has been only a handful of health related services which are universally accessible regardless of nationality and residential visa status, such as those under the Tuberculosis Control Act, the Act Concerning the Treatment of Vagrants found Sick or Dead. Recently, more services such as emergency entrance to maternity facilities (under the Child Welfare Act), subsidies for the care of premature babies and the issuing of the *Boshi kenkō techō* (the Maternal and Child Health Handbook) under the Maternal and Child Health Act, and a regular immunization program (under the Immunization Act) are available regardless of residential status. How much do the migrants themselves know about the availability of these social welfare services? Basically, the overstayers, for fear of getting caught, often avoid going to government offices. Quite a number of them may find it much more comfortable to use medical facilities and services where their language of origin is used, though they may be much more expensive, rather than speaking in Japanese and going through several difficulties.

Exclusion from 'poverty'

Due to the recent tendency towards the decentralization of authority, social security for overstayers is increasingly dependent on each local authority for interpretation and policy decisions. Overstayers can receive completely different social services depending on where they live. In that sense, the welfare services for them can hardly be called their 'right.' They are provided only ever as a favour. In post-War Japan, 'protection' and 'compounding' have been the method of dealing with people with housing problems. As mentioned above, many overstayers practically have their own residences and look after their own lives. However, with respect to healthcare and social security, they are excluded from services on the grounds that they do not have an address. If they are considered in this way as having housing problems and having 'no fixed address,' it is possible to argue that they are entitled to public assistance. Yet, as Masami Iwata (1995) has pointed out, one has to first belong to a society (a nation) to be eligible for social welfare services. These are universally applicable only to those people who belong. Those who do not belong are dealt with, classified and excluded according to a different set of principles. Overseas visitors who overstay cannot even be classified as being in poverty, as defined by the social welfare services, which operate in a completely different reality from their daily life and employment. Visitors from abroad who overstay are left outside the healthcare and social security systems. Having said this, there have not been many instances suggesting the necessity for healthcare and social security for migrant worker overstayers, maybe because most of them are young and they can going back home as a last resort. Not all overstayers, of course, owe a large amount in medical fees to the hospitals. Rather, most of them do not even consider themselves to be eligible for healthcare and social security services, because they have internalized their illegitimacy (that is, 'I am carrying out illegal activities in Japan').

Japanese society, though primarily considering overstayers to be 'illegitimate', exploits their labour power at the foundation of its economy. It has continued to exclude them from healthcare and social security, though they are obliged to pay taxes. They are expected to be super human workers, who do not require healthcare or social security. Once they are unable to work, they always have an exit option, either voluntary or involuntary, like throwing out unwanted waste.

Work cycles and patterns of consumption

New migrants' motivation to stay in Japan besides working

New migrants presumably come to Japan to work and earn money, but some of them seem to ' live it up,' in much the same consumerist fashion as their Japanese counterparts. This is not something peculiar to migrants, as the reality of poverty seems to be so well hidden in Japanese society itself, in spite of all the talk about prolonged economic stagnation. Hiroshi Komai, having arrived at the conclusion after various surveys, that not all new migrants come to Japan just to work, has put them into various categories. Among these is what he calls a 'self-fulfilment' group (Komai 1999: 88–92). His definition of the group is rather vague, but it includes people, mostly single males, whose motivation in coming to Japan is because they are interested in it and they love life in Japan.

The NGOs I mentioned at the opening of this chapter organized Japanese language classes and computer courses for overseas migrants on weekends and evenings. It also organized parties on a regular basis. I was involved in the group for the purpose of active observation. One of the things I found very peculiar was the fact that some of the participants lived miles away from the classes and parties. They kept coming back, paying their own train fares, taking more than an hour each way. In fact, hardly any of the many new migrants living in the neighbourhood of the office of this NGO took part in the classes or parties. At the time, I tried hard to explain this using ethnicity or ethnic networks as the reason. Thinking about it now, maybe they were looking for something they could not get from daily work and sending money back home, even though that might have been their primary motivation in coming to Japan. As a matter of fact, some of the participants of the classes and parties confessed their reason for coming there was because 'I want to find Japanese friends.'

Overstaying: purpose and reality

Elsewhere, there are migrant workers who are very practical about life in Japan. Their purpose in coming to Japan is purely to earn money and to send it back home. Most of these 'successful examples of migrant workers' are couples (without children) hard at work, who are very clear about their motives and they actually send a large amount of money back home. A Korean man in his fifties who in 1995 arrived with his wife from Chejudo , was earning ¥350,000 a month doing welding. With his wife working at a restaurant, they were earning a total of ¥650,000 a month, out of which they were sending between ¥350 to ¥450,000 back home. 'A couple more years of hard work here, then we will go home and take it easy,' he said. Examples like that of this couple are not very common. Single people in particular find their daily expenses can significantly increase as their stay in Japan continues. Their expenses may not just be for food and entertainment, but also sometimes for gambling.

Another Korean man in his thirties originally came to Japan in 1989 to study at a language school. After that, he overstayed his visa and worked. At the time of the interview, he was employed to put up advertising billboards, earning a monthly income of about ¥300,000. He said he spent most of his income on food, entertainment and gambling like pachinko, and sent no money at all back home.[5]

It is not unusual for us to realize over time that we cannot always fulfil what we originally set out to do. Our future plans and predictions change. This is of course the case with new migrants who intend to come to work in Japan for a short period. The difference is, for new migrants, failure to reach their aims and targets (most likely a target amount of money to send back home) means in most cases the extension of their stay. It is particularly true when they are living with children of growing age that many migrants may not be able to save as much as they intended, because the children's education, upbringing and living expenses can be quite a burden. When they are clear about their future plans after returning home and clear about the amount of money they are aiming to save while in Japan, most of the migrants, regardless of their residential status, save their incomes in Japan steadily or send money home. Those who defer their departure date, on the other hand, tend to spend more on day to day concerns.

Migrant workers' supportive contribution

According to UN statistics, there were 175 million migrants throughout the world in 2002, which is nearly twice as many as in 1975. With regard to their migrant destinations, fifty-six million went to Europe, fifty million went to Asia and forty-one million went to North America. Most of them are from so-called developing countries, heading to the economically developed countries.[6] Many lives were lost in the September 2001 terror attacks in the US. The victims of terrorism most of us came to know through the media, were white collar workers working in the World Trade Centre buildings and fire-fighters. In fact, there are said to be many more victims who lost their lives on that day, yet their names are not known and their existence has been disregarded. It is still difficult to find out the exact numbers. This is because they were migrant workers from Latin America, most of whom had entered the US illegally or on false passports. What this tells us is that the lowly paid terminal work in the service and manufacturing industries in developed countries is done by a mainly migrant workforce.

However, their existence and their working conditions are often completely ignored. Ken Loach, the British director of many films dealing with the working class, portrayed the life and the struggle for his rights of a migrant who worked as a janitor in the business district of Los Angeles, in *Bread & Roses* (2000). There is a scene in the film where high heels and leather shoes march past while he is kneeling down cleaning the floor. Naturally, neither he nor they exchange a glance. As far as the white collar workers are concerned, it does not matter who is there. They may not even consider the janitor as a worthwhile being to speak to. The scene symbolizes that relationship very well.

Work for further consumption: never-ending work away from home

In spite of what goes on in the countries they go to and work in, migrant workers overseas are seen as 'heroes' back home by their governments, their economies, and, of course by their families. The Philippines government released a new national bond, called Bagong Bayani (New heroes), intended for Filipino workers overseas. This is proof that the money sent home by more than seven million Filipino workers all around the world is an important source of foreign currency for the country.[7] In this way, migrant workers from developing countries on the one hand support the lower end of the economies of the developed countries, and on the other hand, they are subjected to constant pressure from home to send money.

Many of the new migrants come to Japan aiming to earn money and send it home. Most of the studies and documentaries concerning migrant workers sending money back home, tend to portray them favourably. As far as the individual workers are concerned, they come to Japan to improve their own living standards and those of their families. The other side of the coin is that this could bring about the family's dependency on migrant workers for their well-being. Many new migrants plan to save enough money in Japan to start a business when they return home.[8] Of course there are some successful examples, but there are quite a few business failures and bankruptcies due to a lack of business experience. They then go overseas again to make some more money, becoming what is known as 'repeat migrants.'[9] There are also cases of family breakdown, because the working migrants have to live away from their homes. Even amongst those migrants coming to Japan with their whole family, because the parents are so focused on work that they pay little attention to their children, there are cases of deterioration in the relationship between the parents and children, and an alienation from schools and the neighbouring community.[10]

Migrant workers head overseas looking for a little more affluence for the family, not for excessive luxury, but how many of those initial dreams come true? As I mentioned above, the longer they stay in Japan, the more accustomed many migrant workers become to the way of life here, and to the consumer society. We tend to see migrant workers just as 'working beings' but they are also members of our consumerist society. The most striking thing I found when I visited a slum in Bangkok, Thailand, was the fact many families had TVs, even though they had to finance long term loans. New commodities they had not seen before were featured on the screens, enticingly displayed in advertisements. A volunteer who guided me around the slum said since the arrival of TV, people had been involved in more borrowing in order to consume more. This kind of situation, looking back now, is probably what Zygmunt Bauman is talking about in the following.

> In a synoptical society of shopping/watching addicts, the poor cannot avert their eyes; there is nowhere they could avert their eyes to. The greater the freedom on the screen and the more seductive the temptations beckoning from the shopping-mall displays, the deeper the scene of impoverished reality, the more overwhelming becomes the desire to taste, if only for a fleeting moment, the bliss of choosing. The more choices the rich seem to have, the less bearable to all is a life without choosing (Bauman 2000: 88).

New migrants are placed in an insecure position as far as their housing is concerned, and overstayers especially are not even considered as eligible for medical insurance and social security. When we look just at these visible exclusions, we tend to conclude that the situation the new migrants are facing is almost all derived from systematic factors. Yet it is their consumption patterns that tie them down where they are in the end, even though they seem to choose it by themselves and to embrace it. Maria Mies, quoting Manfred Max-Neef, points out the falseness of the reciprocal consumption model the middle class of the developed countries presents both to their own lower class and to the people in developing countries (2000). Being 'exported' overseas and copied at home, this kind of consumption pattern brings further subjugation, more debts, more imbalances at home, and the loss of cultural identity. Striving to work more to satisfy the constantly aroused desire for consumption in those people willing to go overseas for work, and in their families who receive money from them, means that they are locked in the cycle between work away from home and consumption. This leads to the stabilization of the poverty class. This needs to be recognized as a problem applicable to migrant workers not just in Japan, but also throughout the world.

11 A jail without bars, the social world of the street dwellers

Akihiko Nishizawa

A jail without bars

A city jail in the open

Street dwellers live in their own unique environment, in isolation from the majority of city residents. Our organized and settled society, the domain of 'national good citizens', rejects street dwellers and excludes them on the grounds that they have an empty space in their curricula vitae, that they have no fixed address and no guarantors. The social welfare administration, *Seikatsu hogo* (Public Livelihood Protection) which is essentially intended for traditional families, systematically excludes them. They are intentionally neglected and are not given the chance to return to organized and settled society. In addition, the majority of residents consider street dwellers to be an unpleasantness 'that should not be there,' and try not to notice them. Despite their increasing number, and their increasing visibility, this problem is no nearer to being solved. The disregard of mainstream Japanese society means that even places they know well become alien to them, and their particular environment seems to be enclosed by invisible bars.[1] This chapter describes the environment where street dwellers lead their lives, as a 'jail without bars.' This particular jail is characterized by exclusion, self abnegation, and a high death rate.

First, a jail without bars is an environment of rejection. As mentioned above, in an organized and settled society there are no possibilities for street dwellers to improve their way of living. There are no jobs for them and no shelter for them to move into. The welfare office offers them no life-line, continually reminding them that they are subhumans to whom the concept of human rights no longer applies. Of course, if they are classified as 'elderly' they are eligible for protection under the *Seikatsu hogo* system. If they are recognized as being 'sick,' as long as they continue to be so, they might be given medical assistance. But if they are not 'old' enough or 'sick' enough, or 'women with children' who can receive paternalistic treatment if they are prepared to put up with certain stigma, they have no alternative other than to continue living on the streets. Some are determined to stick it out until they are 'old' enough, but it is a long and arduous journey and there is no guarantee that they will get there.

Second, a jail without bars is a zone of self abnegation. It must be remembered that its inmates were once residents of organized and settled society as well. To them, their existence as street dwellers is experienced as a state they cannot bring themselves to accept. Because of this, living on the streets is accompanied by extremely of self esteem. As we shall see later, street dwellers do not just see themselves as objects rejected by society. In many cases, they are tormented by the twisted values that they used to be familiar with, such as the virtue of financial independence and the contemptibility of being dependent. In addition, they rely on these same values in their struggles to regain self confidence. For example, they tend to feel more independent if they are not on the *Seikatsu hogo* benefit or relying on food handouts.[2] However, such attempts at independence more often than not fail in the harsh struggle for survival. Their goal of maintaining their dignity gradually recedes from them.

Third, a jail without bars is a place to wait for physical destruction. The well-being of street dwellers quickly deteriorates in their terrible living conditions. Exhausted from being pushed endlessly against invisible bars, street dwellers are driven by hopelessness and their lives are dominated by despair. In the jail without bars their lives are just a waiting period before death. This reminds us of Yoshiro Ishihara stating about the lives of post WW2 internees in Siberia. The internees were 'surviving on only a faint desire for life, reasoning to themselves that they would not die for at least a short while.' (Ishihara 1997[1972]: 13)

A bare existence

According to Giorgio Agamben, the nature of internment does not lie in the act of killing. Internment is a state where the 'rule of law is totally suspended,' where 'exceptions become the rule.' It is not just outside the law, and it is not simply excluded from it, but it is also 'included through its exclusion itself.' Having no right to decide on matters of life and death, the internees of those exceptional places, are deprived of subjectivity, the individual's usual expectations and potential for life, and reduced to a 'bare existence' with no emotions or dignity (Agamben, 2000: 43–50). The street dwellers discussed here are also unusual examples of rejected non-humans. A jail without bars is an exceptional space which reduces and discourages rebellion from street dwellers, it leads them to the conclusion that everything is the result of their own wrong doing, and causes them to remain suspended in these conditions just waiting for a waiting death. In this sort of exceptional space, street dwellers are trapped by forces that nullify their existence and reduce them to a bare existence.

Isao Nukada found that there were three characteristics of 'lonely deaths' among the residents of temporary shelters who were victims of the great Hanshin and Awaji earthquake. They were 'unemployed males, living alone' with 'little contact with neighbours.' They were 'suffering from chronic diseases,' and were 'on low incomes, earning around one million yen a year.' Nukada concluded that those who die lonely deaths after suffering a severe setback in their lives were people who had already been living in poverty, who were already suffering from chronic sickness, were alienated from their immediate surroundings and were unable to across essential services such as medical treatment. These people simply disappear from the world (Nukada 1999). In their desperation, they may decide to take their own lives, or 'commit slow suicide' by abusing alcohol. As far as their economic backgrounds are concerned, street dwellers and those who die lonely deaths are extremely similar. In fact some of the deceased Nukada discusses include day labourers who would have obtained work through the yoseba in Kamagasaki. Through his analysis of 'lonely deaths,' Nukada has stumbled upon an impoverished class concealed at the bottom of Japanese society. If we place street dwellers within the scope of the impoverished class, they have already been dying lonely deaths, and are still dying today. This is precisely why it is apt for Masami Iwata to compare the 'routine "despair" of "homeless" people' to 'slow suicide.' (Iwata 2000: 275)

Nozomu Shibuya suggests that it is possible 'to see the numbers of lonely deaths as an effect of the ruling power, and an effect of the raw political power that determines life and death.' (Shibuya 2003: 197–215) 'In globalizing neo-liberal social reorganization,' he says, a new ruling style is emerging in the 'internment, refugee camps, temporary shelters, and handling of the homeless and the destitute, and in the emerging "fourth world".' There, 'where the exception is the rule, people are left waiting forever, in between death and life. Dehumanized, they are allowed to prolong their lives as animals.' A jail without bars that leads the inmates to 'slow suicide' and a bare existence, is connected to the dehumanizing spaces which can be found here and there in contemporary society. But 'slow suicide' is not the same as suicide itself. On the contrary, it embodies something that runs counter to suicide. The 'slow suicide' of the street dwellers has the appearance of clinging on to life. If you fail to see that, you do not understand the real world of the street dwellers. It is indicative that Nukada says the following about street dwellers in Kamagasaki, when talking about their attitude to suicide, although this is somewhat divorced from his main context.

> Many residents of this area I have spoken to during the last few days could be considered to be amongst life's losers in some ways. But even though they have been pushed to the limit they still show a spirit of survival. Every time I come here, I cannot help being amazed at their vitality (Nukada 1999: 233–234).

If we accept the existence of a kind of magnetic force that acts to create a jail without bars, it becomes necessary to ask fresh questions. Are street dwellers really only leading a nullified existence? Can we not see the life force of possibility and potential among them in their resistance to the forces trying to reduce them to a bare existence? If we can, what kind of 'cogitation' (Agamben 2000: 18–19) then, will help them to generate such life forces? Probably the fact that the jail does not have bars is significant. This jail is open to the city. Under this premise, to begin with, I would like to think about the counter currents which are part of the social reality of the city. I will attempt here to describe the social reality of the street dwellers, and in the process I will also focus on those counter currents.

Metropolitan Tokyo's peripheral street dwellers

Below, I will describe the social reality of the street dwellers, relying mainly on interviews with four men living out on the streets in Hiratsuka city in Kanagawa prefecture, situated in an industrial zone on the outskirts of metropolitan Tokyo, as well as a survey of 251 street dwellers throughout the prefecture (excluding Yokohama and Kawasaki cities).[3] In order to make the findings more applicable to the social reality of street dwellers in general, I will refer from time to time to those people sleeping out in the twenty-three wards

Table 11.1: Survey results of street dwellers

Survey location	Survey time	Number surveyed	Occupation immediately before becoming a street dweller — construction and earth moving	Occupation immediately before becoming a street dweller — temporary occupation	Accommodation before living on the street was of an unstable type as temporary workers' sheds, dormitories, temporary shelters and so on	Current occupation[b]
(1) Around Shinjuku railway station (in Tokyo)	September 1994	210	60.0	-	-	No work 73.8, day labouring in construction and earth moving 13.3, 'transport, bookshops and so on' 3.8
(2) Around Shinjuku railway station (in Tokyo)	March 1996	238	(46.2)[a]	-	-	-
(3) Throughout the city of Ōsaka (in Ōsaka prefecture)	August and September 1999	672	75.5	85.6	Multiple answers. Boarding house 39.2, temporary workers' sheds 36.9, company housing and live-in work 8.1.	Multiple answers. No work 20.0.(Among those who answered as having worked) day labouring 7.3 (49 people), collection of reusables 69.7 (468 people)
(4) Toshima, Shinjuku and Shibuya wards (in Tokyo)	October and November 1999	303	64.4	63.0	60.7	-
(5) Sanya and Ueno districts (in Tokyo)	November and December 1999	208	73.4	70.8	66.0 An 'overwhelming number' responded 'no income at all.'	'Contract work' 22.6 and odd jobs 11.1
(6) Four principal areas in the twenty-three wards (in Tokyo)	March 2000	710	(34.5)[a]	61.3	66.2	No work 50.6. Among those who had work (multiple answers), day labouring on construction sites 40.6 (142 people), odd jobs 46.5 (200 people)
(7) Around the principal cities (in Kanagawa prefecture)	February 2001	251	52.4	53.3	45.0	No work 51.0, day labouring at construction or earth moving sites 10.1, odd jobs 38.9

(8) Various areas of Ōsaka prefecture (excluding Ōsaka city)	From March to June, 2001	406	59.2	59.3	47.4	No work 19.3, day labouring 8.1 and collection of reusables 71.4
(9) Six principal urban areas (in Nagoya)	May and June 2001	261	70.7	69.1	54.4	No work 28.8. Among those who answered as having worked (multiple answers), as day labourers at construction or earth moving sites 25.3 (57 people), collection of reusables 58.2 (131 people)

Notes:

a: The figures seem low, because builders and others have been put into the other categories. This is due to the way the categories were set out in the surveys.

b: Readjusted figures. Strictly speaking, we cannot compare these figures because the time frame and the timing specified as 'current' is different in each survey.

Sources:

(1) *Shinjuku nojuku rōdōsha no seikatsu shūrō hoshō wo motomeru renraku kaigi* (1995), Shinjuku homeless (Homeless in Shinjuku).

(2) *Toshi kōreisha seikatsu kenkyu kai* (1997), *Shinjuku hōmuresu no jittai '96* (The facts about homeless people in Shinjuku, 1996).

(3) Ōsaka shiritsu daigaku toshi kankyō mondai kenkyū kai (2001), *Nojuku seikatusha (hōmuresu) ni kansuru sōgōteki chōsa kenkyū hōkokusho* {A report from a comprehensive investigative study of street dwellers (homeless people)}.

(4) Nojukusha jinken shiryō sentā Tokyo seibu ken kikitori chōsa purojekuto chīmu (1999), 'Dai shitsugyō jidai no nojukusha zō wo saguru: Tokyo seibu ken 300 nin kikitori chōsa (Searching for a model for homeless people in the era of massive unemployment: face to face interviews with 300 homeless people in the western region of Tokyo)', *Shelter-less*, 4.

(5) Toshi seikatsu kenkyūkai (2000), *Heisei 11 nendo rojō seikatsusha jittai chōsa* (The 1999 fact finding study of street dwellers).

(6) Kanagawa toshi seikatsu kenkyūkai (2001), *Kanagawa kenka nojukusha chōsa chūkan hōkokusho* (The interim report on a study of street dwellers in Kanagawa prefecture).

(7) Ōsaka furitsu daigaku shakai fukushi gakubu toshi fukushi kenkyūkai (2002), *Ōsaka fu nojuku seikatusha jittai chosa hōkokusho* (The report from the fact finding study of street dwellers in Ōsaka prefecture).

(8) Kiso seikatsu hoshō mondai kenkyūkai (2001), *2001 nen Nagoyashi 'homuresu' kikitori chōsa chūkan hōkokusho* (The 2001 interim report on a face-to-face survey of 'homeless' people in Nagoya city).

of Tokyo and in Ōsaka as well. What I will discuss here are not the attributes of individuals or of individual areas, but rather the characteristics of the particular class.

Having said that, we should not disregard completely the differences between particular areas. To start with, we should note the peculiarities of metropolitan Tokyo. Street dwellers, both in centres like Shinjuku, Ueno and Sumidagawa park and on Tokyo's periphery in Kanagawa prefecture, are, compared to their counterparts in central and peripheral Ōsaka and in Nagoya city, almost certain to have no income at all, and are less likely to be engaged in odd jobs (see the Table 11.1). This suggests that those in Tokyo have fewer opportunities for survival than their counterparts elsewhere. I would not go any further on this point here, but this is attributable this to the greater pressure for homogenization and national conformity existing in Tokyo, because it is the site of the imperial house and the nation's capital (see Chapter 2 for the pressure towards national conformity in Tokyo). Also we should note the difference between the city centre of the megalopolis and its periphery. In the peripheral areas, in contrast to the city centre, street dwellers are less likely to have lived in unstable accommodation (such as temporary workers' sheds, temporary shelters, and dormitories) before becoming street dwellers. They are slightly less likely to have worked as day labourers at construction or earth moving sites, and other temporary occupations. This trend is clear when you compare Ōsaka city centre and the rest of the prefecture. In the city centre where there is an established day labourers' market, many street dwellers tend to have been day labourers before living on the street. But in an area where there is no established day labourers' market, they begin sleeping out on the streets straight away. This shows that the existence of the underclass labour market with its associated accommodation and other facilities, acts as a shock absorber, preventing people from immediately ending up on the street. It also suggests that the lack of the labour market, or its closing, forces more people directly onto the street without going through day labouring. Considering all this, the significance of discussing street dwellers on the periphery of metropolitan Tokyo is that it reveals clearly the social reality of a jail without bars, as a characteristic of social class. This area is in a place where the pressure to conform is strong. Yet, on the outskirts, we see many diverse street dwellers that have not been through the day labouring process. We can see the characteristics of a counter current clearly as well.

A cogitation on distance

Collectivization

Observation of the actual interaction that takes place amongst groups, organizations or simple gatherings helps the understandings of their structural principals. To describe the social reality of the street dwellers, I would like to start with now they combine in public spaces, as they form and then disappear one after the other. Such groupings have become more visible particularly since the 1990s because of the increase in the number of street dwellers. We must note, however, that these groupings do not happen amongst the majority of people living on the street and their power of social cohesion is limited. All groups and organizations have their origins. For an analysis of them among the street dwellers we must begin with the social conditions that generate these groupings.

The areas where we find many street dwellers overlap with areas where many urban underclass people have lived. But even among these areas there are not many places where people can sleep out. The places that can be used include public parks, river banks, beaches and streets which are deserted at night. People cannot live in places where they are frequently chased away. Because of this they are forced to gather in a limited number of places. Among these chance collections of people a neighbourhood is formed with its own system of operating based on mutual understanding, and groups are formed to do odd jobs together like collecting empty cans and old magazines. As a result, these groups help maintain the lives of the street dwellers, by exchanging information and knowledge about odd jobs and day labouring, about locations to collect food, about the timing and locations for food handouts and about how to set up temporary shelters with tarpaulin sheets and cardboard. When I say 'as a result,' this is because these groups are not intentionally formed to perform such tasks. The street dwellers' world is intense. Whether they try to or not, they cannot avoid seeing others in the same predicament as they are in. They can obtain information and knowledge about how to live on the streets, without being neighbours or partners in odd jobs. They can do this just by trial and error. Because of this, there are many who try to go it alone, avoiding contact with others as much as possible. At the *yoseba*, there are many unspoken rules which help to maintain distance from others, like 'do not talk too much about your own past' and 'do not get involved too much with others,' (Nishizawa 1995:

106–113) and similar rules with the same purpose can be observed among street dwellers who share a strong class connection with the *yoseba* workers. Let us look at some neighbouring groups in their areas of habitation.

The habitation areas

> I get on well with people here. They are all good people. We do work and other things separately. There used to be four of us here, but now there are only two. The rest have moved closer to the railway station. I am not sure why. We don't ask those things. I go my way, while the others go theirs. Of course we often bump into each other, and we do have a chat then. We ask after each other, like how things are. When they come around and ask me if they can stay. I say of course. They might end up staying here forever. They might turn up one day and stay for a while. Then all of a sudden, they might go away somewhere (Mr A., seventy years old, spoken on August 6, 2002).

> It's just as well this place has not been attacked yet. The children. Those kids. They come in huge numbers. In summer. It would be terrible if we got attacked here. We often talk about the possibility. The kids hang around there all night, you know. Here, me and the other one, and over here, there are two more. Four of us are here now. We met here. We don't know who everyone is at all. We don't know when we are going to be here. Some of us, we just met by chance or have been introduced by the others. Some have just drifted in here. We take meals separately. We do it all individually. When something happens, they come around for help, and I do help, if asked. If I get something special, I go around and share it. But that's about it. We are not living communally. We would be exhausted if we did anything more. We don't meddle in each others' affairs too much (Mr. B., sixty-three years old, spoken on August 12, 2002).

For a start, the criteria for joining in the habitation area are vague things like being 'good people,' or they 'happen' to drift in. It is all decided in the loose flow of things. When they like, the street dwellers float away from one habitation area to another, in the same way as they moved in. Those who are left behind do not mind at all. Yukihiko Kitagawa sums this up as follows. 'Dissolving the relationship with particular fellow street dwellers, and the subsequent departure or eviction from particular groups, does not necessarily lead to isolation. The increase in numbers and the concentration of street dwellers mean that there always are more opportunities for him to establish a relationship with other street dwellers.' (Kitagawa 2001: 71) As well as the easiness with which people can come and go from groups, the unspoken rule of keeping a distance between themselves is considered most important and this regulates interaction within the group.

Of course, how powerfully the rule operates to regulate behaviour depends on each habitation area. Mr B says that in his area, the group takes meals separately, and in fact the way a group takes meals can be an important yardstick to measure the distance between the members of the group. As we will see later, how they obtain food or how they obtain money to feed themselves is a crucial issue that can maintain or break up the group. It could be said that taking meals separately is a wise decision which helps a group to maintain a loose connection, and avoids internal feuds. Of course, unlike Mr B's habitation area where the rule of distance is predominant and meals are taken individually, there are groups where people take meals together sometimes or in some cases, they eat together all the time. We see some groups, not just in the peripheral areas of the city but also in the area close to the city centre, where a separate 'dining area' has been set up in their shacks, or an outdoor kitchen has been set up and the meal is shared around the fire. In Hiratsuka, we saw a group that included a family (a mother and her son), where the mother was in charge of cooking.[4]

It seems people choose a group depending on their willingness at the time to comply with the specific degree of adherence to the rule of distance of that individual group. However, it is true that they tend to prefer an independent life without the restrictions of living with others when they have been living on the street for more than twelve months. The reality here indicates that they have to learn the rule of distance. According to the data from a survey done in Kanagawa prefecture, 42.9% of street dwellers with less than one year's experience shared their meals with others. However, the figure dropped to 27.2% among those who had been on the street for more than one year and less than three. The figure stabilized somewhat, to 26.5% for those who had lived on the street for between three and five years, and 32.4% for those who had done so for between five and seven years. If they are so concerned about personal distance, why do they form a group in the first place? In the case of a habitation area, the problem of fear is behind this collective activity. With increasing numbers of street dwellers it has become harder to find a place to hide, and more necessary for them to protect themselves by collecting together against sudden assaults by juveniles while they are asleep, and against violence by drunks. Also, if they find 'good people', though their judgement about this can often be wrong, they can include them in the group for the time being, although petty theft and cheating tend to be the causes of mutual mistrust. A jail without bars is an exceptional space where violence and theft can escalate to dangerous levels if left unchecked. In being subjected to such violence street dwellers are, from the start, set apart from others. Because they are living with constant fear, they construct their habitation areas to shelter themselves if only temporarily against those predators who threaten their existence. For their survival as individuals and as a group, they maintain their personal distance within the group.

Work mates

Rational reasons exist as to why working relationships are formed, such as maximizing profits through the division of labour and balancing out unstable incomes. Maintaining these kinds of relationships, however, is much harder than those related to the habitation areas.

> I hardly ever do it (work with other people). Why? Because of betrayal. They cheat you when you trust them. The trust backfires. When they first come in here because I'm sorry for them, I tend to give them a bit of money. I give some change to the smokers, out of the change I get when I buy cigarettes. I help them with food. But as soon as they get money, they don't want to know you. They betray you. After I was deceived by two people, I decided not to make friends any more. I really hate being lied to more than anything. Of course, it's different if you lie to protect others. Your partners slacken off and become lazy. You work hard and earn some money and come back with something. They just freeload off you. It's no good making friends at all. It's not like working in a company here (Mr C., fifty-two years old, spoken on August 8, 2002).

> I have worked with mates (collecting empty cans) before. It didn't work out. We would go halves, no matter how much you or the others collected. We tended to become dependent on the others, or we would begin wondering what the fair share should be, like why do I only

get half even though I worked harder, that kind of thing. It will never work no matter what (Mr A.).

Whether we are talking about Mr C who wanted to take on a more leading role, or Mr A who wanted to stabilize his fluctuating income as much as possible through working with others, I believe there are some common factors that work against the wishes of street dwellers in general. In a jail without bars, a belief in 'egalitarianism,' the idea that everyone there is pretty much the same as you are, is the primary and most dominant notion. When you find yourself there, and recognize there are people there in a similar predicament to you, it helps to soften the feeling that you have lost your self respect somewhat. However, because it replaces subjective judgement with objective values, the capitalist cash economy acts to revive the feeling of a lack of self worth which had been lessened by seeing other people in the same state as you. If you are earning more than your partner, you feel you are a sucker being exploited by your partner. Should you earn less than your partner on the other hand, you cannot help feeling worried that you are inferior to your partner. People in this situation are very sensitive to perceived 'insults.' As a result, an 'egalitarian' group can easily fall apart once money becomes involved. The 'self protective behaviour' observed by Kitagawa in a group in Shinjuku that 'you should not let others know how much money you have in your possession, even though they are your acquaintances' seems to have become the norm in this kind of context (Kitagawa 2002: 259–260).[5]

Certainly, keeping a certain distance in relationships similar to those I have just discussed can occur in various spheres of urban society. However, urban life in general is becoming more pluralistic and diversified, and a place where the rule of personal distance is strictly enforced seems to many urban residents to be exceptional. A jail without bars, however, is filled with singular life values and street dwellers are surrounded by a prescribed distance. The general prevalence of the rule of distance is indeed partly due to the fact that most of its inhabitants have an 'unspeakable past,' but, in addition to that, it is also necessary to understand the phenomenon as a result of the imprisonment of people in a jail without bars. The inhabitants there are subject to low self esteem, and they find themselves abandoned in the jail without bars. They have a type of equality there, but only that of a negative existence. In this jail without bars the inhabitants all look at each other with disdain, and it is also full of deep seated mutual distrust. The rule of distance is another social reality, just like all other skills developed by street dwellers to get by on the street, because no matter how much distrust they have for each other, they have to attempt to build a social life as a group and share what little comfort there is. Insights on social distance like 'they go their way, and I go mine,' 'we don't meddle in each other's affairs' and 'it's better if we don't make friends' are expressions of philosophy reached by the street dwellers after failures during their lives, judgements on fellow human beings and their society, or a 'compromise in life' as stated by the philosopher Shunsuke Tsurumi.

However, it has been reported that there are some examples of groups doing odd jobs which operate hierarchically like a boss and his workers, even though this contradicts the rule of distance, as it involves a ruler and the ruled (Kitagawa 2001: 69–70). Mikio Sumiya once pointed out that there was 'paternal system almost like a boss and worker relationship' operating in the urban odd jobs industry, which is different from 'modern paid labour' (Sumiya 1964: 66). This is observed amongst today's urban odd jobs operators as well. In fact, many street dwellers are happy with the idea of that kind of feudalistic relationship, having spent their working lives as day labourers or as employees of small businesses. Being alone and helpless, many of them are attracted to the idea of relying on a boss. But the attraction of becoming someone's workman is limited, and such a relationship can be easily broken up by betrayal either by the boss or the workers. The frailty and limitation of this relationship, rather than the feudalistic relationship itself, characterize the life of the street dwellers more clearly.

Mr C, quoted above, wanted to become a boss, and was never satisfied as a worker or a junior partner.

> Electrical goods. Radio cassette players and other smaller things, I go around collecting them, three times a week. Been doing that for nearly eight years now. The catch is drastically reduced of late. A lot of days I come home empty handed. I've stopped going a long way, so I can't find much, because I only get exhausted (laughter). I usually get up at about four. Still dark. Yeah, around four. I get going about five. Finish working around nine thirty. They come around collecting, you know. By then. The vehicles come around (Mr C).

The vehicles he mentions here are not from the council garbage collection.

At first, I didn't know the basics of anything at all. Was at a loss. About the end of January, I guess, the middle of winter and it was cold. I would go into the gardens and steal some mandarins. I didn't know anything about collecting electrical goods. A guy (also a street dweller) I happen to see every now and then, told me one day there's a Daiei shopping centre that will buy anything saleable. I dealt with the shop, I think, for about twelve months or so since then. The president of the shop in the Daiei complex, or he might be the shop manager, was a friendly kind of guy, probably ten or so years older than me, would buy electrical goods, leather jackets, cameras, watches and stuff. But the maximum he would pay was only ¥1,000 or ¥1,500, no matter how good the stuff was we brought in. That'd be all we'd get. So I started dealing with the guys coming around in the vehicles. For electrical goods and CDs, I would be paid ¥500 or ¥1,000 each, no problem. I would also take CDs and game stuff (gaming software) to a 'Book Off' store near the railway station. To that chain store dealing in second hand goods. How much would I make? Well, let me think. I make nothing at all when I don't find anything. Absolutely zilch. I go up to this guy who walks around here looking for antique stuff. I would ask him 'please lend me ¥2,000, ¥3,000,' and borrow some money. He's living in a rental flat all right. He's just looking for antique stuff. It is his work, I suppose. While I was looking around for the stuff, we started talking and after a while we became friends. He asked me to let him know if I come across antique stuff. We amateurs don't know what are good antiques, though. He prices the stuff I bring in, like ¥1,000, and takes that amount from my debt. I borrow some money, and I pay it back in goods. Like watches. There are a lot of people cruising around in cars looking for the stuff, a lot of harassment as well. There used to be whole lot more. A van ran into me from behind, like boing! What a pain! They kick you out. Because I was trading with other people. I was selling my stuff to other people. I tend to go to whoever pays more, you know (Mr. C).

Mr. C has a debt to the 'antique dealer' and because he feels indebted, he feels he has to look for 'antique stuff' all the time. We can see here the start of a boss and worker relationship. From Mr. C's point of view, however, the antique dealer is still counted as a friend. There are many who are trying to exploit Mr. C and others. For the time being anyway, that means more choices for the street dwellers that can go to 'whoever pays more.' As long as there are alternatives, the street dwellers can avoid becoming someone's worker and remain free from working exclusively for a boss. A 'friend' means someone who they can keep at a neutral distance in terms of the balance of power.

The social world of the street dwellers

The social world

In general, the way a group or an organization exists is the major factor in deciding how its members behave. However, our world is more and more pluralized with various changes taking place such as intensifying industrialization, urbanization, and the development of the information society, and the significance of the reference group which is outside the definition of a group or an organization, has increased greatly. T. Shibutani redefines the social world as a way to loosely understand various reference groups (Shibutani 1955, 1986). The social world means a collection of individuals who come together as a result of sharing a similar perspective on life, and framework of behaviour. Its members reaffirm their shared perspective and behavioural codes through their interaction with each other. It is appropriate to call the world of the street dwellers a social world, not a group or organization, since no qualifications are required to become street dwellers in the first place. Let us now examine the social world where the street dwellers place themselves, from where their various interactions and collective lives arise, despite the fact that their actions and inner selves are severely restricted by it.

The reconstruction of self identity

Living on the street is hard. The body quickly weakens and the wish to stay alive wanes. In spite of the adverse conditions, many of the street dwellers are workers or are at least willing to work, as numerous investigations suggest. Some street dwellers keep on waiting for day labouring work. They can certainly bring in a considerable amount of money when work is available, but the opportunities come so infrequently that they are not able to sustain themselves. Others prefer to 'create jobs.' Thus we have the start of urban odd jobs like collecting empty tins, copper wire, magazines and books and selling them to the dealers. This is also hard work and it hardly pays anything. The street dwellers have to rise early in the morning, walk around for miles and they make an average of scarcely ¥30,000 a month. If they cannot cope with this, either physically or mentally, they have to rely on scavenging leftovers from the restaurants or collecting lunch boxes which are past their use-by date and takeaway stuff from the convenience stores. Of course they generally tend to do everything, day labouring, odd jobs and scavenging food, whatever comes their way. The size of the day labourers' market for construction and earth moving work differs from one region to another. The conditions in which odd jobs are viable are also different. It is therefore difficult to generalize concerning the national trend for the way in which street dwellers earn their livelihood. What I must stress here, though, is that there is more than one means for survival, no matter how limited these means might be. We would need to seek the meaning of why they are choosing a particular one or something else, in the context of their justification of the reconstruction of themselves.

> I collect tins. To survive. I go around at night. On the nights when they put out (recyclables), you know. We do get harassed these days, like, you shouldn't take them away and so on. I try to sneak around so that they won't notice me. I take collected tins to a dealer in Hiratsuka. At first, I felt so embarrassed that I could hardly do it. I was taught (by fellow street dwellers) where to look for tins, how to collect them, the address of the dealer and so on. It took me a while to get used to it. It's not every day, you know, the first, second such and such day of the month, you know. If the collection days happened every day, that would be great. I can't find anything on the fifth such and such day, for a week. Sometimes there are collections twice or three times a week. There are quite a few people going around. We have to beat the others to it, you know. Get there earlier than the others. If someone's there already, I move on to the other spots. I do say hello to fellow tin collectors when I bump into them. I will ask 'How's things?' you know. It's very hard. I haven't eaten a meal (with rice) for a while. I have to cover a huge distance. On a push bike. It's a tough ask for an old man like myself. The hardest job is to transport the collected stuff. I know some people who do nothing, surviving on the chuck out lunch boxes they can beg from the convenience stores. We can't do that. I have to work hard, with my own body, to survive. That's why I can't afford expensive stuff. I have to live on cheap bread, cheap two minute noodles in winter, cheap packaged fried noodles, this time of the year. As a result, my diet is totally unbalanced (Mr A).

For Mr A who had lived in Hiratsuka for a long time working on construction sites, collecting tins is 'embarrassing' and 'hard' work.

He accepts that it is the only game in town. He is looking for an alternative way of living from just a bare existence, denouncing his fellow street dwellers who 'beg for lunch boxes from the convenience stores' (they are excluded from the category of 'we'). He differentiates himself from them, buying his food from his earnings. Mr D, on the other hand, who lived for a long time in a workers' shack on a construction site, still waits for the construction firm bosses and recruiters to one day show up offering 'good jobs' like in the good old days.

> The recruiters would come around even to places like this, asking if I would like to work. I would say, well, I don't mind. But I would make only ¥6,000 from a whole day's work. They would deduct money for breakfast and lunch, smokes and so on, leaving me with hardly anything. They would take just about everything. The recruiters come from Tokyo or Yokohama. There isn't any work locally. Till October last year I was at Ōimatsuda. I was living in a workers' shack run by the local boss. After I left there, because it started raining, I took shelter from the rain on the underground path over there, in Hiratsuka. I ended up staying there till the second or third of February. Then, there was a good spot in this park, so I thought this will do and moved in. It dragged on and I'm still here. Come September or October, I've got some work lined up, you know. I can go back to day labouring, you know. I've got a lot of places to go, if I want to. I've got a set of my work clothes, underwear and footwear ready all the time, because there are people coming around looking for workers. I've got a lot of things still to do, you know. I don't want to stay here longer than necessary, if I can avoid it. So, I'm waiting. Waiting for the good work to come around (Mr D, sixty-four years old, spoken on August 12, 2002).

Though he may still see himself as a worker, he has in fact got to rely on unsold goods from convenience stores for his survival. He is no different from many of the street dwellers in that respect. Yet he has his own yardstick, by means of which he differentiates himself from the others.

> As for meals, sometimes I have one, and other times I don't have one. I used to be able to feed myself with food scraps at the back of restaurants and eateries. Those places are rather scarce now. I don't like to rely on people's charity too much, you know, but, having passed the age of sixty, I can't help.... These days, I survive mostly on the

> stuff from convenience stores. My friends told me where to go. It depends on the stores, you know. And on people there. Some people are easier to talk to, while others are more difficult, you know. Younger men are no good. The older staff are much easier. That's the difficult bit. So, everybody does this (taking stuff away without asking). In the morning, about two or three o'clock, they sneak into the storage area and steal the stuff. It's three or four days past its use-by date. I myself can't do that. I have to go up there and ask for the stuff that is only a day or so out of date.

Mr D stresses he has the street skill to obtain 'the stuff that is only a day or so out of date,' unlike the others who have to eat 'the stuff three or four days past its use-by date.' However, he was much more interested in talking about the following than about the thrown-out lunch boxes from the convenience stores.

> You might be walking down the street and see a farmer. An old codger, if you know what I mean. I ask him if I can take this or that. He usually says, please help yourself. So I come home with daikon radish and all the rest and cook them. Seasoning is the most important. Stuff like salt and shōyu. If you have salt and shōyu, it will be fine. I have utensils. I've hidden them in a secret place. I have to hide them so that they won't be stolen, you know. Well, it doesn't matter so much if they get stolen. All I have to do is to look for replacements (Mr D).

His self respect has been satisfied with the work he has found, though only for the time being, while he is waiting for the next 'good job' to arrive.

> (Most recently) I've done things like tidying up. In town, I sometimes help loading the trucks. Even for a day, if there is work, like tidying up around a house, it's fine. I make only ¥5,000 or so though. I stumble onto that kind of work. I'm happy to give it a go if the lady of the house looks kind. If she's cross looking, I might walk away. I just don't like sitting still you know. Even if I don't have anything to do, I'll just go out and wander around here and there. I like walking around (Mr D).

According to the requirements of his way of life, he evaluates his social skills such as being able to read the expressions of people and to negotiate with others, and he is proud of his life skills such as being able to provide himself with a steady supply of salt and shōyu. By his yardstick, he can measure the difference between himself and the rest of the street dwellers. His unique philosophy and his attitude of valuing social and life skills, things that make his life more fulfilling, must have been developed as a result of the long years he has spent since leaving the child welfare facility, and living alone working as a day labourer. Mr D's self preservation skills are finely honed and his view on odd jobs is unique. He considers it is inappropriate for him to be engaged in odd jobs like collecting empty tins.

> I would never (be engaged in things like tin collection). Saw it for the first time after I arrived here. From Monday to Saturday, everyone goes out late at night to collect tins. They go around and pick up the tins, which are all stored neatly in (recycling) boxes. Why bother? The dealer will only give you ¥3,000 or so for a bag, thirty kilos of tins (Mr D).

Having said that, he does not mind going around collecting unwanted goods in bulk and 'trading' them with his 'friends.'

> ... Me, too, having been here for a long time, I have made friends, you know. In town, I pick up some bulky stuff and barter it. I never sell it for money. I only swap it for food. We estimate the worth of the stuff I pick up, like ¥2 or 3,000, then I barter it for what is fair, you know. When I'm short of money, I can manage by bartering. I'm a stranger to money now (Mr D).

Even though he has to refer to the market value, it means a lot to him to barter his goods rather than selling them. In reality what he does is working at odd jobs, but, because he does not convert the stuff he collects into money, he is able to retain his pride as a worker. Psychologically he is also able to stay away from the cold cash economy. As we have seen so far, street dwellers develop their value judgements and their justification for 'what they do' and 'what they don't,' depending on their different methods of survival. Their justification can be based on the dominant value standards they inherited from the organized and settled societies to which they once belonged. They use those standards to compare themselves to others and by dismissing others as inferior according to those standards, they can view themselves as slightly superior beings (like Mr B who values most his financial independence). Alternatively, they might use their own individual standards to place others in a negative light so that they can feel superior (like Mr D who boasts about his own social ability and life skills). Through that process, they can differentiate themselves from their fellow street dwellers. They can also differentiate their life from a bare existence.

Counter currents found in the social world

Masami Iwata remarks on the following:

> One of the things that impressed me when listening to their interviews is the way they see the world through the use of three different terms, 'me,' 'them (meaning other street dwellers),' and the 'society out there.' Often, the immediate concern 'me' is discussed as a quite separate existence from 'them,' the other homeless people. When dealing with this issue, non-homeless people tend to have a dichotomical perspective of 'us' ('society in general') and 'them' ('homeless people'). Against this perspective and through the way they emphasize that 'me' is not to be identified with such a group as 'homeless people' it is clear that this is something that is very important to them (2000:247–248).

Indeed '*me*' seems to intend to stay far away from '*them*,' out of the fear of losing '*my*' identity among '*them*.' However, the important thing to note is that when street dwellers attempt to cling to their own identity, *me* needs *them* as a referencing framework. Street dwellers enter their social world by accepting their difficult predicament and by recognizing that there are many who share this predicament. By sharing the rule of keeping a certain distance from each other and learning how to survive, they become engaged more deeply in their social world. Of course their world is enforced strongly by the existence of a jail without bars. It is a world they despise, but it is also a buffer for them as they struggle against a bare existence, as it gives them a reference point to regain their identities through comparison with others. If that world disappeared, they would be completely isolated and lose their sense of identity. The social world of the street dwellers thus provides a basis for their proof of existence. Going back to Nukada's argument, can we conclude that the sense of despair which may lead to the lonely deaths of these lower class people who have been segregated in temporary shelters where they are an isolated minority group, is derived from the fact that they have no reference point for their relationships from which they can reconstruct their self identities?

There are contact opportunities among the street dwellers, as well as a sense of personal distance. They can exploit each other, and these opportunities give them a vitality which helps to slow the number of suicides or that may even put a stop to 'slow suicides.' The street dwellers are exposed to the city. That fact enables them to construct their social world, to fulfil themselves, and to edge away from a bare existence, even though it appears that as a group that is the sort of life they are leading. The city is also a place that enables some street dwellers to say, 'I have still got a lot to do.'

12 Improving poverty stricken areas: A rehabilitation project for *Shima Danchi* public housing

Yosuke Hirayama

The rehabilitation of the *Shima Danchi*

At the *Shima Danchi* public housing area in Gobo city in Wakayama prefecture, the buildings were ageing and deteriorating and the residents were finding themselves in increasingly difficult circumstances. The problems were so intractable that the area had become poverty stricken. To deal with this situation, a project to rehabilitate the *Shima Danchi* was devised and put into practice. This is an inspiring project with a very fresh approach. The project to rehabilitate the *Shima Danchi* was really a 're-rehabilitation of a rehabilitation project'. The *Shima Danchi* public housing was first established as a result of a project to rehabilitate a deteriorated residential area with public housing construction. The key elements in contemporary housing policy for low-income people were the clearing and removal of degraded residential areas and the provision of public housing (Hirayama 2003, 2007; Hirayama and Ronald 2007), and *Shima Danchi* was created in just this way. However, the *Shima Danchi* project could not be maintained in a stable manner, and soon reverted to its degraded state. A housing estate created on the degraded area became a new degraded area. The rehabilitation project was intended to tackle this situation.

In this chapter, I will explore the project to rehabilitate the *Shima Danchi* and argue what this means to improve impoverished residential areas and rejuvenate degraded public housing areas. Why did the original project for improvement fail? Can such a rehabilitation project ever succeed? Why is there a cycle of problems, where a degraded housing area is rehabilitated and becomes degraded again only to require another rehabilitation project? How can we possibly break out of this cycle, and what strategies are needed?

I have been involved in the rehabilitation project for the long term. The *Shima Danchi* was in a bad state. It was obvious something had to be done. Various people had been involved in the rehabilitation of the area, but along the way a wide rage of problems had arisen. What, in the first place, does it mean 'to improve', 'to better', or 'to rejuvenate'? We needed to think about what these concepts mean. Some epistemological analysis for measuring the state of a poverty stricken area and understanding its structure has been conducted in Japan's academic circles, but there had not been much discussion of the strategies involved and how to actually implement these.

The rehabilitation of *Shima Danchi* was carried out as a practical, on the ground project. Most of the measures which were incorporated originated during the process from the participants. In order to determine what should be done to improve impoverished residential areas, instead of just being absorbed in theoretical study and abstract debate, an ongoing discussion was implemented, based what actually happened as the work is being done. Below I will present and analyse some of the problems and solutions I encountered during the rehabilitation process.

The rehabilitation project

The *Shima Danchi*, the biggest public housing estate in Gobo city, is situated in a *dowa* area along the Hidaka River. In *dowa* areas, residents are said to be descendants of an outcast group under the cast system of the feudal era and have been discriminated against in marriage and employment in even modern times. The government have implemented various measures to improve living conditions in *dowa* areas particularly in terms of housing, physical environments and employment. Constructed between 1959 and 1969, the *Shima Danchi* complex had in all ten blocks providing homes for 226 families. Nine buildings were medium height apartment blocks, with 218 apartments and the remaining one was a two storey block with eight homes. The construction of this public housing complex was heavily influenced by the various natural disasters which had hit the area including Typhoon Jane in 1950, the flooding of the Hidaka River in 1953, the second Muroto typhoon of 1961 and a severe fire in 1964. The housing complex grew out of a need for public housing and temporary emergency accommodation for disaster victims, and it was later renovated under the national government's programme for the upgrade of residential areas.

The degradation of the housing complex was plainly apparent with the extremely inadequate living conditions. Each apartment was only 30.2 to 39.6 square meters, and most of them had only a toilet and no bath. This small size had forced the occupants to try to renovate, in particular converting the verandas into bathrooms, and extending the living areas in the first floor apartments. These numerous random extensions and renovations had led to chaos throughout the whole complex. The residents were on low incomes, with most of them unemployed, the family units were unstable and many residents were affected by disease or disability. In 1989, the city administration set up a task force for *Shima Danchi* improvement to address the predicament. The task force carried out a fact finding investigation in the summer. It was the first investigation done of the *Shima Danchi*, which also provided contact opportunities between the residents and city bureaucrats.

In the following year, a group including myself was contracted by the city to carry out a more comprehensive fact finding investigation. Based on this investigation, we put forward a basic direction for a rehabilitation programme. The crux of our recommendation was, firstly, that it should be a 'comprehensive programme' incorporating a social work programme for individual households, a housing programme centring around the reconstruction of the buildings, and a community building programme. Secondly, the council should set up an office solely dedicated to the programme, and that it should be 'horizontal' and be 'on site.' Thirdly, the programme should involve the residents on a continual basis. These recommendations became the basis for the rehabilitation programme.

Office for the Rehabilitation

In April 1992, the council administration opened an on-site Office for the Rehabilitation of the *Shima Danchi*. The Office had a 'horizontal' organizational structure, corresponding to a division in the city government structure, staffed by six city employees from various sections including environment, welfare, *dowa* reconciliation, children and education. This must have been the first of such administrative offices in the nation. With the opening of the Office, the rehabilitation programme itself was ready to go. The residents reorganized the existing 'committee for community building' into a 'gathering for review' committee. A channel was thus set up, by which the Office would implement a 'comprehensive programme' which the residents could take part in through their 'gathering for review' organization.

Structurally speaking, the Gobo city council now had two divisions handling public housing matters, the Public Housing Division and the Office for the Rehabilitation of the *Shima Danchi*. The former would handle the maintenance and administration for the whole of the public housing in the city. The latter dealt exclusively with the rehabilitation programme, with the responsibility to speak on behalf of the *Shima Danchi* residents.

The initial task of the Office in the early days was to set up a relationship between the executive power and the residents. There was no denying that the city government had ignored the predicament of the *Shima Danchi* for a long time. To get the ball rolling for the rehabilitation programme, the Office staff had to first win the trust of the residents through continuous daily contact with them. The main task of the rehabilitation programme was the physical rebuilding of the residential buildings but the Office first concentrated on the social work and community building programmes. Through the social work programme, individual problems in each household were dealt with, and the community building programme was extremely effective in encouraging communication among the residents. The decision to prioritise these programmes was based on the belief that the physical rebuilding alone would not be sufficient to rehabilitate the area.

Towards an organic neighbourhood

The Osaka office of the Gendai Keikaku Kenkyujo, an architectural firm with prominent records of progressive planning and design related to public housing construction throughout Japan, joined in the programme as expert architectural advisor in 1993. The Gendai Keikaku and I worked together on the basic concept of the housing programme (Egawa, Hoshida, Maitani, Hirayama 1994). It was decided that the rebuilding programme would secure another plot nearby and utilize two sites, in order to avoid creating excessively dense living conditions by rebuilding on the existing site alone. The idea was to construct the housing on the new site first, then to get on with rebuilding work on the existing site. The basic concept of the architectural plan was to construct an organic neighbourhood. The *Shima Danchi* then was totally alien to its surroundings being monotonous, box-shaped and very densely populated. In order to alter this situation, the new *Danchi* was designed as an organic neighbourhood which would fit with its surroundings. Specifically, one of the features of the architectural plan was to segmentalise the volume of the physical buildings to blend in with the surrounding areas. This was expected to lead to the buildings' aestheticism within its local area. The complex was planned to have courtyards surrounded by the residential buildings but also be open to its surroundings, while the buildings were to have communal spaces such as common rooms, open corridors, and hanging gardens, designed to be integrated horizontally and vertically (see figure 12.1).

The construction of the organic neighbourhood progressed slowly. Instead of locking in the whole construction plan at the start, we opted to proceed with a small portion of the design and construction, reviewing them every year. The programme on the newly acquired site was estimated to require five financial years, while the project on the existing site would need four. The project that evolved gradually would be more effective, as we could reflect on the progress at the end of each financial year, and we could also deal with any newly emerging problems as they arose. In relation to the building code, this project was not presented as a design for one *Danchi* complex, but was accepted as a yearly ongoing renovation. Compared to locking in the design for one complete *Danchi* complex, our approach of yearly ongoing renovations was more suited to the project. Instead of being completed in one go, an organic neighbourhood ought to grow naturally.

Introduction of the workshop approach

When the renovation project kicked off in 1995, a workshop system was introduced to facilitate the residents' participation (Hirayama 1998, 2002). Workshops were set up where the residents, council workers and experts could get together to talk, interact, co-operate and work on the plan for rebuilding and rejuvenating the *Danchi* complex. The workshops were made up of the 'gathering for review' committee and the existing residents, the city government's Office for Rehabilitation and our group of experts. The residents were organized into different workshops according to the year they were scheduled to move in. The assiduous work on planning through the workshop system has developed into the core characteristic of the project, which remains still strong even today.

The construction planning at the workshop evolved around the participants' exchange of questions and answers. An outline of

Figure 12.1: Floor plan for the second floor of Green Heights

buildings and their layout was prepared first, tentatively, by the experts. A design process through continuous discussion with the residents progressed in the following order. With this tentative plan in hand, the experts paid 'door to door' visits to residents, and learned about their way of living and their future needs. Then the layout of the block showing which family would live in which part of the block was decided. After consideration of the residents' wishes, the layout of each apartment unit was then decided. The position of the common rooms, tree planting and rooftop gardens, external wall colours, how to dispose of garbage, the way of managing the community and other uses of common space were then decided. Following the completion of the construction each year, a follow up survey was conducted to find out if residents were happy with the results.

The first block was finally completed at the end of 1997. The new *Danchi* complex on the new site was named the *Gurin Haitsu* (Green Heights) by the residents. It had been nearly nine years since the task force for *Shima Danchi* improvement was set up, and almost six years since the Office for the Rehabilitation of the *Shima Danchi* had been established. In the autumn of 2001, with the completion of the fifth residential block, construction on the new site was complete, and so was the first stage of the rejuvenation project itself. At the time of writing, the project is continuing on the former site of the *Shima Danchi*, with the construction of the residential blocks under way. Incidentally, the project was awarded the Nihon Toshi Keikaku Gakkai Kansai Machizukuri Sho (Award for community development in the Kansai area from the City Planning Institute of Japan) and the Wakayamaken Furusato Kenchiku Keikan Sho (Wakayama prefecture's fine architectural urbanscape design for a hometown award) in 2000 and the Nihon Toshi Keikaku Gakkai Keikaku Sekkei Sho (planning and design award from the City Planning Institute of Japan) in 2002. It has certainly played its role in raising awareness of the importance of paying social attention to redeveloping deprived residential areas.

Who to help?

The rehabilitation programme was initiated to help the residents of a degraded residential area. Residents who had had to put up with inadequate environments, surrounded by desolation, will be able to improve their living conditions after moving into a freshly built residential block. However, just who the rehabilitation programme is aimed at assisting is a complex issue.

Programs to improve conditions in deprived residential areas inevitably have to divide poor people into those worth helping and those not. For the residents to move out of an existing deteriorated residence into a new residence, they have to have the necessary 'qualifications' to cross the 'boundary'. The programmes do not automatically assume that the residents of the deprived areas are worth helping. Only those with the 'qualifications' to cross the 'boundary' can attain the status of 'worth salvaging'. Pre-War investigations and studies into the improvement of degraded residential areas found that such programmes clearly decided which households could cross the 'boundary' and which could not (Sumita 1982). This rule still exists in today's similar programmes.

The households who wish to move to a new residential block are required to have the following qualifications. To take part in the rehabilitation programme, first of all, the occupants have to be legitimate leaseholders. They have to have paid their rent, their tax, their dues for national health insurance and so on. To be able to move into a new block, they have to have the means to pay the rent and maintenance expenses at the new place, as well as a guarantor.

As the rejuvenation of the *Shima Danchi* project went on, people without the necessary qualifications began to emerge. At the *Shima Danchi*, there are many residents whose rent is in arrears, who have 'purchased' public rental properties, who cannot easily find a guarantor, who are not living in the residential properties but just using them as storage space, and who are not legitimate residents. The city government had for a long time, turned a blind eye to the chaos in the *Shima Danchi* management. The qualifications related issues had been left to grow and become more complicated. The rent and maintenance expenses at the *Shima Danchi* had been relatively low. At the new complex these would rise sharply. Those residents on low incomes would not necessarily be able to pay for the increased rent and maintenance expenses.

The existence of a boundary in the rejuvenation project would not only put pressure on the residents, but also undermine the foundation of the project's existence itself. In the early days of the project, many residents from the existing *Danchi* applied, and the qualified ones succeeded in moving into the new blocks. As the project progressed, however, the number of applicants went down drastically. This was because the proportion of unqualified applicants among the remaining residents increased. The project would come to a halt as long as these unqualified residents remained, because, even though the buildings were complete, the residents for whom the new housing complex was built would not be able to move in. Before calling for applications for participants in the fourth stage of the programme, the Office for the Rehabilitation of the *Shima Danchi* conducted an investigation into the qualification issue. They decided to do this because they were worried that the project would not attract enough applicants. The result of the investigation revealed that many households were hesitant to apply, because they were anxious about the burden of increased rents, or the fact that their rent was in arrears, that they were not the holders of tenure, and so on.

The rehabilitation project is now in its final phase and calling for participants in the seventh stage. It is, however, noticeable that a significant number of remaining residents in the existing *Danchi* blocks are unqualified people. At the time of writing, there are forty-six households left in the old blocks. Of them, thirteen are not actually living there, while eleven of them have rent in arrears, and eleven of them are not legitimate tenure holders. Their ability to pay the increased rent is very low. Most of the qualified households have already moved into the new blocks. The proportion of residents with some problem or other is inevitably very high among the remainder.

We saw a marked difference in the approach to the qualification problems between the two city council divisions, the Office for the Rehabilitation of the *Shima Danchi* and the Public Housing Division. The former, having the role of representing the residents and promoting the project, suggested lowering the qualification standard. The latter, in charge of all the council public housing in Gobo city, could not give its consent to allow the residents of the *Shima Danchi* any special concessions. From the latter's point of view, the unqualified households had to go. The Office for the Rehabilitation of the *Shima Danchi* made various attempts to help the unqualified households become qualified. As a start, through the social work programme, help was offered to the residents to sort out the problem of unpaid rent and to correct the tenure titles. Some households, thanks to this help, were able become qualified and cross over the boundary. Secondly, the Office made changes to the qualifications, making the boundary easier to reach. In applying for the first and second stages, for example, the residents were asked to produce proof of their qualifications at the time of application, but from the third stage on, they only needed to produce it by the time they were going to move in.

Yet, the effort made solely by the Office could not remove the boundary. No matter how carefully the social work was conducted, there were households owing an enormous amount of rent, households on low incomes which could not possibly afford a rent increase, and households which could not adjust their leases. The easing of the qualifications did not mean the eradication of the boundary and there remained households which could not cross it. The Public Housing Division then began dealing with what it considered to be illegal squatters. It defined the residents who were not the legitimate holders of lease tenure to be squatters, and they were required to vacate the property and pay compensation. For the Public Housing Division, the eviction of illegal squatters would normalize the administration of the *Danchi* blocks. However, the legal ruling for how to deal with illegal squatters is not necessarily clear cut. It is legally possible for the executive power of the public housing to evict illegal occupiers. It is, however, very difficult for them to go to court and win the case, because their negligence in allowing the administration to fall into chaos would come under consideration. It was expected that squatters, whom the local government had overlooked, would not agree to pay compensation for their housing.

The definition of illegal squatters was awkward, and the measures taken by the city council's Public Housing Division were full of contradictions. For example, it tended to accept applications from people who were legal lease holders and had paid their rent on time, even if they were, in a strict sense, illegal because they were using the apartments for storage and not living there. On the other hand, residents who did not have legitimate tenure of their apartments, even though they actually resided there, and paid their rent on time, were considered to be squatters and would have difficulty securing an apartment in the new blocks.

The existences of a boundary and qualifications in the project have been used to define the parameters of those who are worth salvaging from among the deprived. The Office for the Rehabilitation of the *Shima Danchi* demanded that the parameters be widened, while the Public Housing Division wanted those households who were 'not worth salvaging' to be evicted. Yet, the measures taken by the both offices in dealing with the boundary had limitations. The complex problem of just who to "salvage" in the revitalization project presented itself.

Who decides?

Plural 'voices'

The defining characteristic of the *Shima Danchi* rejuvenation project was the introduction of the workshop system. Jurisdiction over public housing belongs to the local administration. However, at the project's workshop sessions we have seen not just executive power, but many concerned people voicing their opinions. Through the workshops, instead of the administrative voice with its overtones of legal authority totally dominating the project, it became possible for many voices to be heard. When a *Danchi* must be rebuilt, there always is the contentious question of who decides how this is to be carried out. All the people concerned with this project have treated the question as one that needs to be continually re-examined, instead of being simplified.

The workshop is comprised of the residents, city government bureaucrats and experts. In any project concerning public housing the participants are expected to perform their roles according to the definitions spelt out in the project. The residents are the object of the administrative measures. The government officials take on the mantle of authority and conduct the project. The experts provide their clients, the city council, with advice in their field of expertise. The three participants can perform their assigned functions and establish an effective working relationship, without their roles overlapping. The participants in the *Shima Danchi* renewal project, however, do not necessarily remain in their assigned roles during the workshop discussions. The relationship between the residents and the executive power in this project is clearly different from that in other projects involving the rebuilding of public housing. Issues such as who will live where, the layout of the apartments and how the maintenance of new *Danchi* blocks is to be are all discussed in the workshops. The city council, without resorting to its ultimate power of veto, incorporates the residents' wishes. The residents take part in a discussion which ranges beyond the basic object of the project. The relationship between the parties is difficult to explain simply. Whether the city administrators or the residents have the final say on any subject, or whether they can come to a mutual agreement, is not formulated in a clear cut manner. Their relationship is not standardized but changes constantly due to the different issues raised in the workshops.

As noted, two divisions of the city government have been involved in this project. Accordingly, there has not been a sole voice of executive power. We have had many occasions where the Office for the Rehabilitation of the *Shima Danchi* has differed in its opinion from that of the Public Housing Division. The former, because it is located on site and has the role of representing the residents as well, naturally has a different view of the project from the latter which is responsible for all of the public housing in the city. One of the factors that influence the project is the city ordinance for the maintenance of public housing. The *Shima Danchi* Office tends to make every effort, within the legal limits, to protect the residents' interests, while the Public Housing Division tends to enforce the letter of the ordinance.

The position of the experts in the rehabilitation project is not confined to conventional one. They are expected to provide the clients with technical advice. In this project, too, as is generally the case, the experts and the city administration have a contractual relationship where the former is paid by the latter for their services. At the workshops, however, the experts deal directly with the residents and are asked to help to make their wishes possible. When their wishes do not coincide with those of the administration, the experts have a complicated situation to deal with. As well, unlike experts in general, architects tend to have their own ideas and are looking for an opportunity to express them. The architectural experts do not necessarily respond to the demands of the residents or the executive power unconditionally. They have a tendency to believe in their own professional knowledge and to work on their own ideas.

Decision making

In the area of architectural and urban planning, the issue of how to build consensus has been examined. There is often a pre-programmed pattern in which the city council first provides the plan, the residents make their response and the experts try to get the agreement of all concerned. More often than not, the discussion tends to focus on how to streamline the process of reaching consensus, in other words, on technicalities. The workshop process is, on the contrary, not a means to reach consensus. The promoters of reaching consensus tend to see it as important to singularise the 'voices' presented, while the workshops focus on drawing out the plural 'voices,' the differences, among the participants. Any planning process requires decisions to be made. No project can make progress without these being made authoritatively. The decisions made through workshops are, however, completely different from those made through the consensus building process. If more than one 'voice' exists on particular subject, the consensus for decision making would be only a hypothetical construct and inherently impossible. The process of constructing consensus inevitably singularises the voices and declares that agreement is reached. But at a workshop, decisions are made on a premise of acknowledging the impossibility of reaching agreement. A decision made at a workshop does not represent the product of consensus making for the sake of it, but is a result of listening to more than one 'voice,' one made after paying attention to the dissenting voice to consensus building, or one made with a promise to continue to listen to dissenting 'voices' even after the decision is confirmed.

The rehabilitation project, of course, relies on decisions being made nevertheless. There are many decisions to be made in consultation between the residents, the city Office and the experts, about who should live where, the layout of the buildings, and the rules of community maintenance. In the workshop sessions, those decisions are made after encouraging more than one 'voice' to be heard and acknowledged by all the concerned people. The decisions made this way do not aim at reaching a simple conclusion, but still contain conflict. The workshop is not a process to select and designate the 'right voice.' All three participants insist on their individual standpoints. The residents ask for their needs and wishes to be met, while the executive power wants adherence to the system. The experts voice their expert opinions based on their professional experiences. Plural 'voices' do not necessarily lead to a convergence of these different standpoints. The adherents of consensus building would try to narrow down the parameters of the discussion using one sole 'right voice,' whereas the workshop would avoid the notion of a single 'right voice.' The significance of the workshop lies in the process by which conflicts about decision making are accepted, and more than one point of view can be accepted.

Thorny issues

The residents who are to move into a new block become most enthusiastic when they are working on the layout of their new apartments at the workshops. They come up with their own floor plans about which the residents, administrators and experts have numerous discussions. The residents really enjoy working on the floor plan layout because they can arrange it to suit themselves. However, it should be noted that the decision making process for the floor plans is not straightforward, and sometimes it brings up some difficult issues. An example of this is found in Mr. A's household. Mr. A lived with his wife and his teenage daughter at the time. The household was represented at the workshop by the daughter, then still at junior high school, largely because her father had a drinking problem, and her mother had a mental illness. The final layout decided on in the end, based on their proposal, is shown in figure 12.2. The floor plan is extraordinary, if evaluated from the sensible school of residential design. The final layout sets aside a separate corridor which does not make the best use of space. There are two adjacent south facing Japanese rooms {(1) and (3)}, that can open up into one large room, which is for the father to invite his friends over for a drink. A tiny north facing Japanese-style room, only four *tatami* mats {(4)}, is for the mother. The room for the daughter {(2)} is most the independent room of the house. The kitchen is tiny, with no dining, living or other space to mingle. From this kind of floor plan, we can see that it is not meant for a family but is just a collection of individual spaces. At the same time, we can see that the father is dominant and that the daughter desperately wants her own room.

When the draft floor plan was submitted by Mr. A's household, a lengthy debate erupted among the experts and the city council's Office workers. To those familiar with traditional house layouts, it just looked very odd. The experts voiced a series of critical comments. The space for the mentally ill mother was extremely small. Since she spends most of the day inside, her room should have adequate light and be a reasonable size. Because she cannot express herself, her needs are not reflected in this layout. The experts and the council have to represent her position. Her doctor should be consulted. On the other hand, the father's wishes are over represented and this is what makes this plan look so extraordinary. A floor plan with no family space is noticeably odd and inappropriate for public housing.

The Office accepted these critical comments from the experts, but staff decided to go ahead with the draft proposal as a basis for the final floor plan, taking into consideration the peculiar relationship among Mr. A's family. There is no doubt the father's wishes are overly represented and it is obvious the space for the mother is problematic. However, if the draft is altered, the father's anger will be directed at his daughter who had represented the family at the workshop. This extraordinary draft floor plan is based on the fragile balance in the family. If it was altered by the city, the Office, or by the other experts involved, it might lead to the destruction of this balance. Doubt still remains over the Office's judgement. Certainly it is in closer contact with the family than the experts and is more aware of what is going on in the family, but how deep

Improving poverty areas: Shima Danchi *housing*

Figure 12.2: Floor plan for Mr. A's residence

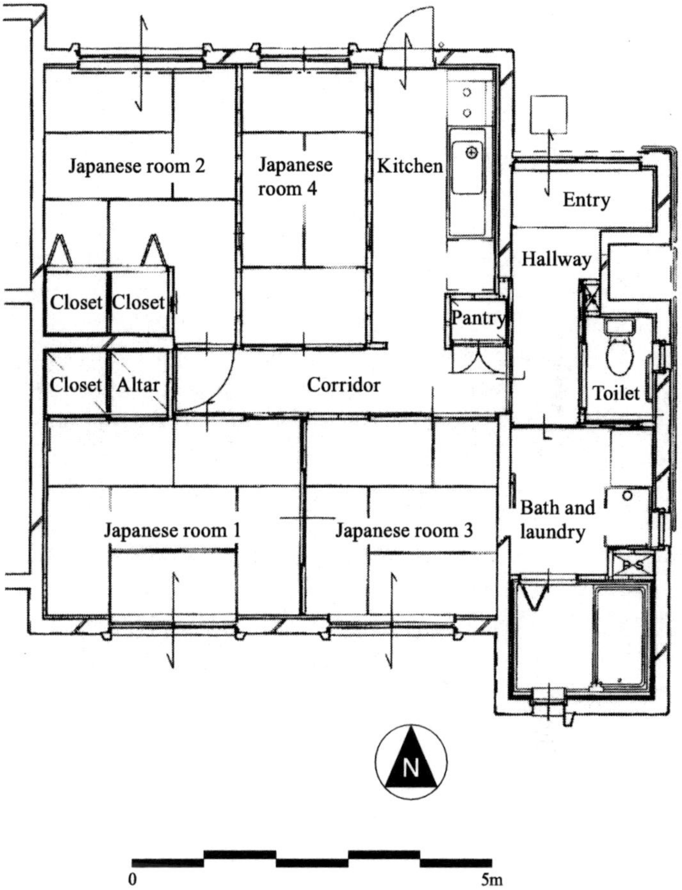

is its understanding? Should the stability of the domestic balance be given more priority than anything else? Is it an inappropriate floor plan for public housing?

The final design, after lengthy debate, was not very different from the original draft. The experience of making Mr. A's floor plan was symbolic of difficulties in addressing the various different opinions expressed in the debates that took place generally during the decision making process of the project. Is Mr. A's household really a household? Whose 'voice' exactly is this household's 'voice'? How can we respond to the mother's 'silent voice'? Is it acceptable for the architects to continue to cling to their accepted definition of rational architecture? These complex conflicts were born out of the many different 'voices' of the 'household', experts and administrators. We found that the rationale for the final decision can never be perfect.

What is desirable?

What is the 'ideal state'?

The act of rehabilitating residential blocks in a deprived area has a lot to do with what is desirable and what is the ideal state we can aim at. The *Shima Danchi* originated as a result of a typical modern housing policy. That is, the clearance of an old degraded residential area and the construction of new public housing blocks. This policy as it progressed has been intended to produce institutionalized spaces. Old, dilapidated, overcrowded and unhygienic housing was demolished, and run down residential precincts were replaced by good quality housing and improved living conditions. The construction of public housing, based on a legal foundation, means building what is recognized as desirable housing. In that sense it is the construction of a model space.

Modern housing policy has established a technique of standardizing design in order to define the 'ideal state' clearly. It is a technique intended to provide standardized accommodation to numbers of unspecified people. The generic idea is based on the principle of the separation of dining and sleeping areas, and the separation of family and individual spaces. Its basic concept is expressed in the floor plan in the form of X number of bedrooms plus dining and kitchen (nDK) and X number of bedrooms plus living, dining and kitchen (nLDK). Standard accommodation is designed for a standard *parents with children* family. The number of people in a household, n would correspond to the size of the (household) dwelling unit. It has been the accepted opinion that an appropriate standard of living would be ensured once these standardized apartments are piled up vertically and placed horizontally, with some additional open spaces, and some consideration for sunlight and air circulation.

The *Shima Danchi* had originally been created as an institutionally regulated space, but evolved out of this regulated framework. Whether the space created by the rejuvenation project can remain in a stable state, without again falling into chaos remains to be seen. There is a similarity between the original project and the second rehabilitation of the original project, as far as the construction of regulated space is concerned. However, what is different between them is the breadth of the range of what is desirable. There is a marked difference between the original construction project for the *Shima Danchi* and the rehabilitation programme, with regard to what is acceptable as desirable spaces.

Modern public housing policy has narrowed down the breadth of the ideal state and decanted numbers of people into it. However, the reality of the *Shima Danchi* where the multi-dimensional problems have been left incompletely resolved, proves that the problem is not just due to physical constraints such as the smallness of the apartments, but is also due to the limitations of the ideal state concept itself. In most public housing projects only standardized accommodation is provided. Those who cannot fit in are simply refused. The extremely simplified life in a *Danchi* tends to alienate the residents. It is assumed that in their 'ideal' apartment, a household consisting of a couple with children will lead a desirable life. The authorities believe that the husband with his regular job, his wife and their kids will lead a life socially defined as 'normal'. But this never corresponds with the reality of a public housing district where many low-income people live. At the *Shima Danchi*, half of the households are not couples with children. There are many problems in the neighbourhood such as unemployment, unstable employment, low income and illness. Imposing an ideal standard there means creating more difficulties for the residents.

By introducing the workshop system to the rejuvenation programme, we attempted to enlarge the boundaries of the ideal state and diversify the possibilities of what this accommodation could be, and the idea of what styles of living could be encompassed. This rebuilding project for the *Danchi* had in its sights the intended residents and their real lives. The experts examined and learned about the lives of individual residents, by visiting each household. The design layout of each apartment was based on the residents' wishes. In the design of the common space, the numerous opinions of the residents were taken into account. The workshop system diversified the ideal state of housing and encouraged people to push the boundaries of what is acceptable as a desirable space. At the time of writing, only a few years has passed since the completion of the first stage of the *Gurin haitsu* blocks. Accordingly, it is too early to say whether or not the high quality living standards of the new *Danchi* can be maintained. However, if different results emerge from the original public housing construction programme and the rehabilitation programme of the original project, it may be due to their different approaches toward an ideal state of public housing.

Housing and the household

A standard house design presupposes that there is a standard relationship between an individual family and individual housing. A standard family consisting of a couple with children is expected to lead its life within a certain style of housing, and this was made possible by the existence of a full time housewife. Families consisting of a couple with children are, however, not standard at all at the *Shima Danchi*. The most common households are single people, single parent families, and elderly only households, without full-time housewives. The lives of these families may not necessarily be contained only within their individual homes. The relationship between the family and the house cannot here be satisfactorily covered by the standard design.

First, more than one family for kinship reasons may use more than one apartment on a flexible basis. Some may have their meals at one apartment, but sleep in a different apartment. Or some may move from one apartment to another, following the changing composition of their family. Families may frequently visit each others' apartments. There are diverse ways they use their houses. Through the results of our door to door survey, we had noticed the existence of this multiple use of housing by quite a number of families in the *Shima Danchi*. The new *Danchi* has inherited this life style (see figure 12.3).

Second, in order for single elderly people to avoid becoming isolated and to be able to socialize, a common lounge space was included in the design of the new block. Elderly residents were therefore not confined to their own apartments, but had access to the lounge for a chat with neighbours over a cup of tea or a meal. The access to the lounge is through a sun room with floor grates, so that they do not need to change their footwear. This is effective in the sense that the elderly residents look at the space as their own. The lounge is regularly visited by home care workers who organize tea parties (see figure 12.4).

Third, an individual home does not necessarily need to suit the life of a family but rather that of the individual family members. Life in the home may not revolve around the interaction between the family members, but the dwelling may be just a space shared by the individual family members. Accordingly, a suitable floor plan may need less space for family interaction. Mr. A's family mentioned above is an example of this. It is common when the whole floor area is smaller than 70m^2, not to have a separate corridor, in order to

Figure 12.3: An example of multiple families using multiple homes

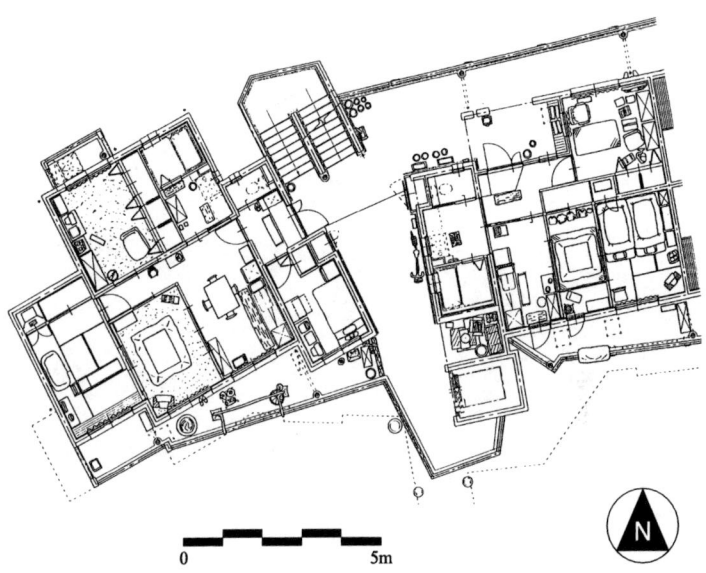

make the best use of available space. But we have examples here of distinctive corridors separating the rooms clearly. We also have floor plans allocating extremely limited space for a family lounge. In these cases, it is not the organic relationship of family members that makes up the household and thus the decisive element in the layout of the floor plan. In these cases, individuals, not the family, influence the layout in order to make sure that they have their own spaces.

What is seen in the new blocks resulted from the spatial planning via the workshops is that the house and the family do not necessarily correspond to each other. We can see the way things are heading here, that a way of living can be shared by multiple families, while, at the same time, be totally individualized within a family. Through the workshop system people have been encouraged to reconsider the way living space can be designed, in terms of the relationship between the house and the family.

Public and private spaces

Public rental housing has a double meaning as a space. On one hand, the housing is constructed as a public space. The citizens have a share of public housing properties via the administrative power. Tax

Figure 12.4: Floor plan for the first floor incorporating a lounge room

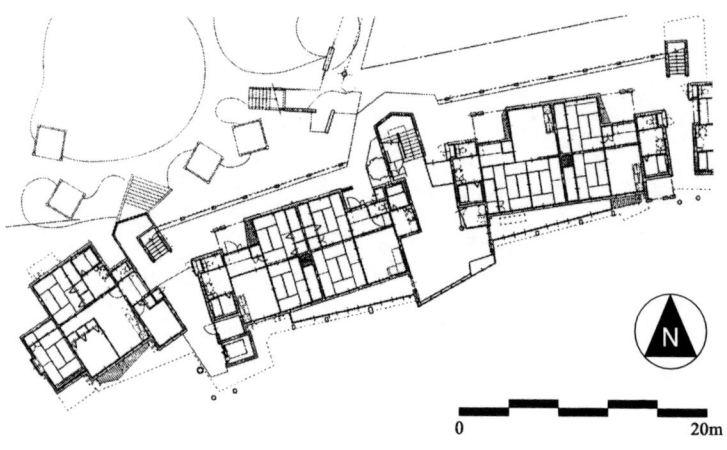

monies, national subsidies and local revenue are used for the physical construction of the public housing. Public rental housing is required to address many different needs since the exiting residents will be replaced by new ones. On the other hand, it also exists as a private space, occupied by specific households. In order to deal with the public/private characteristics of public housing, the standard design has consisted of only one style of space centring on the concept of nDK or nLDK. Standard design works on the assumption that private space that satisfies everyone works as public space for everyone. That kind of standard is, however, just a fiction. The technique of standardization, because it limits itself to a fictional standard which is believed to deliver the ideal state, has created what might be called the 'paradox of standardization.' By oversimplifying what is desirable, the space created is only good for a very limited number of people as a private space, and thus cannot be good as public space as well. A space designed for everyone is, in the end, suitable for nobody. Standardized approach of design has been responsible for the creation of a lot of housing neither private nor public.

In the rehabilitation programme for the *Shima Danchi*, we experimented with a new approach to private and public zoning. We attempted to make the private housing more open, and to make it possible for people to be private within the public space. Basing the layout of each individual apartment on the wishes of the individual household did not mean it would end up as an odd amalgam of private spaces. On the contrary, it led to a creation of public housing dwellings that suited many types of households. The life of a particular family is not exclusive to just that family, but is also a reflection of typical background factors which can be attributed to their ages, the household form, their social class and so on. By working with the layout each household wanted, not only private space is created, but also public space which is suitable for many successive households, because of these general characteristics. The space designed for a particular someone can indeed turn out to be a space suitable for many others. A private yet public space can thus be created.

In the programme for the rejuvenation of the *Shima Danchi*, the floor space has been diversified and the scope of what is desirable has been extended. While the standard layout approach tends to reduce the floor space into the nDKs and nLDKs pattern, we have many connecting room patterns as well. At the *Gurin haitsu*, all the apartments have different floor sizes and plans. This does not mean they form an awkward collection of individualistic apartments, because they still fit in with the general characteristics of households, with the nDKs, nLDKs and connecting room patterns being in the majority. Modern housing policy has treated the connecting room type of design as a leftover from the pre-modern era, and has excluded it from the standard layout design. The characteristic flexibility of the connecting room design has been considered undesirable, because the traditional Japanese style of house design has been seen as lacking in privacy and a clear function for each room, and so making housing modernization more difficult. Our project has rescued the traditional design pattern and incorporated it in the desirable housing layout.

One characteristic of the standard space design is the separation of the private and internal, and public and external spaces. Through our workshops, we came up with spaces that incorporated both of these concepts (see figure 12.5). The residents on the ground floor level consider the outside area as an extension of their living space, and enthusiastically construct flower beds and plant trees. The open air corridors on the upper floor are used as extension of the external living space. The apartments built to the connecting room design are ready to invite external visitors into the space inside. Many residents opted to install sliding doors instead of hinged doors at their entrance, and have verandas alongside. Both sliding doors and verandas have a softening effect on the boundary between the inside and outside of the house. Here we have created housing that

Figure 12.5: An example of internal yet external space

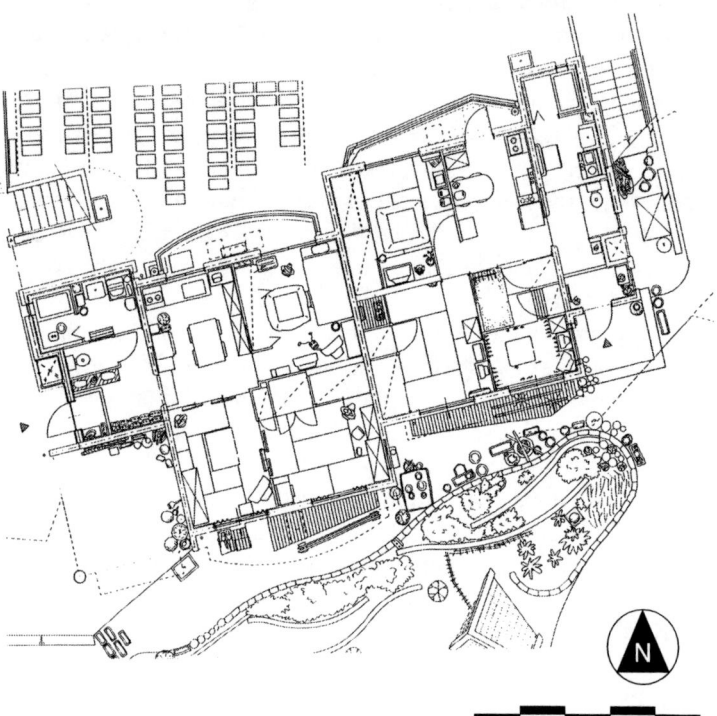

has both more open internal space and private external space. It is reminiscent of concepts such as Bruno Taut's 'external living room' and Frank Lloyd Wright's 'inter penetration of the interior and exterior.'

While *Danchi* housing built according to standard housing design simply piles up and spreads out residences, separating private and public spaces, the organic town created by our project links them through a series of small common rooms, a network of open corridors and gardens in the air. Common rooms, apart from the meeting hall, are embedded in daily living space, within easy reach of small groups of people. Corridors and gardens in the air produce an alternative space and an effective addition to the paths on the ground. They not only function as walkways, but also as informal gathering places, children's playgrounds and a place to relax as well. The project has attempted to embrace the private and public dual nature of public housing, and has created a space where private and public spaces merge organically. Compared to the *Danchi* built to the standard design, the *Gurin haitsu* looks vibrant because public and private spaces are interlaced and full of life.

The improvement of deprived areas

To be honest, I was shocked to see the state of the *Shima Danchi* when I first visited it. The blocks were just piles of old, small and dilapidated apartments. They even looked physically dangerous, because of the residents' unregulated renovations and additions to them. Litter was scattered amongst discarded cars. I was contracted to report on its current state and to come up with a proposal. I looked for positive signs to put in the proposal but all I heard from the people concerned was that "there is no future here."

I believed that this unhappy state of affairs could not be easily resolved. Physical rebuilding alone would not be effective in regenerating the neighbourhood. The residents were alienated from their homes and had lost interest in improving their environment. The whole *Danchi* needed reinvigoration. It seemed essential to get the residents themselves involved in the project. The executive power had to interact with the residents on a daily basis to build up a mutual relationship. Instead of fragmented programmes, the creation of a holistic programme was required. It seemed we needed to approach the task by making use of whatever small 'positive' signs we had.

An endless number of public programmes had been aimed at helping the *Shima Danchi*. They had only managed to make things worse, creating a miserable state of the estate. We had to conclude that something must be wrong with the public policies for the improvement of residential areas, including public housing, the standard design approach and all the other low-income housing policies of our modern society. As for the improvement of deprived residential areas, the criticism has been made that not enough resources have been allocated. We must remember, though, that merely increasing the injection of resources would not improve conditions in deprived areas. What we have to look at closely is the ways those resources are used. When we were faced with the appalling state of the *Shima Danchi*, we had to think seriously about what had gone wrong with the programmes in the past, and how we could correct those mistakes. It had to be done, also, not as a theoretical exercise, but as a practical one.

The way in which improvements are implemented is always straightforward. Where there is a 'problem', a particular 'method' is employed which should lead to a particular 'solution'. But, who defines what a problem is? Why is it a problem? To whom is it a problem? How is it changed towards a solution? To whom is it a solution? What method is employed to solve it? Why that method? All those concerned with the rehabilitation project, consciously or otherwise, have attempted to deconstruct the process of improvement. While the existing policy tends to focus in a narrow way on problem, method and solution, this project has looked carefully at situations that cannot be solved by conventional approach and we have sought a new direction towards a new approach. The staff at the Office for the rehabilitation project did not automatically follow the guidelines for 'who should be salvaged,' but instead made every attempt to break down the boundary and qualifications. The workshops did not rely on a single voice for decision making, but instead created an environment where multiple 'voices' could be heard. The scope for 'what is desirable' has been extended. The *Gurin haitsu* has produced an organic landscape, which is not because of design for its own sake. The residents themselves initiated the layout of their houses, took part in the workshops and discussed how the common space should be set out. The council staff from the Office for rehabilitation and the experts had numerous discussions. All of these things have resulted in expanding the sphere of what is acceptable for a good state.

I think the project has been a success. The old *Shima Danchi* was overcrowded with its small, ageing and out-of-date apartments, without bathing facilities. At the new *Gurin haitsu,* the living conditions have been exponentially improved with much larger living areas, and plenty of sunlight and airflow. The follow up surveys confirm the residents' appreciation of their improved living standards. But what has been achieved by the project cannot be measured by the level of physical comfort alone. The improved living conditions at the *Gurin haitsu* have had a flow-on effect in the residents' lives generally, as we can see in the residents' saying in the follow up surveys. Since moving into the new apartment, they said:

> Our daughter has successfully got married. In the previous *Danchi*, it was almost impossible to invite the partner's parents over.

> Our children have come to invite their friends home more often.

> I feel my health has improved.

> People say I am a much better colour.
>
> I was told that I look much better.
>
> My relatives have come to come and stay for the night.

Most of the residents appreciate where they are now. A rebuilding project would not be too difficult, if the intention was just to rebuild with an enlarged living space. I think, however, that what makes the residents so appreciative is the fact that they have experienced the process of rebuilding themselves, by voicing their opinions, listening to others and going over tough issues. The project has continued on step by step. Nearly every year, we face new challenges and we experiment with new methods. The workshop system has become a part of the landscape, leading to a genuine change taking place at the *Shima Danchi*.

Endnotes

Chapter 1

1 According to Tokyo's Sumida ward's 'Handling guidelines for the assistance of people of no-fixed-address,' 1982.
2 For example, the Tokyo government, because it was having trouble finding a place to accommodate the vagrants who had been illegally occupying public spaces immediately after the War, decided that 'it would help them to become self reliant and to put them up in private accommodation rather than compounding them into *hogo* facilities, if they were capable of working.' The government distributed for free the tents and beds of the former military to the operators of cheap rooming houses from pre-War days, and in return asked them to 'take in' vagrants (Iwata 1995: 68). Because of this, the cheap rooming houses were initially called 'houses of public welfare commissioned by the public services bureau' (Tokyo jōhoku fukushi sentā 1996: 21). On the other hand, by around 1950, most of the vagrants had constructed makeshift shacks and were making a living from the collection of recyclables. The legitimate industry of recyclables collectors became concerned about the widespread growth of unlicensed operators and demanded that the Tokyo government get rid of them. The Tokyo government demanded in return that the industry 'compound' vagrants from the areas around the Imperial hotel in the industry's dormitories, offering loans to update and improve them (Tokyoto shigen kaishū jigyō kyōdō kumiai 1970: 82–85). In this way, the 'recyclable collectors' area, as well as the *yoseba*, by absorbing vagrants, are becoming the 'special areas' of the big cities. A special kind of poverty can be concentrated in particular areas of the city by other policy measures such as residential improvement programmes in the *Dōwa* areas and the construction of public housing. These post-War style slums, as well as the 'foreigners' areas,' being not included by these policies became an issue from time to time.
3 The House of Representatives 'Resolution in regard to the bereaved family assistance (May 12, 1949)' and the House of Councillors 'Resolution in regard to the welfare of War widows and the bereaved families of the War-dead' (May 13, 1949).

Chapter 2

1 Shōzō Fujita argues that the 'establishment of the family registration system under which people are tied to the land (housing) was possible when the modern state connected its territorial notion to its people notion. Only then and there could the vertical notion of the subject and the horizontal

notion of the nationals emerge.' It is an important indication, Fujita notes, that the term 'nationals' came into general use by the Meiji government in its official notices, notes, and announcements, only after the attachment notice to the *Kosekihō* (Family Registration Act) in April 1871. Before then, the term had hardly ever been used (Fujita 1998: 106).
2 Of course, both universal public education and conscription are by themselves devices for standardizing people.
3 Berger and Luckmann typified the 'application examples' of 'conceptual structures' as therapy and nihilation. The Japanese terms I use here, *chiryō* and *impei* correspond to Berger and Luckmann's 'therapy and nihilation.' Setsuo Yamaguchi uses *mukōka* for nihilation when translating into Japanese. But here, I use *impei* to clearly differentiate it from physical nihilation, which Berger and Luckmann touched on, but did not categorize as a separate entity. I treat physical nihilation, *massatsu*, as a separate typification here.
4 Prison is for therapy, nihilation and physical nihilation. The emphasis shifts according to the changes taking place in the surrounding society. According to Bauman, all kinds of panoptical styles of control in prisons in a disciplinary society are 'factories of discipline, more precisely, factories of disciplined labour.' He finds in the 'state of the art' Pelican Bay prison in California, a completely different regulatory system from Panopticon. The inmates there do not have to work, nor do they have access to recreation. They do not mingle with fellow inmates, nor have any direct contact with the prison guards. Apart from remaining there, nothing is expected from them. The prison operates as a 'factory of exclusion, for people habituated to their status as the 'excluded.' (Bauman [2000] 2001: 88–92) He portrays the shift of meaning of these institutions from correctional houses to places of punishment.
5 Georg Simmel mentions the overwhelming nature of the sense of vision in the metropolis. In the metropolis where social distance is the norm, due to limitless degrees of social differentiation, people lead their lives in isolation, and their contact tends to be reduced to the level of 'seeing and being seen.' According to Simmel the masses are the bulk of people who produce and share an 'ordinary' lower stable way of life which everyone can aspire to. Among the urban masses, 'an immeasurable superiority of seeing others over listening to others is firmly entrenched.' (Simmel 1994: 252)
6 There have been hardly any studies done on the female urban underclass. The information is sketchy and incomplete. We are unable to talk about their lives as a whole here as there are no studies done. What Tomoko Kawabata (1998) reports as a 'reluctant acceptance' by the women working in the adult entertainment industry has perhaps a lot in common with the majority of people in the urban underclass. However, Kawabata concludes simply that the reason for their reluctant acceptance is because of legal control, namely the act banning prostitution.
7 In the case of a recently arrived ethnic minority, despite the xenophobic attitude, there is a possibility that some of them can set up an economic foundation of their own, like an ethnic business, by establishing a market of their own among people from the same region or among people who share the same language. However, it would be difficult for a minority group

which simply does not have the numbers to set up its own market. All they could do is to rely on the underclass labour market or to be employed in odd jobs.

8 Mitsuo Nakamura, a labour union activist in Sanya says the following:

> Since the 1980s, it has gradually become common for them to go straight to the work sites without coming to the *yoseba* in the morning. It is the norm now. (...) The relationship between the labourers and the brokers or recruiters is now one on one, shall I say. It's impossible now to go to the job as a group. In other words, everyone is screened out individually, (...) and it is extremely difficult for workers to establish contact with fellow workers, I'm afraid. (...) In the 1970s and 1980s, (...) among those working for cash, or among those workers who preferred to live in the *hamba* for work, workers naturally had mates, friends or whatever. It's becoming the thing of the past, or shall I say, it's almost completely gone from Sanya (cited in Nakamura 1998: 168–169).

Chapter 5

1 The Committee was appointed by the UK government to investigate health inequalities based on the social conditions in the country. *The Black Report* was named after the chairman of the committee, Sir Douglas Black. The report was published in 1980, and had a huge impact not only in the UK but also in other developed nations.
2 'Elderly household' in this survey referred to households made up solely of people over sixty-five years old, and households made up of elderly people and unmarried under eighteen year olds.

Chapter 6

1 The basic method of indexation used in this chapter is based on the method used in Kurasawa and Asakawa (eds) (2004). Please refer to this book as well. The maps used in this chapter are based on the administrative divisions as of 2003. A total of 335 local council areas were examined and represented.

The indices used are below.

Reference number
Title of the map
Data source
Definition

Figure 6-1
The ratio of blue collar workers (1975)
National census
Security, crafts, mining, manufacturing, construction workers/all employed workers

Figure 6-2
The ratio of blue collar workers (1990)
National census
Security, crafts, mining, manufacturing, construction workers/all employed workers

Figure 6-3
The ratio of blue collar workers (2000)
National census
Security, crafts, mining, manufacturing, construction workers/all employed workers

Figure 6-4
The ratio of unemployment (1975)
National census
Number of unemployed people/employable population

Figure 6-5
The ratio of unemployment (1990)
National census
Number of unemployed people/employable population

Figure 6-6
The ratio of unemployment (2000)
National census
Number of unemployed people/employable population

Figure 6-7
The ratio of single mother households (1990)
National census
Number of single mother households/total number of households

Figure 6-8
The ratio of single mother households (2000)
National census
Number of single mother households/total number of households

Figure 6-9
The ratio of public rental housing (2000)
National census
Amount of public rental housing/total number of dwellings

Figure 6-10
The ratio of private rental housing (2000)
National census
Amount of private rental housing/total number of dwellings

Figure 6-11
The ratio of owner occupied houses (2000)
National census
Number of owner occupied houses/total number of dwellings

Figure 6-12
The ratio of elderly single person households (1990)
National census
Number of elderly single person households/total number of households

Figure 6-13
The ratio of elderly single person households (2000)
National census
Number of elderly single person households/total number of households

Figure 6-14
The ratio of people on the Seikatsu hogo benefit (1990)
Demographic statistics of each prefecture
Number of people on the *Seikatsu hogo* benefit/total population $\times$ 1,000

Figure 6-15
The ratio of people on the Seikatsu hogo benefit (2000)
Demographic statistics of each prefecture
Number of people on the *Seikatsu hogo* benefit/total population $\times$ 1,000

Figure 6-16
The number of homeless people (2003)
Survey commissioned by the Ministry of Health, Welfare and Labour
Number of homeless people in each local council area

Figure 6-17
Number of vagrants found dead (1986–1990)
Yamaguchi (2004: 196)

2 When we compare the maps from 1990 and 2000 according to the occupational classifications, there are no major differences and we can conclude that the basic structures remain the same. We can see, however, changes in two indices. One is in the rate of workers engaged in administrative work. In areas like the middle of Kanagawa prefecture and south-eastern Saitama prefecture, we see a clear contrast between the high and low concentrations of these workers. When we take into account the changes since 1975, we can conclude that these workers are becoming more and more concentrated in particular areas. The other change is the rate of workers engaged in transport and telecommunication. They are now concentrated in the 'blue collar belt' and the prefectural border area between Saitama and Ibaraki in the north. We can see a concentration in the eastern areas of Ibaraki and Chiba as well. These are considerable changes since 1975.

3 Because this includes 'unknown' factors, the sum of these percentages does not add up to one hundred. The definition of a single mother household, according to the Ministry of Health, Welfare and Labour which conducts the *Zenkoku boshi setai tō chōsa kekka no gaiyō* (the National Survey of Single Mother Households) every five years, is 'a household with fatherless children (unwed and less than twenty years old) who are looked after by their mothers.' The national census, on the other hand, defines it as a 'general household, either as a result of divorce, death or separation, made up of a female sole parent and unmarried minors less than twenty years old (without other adults).' In other words, we need to note, the national census figures do not include those single mother households which share accommodation with parents or other adults.

4 The basic data for the rate of people on the *Seikatsu hogo* benefit is released in the country areas, by each district in Ibaraki, by each county in Chiba, and by each health Centre jurisdiction area in Kanagawa. Accordingly, each unit in these areas is represented by the same colour.

5 *Kōryoshibōnin*, or 'vagrants found dead' mean those who are found dead on the road, without any identification or without anyone such as relatives to claim their bodies. They were defined by the 1889 *Kōryo byōnin oyobi kōryoshibōnin toriatsukai hō* (The Act Concerning the Treatment of Vagrants found Sick or Dead). The head of the local council is obliged to conduct funerals for these unidentified dead people, according to the Act, and at the same time, publish a public notice in the official circular. For the details of the data processing see (Yamaguchi 2004).

Chapter 8

1 This chapter owes a lot to the work by Alcock (1997) on gender and poverty.

2 A letter to the editor from a woman in her thirties, who had wanted her husband to accompany her home from a child birth clinic, expressing her anger and frustration towards her husband's employer who refused to grant paid leave for child related or any other domestic reasons, saying 'do not spoil your wife.' (The Asahi Shimbun, morning edition, July 28, 2003) Incidents like this illustrate how dominant the household ethics based on the gender division of labour in corporate society still is.
3 According to the 2001 *Josei rōdō hakusho* (White paper on female workers), the female working population is 27.6 million, making up more than forty per cent of the entire workforce. The labour force participation rate for women with spouses is about fifty per cent. The participation rate for women in their late 20s and early 30s with spouses drops because of childbirth and the rearing of children. As far as their own wishes go, nearly forty per cent of women want to go back to work, while a third of women want to 'keep their current job even after giving birth to their babies'. {*Kosei rōdō shō* (Ministry of Health, Labour and Welfare), 2002: 53}
4 When married women are re-employed, seventy per cent of them do part-time work. It is noted that many of them seek part-time job in order to cope with their housework, child rearing, caring and other domestic duties (*Kosei rōdō shō koyō kintō jidō kateikyoku* [Equal employment, children and families bureau, Ministry of Health, Labour and Welfare] 2002: 54–55).
5 Eiichi Eguchi, who studied poverty from the point of view of social class structure, pointed out that it was characteristic of 'unstably employed' women that most of them had experienced family break-up (1979: 215–227).
6 In addition to Aoki (2003) see also Otomo (1985).
7 I analysed the process of families becoming homeless and came up with three patterns (Kawahara 2000). The 'spiral' pattern corresponds to the hidden poverty of women mentioned here. An example of 'hidden poverty' being manifested is an terrible case in which a mother, having left one live-in job for another, ended up in an acquaintance's public housing, where she starved her own child to death and was charged with protector negligence resulting in death (the Okayama district court ruling, Wa, #733, April 23 2003).
8 In this chapter, the term homeless is used to mean the state of having no home, nowhere to go and lacking the basis for stable living. Having no home or nowhere to go is not just a state, but it also contains the elements that could lead to social exclusion such as exclusion from the labour market, daily life which usually revolves around the home, isolation from various social relations and so on (Iwata 2000: 39–41). In Japan, the term homeless is generally used in the narrowest sense, as it is defined as 'those who reside in and lead their lives, for no reason, at parks in urban areas, river banks, roads, railway station buildings and other facilities' in the *Hōmuress jiritsu shien hō* (Act to Assist Homeless People become Financially Independent). Having no home or nowhere to go, however, is not necessarily limited to people living out on the street. It can take various forms. They could be, for example, having to stay against your will with relatives or friends, or getting evicted due to being behind in your rent, or being well enough to leave medical care but having nowhere to go, or they could be having to take shelter at night in cinemas and cafés. Research in the West indicates that women's homelessness tends to be hidden (Edgar

and Doherty 2001). Please note that the term is used in this chapter to include all these states.
9   Ministry of Health and Welfare notification, 'On the protection of women' (Ministry notification #161, December 11, 1946).
10 Article One, stating the reason for the enactment, is interpreted as 'the emphasis of the Act was that prostitutes themselves, with a few exceptions, are seen as unfortunate victims and to be rescued, while the pimps, operators and others involved in the prostitution racket should be punished' {*Hōmushō keiji kyoku* (Bureau of Criminal Affairs, Ministry of Justice) 1963: 21}.
11 Ministry of Health and Welfare notification, 'On the execution of section three of the Anti-prostitution Act regarding protection and rehabilitation' (Ministry notification #89, April 22, 1957).
12 This is based on interviews with the counsellors and directors of *fujin hogo* who were working at the time. They say that since around 1965, the prosecution rate on prostitution has been dropping gradually, and that temporary protection was provided for women 'who came in voluntarily because they could not feed themselves or they were suffering from violence.' Also, the Centre began catering for women with children as well. See also Kamano (1997).
13 Based on the aforementioned interviews in endnote 12. The 1961 law enactment has made it possible for the police to intervene in domestic violence if the offenders are drunk. If this were not the case, the authorities, including the social welfare office would have been rather reluctant to intervene in domestic affairs.
14 Based on the aforementioned interviews in endnote 12. Due to the reluctance on the part of the social welfare office to intervene in domestic affairs, lobbying was done by the people involved in the *Fujin hogo jigyō*, so that their counsellors could handle the cases. See also Kamano (1997). According to the interviewees, those who could not be classified as 'potential prostitutes,' were sheltered at the subsequently mentioned *Seikatsu hogo* facilities and the shelters for vagrant women with children.
15 For this process, see also Shigei (1977).
16 In this notification, the target clients of the *fujin hogo jigyō* are defined as those women 'with such problems as break-up of the family, poverty, being the victims of sexual crimes, and so on, who cannot lead a normal life and who have no other organizations to turn to for help. They may be unlikely to get into prostitution for the time being, but, if not offered assistance they might take up prostitution in the future. Assistance and protection should be provided to these women, from the perspective of prevention.'
17 According to the annual report of programme summery, by this notification, the '*fujin hogo jigyō* now has all women as possible clients, and the difference between the local ordinance and the national act has been removed.' From the statistics as well, the distinction between 'women in need for prostitution' and 'women in general' has also been removed {*Tokyo to josei sōdan sentā* (Tokyo metropolitan women's counselling centre) 1999: 5}.
18 For the historical development of the welfare programs for the homeless people in Tokyo, see Iwata (1995).

19 In relation to this, the term *furō boshi* (vagrant women with children) included, it is said, the families of War widows and, of course those returning from former overseas colonies {*Tokubetsuku jinji kōsei jimu kumiai shakai fukushi jigyōdan* (the Association of the Tokyo 23 special wards for personnel and welfare affairs) 2000: 30}.
20 There was opposition to this change, raised by the workers (Iwata 1995: 104–106; Taguchi et al., 1999: 195–196).
21 In those days, to be admitted at the *boshi ryō* shelter, one had to supply a copy of one's family register, resident register and a health report, as well as proof of income (tax return or equivalent) (Hamanaka 1978: 128–129). It was generally required before admittance, for the client to show an officially sanctioned paper of their marital status.
22 See {The *tokubetuku jinji kōsei jimu kumiai kōseibu, kongo no kōsei kankei fukushi shisetsu no unei no arikata kentō iinkai* (The committee to investigate the future operation of welfare facilities, The association of the 23 special wards in Tokyo for personnel and welfare affairs (1992)}, '*Kongo no kōsei kankei fukushi shisetsu no unei no arikatani tsuite: dai ichiji hōkokusho*' (On the operation of welfare facilities in future: the first report).
23 According to a newsletter from a non-governmental shelter for women in need, before the Domestic Violence Prevention Act came in force, many domestic violence victims were using the shelter. But after that, the number of domestic violence victims using the shelter declined drastically. Instead, the number of women living on the street at the shelter increased {*Josei no ie HELP* (House in Emergencies of Love and Peace) 2002: 1}.
24 It is noted that among homeless women, those with children are more likely to be protected (Passaro 1996: 19–21, Edgar and Doherty 2000: 233).

Chapter 9

1 For example, Hideo Aoki estimates that, as of September 1983, there were at least one thousand people sleeping on the streets in the Tokyo metropolis (Aoki 1989:107).
2 This Act, based on the principle defined in article 25 of the constitution, aims at guaranteeing a basic minimum standard of living to all nationals who are in dire circumstances, providing necessary assistance depending on the severity of their predicament, and assisting them to become self-reliant {Article One, the *Seikatsu hogo hō* (The Livelihood Protection Law)}.
3 This has been the case since its jurisdiction was transferred to the wards from the metropolitan government in 1965. Before 1965, the metropolitan government's Life Counselling and Rehabilitation Centres functioned as the contact points. See Iwata (1995).
4 The separation and exclusion from the welfare system of those considered to be able to work had been happening since the time of the *Seikatsu hogo* Act coming into force. Even then, when the streets were still full of War veterans and the unemployed and others who were referred to in those days as 'vagrants', the application of the *Seikatsu hogo* system was based on this principle, and excluded those who could work from the system's proper targets. See Iwata (1995).

5 In 1994 there was a court case (known as the Hayashi case) which dealt with the appropriateness of turning down an application for *Seikatsu hogo* assistance based on the ability to work as defined in a narrow sense. For the details of the Hayashi case, see chapter six of Katsuhiko Fujii and Matsuo Tamaki (2003).
6 The age at which a person is considered 'elderly' varies from one local government to another, but is generally 65.
7 Temporary workers lodgings are accommodation facilities where construction contractors and illegal recruiters house labourers.
8 One of the slang words used among the labourers who flock to the *Yoseba* is 'aokan' meaning sleeping out on the street. The fact such a word exists shows how common it is for them to face such a predicament.
9 For example, in the case of Sanya in Tokyo, the female population shrank drastically from 1,731, or 13.7% in 1961 to a mere 94 or 1.7% in 1976 (Nishizawa 1995: 78).
10 For example, Isao Imagawa pointed out that it was a common practice at various social welfare offices in the Tokyo metropolitan area in the 1970s to tell the people living on the street within their jurisdiction to 'go to Sanya and stay overnight and then go to the nearest welfare office,' and they would give them their train fare (Imagawa 1987: 76).
11 There are no comprehensive statistics on the upper age limit for jobs at the Yoseba, but based on my own interviews with homeless people (who commute from Shinjuku to Takadanobaba looking for jobs), it seems to have come down since 1995 (around 1995, it was the late 50s, but in 2000, the cut-off age was around 50).
12 For example, in the interim report on the homeless people of eastern Tokyo (Sanya and Ueno districts), Matsuo Tamaki et al (2000: 87) note the case of a construction worker who was fired from his job and forced onto the street, after living and working in the same temporary workers lodging for 8 years, because a test revealed he had high blood pressure.
13 Of course, there are people who have acted to set up support activities, but they are a minority, at least at the present.
14 Whether this takes the form of impounding them in a facility following a forced eviction (such as the removal of the street residents from the underground walkway in Shinjuku, Tokyo in February 1994), or of aiming at a gradual reduction of street homeless from public spaces without the use of force by building a facility first and persuading them to move into it, depends on the context on which each local neighbourhood is based (such as the reaction to each program from the organization set up to assist the homeless, the Neighbourhood Associations). It also affects whether or not help will be limited to temporary impounding (for example, at the emergency shelter at Nagai park in Osaka) or whether continuous assistance will be provided to the interned (for example, the Centres for Self Reliance in Tokyo and Osaka). For more information on the conflicts about the homeless policies between the government, assisting organizations and local residents, see Kitagawa (2002).
15 For example, see the 'Submission on the Handling of Homeless People' (dated September 30, 1999) addressed by the metropolitan parliament to the national government, and the petition from the Osaka Metropolitan

Government, Osaka City Government and the Osaka Chamber of Commerce and Industry (dated August 2000).
16 See for example, the 'letter of demand' issued by the 27 organizations of street homeless people and their supporters, to the government (dated May 22, 2002).
17 Those who are unemployed but considered to have the will and the ability to work, should be first considered for admittance to a Self Reliance Centre if there is one in the local area (*On the application of the* Seikatsu hogo *to homeless people*, notice # 0807001 on August 7, 2002, by the Ministry of Health, Labour and Welfare).
18 Unless otherwise stated, all the figures mentioned below about the Program to Assist Self-Reliance are taken from the table listed in *Tokubetsuku jinji kōsei jimu kumiai* (2002).
19 Based on statistics compiled by the Ministry of Health, Labour and Welfare.
20 Notice from the Director of the Section for Protection, Life and Welfare Division, Social Welfare Bureau of the Tokyo metropolitan government to the heads of the ward welfare offices (dated October 31, 2000) entitled *On the application of the* Seikatsu hogo *system to applicants for the Centre for Self Reliance, under the program to assist street homeless people to become self reliant* (12 Fukuseiho #865).
21 Based on an interview with a worker responsible for the Program to Assist Self Reliance, the Social Welfare Bureau of the Tokyo metropolitan government, on 19 November, 2001. The limits as to the use of the Centre, by the way, were 'relaxed' as of September 2003. Those who had left the Centre previously because of being employed and of 'becoming protected under the *Seikatsu hogo* due to illness or for other reasons' were now allowed to be admitted to the Centre again.
22 The word 'administration' in 'administration and security' here refers not to the administration of the white collar workers, but to the act of physically minding buildings and parking lots.

Chapter 10

1 Of course, we can point out that new migrant street dwellers have not been properly understood, or to be more exact, they have been neglected at the administrative level as well as at the citizens' movement level, because of the complexity of their problems, as they are a minority within a minority. We have to bear in mind that they are accordingly harder to study.
2 At *Gaikokujin shimin daihyōshakaigi* (Kawasaki City Representative Assembly for Foreign Residents) (1996), a suggestion was made to 'establish a local ordinance "tentatively called the Kawasaki city ordinance concerning residential properties" prohibiting discrimination against migrant workers of foreign origin over access to residential properties. In response to this, the Kawasaki city basic ordinance concerning residential properties was introduced in April 2000. In their first session *Gaikuseki kenmin Kanagawa kaigi* (the Kanagawa Foreign Residents' Council), proposals were made to develop a housing support system to improve the discriminatory conditions for foreigners trying to gain access to residential properties.

See: *Gaikokujin shimin daihyōshakaigi* (Kawasaki City Representative Assembly for Foreign Residents) *http://www.city.kawasaki.jp/25/25zinken/home/gaikoku/kaigi/index.htm*; and *Gaikokuseki kenmin Kanagawa kaigi* (Kanagawa Foreign Residents' Council) (International division, community relations department, Kanagawa prefectural government) *http://www.pref.kanagawa.jp/osirase/kokusai/seisaku/gaikokuseki/gaikokuseki-index.htm*.

3 See for example, Tsuzuki, Kurumi (1998), 'Esunikku komyuniti no keisei to "kyōsei": Toyodashi H danchi no kinnen no tenkai kara' (The birth of an ethnic community and "co-habitation": recent developments at the H danchi in Toyota City) *Nihon toshi shakaigakkai nenpō* (Annual report of the Japan academy of urban sociology), July 1998, Nihon toshi shakai gakkai.

4 In the verdict from the subsequent appeal court, though, it was declared to be sound not to consider the plaintiff as 'a person with an address,' and therefore, not to recognize his right to health insurance. For the details, see the Ijū rōdōsha to rentai suru zenkoku nettowāku (the Solidarity network for migrants Japan), *M-netto*, no. 37 (April 2001) and no. 48 (April 2002).

5 Both these interviews were conducted in August 1997. The ages given are as at the time of interview.

6 United Nations Population Division, 'International migration report 2002.'

7 According to the *Asahi Shimbun* (morning edition, November 21, 2001).

8 According to a survey conducted by Takamichi Kajita and others with Brazilians of Japanese ancestry, to the question 'what would you like to do when you get back in Brazil?,' more than forty per cent of them said they 'would set up a business.' (1999: 17–18)

9 For the activities dealing with these repeat migrants by citizens volunteer organizations, see the following. Chiho Ogaya, Nanako Inaba, Kimiko Ogasawara, Kiyoko Tanno and Naoto Higuchi, 'Ijū rōdōsha no enpawāmento ni mukete: shien soshiki ni yoru torikumi wo chūshin ni' (Towards the empowerment of migrant workers: activities by support organizations), *Ibaraki daigaku chiiki sōgō kenkyūjo nenpō* (Annual journal of the Institute of integrated regional studies, Ibaraki University), No. 34 (2001), Ibaraki daigaku.

10 The alienation of migrants' children brought to Japan by their parents, may not be the direct cause of the 1997 case in which a Brazilian boy of Japanese descent was bashed to death by a group of Japanese boys. However, it certainly was one of the background reasons. Refer to the following and others. Nishino, Rumiko (1999) *Erukurano ha naze korosaretanoka: Nikkei Burajirujin shōnen shūdan rinchi satsujin jiken* (Why was Herculano killed: the mob lynching of a Brazilian boy of Japanese descent), Akashi shoten.

Chapter 11

1 For the geographical limitations imposed on the habitation areas of street dwellers, see Nishizawa (2005a).

2 According to Shingo Tsumaki, there are many street dwellers that hate 'handouts,' and refuse assistance from the government or supporting organizations. This is, according to him, 'their form of resistance because they are governed by the "life ethic" that they should attain "independence by working".' Submission to this ethic, which is only the 'capitalist logic' of a 'civil society,' means they 'drop out' from the 'civil society' and then live on the streets, paradoxically in a civil society, because street dwellers do not wish to rely on anybody for their survival (Tsumaki 2003). If their struggle for survival is 'paradoxical' in a 'civil society,' we are able see the context in which it may become a form of social resistance by itself. But it is not that simple because it becomes 'paradoxical' only when it deals with the increasing number of street dwellers or complaints from neighbouring residents. For the street dwellers, 'their "life ethic" that they ought to attain "independence by working" ' is first and foremost an internalized mechanism, driving them to continual self-abnegation. It is also these sorts of values which force them to 'give up' and give in to 'despair' in their jail without bars, and which push them into a bare existence. If this is the case, it is not 'paradoxical.' The channel through which they daily struggle for survival can lead to social resistance, see Nishizawa (2005b).

3 This survey was carried out under contract to the prefectural government, and conducted by a team of concerned citizens, supporting organizations and scholars including myself and students, between February 11 and 16, 2001, on the river banks of the Sagamigawa in Atsugi and Ebina cities, Hiratsuka city, Fujisawa city, Odawara city, Sagamihara city and Chigasaki city in Kanagawa prefecture. The questionnaires were composed following a discussion amongst the team. The investigation was carried out in five cities with large homeless populations and in their environs, excluding Yokohama and Kawasaki cities, based on the results of a visual survey, *'Heisei 11 nendo Kanagawaken homuresu jittai chōsa'* (The 1999 fact finding study of street dwellers in Kanagawa prefecture). With the results of the *jittai chōsa* and suggestions from the local supporting organizations in mind, the areas where street dwellers were living were first recorded while the flyers asking for contributions to the survey were being distributed (between February 5 and 10). That record was translated onto the map, and then the interviews were conducted. We counted 397 homeless people of whom 251 responded to the questionnaires. The results of this investigation were compiled in the *Kanagawa toshi seikatsu kenkyūkai* (2001) *Kanagawa kenka nojukusha chōsa chūkan hōkokusho* (The interim report on a study of street dwellers in Kanagawa prefecture).

4 This woman and her son were hoping to leave their life on the streets as soon as possible by applying for the *Seikatsu hogo* benefit.

5 Kitagawa also mentions an 'unspoken rule' that 'when you are given scavenged food, you should not ask for the details of how and where it was obtained.'

References

Agamben, Giorgio (2000), *Jinken no kanatani: Seiji tetsugaku nōto* {Beyond human rights: political philosophy notes (Mezzi senza fine)}, translated by Takakuwa, Kazumi, Tokyo: Ibunsha.
Aihara, H. and Iki, M. (2002), 'Effects of socio-economic factors on suicide from 1980 through 1999 in Osaka prefecture, Japan' *J Epidemiol*, 12(6), pp. 439–449.
Aihara, H. and Iki, M. (2003), 'An ecological study of the relationship between the recent high suicide rates and economic and demographic factors in Japan,' *J Epidemiol*, 13(1), pp. 56–61.
Ainoya, Yasutaka (2002), 'Shakai hoshō to shiteno kokumin kenkō hoken seido (The national health insurance system as social security),' *Shakai hoshō* (Social security), 34(384), pp. 13–21.
Alcock, Pete (1997 [1993]), *Understanding poverty* (2nd edn), London: Macmillan Press Ltd.
Aoki, Hideo (1989), *Yoseba rōdōsha no sei to shi* (The lives and deaths of yoseba workers), Tokyo: Akashi shoten.
Aoki, Osamu (2003), 'Hinkon no sedaiteki saiseisan no kōzō (2)' {the structure of generational recreation of poverty (2)}, *Hokkaido daigaku daigakuin kyōikugaku kenkyūka kiyō* (Journal of educational studies, Graduate school, Hokkaido University) 89, pp. 211–237.
Axinn, June (1990), 'Japan: A Special Case', G.S. Goldberg, and Eleanor Kremen, (eds), *The feminization of poverty: only in America?* New York: Praeger.
Baishun taisaku kokumin kyōgikai kaihō (The report of the National Association against Prostitution), 1957–64.
Bane, Mary Jo and David T. Ellwood (1986), 'Slipping into and out of poverty: the dynamics of spells,' *The journal of human resources* 21(1) pp. 1–23.
Baudrillard, Jean (1995), *Shōhi shakai no shinwa to kōzō, fukyūban* (The consumer society: myths and structures, trade edition), Hitoshi Imamura et al (translation), Tokyo: Kinokuniya shoten.
Bauman, Zygmunt (1998), *Work, consumerism and the new poor*, Buckingham and Philadelphia: Open University Press.
Bauman, Zygmunt (2000a), "Social uses of law and order" in Gerland, David and Sparkes, Richard (eds), *Criminology and social theory*, Oxford University Press, Fukumoto, Keisuke (translation) (2001), "*Hō to*

chitsujo no shakaiteki kōyō (Social uses of law and order)," *Gendai shisō*, vol.29–7.
Bauman, Zygmunt (2000b), *Liquid modernity*, Cambridge: Polity Press.
Beier, A.L. (1986), Masterless Men: The vagrancy problem in England 1560–1640, London and New York: Methuen.
Benzeval, M and K. Judge, (2001), 'Income and health,' *Soc Sci Med*, 52(9), pp. 1371–1390.
Berger, Peter L. and Thomas Luckmann (1966), *The social construction of reality: A treatise in the sociology of knowledge*, Doubleday & Company, Yamaguchi, Setsuo (translation) (1977) *Nichijō sekai no kōsei: aidentiti to shakai no benshōho* (The construction of daily reality: dialectic of identity and society), Tokyo: Shinyosya.
Booth, Charles (1970), *Life and Labour of the people of* London, Vol.1. New York: AMS Press.
Cabinet Office, Government of Japan (2002), *Heisei 14 nen ban kōrei shakai hakusho* [2002 White paper of the ageing society], Tokyo: Ministry of Finance Printing Office.
Coe, Richard D. (1978), 'Dependency and poverty in the short and long run,' in Greg J. Duncan and James N. Morgan, (eds), *Five thousand American families: patterns of economic progress*, vol. 6, Ann Arbor: Institute for social research, University of Michigan Press, pp. 273–296.
Deleuze, Gilles (1996), Hiroshi Miyabayashi, (translation) *Kigō to jiken: 1972–1990 nen no taiwa (kaiteiban)* {Symbol and incidents: conversations taking place between 1972 and 1990 (revised edition)}, Tokyo: Kawaide shobō shinsha.
Diaz, T. et al (1994), 'Socio-economic differences among people with AIDS,' *Am J Prev Med*, 10(4), pp. 217–222.
Doherty, Joe (2001), 'Gendering homelessness,' B. Edgar, and J. Doherty, (eds.) *Women and homelessness in Europe*, Bristol: The Policy Press, pp. 9–20.
Duncan, Greg J. and Willard L. Rodgers (1988), 'Longitudinal aspects of childhood poverty,' *Journal of marriage and the family* 50(4) pp. 1007–1021.
Duran-Tauleria, E. and R.J. Rona (1999), 'Geographical and socio-economic variation in the prevalence of asthma symptoms in English and Scottish Children,' *Thorax*, 54(6), pp. 476–481.
Edgar, Bill and Joe Doherty (eds) (2001), *Women and homelessness in Europe*, Bristol: The Policy Press.
Egawa, Naoki, Itsurō Hoshida, Yoshiaki Maitani, and Yōsuke Hirayama, Yosuke (1994), *Gobo shi Shima Danchi saisei keikaku kihon koso hokokusho* (Report on the basic concept for the rehabilitation project of the *Shima Danchi* in Gobō city), Gobo shi: The City of Gobo.

Eguchi, Eiichi (1979), *Gendai no 'tei shotoku sō' jo* (Today's 'low income earning class' vol. 1), Tokyo: Miraisha.

Eguchi, Eiichi, Yukiyasu Nishioka and Yuji Kato (eds) (1979), *Sanya: Shitsugyō no gendaiteki imi* (Sanya: the contemporary meaning of unemployment), Tokyo: Miraisha.

Eijing sōgō kenkyū sentā (1998), *Senshinkoku ni okeru saishin no kōreika taisaku* (The latest measures to deal with an ageing society in developed countries).

Fujii, Katsuhiko and Matsuo Tamaki (2003), *Henken kara kyōsei he: Nagoya hatsu, homuresu wo kangaeru* (From prejudice to co-habitation: from Nagoya, thoughts on the homeless issue), Nagoya: Fubaisha.

Fujimura, Masayuki (1998), 'Fukushi kokka, chūryū kaisō, fukushi shakai (The welfare state, the middle class and the welfare society),' *Shakaigaku hyōron* (Sociology review), Vol. 49, No.3.

Fujita, Shōzō (1998), 'Tennōsei kokka no shihai genri (Governing principles of Japan's imperial nationhood,' in Fujita Shōzō chosakushū (Collected works of Shōzō Fujita), Tokyo: Misuzu shobō.

Furugori, Tomoko (1997), 'Sangyō kōzō no henka to tayōka suru koyō keitai' (The changing industrial structure and diversification of employment), *Nihon rōdō kenkyū zasshi* (Journal of Labor Studies in Japan), 448, pp. 29–38.

Geremek, Bronislaw (1993[1989]), *Awaremi to shibarikubi* (Pity or the gallows, *Litość i szbienca*), Mari Hayasaka (trans.), Tokyo: Heibonsha.

Glendinning, Caroline and Jane Millar (eds) (1987), *Women and poverty in Britain*, Brighton: Wheatsheaf.

Goldberg, G.S. and Eleanor Kremen (eds) (1990), *The feminization of poverty: only in America?*, New York: Praeger.

Hamanaka, Jōji (1978), 'Boshi ryō eno sochi ni tsuite' (On measures concerning the accommodation of women with children),' *Boshi kenkyū* (A study of single mother families), 1.

Handler, Joel F. (1992), 'The modern pauper: homelessness in welfare history,' Marjorie J. Robertson, and Milton Greenblatt (eds), *Homelessness: a national perspective*, New York: Plenum Press.

Harada, Katsumasa and Fumio Shiozaki, (1979), *Tokyo: Kanto dai shinsai zengo* (Tokyo: before and after the great Kantō earthquake), Tokyo: Nihon keizai hyōronsha.

Harada, Ken, Hidehiro Sugisawa, Erika Kobayashi, et al (2001), 'Kōreisha no shotoku hendō ni kanrensuru yōin: jūdan chōsa niyoru hinkon no dainamikusu kenkyū' (Factors related to income change among elderly: dynamics of poverty based on a longitudinal survey), *Shakaigaku hyōron* (Japanese sociological review) 52(3): 382–397.

Harvey, David (1989), *The condition of Postmodernity*, Oxford: Blackwell.

Hawker, Jeremy, Surinder S Bakhshi, Shaukat Ali and C Paddy Farrington

(1999), 'Ecological analysis differences in the relation between tuberculosis and poverty' *BMJ*, 319, 1999, pp. 1031–1034.

Hayakawa, Kazuo (1997), *Kyojū fukushi* (Residential welfare), Tokyo: Iwanami shoten.

Hayakawa, Kazuo and Yoshihiro Okamoto (1993), *Kyojū fukushi no ronri* (The logic of residential welfare), Tokyo: Tokyo daigaku shuppan kai.

Heywood, Frances, Christine Oldman and Robin Means (2002), *Housing and home in later life, Buckingham*, Basingstoke: Open University Press.

Hi hogosha zenkoku issei chōsa (The national simultaneous survey of the *hi hogo* people), annual editions Tokyo: Kiseirodosho.

Hiejima, Toshikazu (2002), 'Fukuoka shi no kokuho gyōsei: inochizuna no hokenshō toriageruna (The management of national health insurance at Fukuoka city: do not take away the health insurance cards as they are our lifeline),' *Shakai hoshō* (Social security), 34(384), pp. 22–25.

Hill, Martha S. and Stephen P. Jenkins (2001), 'Poverty among British children: chronic or transitory?,' in Bruce Bradbury, Stephen P. Jenkins, and John Micklewright (eds), *The dynamics of child poverty in industrialised countries*, Cambridge: Cambridge University Press, pp. 174–195.

Hills, John, Julian le Grand and David Piachaud (eds), (2002), *Understanding Social Exclusion*, Oxford: Oxford University Press.

Hirayama, Yosuke (1998a), *Wakushoppu haujingu: Shima Danchi saisei jigyo no purosesu to sono imi* (The housing workshop: the process of the *Shima Danchi* rehabilitation project and its meaning), Gobo shi: The City of Gobo.

Hirayama, Yosuke (1998b), Sumai no kaizen wo mezashite: *Shima Danchi* saisei jigyo no keiken to sono imi (Towards the improvement of housing: the experience of the *Shima Danchi* rehabilitation project and its meaning), Gobo shi: The City of Gobo.

Hirayama, Yosuke (2003), Housing policy and social inequality, in Misa Izuhara (ed.) *Comparing Social Policies: Exploring New Perspectives in Britain and Japan*, Bristol: Policy Press.

Hirayama, Yōsuke (2004), Fukanzen toshi: Kōbe, Nyū yōku, Berurin (Incomplete cities: Kōbe, New York, Berlin), Gakugei shuppansha.

Hirayama, Yosuke (2007), Housing and state strategy in post-war Japan, in Richard Groves, Alan Murie and Christopher Watson (eds.) *Housing and the New Welfare State: Perspectives from East Asia and Europe*, Aldershot: Ashgate.

Hirayama, Yosuke and Richard Ronald (eds) (2007) *Housing and Social Transition in Japan*, London: Routledge.

Hōmushō keiji kyoku (1963), 'Baishun bōshi hō kaisetsu' (Comments on The anti-prostitution act), *Kensatsu shiryō*, 123.

Horie, Hiroshi (2001), 'Wakayama ken ni okeru kekkaku rikanritsu no suii to chiiki kakusa ni kansuru kenkyū (A study of changes in tuberculosis morbidity and the local differentials in Wakayama prefecture),' *Wakayama igaku* (Medicine in Wakayama), 52(4), pp. 368–376.

Hoshino, Shinya (2000) *'Senbetsuteki fuhen shugi' no kanōsei* (The possibility of 'selective universalism'), Tokyo: Kaiseisha.

Imagawa, Isao (1987), *Gendai kimin kō: Sanya wa ikanishite keisei saretaka* (On the discarded people of our time: how did Sanya come into being?), Tokyo: Tabata shoten.

Inaba, Tsuyoshi (2002), 'Kibō wo takuseru shien sisutemu no kōchiku o! Tokyo ni okeru jiritsu shien jigyō no genjō to kadai (Build a system of assistance that nurtures hope! The current state and problems in the program to assist self reliance in Tokyo)' *Shelter-less*, 13, pp. 56–63.

Ishihara, Yoshirō ([1972] 1997), *Bōkyō to umi* (Longing for home and the sea), Tokyo: Chikuma bunko.

Ishii, Yuka and Nanako Inaba (1996), 'Jūtaku mondai: Kyojū no chōkika no nakade' (The housing problem: as the period of residence lengthens), in Takashi Miyajima, Takamichi Kajita, Naoto Higuchi, Yuka Ishii, Nanako Inaba, Aya Sadamatsu, Yukiko Tsujiyama, Haruo Ohta, Kousei Sakuma, Chinami Kasama, Toshio Iyotani, Dietrich Thränhardt (eds), *Gaikokujin rōdōsha kara shimin he: chiiki shakai no shiten to kadai kara* (From overseas migrant workers to citizens: from the perspective and issues of neighbourhood), Tokyo: Yūhikaku.

Iwata, Masami (1995), *Sengo shakai fukushi no tenkai to daitoshi saiteihen* (Social welfare in post-war society and the lowest level of the megalopolis), Kyoto: Minerva shobō.

Iwata, Masami (1997), 'Gendai no hinkon to hōmuresu (Contemporary poverty and homeless people),' Yōko Shōji, Hiroshi Sugimura and Masayuki Fujimura (eds), *Hinkon, fubyōdō to shakai fukushi* (Poverty, inequality and social welfare), Tokyo: Yuhikaku.

Iwata, Masami (1999), 'Josei to seikatsu suijun hendō: hinkon no dainamikkusu kenkyū' (Women and the fluctuation of living standards: a study of poverty dynamics) in Yoshio Higuchi and Masami Iwata (eds), *Paneru dêta kara mita gendai josei* (Contemporary women seen from panel data) Tōyō keizai shinpō sha, pp.171–191.

Iwata, Masami (2000), *Hōmuresu/gendai shakai/fukushi kokka: Ikiteiku basho wo megutte* (Homelessness/contemporary society/welfare state: thoughts on where we live), Tokyo: Akashi shoten.

Iwata, Masami (2001), 'Shakai fukushi ni okeru taishōron kenkyū no tōtatsu suiiki to tenbō' (The level of attainment and prospect of the theory of object in social welfare), *Shakai fukushi kenkyū* (Studies of social welfare), 80, pp. 27–33.

Iwata, Masami (2003), 'Atarashii hinkon to 'shakaiteki haijo' he no shisaku

(Policy enforcement on new poverty and 'social exclusion')', in Katsuyoshi Uyama and Ryōji Kobayashi (eds) *Atarashii shakai fukushi no shōten* (The focus of new social welfare), Tokyo: Kōseikan.

Iwata, Masami and Chizuka Hamamoto (2004), 'Defure fukyōka no "hinkon no keiken"' ("Poverty experience" under deflationary recession), Yoshio Higuchi, Kiyoshi Ōta and Kenkyūjo Kakeizai (eds) *Josei tachi no Heisei fukyō* (The Heisei recession for women), Tokyo: Nihon keizai shimbunsha.

Iwata, Masami and Keiko Kawahara (2001), Hōmuresu mondai to Nihon no seikatsu hoshō sisutemu (The homeless problem and Japan's livelihood protection system), *Sōsharu wāku kenkyū* (A study on social work), 27(3), pp.4–11.

Iwata, Masami, et al (2002), 'Sengo shakai fukushi taishō kategorî no hensen: Tokyoto shakai fukushi jigyō wo jirei to shite' (The transformation of social welfare target categories in the post-war era: examples from the social welfare programmes of the Tokyo Metropolitan Government), Nihon joshi daigaku, *Shakai fukushi*, No. 42.

Iwata, Masami, Taku Okabe and Hiroshi Sugimura (eds), (2003), *Kōteki fujo ron* (On public assistance), Minerva shobō.

Izuhara, Misa (2000), *Family change and housing in post-War Japanese society: the experiences of older women*, Aldershot: Ashgate.

Jalan, Jyotsna and Martin Ravallion (2000), 'Is transient poverty different? Evidence for rural China,' *The journal of development studies* 36(6) pp. 82–99.

Jenkins, Stephen P. (2000), 'Modelling household income dynamics,' *Journal of population economics* 13 (4) pp. 529–567.

Johansson, S.E. and J. Sundquist, (1997), 'Unemployment is an important risk factor for suicide in contemporary Sweden,' *Public health*, 111(1), pp. 41–45.

Josei no (*HELP*) (2002), *Nettowāku nyūsu* (Network news), 51.

Kajita, Takamichi (1999), 'Dekasegi 10 nen go no Nikkei Burajiru jin: 1998 nen no nikkei jin rōdōsha ankêto chōsa ni motozuku saikenshō' (Brazilians of Japanese descent a decade after they arrived in Japan to work: a revaluation based on a survey with migrant workers of Japanese ancestry in 1998), *Kokusai kankeigaku kenkyū* (The study of international relationships) No. 25 (March 1999), Tsudajuku daigaku.

Kamano, Rei (1997), 'Fujin hogo jigyō no rekishi' (A history of the program to assist women in need), *Seikatsu to fukushi* (Life and welfare), 497.

Kanagawa jichitai no kokusai seisaku kenkyūkai (2001), *Kanagawa ken gaikokuseki jūmin seikatsu jittai chōsa* (Research into the way of life of residents of foreign nationality living in Kanagawa prefecture). Kanagawa: Kanagawa Prefectural Government.

Kanagawa toshi seikatsu kenkyūkai (ed) (2001), *Kanagawa kenka nojukusha* chōsa chūkan hōkokusho: Atsugi, Ebina, Odawara, Sagamihara, Chigasaki, Hiratsuka, Fujisawa and Yokosuka no kakushi ni okeru (An interim report of the investigation into street dwellers in Kanagawa prefecture: at Atsugi, Ebina, Odawara, Sagamihara, Chigasaki, Hiratsuka, Fujisawa and Yokosuka), Kanagawa toshi seikatsu kenkyūkai.

Kano, Masanao (1983), *Senzen, 'ie' no shisō* (Pre-war times, thoughts on the 'family'), Tokyo: Sōbunsha.

Kawabata, Tomoko (1998), 'Baishun no kinshi no shakaiteki imi: kokka to jendā no kakawari kara' (The social meaning of the ban on prostitution: from the interaction between the state and gender), *Shakaigaku ronkō* (Sociological discourse), vol. 19.

Kawahara, Keiko (2000), 'Shukujo teikō shisetsu riyō kazoku no hōmuresu ka katei – hōmuresu kenkyū no tame no yobiteki kōsatsu' (How the families who patronize facilities offering shelter accommodation become homeless: a preliminary analysis for the study of homelessness), Nihon joshi daigaku shakai fukushi gakka, *Shakai fukushi* (Social welfare), 40, pp. 110–124.

Kawakami Ikuo (2001), *Ekkyō suru kazoku: zainichi Betonamukei jūmin no seikatsu sekai* (Families crossing the border: the lives of residents of Vietnamese origin), Tokyo: Akashi shoten.

Keisatsuchō seikatsu anzenkyoku chiikika (2002), *Heisei 13 nen chū ni okeru jisatsu no gaiyō shiryō* (Summary document of suicides in 2001).

Kida, Tetsurō (1960), 'Sengo shakai jigyō riron taikeika no shokōsō' (Various concepts on systematically theorizing the social programmes of the post-war era), Nihon shakai jigyō daigaku kyūhin seido kenkyūkai (ed) *Nihon no kyūhin seido* (A system for assisting the poor in Japan), Tokyo: Keisō shobō.

Kim, Chan Jong (1997), *Zainichi Korian hyakunen shi* (A one hundred year history of Korean residents in Japan), Tokyo: Sangokan.

Kimoto, Kimiko (2000), 'Rōdō to jendā' (Work and gender), *ōhara shakai mondai kenkyūjo zasshi* (Journal of the Ohara Institute for Social Research), 500, pp. 2–16.

Kinoshita, Reiko, Yoshimichi Yui and Keiji Yano (eds) (2006), *Shinguru josei no toshi kūkan* (The urban space for single women), Daimyōdō.

Kinra, Sanjay, Robert P. Nelder and Gill J. Lewendon (2000), 'Deprivation and childhood obesity,' *J epidemiol Community health*, 54(6), pp. 456–460.

Kiso seikatsu hoshō mondai kenkyūkai (2002), Nagoyashi 'homuresu' kikitori chōsa *tō ni kansuru saishū hōkokusho 2002 nen 12 gatsu* (The final report on the interviews and other investigations into 'homeless people' in Nagoya city, December 2002).

Kitagawa, Yukihiko (2001), 'Nojukusha no shūdan keisei to iji no katei: Shinjuku eki shūhen wo jirei to shite (Group formation and sustenance process among homeless people: a case study on Shinjuku district), *Kaihō shakaigaku kenkyū* (The liberation of humankind: a sociological review), 15, pp. 54–74.

Kitagawa, Yukihiko (2002), 'Hōmuresu mondai' no kousei: Tokyo wo jirei to shite {(Con)structuring the 'homeless problem': a case study on Tokyo}, *Kaihō shakaigaku kenkyū* (The liberation of humankind: a sociological review), 16(1), pp. 161–184.

Kodama, Tōru, Tamiko Tsuru, Nakamura Kengo and Hirakawa Shigeru (2003), ōbei no hōmuress mondai (jō) jittai to seisaku (Homeless problems in Europe and in the US (first volume): the reality and policies), Kyoto: Hōritsu bunka sha.

Koh, Sun Hui (1998), *20 seiki no tainichi Saishūtō jin: sono seikatsu katei to ishiki* (Japanese residents from Chejudo in the twentieth century: their lives and their consciousness), Tokyo: Akashi shoten.

Kokuho shimbun (The national health insurance press) (2000), October 10; December 1.

Kokuho shimbun (The national health insurance press) (2002), January 20.

Komai, Hiroshi (1969), 'Sanya hiyatoi rōdōsha no shakaiteki idō – shokuan siryō ni motozuku – shiron (Tentative thoughts on social transformation of the day labourers of Sanya, based on statistics from the official employment service agency), *Jinkō mondai kenkyū* (Journal of population problems), 110, pp. 40–48.

Komai, Hiroshi (1999), *Nihon no gaikokujin imin* (Overseas migrants in Japan), Tokyo: Akashi shoten.

Komamura, Kōhei (2003), 'Teishotoku setai no suikei to seikatsu hogo seido' (Low income earning households and the *Seikatsu hogo* system), Kido Yoshiko kyōju taikan kinen ronbun henshū iinkai, *Shakai hoshō kenkyū no kako to genzai kara mirai he* (The study of social security, from the past, to the present and the future), Tokyo: Kido Yoshiko kyōju taikan kinen ronbun henshū iinkai.

Kōsei rōdō shō (ed.) (2002), *Heisei 14 nen ban kōsei rōdō hakusho* (White paper on welfare and labour, 2002 edn).

Kōsei rōdō shō daijin kambō tōkei jōhōbu (ed) (2002), *Heisei 12 nendo shakai fukushi gyōsei gyōmu hōkoku* (The 2000 business summary of social welfare administration), Kōsei tōkei kyōkai.

Kōsei rōdō shō koyō kintō jidō katei kyoku (2002), *Heisei 13 nen ban josei rōdō hakusho: hatraku josei no jitsujō* (White paper on female workers: the reality of working women, 2001 ed.), 21 seiki shokugyō zaidan.

Kōsei rōdō shō koyō kintō, jidō katei kyoku (ed) (2001), *zenkoku boshi setai tō chōsa kekka no gaiyō Heisei 10 nendo* (The 1998 national survey of single mother households), Kōsei rōdō shō koyō kintō, jidō katei kyoku.

Kōseishō (1950), *Kōseishō shakaikyoku no 10 nen* (The ten years of the Social Welfare Bureau, Ministry of Health and Welfare).

Kōseishō hoken iryō kyoku shitsubyō taisaku ka (1996), *'Kōshū eisei shingikai seijinbyō nanbyō taisaku bukai gijiroku* (Minutes from the section meeting in dealing with adult diseases and difficult diseases, at the council for public health),' October 21 and December 15.

Kōseishō hoken kyoku (ed) (2000), *Heisei 12 nen ban iryō hoken jitsumu roppō* (2000 edition, six major acts concerning practical medical insurance affairs), Hōken.

Kōseishō shakaikyoku hogoka (1981), *Seikatsu hogo 30 nen shi* (A thirty year history of the *Seikatsu hogo*), Tokyo: Shakai fukushi chōsakai.

Koyama, Shinjirō (1950) *Kaitei zōho, Seikatsu hogo no kaishaku to unyō* (Revised and enlarged edition, The *Seikatsu hogo*, its interpretation and operation), Tokyo: Chūō shakai fukushi kyōgikai.

Koyama, Shinjirō (1951), *Seikatsu hogo hō no kaishaku to unyō (kaitei zōho)* {The interpretation and operation of the *Seikatsu hogo* Act (revised and extended edition)}, Tokyo: Chūō shakai fukushi kyōgikai.

Kozawa, Hajime (1934), *Kyūgo jigyō shishin* (Guidelines for relief activities), Tokyo: Ganshōdō shoten.

Kumazawa, Makato (2000), *Josei rōdō to kigyō shakai* (Women's work and the corporate society), Tokyo: Iwanami shinsho.

Kurasawa, Susumu (ed) (1986), *Tokyo no shakai chizu* (A social atlas of Tokyo), Tokyo daigaku shuppankai.

Kurasawa, Susumu (ed) (1999), *Toshi kūkan no hikaku shakaigaku* (The comparative sociology of urban spaces), Hōsō daigaku kyōiku shinkōkai.

Kurasawa, Susumu and Tatsuto Asakawa (eds) (2004) *Shinpen Tokyo ken no shakai chizu 1975–90* (New edition: A social atlas of metropolitan Tokyo between 1975–90), Tokyo daigaku shuppankai.

Kuroda, Kenji and Yoshimi Sumida (2002), 'Kōreisha ni okeru nichijō seikatsu jiritudo teika no yobō ni kansuru kenkyū (dai2 hō) {A study in preventing elderly people from losing their independence in daily life (second report)},' *Kōsei no shihyō* (Index for health and welfare), 49(8), pp. 14–19.

Kuroki, Toshikatsu (1958), *Nihon shakai jigyō gendaika ron* (On modernizing the social programmes in Japan), Tokyo: Zenkoku shakai fukushi kyōgikai.

Kusama, Yasoo (1936 [1987]), 'Donzoko no hitotachi' (People in dire straits), *Kindai kasō minshū seikatushi 1: hinmingai* (The journal of life of contemporary underclass people: skid row), Akashi shoten.

Lepietz, Alain. et al. (2002), 'Rethinking Social Housing in the Hour-Glass Society', in Ali Madanipour, Göran Cars and Judith Allen (eds) *Social Exclusion in European Cities*, London: The Stationery Office.

Lewis, Jane (1992), 'Gender and the development of welfare regimes,' *Journal of European social policy*, 2(3): pp. 159–73.

Machimura, Takashi (1994), *'Sekaitoshi' Tokyo no kōzō tenkan: toshi risutorakucyuaringu no shakaigaku* (The structural change in 'the world city,' Tokyo: a sociology of urban restructuring), Tokyo daigaku shuppankai.

Machimura, Takashi (1998), 'Baburuki ikō ni okeru toshi kaisō hendō: Tokyo wo jirei ni (The change to urban classes since the bubble economy period: examples from Tokyo),' Kurasawa sensei taikan kinen ronshū kankō kai (ed) *Toshi no shakaiteki sekai* (The social world of the city), UTP seisaku sentā.

Madanipour, Göran Cars and Judith Allen (eds) (2002), *Social Exclusion in European Cities*, London: The Stationery Office.

Majeed, Azeem et al (2000), 'Cross sectional study of primary care groups in London' *BMJ*, 321, pp. 1057–1060.

Marshall, Thomas H. (1981), *The right to welfare, and other essays*, London: Heinemann.

Maruyama, Masao (1964) *Zōhoban gendai seiji no shisō to kōdō* (Contemporary politics, theory and action, revised edition), Tokyo: Miraisha.

Marx, Karl (1965), *Das Capital*, Volume 1. Moscow: Progress Publisher.

Matsubara, Yasuo (1990), 'Famirî sapōto no kyoten to shiteno boshi seikatsu shien shisetsu' (Facilities to assist the lives of single mother families as a basis for family support), Yasuo Matsubara (ed), *Boshi seikatsu shien shisetsu* (Facilities to assist the lives of single mother families), Tokyo: Eideru Kenkyūjo.

Matsuzawa, Tetsunari (1988), 'Yoseba no keisei, kinō, soshite tatakai' (The formation of the *yoseba*, its function and its struggles), *Yoseba*, 1, pp. 169–198.

Mcloone, Philip and F. Andrew Boddy, (1994), 'Deprivation and mortality in Scotland, 1981 and 1991,' *BMJ*, 309, pp. 1465–1470.

Mies, Maria (2000), 'Gurobarizêshon to Jenddā: Orutanatibu pāsupekutibu ni mukete' (Globalization and gender: towards an alternative perspective), Furuta, Mutsumi (translation), in Kenko Kawasaki et al (eds), *Anpeido wāku towa nanika* (What is unpaid work?), Tokyo: Fujiwara shoten.

Mizota, Yuri et al. *Tokyo to ni okeru chūnen danshi shibō no chiikisa to sono shakaiteki haikei* (The local differentials and the social background to deaths of middle aged men in Tokyo), unpublished.

Mizuoka, Fujio (ed) (2002), *Keizai shakai no chirigaku: gurōbaru ni, rōkaru ni, kangae soshite kōdō shiyō* (The geography of economy and society: let us think and act globally and locally), Yūhikaku.

Mori, Hirotaka and Tagayasu Tanaka (1999), 'Gifu ken no kekkaku ni kansuru kenkyū (A study of tuberculosis in Gifu prefecture),' *Gifu ken hoken kankyō kenkyūjo hō* (Journal of Gifu prefecture's institute of health and environment), 7, pp. 5–12.

Naikakufu (2002) *Heisei 14 nen ban kōrei shakai hakusho* (The white paper on the aging society), Tokyo.

Nakagawa, Kiyoshi (1985), *Nihon no toshi kasō* (Japan's urban underclass), Tokyo: Keisō shobō.

Nakagawa, Kiyoshi (2000), *Nihon toshi no seikatsu hembō* (The transformation of life in Japan's cities), Tokyo: Keisō shobō.

Nakagawa, Kiyoshi (2002), 'Seikatsu hogo no taishō to hinkon mondai no henka

(Changes seen in the clients of public assistance and the poverty issue),' *Shakai fukushi kenkyū* (social welfare studies) 83: 32–42.

Nakamura, Mitsuo (1998), 'Yoseba to hamba no 10 nen: Sanya wo chūshin ni' (A decade of the yoseba and hamba: mostly observed from Sanya), *Yoseba* (Yoseba) 11, Renga shobō shinsha.

Nakamura, Mitsuo (1999), 'Hamba kyojū gata no kiga chingin: Ueno no rōdō sōdan kara' (The starvation wages of hamba living: based on a labour consultation at Ueno), *Kikan Shelter-less* (Quarterly Shelter-less), No.4.

Nakano, Tsuya (1973), 'Tokyo to no fujin hogo gyōsei no ayumi' (The history of the program to assist women in Tokyo), Tokyo to minsei kyoku, *Tokyo to no fujin hogo* (Protection of women in the Tokyo metropolis), pp. 277–300.

Narita, Kozo (1987), *Daitoshi suitai chiku no saisei* (The rehabilitation of the derelict areas of the megalopolis), Daimyōdō.

Nasubi (2003), '"Hōmuresu jiritsu shien tokubetsu sochi hō" seiritsugo no gyōsei dōkō to mondai' (The adjustments and the problems for administration following the "Special Act to Assist Homeless People to become Self Reliant"), *Yoseba*, 16, pp. 171–180.

Nishimura, Miharu (1984), 'Fujin hogo jigyō ni okeru 'yō hogo joshi' kitei wo megutte' (In regard to the definition of 'women in need of protection' specified in the program to assist women in need), Nihon joshi daigaku shakai fukushi gakka, *Shakai fukushi* (Social welfare), 25, pp. 33–44.

Nishizawa, Akihiko (1995), *Impeisareta gaibu: toshi kasō no esunogurafi* (Hidden in the open: the ethnography of the urban underclass), Tokyo: Sairyūsha.

Nishizawa, Akihiko (1997) 'Toshi kasō to shiteno nojukusha, "homuresu mondai" to sono kōzōteki haikei ni tsuiteno nōto' (Street homeless people as the urban lower class: notes on the "homeless problem" and its structural background), *Gendai Nihon shakai ni okeru toshi kasō shakai ni kansuru shakaigakuteki kenkyū, Heisei 7–8 nendo mombushō kagaku kenkyūhi hojokin sōgō kenkyu (A) seika hōkokusho [kadai bangō 07301068]* (A sociological study on the urban lower class in contemporary Japanese society, a comprehensive study carried out under the Ministry of Education Scientific Research Grant, (A) the report of the study [project number: 07301068]).

Nishizawa, Akihiko (2002), Teito ron nōto (Notes on the imperial capital), *Posuto koroniaru to hi seiō sekai (Kanagawa daigaku hyōron gyōsho 10)* {Post colonialism and the non-Western world (Critical essays from Kanagawa university 10}, Tokyo: Ochanomizu shobō.

Nishizawa, Akihiko (2004), 'Shokugyō kaisō kara mita Tokyo ken (The greater Tokyo area seen from the point of view of the occupational classes)' in Susumu Kurasawa and Tatsuto Asakawa (eds) *Shinpen Tokyo ken no shakai chizu 1975–90* (New edition: A social atlas of metropolitan Tokyo between 1975–90), Tokyo daigaku shuppankai.

Nishizawa, Akihiko (2005a), 'Hōmuresu no kūkan' (The personal space of homeless people), in Shunya Yoshimi and Mikio Wakabayashi (eds), *Tokyo sutadīzu* (Tokyo studies), Tokyo: Kinokuniya shoten.

Nishizawa, Akihiko (2005b), 'Bourei no koe: nojyukusya no aragai to teikō' (Ghosts with a voice: the resistance and struggles of street dwellers), in Ayumi Kariya (ed) *Hurachina kibou: homuresu / yoseba wo meguru syakaigaku* (Hope that exceeds limit: a sociology of homeless people and the *Yoseba*), Kyoto: Shōraisya.

Nomura, Masami (1998), *Koyō fuan* (Employment uncertainty), Tokyo: Iwanami shinsho.

Nukada, Isao (1999), *Kodokushi: hisaichi Kōbe de kangaeru ningen no fukkō* (Lonely deaths: a human renaissance at ground zero Kōbe), Tokyo: Iwanami Shoten.

Obinata, Sumio (1993), *Keisatsu no shakaishi* (The social history of the police), Tokyo: Iwanami shinsho.

Obinata, Sumio (2000), *Kindai Nihon no keisatsu to chiiki shakai* (The police in contemporary times and local communities), Tokyo: Chikuma shobō.

Ogawa, Masaaki (1960), Sangyō shihon kakuritsuki no kyūhin taisei' (A system for assisting the poor at the dawn of industrial capitalism), Nihon shakai jigyō daigaku kyūhin seido kenkyūkai (ed) *Nihon no kyūhin seido* (A system for assisting the poor in Japan), Tokyo: Keisō shobō.

Okada, Tōtarō (1984), *Fukushi kokka to fukushi shakai* (The welfare state and welfare society), Tokyo: Aikawa shobō.

Okamoto, Hiroyuki (2000), 'Hokkaidō ni okeru jisatsu no ekigaku (Epidemiology of suicides in Hokkaidō),' *Hokkaidō kōshū eiseigaku zasshi* (Journal of public hygieiology of Hokkaidō), 13(2), pp. 179–183.

Ōkawa, Akihiro (2001), 'Gaikokuseki shimin to shakai hoshō, fukushi seido' (Social security and welfare systems, and citizens of foreign origin), NIRA/ shichizunshippu kenkyūkai, *Tabunka shakai no sentaku: shichizunshippu no shiten kara* (Multicultural choice: from the point of view of citizenship), Tokyo: Nihon keizai hyōronsha.

Okazaki, Kyōko (2003), *Herutā sukerutā* (Helter skelter), Tokyo: Shōdensha.

Oki, Norio et al (2001), 'Hai kekkaku kanja no jushin to shindan no okure ni kanren suru yōin (The factors delaying medical consultation and diagnosis of lung tuberculosis sufferers),' *Hyōgo kenritsu eisei kenkyū jo nenpō* (Annual report of the Hyōgo prefecture institute for health), 35, pp. 82–88.

Onuma, Tadashi (1974), *Hinkon: sono sokutei to seikatsu hogo* (Poverty: its measurement and the *Seikatsu hogo*), Tokyo: Tokyo daigaku shuppankai.

Osaka shiritsu daigaku toshi kankyō mondai kenkyūkai (2001), *1998–1999 nendo {nojuku seikatsusha (hōmuresu) chōsa} chōsa hōkoku* {An investigative report on street dwellers (homeless people) in the years between 1998 and 1999}. Osaka: Osaka shiritsu daigaku toshi kankyō mondai kenkyūkai.

Osawa, Machiko (1993), *'Kigyō chūshin shakai wo koete: gendai Nihon wo jendā de yomu* (Beyond corporate centrism: analysing contemporary Japanese society through gender perspectives), Tokyo: Jiji tsūshinsha.

Osler, M., E. Prescott, M. Grønbæk, U. Christensen, P. Due and G. Engholm (2002), 'Income inequality, individual income and mortality in Danish adults,' *BMJ*, 324, pp. 13–16.

Ōtomo, Nobukatsu (1985), 'Boshi setai chōsa hōkoku – hi hogo boshi setai chōsa wo chūshin ni shite' (Report on single mother households: centred on those receiving benefits), *Seikatsu mondai kenkyū* (Study on life issues), 1, pp. 37–120.

Otto, Birgit and Jan Goebel (2002), 'Incidence and intensity of permanent income poverty in European countries,' *EPAG working paper* 28.

Ozawa, Martha N. (1990), 'America ni okeru hinkon no joseika' (The feminization of poverty in the USA), *Kikan shakai hoshō kenkyū* (The quarterly of social security research), 26 (3), pp. 228–242.

Passaro, Joanne (1996), *The Unequal Homeless: Men on the streets, women in their place*, New York: Routledge.

Pāto taimu rōdō kenkyūkai (2002), Pāto rōdō no kadai to taiō no hōkōsei (saishū hōkoku) {Current problems and the future direction of part time work (final report)}, July 2002. http://www.mhlw.go.jp/shingi/2002/07/s0719-3f.html

Phillimore, P. et al (1994), 'Widening inequality of health in Northern England, 1981–91,' *BMJ*, 308, pp. 1125–1128.

Reading, R. et al (1994), 'Do interventions that improve immunisation uptake also reduce social inequalities in uptake?' *BMJ*, 308, pp. 1142–1144.

Roberts, I. and C. Power, (1996), 'Does the decline in child injury mortality vary by social class?' *BMJ*, 313, pp. 784–788.

Rodgers, Joan R. and John L. Rodgers (1993), 'Chronic poverty in the United States,' *The journal of human resources* 28(1) pp. 25–54.

Rose, D. and D. Pevalin, (2002), *A researcher's guide to the national statistics socio-economic classification*, London: Sage.

Saife, B. et al (2000), 'Socio-economic characteristics of adult frequent attenders in general practice,' *Family Prac*, 17(4), pp. 298–304.

Sasaki, Yuka et al (1996), 'Yū shōjō jushin rei ni okeru kekkaku shishō rei no shakai haikei no kentō (Discussion of the social factors contributing to deaths from tuberculosis, following symptomatic consultation examples),' *Kekkaku* (Tuberculosis), 71(7), pp. 427–430.

Sasaki, Yuka et al (2002), 'Kōhan kūdō gata (b13) hai kekkaku shō rei no rinshōteki kentō {Clinical discussion on far-advanced cavitary type (b13) lung tuberculosis},' *Kekkaku*, 77(6), pp. 443–448.

Satō, Hideki and Kazuo Nakajima (1997), 'Chiiki kōreisha no yokuutsu jōtai wo kitei suru yōin (Factors defining depressive moods among elderly people in country areas),' *Kōsei no shihyō* (Index for health and welfare), 44 (13), pp. 10–16.

Seikatsu hogo no dōkō (Trends in the *Seikatsu hogo*), annual editions Tokyo: Chūō hōki shuppan.

Shakai fukushi gyōsei gyōmu hōkoku (fukushi gyōsei hōkoku rei) {The business report, social welfare administration (examples of the report on welfare administration)}, annual editions, Tokyo: Kōsei tōkei kyōkai.

Shibutani, T. (1955), 'The reference group as perspective,' *American Journal of Sociology*, 60: pp. 60–65.

Shibutani, T. (1986), *Social Processes*, Berkeley: California University Press.

Shibuya, Nozomu (2003), *Tamashii no rōdō: neo riberarizumu no kenryoku ron* (Labour with soul: on power by neo-liberalism), Tokyo: Seidosha.

Shigei, Takeyo (1977), 'Fujin fukushi jigyō no aratana hōkō o mosaku site' (In search of a new direction for the welfare programs for women), *Fujin mondai konnwakai kaihō* (Journal of the discussion group on women's issues), 27, pp. 26–30.

Shigeta, Shinichi (1960), 'Senjika ni okeru kōtekifujo no dōkō' (The development of public assistance during the war), Nihon shakai jigyō daigaku kyūhin seido kenkyūkai (ed) *Nihon no kyūhin seido* (A system for assisting the poor in Japan), Tokyo: Keisō shobō.

Shōya, Reiko (1996), *Gendai no hinkon no shosō to kōteki fujo* (Various aspects of today's poverty and public assistance), Kyoto: Keibunsha.

Simmel, Georg (1994), Tadashi Iyasu (translation), *Shakaigaku (ge)* {Sociology (latter half)}, Tokyo: Hakusuisha.

Simon, P.A. et al (1995) 'Income and AIDS rates in Los Angeles county' *AIDS*, 9(3), pp. 281–284.

Smith, M. Y. et al (2000), 'Housing status and health care service utilization among low-income persons with HIV/AIDS,' *J Gen Intern Med*, 15(10), pp. 731–738.

Sonobe, Masahisa (2001), *Gendai daitoshi shakai ron: bunkyokuka suru toshi?* (On contemporary megalopolis society: are the cities polarizing?), Tokyo: Tōshindō.

Spance, D. P. et al (1993), 'Tuberculosis and poverty,' *BMJ*, 307, pp. 759–776.

Stevens, Ann Huff (1999), 'Climbing out of poverty, falling back in: measuring the persistence of poverty over multiple spells,' *Journal of human resources* 34(3) pp. 557–588.

Stirling, A. M. et al (2001), 'Deprivation, psychological distress, and consultation length in general practice' *Br J Gen Prac*, 51(467), pp. 456–460.

Sudō, Yachiyo (2003), 'Domesutikku baiorensu to sōsharu wāku' (Domestic violence and social work), *Sōsharu wāku kenkyū* (A study of social work), 29 (1). pp. 10–17.

Sugimoto, Kiyoe (1986), "Hinkon no joseika' genshō to Rêgan fukushi seisaku' (The 'feminization of poverty' phenomenon and Reagan's welfare policy), *Shakai fukushi kenkyū* (A study of social welfare), 38, pp. 91–97.

Sumita, Shoji (1982), *Jutaku kyokyu keikaku ron* (On the supply plan for housing), Tokyo: Keiso shobo.

Sumiya, Mikio (1964), *Nihon no rōdō mondai* (The labour problems of Japan),Tokyo: Tokyo daigaku shuppankai.

Taguchi, Shinichi, Masaharu Kondō and Akira Shimizu (1999) *Haha to ko no kizuna* (The bond between mother and child), Sangaku shuppan.

Takahashi, Yūetsu (1992), *Daitoshi shakai no risutorakucharingu* (The restructuring of the megalopolis society), Tokyo: Nihon hyōronsha.

Takasawa, Takeshi (2000) *Gendai fukushi shisutemu ron* (On the contemporary welfare system), Tokyo: Yūhikaku.

Takegawa, Shogo (2001), *Fukushi shakai* (The Welfare Society), Tokyo: Yūhikaku aruma.

Takenaka, Hideki (1990), 'Nyūtaun no jūtaku kaisō mondai (The residential class problems of the new town)' in Susumu Kurasawa (ed) *Daitoshi no kyōdō seikatsu: manshon, danchi no shakaigaku* (Communal living in the megalopolis: the sociology of apartments and residential blocks), Tokyo: Nihon hyōronsha.

Tamaki, Matsuo (1999), 'Yoseba to gyōsei: Sasajima wo omona jirei to shite' (The yoseba and the government: an example from Sasajima), in Hideo Aoki (ed.) *Basho wo akero! Yoseba/hōmuresu no shakaigaku* (Open up the space! The sociology of the yoseba/homeless people), Kyoto: Shōraisha.

Tamaki, Matsuo (2002), 'Tokyo to hōmuresu jiritsu shien jigyō no nani ga mondai nanoka' (What are the problems of the Tokyo metropolitan government's program to assist self reliance?) *Shelter-less*, 15, pp. 19–31.

Tamaki, Matsuo and Keiko Yamaguchi (2000), 'Nojukusha no shūrōmen: Tokyo tōbuken (Sanya, Ueno) no nojukusha kikitori chōsa hōkoku' (On the employment of street dwellers: a report on interviews of face to face interviews with street dwellers in eastern Tokyo (Sanya and Ueno), *Kikan Shelter-less* (Quarterly Shelter-less), No.5.

Tamaki, Matsuo and Keiko Yamaguchi (2000), 'Nojukusha zōdai no haikei to yoseba no henyō: "Sanya, Ueno chōsa" kara miru hanba rōdō no jittai' (The background behind the increase in the number of street homeless people and changes at the yoseba: the realities for the labourers in the temporary workers sheds seen from an "survey in the Sanya and Ueno districts"), *Yoseba*, 13, pp. 76–90.

Tanii, Miyuki et al (1999), 'Arukōru senmon byōtō ni okeru chōki nyūin no haikei ni tsuite (The background of long term patients hospitalised in the specialised alcoholic treatment wards),' *Rinshō seishin igaku* (Clinical psychiatric medicine), 28(5), pp. 545–553.

Tanno, Kiyoto (2003), 'Burōkā no shakaigaku: pin pointo ijū to "chiiki rōdō shijō"' (The sociology of brokers: pinpointing migration and the "local labour market"), *Gendai shisō*, volume 31, number 6 (May 2003), Seidosha.

Tōki rinji shukuhaku jigyō kentōkai (1998), *Tōki rinji shukuhaku jigyō kentōkai rojō seikatsusha jittai chōsa hōkokusho* (The report of a survey of street homeless people by the discussion group on temporary accommodation establishments during the winter), Tokyo: Tōki rinji shukuhaku jigyō kentōkai.

Tokubetsuku jinji kōsei jimu kumiai (2002), *Kōsei shisetsu, shukusho teikyō shisetsu, shukuhakujo, jigyō gaiyō, Heisei 14 nendo* (The 2002 business summary of correctional facilities, facilities offering temporary accommodation and accommodation facilities), Tokyo: Tokubetsuku jinji kōsei jimu kumiai.

Tokubetsuku jinji kōsei jimu kumiai (2003), *Kinkyū ichiji hogo sentā ōta ryō riyōsha jittai chōsa* (A survey of the users of the ōta dormitory in the Emergency Temporary Protection Center), Tokyo: Tokubetsuku jinji kōsei jimu kumiai.

Tokubetsuku jinji kōsei jimu kumiai shakai fukushi jigyōdan (2000), *Chiiki shakai deno jiritsu wo sasaete: Tokyo 23 ku kyōdō keiei no kōsei kankei shisetsu 30 nen no ayumi* (In support of independence in the local community: a 30 year history of the joint operation of welfare related facilities among the 23 wards of Tokyo).

Tokubetuku jinji kōsei jimu kumiai kōseibu, kongo no kōsei kankei fukushi shisetsu no unei no arikata ō iinkai (1979), *Kosei shisetsu no arikata ni tsuite hōkoku oyobi fuzoku shiryō* (Report on how welfare facilities should be, with accompanying data).

Tokunaga, Masako (1996), 'Arukōru izonshō no chōki yogo kenkyū (A study of the long term prognosis for alcohol dependency),' *Arukōru izon to adikushon* (Alcohol dependency and addiction), 13(3), pp. 229–237.

Tokyo jōhoku fukushi sentā (1996), *Jōhoku fukushi sentā 30 nen no ayumi* (The thirty years of operation of the Jōhoku Welfare Centre).

Tokyo to fujin sōdansho/Tokyo to fujin sōdan sentā, *Jigyō gaiyō* (Annual report of programme summary), annual editions. Tokyo: Tokyo metropolitan government.

Tokyo to fukushi kyoku (2000), 'Josei no tayō na sōdan ni ōjite: domesutikku baiorensu nado de koe wo agehajimeta josei tachi. Tokyo to josei sōdan sentā' (Responding to various calls from women: women raising their voices against such problems as domestic violence, by the Tokyo municipal women's counselling centre), *Shakai fukushi* (Social welfare), 489.

Tokyo to fukushi kyoku (2001), *Tokyo no hōmuresu: jiritsu heno aratana sisutemu no kōchiku ni mukete* (Homeless people in Tokyo: towards the construction of a new system for self reliance), Tokyo: Tokyo to fukushi kyoku.

Tokyo to josei sōdan sentā (1997), *Kakushu shiryō ni miru josei sōdan jigyō no 40 nen* (Forty years of women's counselling from various data).

Tokyo to josei sōdan sentā, *Jigyō gaiyō* (Annual report of programme summary), annual editions. Tokyo: Tokyo metropolitan government.

Tokyo to minsei kyoku (1948), *Minsei kyoku nenpō* (Bureau of social services annual report).

Tokyo to minsei kyoku (1973), *Tokyo to no fujin hogo* (The protection of women in the Tokyo metropolis), Tokyo: Tokyo metropolitan government.

Tokyo to shakai fukushi kyōgikai boshi fukushi bukai (1998), *Kinkyū ichiji hogo jigyō ni kansuru chōsa hōkoku to sinpojiumu, siryō* (An investigative report into the emergency protection program and symposium: handout).

Tokyo to shakai fukushi kyōgikai boshi fukushi bukai (2003), *Heisei 14 nendo Tokyo no boshi seikatsu sien shisetsu jittai chōsa* (A survey of the reality of the facilities to assist the lives of single mother families, 2002 ed.).

Tokyo Uimenzu puraza (2003), *Plaza*, 13.

Tokyofu shakaika (1936), *Zaikyo Chōsenjin rōdōsha no genjō* (The current state of Korean workers living in Tokyo).

Tokyoto minseikyoku nenpō (The annual report from the Tokyo Metropolitan Government Public Service Bureau), 1948–1960.

Tokyoto shigen kaishū jigyō kyōdō kumiai (1970), *Tōshikyō 20 nen shi* (A twenty year history of the Tokyo Resource Recovery Programme Co-operatives).

Toshi seikatsu kenkyūkai (2000), *Heisei 11 nendo rojō seikatsusha jittai chōsa* (An suevry of the lives of street homeless people in 1999), Tokyo: Toshi seikatsu kenkyūkai.

Townsend, Peter (1974), Poverty as relative deprivation: resources and style of living, In Wedderburn, D. (ed.), *Poverty, inequality and class structure*, Cambridge: Cambridge University Press.

Toyoda, Tetsuya (1999), 'Shakai kaisō bunkyokukaron to toshi no kūkan kōzō: Tokyo tokubetsuku no jirei (On the polarisation of social classes and urban spatial structures: examples from the ward areas of Tokyo)' in Narita, Kozo (ed) *Daitoshiken kenkyū (jō)* (Studies of the megalopolis sphere, vol 1), Daimyōdō.

Tsukahara, Yasuhiro (2001), 'Shūnyū jōkyō to shūgyō kōdō, dōkyo kōdō (Employment and cohabitation in relation to income status)' in Hiraoka, Kōichi (ed) *Kōreiki to shakaiteki fubyōdō* (The ageing society and social inequality), Tokyo daigaku shuppankai.

Tsumaki, Shingo (2003), 'Nojuku seikatsu: 'shakai seikatsu no kyohi' to iu sentaku' (Sleeping out: the choice of 'refusing a social life'), *Sosioroji* (Sociology), 48–1.

Ukai, Shinichi (1994), *Gendai Nihon no seizōgyō: kawaru seisan shisutemu no kōzu* (Manufacturing industries of contemporary Japan: the structure of the changing production system), Shinhyōron.

United Kingdom Department of Health (1999), *Our Healthier Nation.*
United Kingdom Office for National Statistics (1997), *Health inequalities.*
United Kingdom Office for National Statistics (2000), *Health statistics quarterly 04 and 11.*
United States of America Census Bureau (2002), Current population survey, 1988–2002 annual demographic supplements in *Health insurance coverage: 2001.*
United States of America Department of Health and Human Services (2000) *Healthy People 2010.*
Vinamaki, H. et al (1995), 'The association between economic and social factors and mental health in Finland,' *Acta psychiatr Scand*, 92(3), pp. 208–213.
Wakabayashi, Mikio (1996), 'Kūkan, kindai, toshi: Nihon ni okeru (kindai kūkan) no tanjō' {Space, contemporary, cities: the birth of (contemporary space) in Japan}, Shunya Yoshimi (ed.), *21 seiki no toshi shakaigaku 4: toshi no kūkan, toshi no shintai* (The urban sociology of the 21st century 4: urban space, urban body), Kyoto: Keisō shobō.
Weich, S. and G. Lewis, (1998), 'Poverty, unemployment, and common mental disorders' *BMJ*, 317, pp. 115–119.
Williams, J.C. (1998), 'Domestic Violence and Poverty: The Narratives of Homeless women,' in *Frontiers: A Journal of Womens Studies*, vol. 19, pp. 143–165.
Willis, Paul (1977), *Learning to labour: how working class kids get working class jobs.* Farnborough: Saxon House.
Yamaguchi, Keiko (2001), 'Tokyo Sanya ni miru hōsetsu to haijo no kōzō: nojukusha no zōka to yoseba no henyō ni tsuite' (The structure of inclusion and exclusion seen in Tokyo's Sanya: on the increase in the number of street dwellers and the changes to the yoseba), *Kaihō shakaigaku kenkyū* (Study of liberated sociology), 15.
Yamaguchi, Keiko (2004), 'Hinkon no kūkan bumpu' (The spatial spread of poverty) in Susumu Kurasawa and Tatsuto Asakawa (ed) *Shinpen Tokyo ken no shakai chizu 1975–90* (New edition: A social atlas of metropolitan Tokyo between 1975–90), Tokyo : Tokyo daigaku shuppankai.
Yamaguchi, Keiko (2004), 'Tokyo Sanya ni miru hōsetsu to haijo no kōzō: nojukusha no zōka to yoseba no henyō ni tsuite (The structure of inclusion and exclusion seen in Tokyo's Sanya: on the increase in street dwellers and the changes to the yoseba),' *Kaihō shakaigaku kenkyū* (The study of liberated sociology), 15.
Yamamoto, Kahoruko (1998), 'Fîrudo nōto' (Field note), document attached to master's thesis, Keio University (unpublished).
Yamamoto, Kahoruko (2000), '"Āban esunisiti" saikō: nyūkamā no kategorîka mondai wo megutte' (A Reconsideration of "Urban Ethnicity": A New Approach to the issue of Migrants Workers in Japan), *Nenpo shakaigaku*

ronshū (The Annual Review of Sociology), No.13 (June 2000), Kantō shakaigakkai.

Yamazaki, Yoshihiko (1989), *Toshika to jumyō no kankei ni kansuru kenkyū* (A study of the correlation between urbanization and longevity), Chiiki shakai kenkyūjo hōkokusho.

Yokohamashi gyōsei mondai jishukenkyu B kōsu fujin boshi mondai kenkyūkai (1983), *Fujin hogo jigyō toha nanika* (What is the *Programme for Assisting Women in Need*?).

Yokoyama, Gennosuke (1985), *Nihon no kasō shakai (shimban)* {The underclass of Japan (new edition)}, Tokyo: Wanami bunko.

Yui, Yoshimichi (1999), *Chirigaku ni okeru haujingu kenkyū* (Housing study in geography), Tokyo: Daimyōdō.

Yui, Yoshimichi and Keiji Yano, (2002), 'Shinguru agein no jūtaku mondai: Tokyo 23ku no hitori oya setai' (The housing problem of separated singles: sole parent households in Tokyo's twenty-three wards) in Wakabayashi, Yoshiki, Kamiya, Hiroo, Tokyo: Daimyōdō.

Index

Alcock, Peter 2, 12, 13, 186, 191, 292

Bauman, Zygmunt 44, 240, 289
Booth, Charles and Seebohm Rowntree 4, 6, 158
bubble economy, The 56, 65, 81, 93, 137, 138, 140, 159, 160, 161, 232

class 4, 5, 6, 38, 41, 46, 54, 60, 111, 112, 113, 115, 116, 117, 118, 119, 131, 136, 139, 154, 239, 240, 248, 283, 293
 and low income 16, 17
class consciousness 112

Deleuze, Gilles 57, 60
displacement 42

family registration
 and exclusion from citizenship 39, 41, 288
Foucault, Michel 43
France 6, 229, 231

Geremeck, Bronislaw
 labour and poverty 3, 13, 32
globalisation 6

Healthy Japan 21 129, 130, 131
Healthy People 2010 (US) 118
hi hogosō; *hi hogosha* (trans. the poor; 'welfare beneficiaries') 14, 16, 17, 18, 19, 23, 31, 37, 157, 158, 159, 160, 161, 163, 164, 166, 168, 170, 172, 173, 176, 177, 178, 180, 182, 183
homeless, the 11, 20, 21, 22, 23, 25, 26, 27, 31, 34, 35, 56, 58, 59, 60, 119, 136, 151, 152, 153, 154, 155, 156, 158, 168, 185, 192, 193, 194, 196, 198, 199, 200, 203, 205, 206, 207, 208, 210, 211, 212, 213, 215, 216, 217, 218, 219, 220, 221, 222, 223, 224, 228, 229, 233, 242, 243, 244, 245, 248, 249, 250, 251, 253, 254, 255, 256, 257, 258, 260, 261, 292, 293, 294, 295, 296, 297, 298, 299
boshi (single mothers and their children) 28, 29, 30, 34, 144, 198, 199, 200, 201, 202, 203, 206, 207, 208, 292, 295
hamba (temporary workers sheds) 51, 56, 290
sanya (single male only day labourers accommodation) 25, 52, 53, 54, 59, 152, 156, 213, 223, 290, 296
vagrant men 20
women in prostitution 30, 31, 33, 34, 194, 196, 197, 198, 199, 200, 294

yoseba (billeted day labourers) 25, 26, 30, 34, 51, 53, 55, 56, 59, 158, 228, 244, 249, 288, 290, 296

income disparity 62
income security 19, 22, 29, 35, 36

Korea 50

labour market 6, 8, 17, 25, 32, 44, 51, 54, 55, 56, 58, 105, 106, 156, 158, 187, 188, 189, 190, 191, 192, 206, 220, 223, 224, 231, 248, 290, 293

Marshall, T.H. 4, 33
Marx, Karl 4, 5
Medicare (US) 117
megalopolis, The 41, 45
Ministry of Health, Welfare and Labour 23, 151, 292

nationalism 61
Negri, Antonio 57
nihilation 43, 44, 45, 46, 47, 50, 51, 52, 53, 54, 55, 58, 59, 60, 289

Our Healthier Nation (UK) 114, 115

post-war social conditions 87, 107
poverty 1, 2, 3, 4, 5, 6, 7, 8, 9, 10, 11, 12, 13, 14, 15, 16, 17, 18, 19, 20, 21, 23, 24, 25, 27, 28, 30, 31, 32, 33, 34, 35, 36, 37, 38, 39, 40, 41, 43, 49, 52, 54, 56, 59, 62, 63, 64, 65, 67, 69, 72, 73, 76, 78, 79, 80, 81, 82, 84, 85, 86, 87, 88, 103, 105, 108, 110, 111, 112, 113, 114, 116, 118, 119, 120, 122, 131, 132, 133, 134, 136, 138, 139, 140, 148, 149, 151, 153, 154, 155, 156, 157, 158, 159, 160, 161, 163, 164, 165, 166, 168, 170, 172, 176, 177, 182, 183, 184, 185, 186, 187, 188, 189, 190, 191, 192, 206, 207, 209, 210, 213, 226, 227, 228, 232, 235, 236, 241, 244, 263, 264, 288, 292, 293, 294
absolute poverty 112
and belonging 34
and citizenship 289
and depression 78, 79, 123, 133, 140
and education 84
and employment 6, 8, 17, 25, 32, 44, 51, 54, 55, 56, 58, 105, 106, 156, 158, 163, 170, 186, 187, 188, 189, 190, 191, 192, 206, 220, 223, 224, 231, 248, 252, 290, 293
and health insurance 18, 37, 117, 118, 120, 122, 125, 126, 129, 173, 176, 270, 298
and housing 136
and its classification 72, 73, 78, 79, 81, 87, 111, 113
and life expectancy 86, 111, 124
and local government 17, 26, 29, 49, 50, 53, 87, 89, 92, 95, 98, 101, 103, 104, 105,

106, 109, 139, 144, 145, 149, 151, 154, 155, 214, 230, 231, 232, 263, 264, 266, 271, 272, 273, 274, 276, 277, 278, 279, 281, 283, 284, 285, 288, 290, 292, 293
- and migrant workers 30, 226, 227, 228, 229, 230, 231, 232, 233, 234, 235, 236, 237, 238, 239, 240, 241, 297, 298
- and morbidity rates 111, 112, 116, 122, 132, 152, 292
- and mortality rates 29, 34, 63, 83, 94, 98, 99, 101, 102, 106, 107, 108, 109, 111, 112, 114, 115, 116, 119, 121, 124, 130, 131, 132, 133, 134, 147, 157, 182, 187, 190, 242, 243, 244, 261, 292, 293, 298
- and older women 7, 63, 86, 87, 88, 92, 93, 95, 96, 97, 98, 99, 101, 102, 103, 104, 105, 109, 215
- and policy categorisation 27, 260
- and quality of life 18, 37, 111, 117, 118, 120, 122, 125, 126, 129, 173, 176, 270, 298
- and rental accommodation 88, 89, 93, 94, 95, 97, 99, 100, 101, 102, 104, 105, 110, 146, 149, 151, 154, 156, 230, 231, 232, 270
- and social inclusion / exclusion 5, 6, 7, 8, 9, 10, 11, 37, 39, 40, 41, 43, 46, 48, 50, 52, 54, 56, 58, 59, 60, 96, 114, 121, 183, 210, 211, 214, 217, 226, 234, 242, 243, 289, 293, 295
- and suicide 44, 121, 123, 124, 134, 244, 245
- and the Japanese household 10, 64, 65, 67, 69, 72, 73, 75, 76, 84, 85, 88, 89, 92, 93, 95, 96, 97, 98, 99, 100, 110, 111, 116, 144, 146, 149, 230
- and urban spatiality 10, 45, 47, 48, 49, 51, 52, 54, 59, 67, 136, 137, 138, 139, 140, 155, 187, 232
- and women's life chances 27, 30, 31, 34, 52, 88, 186, 187, 188, 189, 190, 191, 192, 194, 195, 196, 198, 201, 202, 203, 205, 206, 207, 208, 213, 289, 293, 294, 295
- and women's marital status 7, 15, 17, 28, 29, 30, 34, 37, 39, 55, 78, 79, 80, 83, 87, 89, 96, 101, 102, 103, 104, 106, 107, 108, 110, 123, 133, 139, 144, 149, 154, 156, 164, 166, 168, 169, 170, 172, 182, 184, 186, 187, 189, 190, 191, 192, 198, 199, 200, 202, 203, 204, 206, 290, 291, 292
- and the working class 137, 139, 140, 141, 144, 153, 154, 155, 290, 291, 292
- as a moral problem 2, 33
- as a policy category 13, 38
- as perceived by the observer 1
- chronic poverty 63, 67, 72, 73, 75, 76, 79, 80, 81, 82, 83, 84, 85, 177, 182

our own poverty / their poverty 4, 5, 6, 7, 97
relative poverty 112
transient poverty 63, 72, 73, 75, 76, 79, 80, 81, 85, 177, 182
public housing programmes 17, 26, 29, 53, 87, 89, 92, 95, 98, 101, 103, 104, 105, 106, 144, 145, 151, 154, 155, 214, 230, 231, 232, 263, 264, 265, 266, 267, 269, 270, 271, 272, 273, 276, 277, 278, 279, 280, 281, 282, 283, 284, 285, 286, 287, 288, 293

retirement 78, 80, 96, 97, 100, 106, 109

Scandinavian countries 112, 120, 121
social change
  the vanishing middle class 7
social exclusion 3, 5, 6, 7, 8, 9, 10, 11, 16, 17, 18, 26, 37, 39, 40, 41, 43, 45, 46, 48, 50, 52, 54, 56, 58, 59, 60, 96, 101, 114, 117, 121, 158, 176, 183, 207, 210, 211, 212, 213, 214, 215, 217, 218, 223, 224, 226, 234, 236, 242, 243, 258, 283, 289, 293, 295

The Black Report (UK) 112, 290
Tokyo 10, 11, 21, 22, 24, 25, 39, 40, 43, 46, 48, 49, 50, 52, 53, 59, 88, 132, 136, 137, 138, 140, 141, 144, 147, 148, 150, 151, 152, 153, 154, 155, 161, 186, 192, 193, 194, 195, 197, 198, 199, 200, 201, 202, 203, 205, 208, 211, 212, 213, 216, 217, 220, 221, 223, 224, 226, 227, 235, 245, 248, 258, 288, 294, 295, 296, 297
Tokyo urban underclass, the 10, 39, 40, 41, 42, 43, 44, 46, 48, 49, 50, 51, 52, 53, 54, 55, 56, 58, 228, 249, 289
Townsend, Peter 1, 2, 113

United Kingdom, the 92, 97, 111, 112, 113, 115, 116, 122, 124, 131, 290
United States, the 6, 52, 63, 81, 112, 117, 118, 131, 186, 238
urban space in Tokyo 136, 137, 138, 139, 140, 155

welfare state, the 1, 2, 4, 6, 7, 8, 18, 25, 43, 52, 54, 188
welfare state policy
  and exclusion from citizenship 40, 42, 46
  and individual responsibility 8, 19, 35, 36, 37, 173, 176, 200, 202, 208, 235
  homogenisation of the population 41, 43, 45, 47, 48, 53
  ippan kyūgo (General relief) policy 14
  Kyūgo hō (Relief Act) 14, 15, 27, 158, 171
  preventative policy 13
  Seikatsu Hogo Act (Public Livelihood Protection Act); policies and

programmes 10, 15, 16, 17, 18, 19, 20, 22, 23, 24, 26, 28, 31, 32, 33, 34, 36, 37, 38, 54, 58, 59, 64, 69, 73, 76, 92, 93, 122, 133, 134, 139, 147, 149, 153, 154, 155, 156, 157, 158, 159, 160, 161, 163, 164, 165, 166, 167, 168, 170, 171, 172, 173, 176, 177, 178, 180, 182, 183, 193, 198, 199, 200, 203, 204, 211, 212, 213, 215, 217, 218, 219, 220, 221, 222, 223, 224, 242, 243, 291, 292, 295, 296, 297, 299

seikatsu hogo and work 32, 33

self reliance programmes 23, 37

tokushu kyūgo (specific relief) policy 14

work 6, 8, 13, 17, 25, 32, 44, 50, 51, 54, 55, 56, 58, 105, 106, 107, 108, 126, 156, 158, 167, 187, 188, 189, 190, 191, 192, 206, 213, 214, 215, 220, 223, 224, 231, 232, 236, 248, 249, 254, 256, 258, 289, 290, 293